Action Analysis for Animators

Action Analysis for Animators

Chris Webster

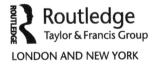
Routledge
Taylor & Francis Group

LONDON AND NEW YORK

First published 2012 by Focal Press

Published 2017 by Routledge
2 Park Square, Milton Park, Abingdon, Oxon OX14 4RN
711 Third Avenue, New York, NY 10017, USA

First issued in hardback 2017

Routledge is an imprint of the Taylor and Francis Group, an informa business

Library of Congress Cataloging-in-Publication Data
Webster, Chris, 1954-
 Action analysis for animators / Chris Webster.—1 [edition].
    pages cm
  ISBN 978-0-240-81218-2 (pbk.)
 1. Animation (Cinematography) I. Title.
 TR897.5.W428 2012
 777–dc23

                                                          2012003486

ISBN 13: 978-1-138-40322-2 (hbk)
ISBN 13: 978-0-240-81218-2 (pbk)

Typeset by: diacriTech, Chennai, India

For my granddaughter, Madlenka, and for my mother, Connie

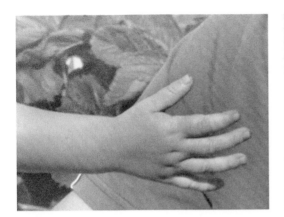
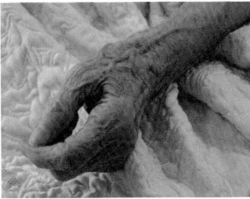

Contents

Contents

Contents

Contents

Acknowledgments

Everybody knows that trying to balance all of the commitments we face in life, either the ones we take on voluntarily or those we are pressed into, is a difficult task. I am certainly not alone in that. The particular pressures I attempt to balance include teaching my very bright undergraduate and postgraduate students, maintaining and developing my own animation practice, coping with the ups and downs of family life, and coping with the regular disappointment of unsuccessful fishing trips—oh, and of course, writing this book. For those more capable of achieving such a balancing act I feel nothing but delighted and a more than a little awe.

For me this rather modest book has been something of a mammoth task, one that has left its mark. This is perhaps testament to my own inadequacies and shortcomings rather than reflecting the weight and intellectual gravitas of which there is little, of what I now offer up to the reader. Even this I would have found nearly impossible without the help and support of a string of people who deserve a medal as big as a frying pan, but unfortunately they will have to make do with this modest though heartfelt thanks and acknowledgment. Without the following people (and others who I have had to omit for reasons of space and my poor memory) you would not be reading this right now, not that they are to blame for any of it!

First and foremost a million thanks must go to Katy Spencer at Focal Press for whom editor seems a ridiculously modest title for what she has done to get this work anywhere near a bookshelf. My sincere thanks go to her for extending huge levels of patience, understanding, and support that can only be matched by his holiness the Dalai Lama. Her patience was a wonderful thing to behold, something that I never really deserved but always received. Thank you.

Thanks also to Sarah Binns at Focal press for making sense of the material that trickled through at a pace so slow it made watching paint dry look like an extreme sport.

I am delighted to extend my many thanks to my longtime friend and colleague Mary Murphy, with whom I have had the privilege to work for the best part of ten years. I was delighted when she agreed to take on the role as the technical editor for this book.

I received the greatest assistance from my students, for which I am most grateful, and humbled by their commitment and talent. There are far too many to name individually but one student above the rest deserves my appreciation and thanks. So I extend my deepest thanks to Dominique Bongers for all of the days she spent during her time as one of my postgraduate animation students working as an unpaid volunteer research assistant. Over many months she carried equipment, undertook filming duties (very often performing in front of the camera), and even remembered where I left my reading glasses, though in fairness they were usually perched on top of my head.

Thanks to senior technical instructor Dave Neal for sharing his interest in wildlife filmmaking and high-speed photography and his invaluable technical support, and to Bob Prince for the same.

A big thank you must go to the owners of Noah's Arc Wildlife Park in Bristol for their help and access to their facilities, and to Chris, the bird handler there.

Again I acknowledge the contributions from my many students, too many of them to name individually but you know who you are, without whom this project would have been impossible. I am surprised and delighted at how many of them were happy to help with undertaking the actions recorded for the illustrations for this research. The term *happy* may be stretching it a little but they were at least willing (and I use this term very loosely here) to help out by undertaking all manner of jumping, running, dancing, lifting, throwing, and other silly things in front of the camera.

A big thank you must go to all my colleagues in the Bristol School of Animation within the University of the West of England who have shown me inordinate levels of tolerance that made this project achievable: Mary Murphy, Rachel Robinson, John Parry, Arril Johnson, Nic Homoky, and Julia Bracegirdle; and Ian Friend for all his technical assistance, advice and support and for dragging me kicking and screaming into the 19th century, even he couldn't manage to get me into this century.

Naturally my family deserves a special mention here because without them *nothing* would be possible. My wife Pauline deserves a particular mention and all of my love. She has enough to put up with my extended absence while I am on my unsuccessful fishing trips and then coping with the periods of depression on my returning home from them, let alone when I shut myself away in my studio to hammer away at the keyboard of my laptop. All the while she kept me supplied in endless cups of tea, wonderful food, and her love and patience. My three grown up children, Marc, Richard, and Rachel, also made a contribution in their own unique ways, especially my daughter who, never one to shun the limelight, made a very eager and willing subject for some of the sillier actions. Perhaps the best contribution of all was made by my lovely granddaughter Madlenka who made such a willing and rather beautiful subject. This book is dedicated to her.

Introduction

It has been said that art is a marriage between craft and imagination, skills, and inventiveness coming together in a fine balancing act to achieve results that speak to the soul as well as the mind. Craft without concept, imagination, or invention is reduced to a cold technical proficiency, eye candy, and the facile demonstration of dexterity, which are ultimately unsatisfying. I suppose it could be argued, then, that creating art without underpinning craft skills is in danger of becoming an esoteric exercise, an intellectualization of the human experience. The former (craft without concept) hides the lack of ideas under the high gloss of often expensive production values, whereas the latter (imagination without craft) seems to purposely distance its maker from the audience (if an audience is considered at all). All too often I have seen art being achieved by decrying craft as a second-rate activity. Unfortunately, this appears to make the results intentionally cold, distant, and rather aloof. It is my belief, for what it's worth, that it is important for artists, designers, filmmakers, and a wide range of other creative individuals to be truly creative in a manner that reaches, is understood, and is appreciated by a wider audience, so it is vital to strike a balance between imagination and craft.

Imagination and inventiveness are vital aspects of any creative endeavor. For the student of animation it is this imaginative inventiveness, which often begins at a very early age, that marks the starting point in a developing practice. However, it is detailed information, sound knowledge, and a deep understanding of those things that are pertinent to the craft of production and creative processes that not only underpin the art form but may become the starting point for a creative endeavor. Such knowledge and understanding provide a firm foundation for the creative development of a practice and, through practice, provide a range of practical skills for artists on which to build, over time enabling them to fully develop their individual and distinctive creative voices. Armed with the appropriate craft skills, we can all begin to explore the unlimited possibilities our imaginations will offer.

In writing this text it is not my intention to try to cover all possible subjects related to animated dynamics or the study of motion that may be of interest to the animator or artist. Such an ambitious aim would be simply too enormous for this or any other single book or other media. Indeed, this effort represents my own research interests, which, although they are quite wide, have only managed to scratch the surface of a subject: dynamics and action analysis. This text is intended to assist animators, designers, artists, and people working in other related areas who are interested in the analysis of movement and the creation of animation. A great many scientific texts deal with specific subjects to a much deeper level than I have covered here. I must at the outset make it clear to the reader that I come from an arts background and my own practice is specialized in traditional animation methods; therefore, for the most part this book reflects my practice in animation, though I have attempted to steer away from making it specifically relevant to any one animation discipline. How successful I have been in that attempt I shall leave you to decide.

Although I am clearly not a biologist or zoologist and am only an amateur and rather inadequate naturalist, my interest in wildlife, particularly birds and fish, has been with me since childhood. My interest in the details of animal locomotion stems from my work as an animator. It is my greatest hope that this text will help introduce readers to the subject and encourage them to seek out other texts and resources that deal with the subject either in more detail or by providing a different take on it. Serious students of any art or craft should look to a range of sources from a variety of practitioners and in doing so help themselves develop their own independent studies. In sharing that knowledge and understanding, they may in turn add to the breadth of knowledge. The suggested reading list presented in this text may assist you in identifying some of these resources.

On more than one occasion I have heard young animation students say that using reference material is, in some undefined way, "cheating." Although this attitude never ceases to amaze me, I have now heard this so often it no longer takes me by surprise. I believe these studetns think that unless they have discovered everything for themselves through research, systematic experimentation, or simple trial and error or by working completely from their imagination or from what they *think* they already know, they are simply copying and not engaging in an original creative endeavor. This is a huge mistake but is one some students persist in.

Artists and designers have always shared knowledge and information and looked to the work and findings of others as well as other resources and processes to assist their efforts. The 15th-century renaissance artist Piero della Francesca and his understanding of geometry and perspective, the color work of J. M. W. Turner and later Henri Matisse, the groundbreaking work on the human form by Michelangelo, and the anatomical drawings of Leonardo da Vinci were not works of the imagination but of research. Their work was only possible through a deep understanding of their subjects. Such in-depth understanding is not due to their intuition alone; it can only come through long-term serious study and analysis. Such a deep level of understanding is achieved through practice and a range of research methods: the combination of first-hand experience, primary sources of research, the work of contemporaries in both their own fields and other fields, and the experiences, work, and findings of other practitioners that preceded them.

I doubt that the attitude toward "cheating" that I have found in some of our animation students is restricted to the study of animation; I am sure that teachers in other disciplines share similar experiences with some of their students. I believe it is our duty as teachers to encourage serious research but also to get across to our students that we can *all* learn from anywhere and everywhere, and anyone. We must not be afraid to learn from each other; we are *all* teachers and, above all, *all* teachers are students, too.

When learning any new skill, craft, or art, the importance of thorough research and good reference material cannot be overstated. For the most part this effort will entail not a single source of reference or just one kind of reference material but a range of items and media; photographs, written texts, movies, drawings, models, and paintings, each of which may have a discrete and distinctive part to play. We should get it into our heads from the start that there are no (or at least very few) limits to what we can use to aid our progress in seeking new knowledge; nothing should be considered out of bounds. We are very lucky as animators because even though the art form of animation is still very much in its infancy, we have available to us a mass of work created by earlier animators. The pioneers of animation had no reference sources that were specifically aimed at animators, yet in shaping the art form they made some of the greatest animation that has ever been created. We are truly standing on the shoulders of great men.

There are a number of principles that we can learn about a whole range of things that may be of use to us as artists—everything from color theory, perspective, and laws of motion to animation timing. Principles are very important; clearly, without the understanding and application of certain design and engineering principles, bridges would collapse, airplanes would fall from the sky, our clothing wouldn't hang together, our houses and homes would crumble to dust, and our cars would tear themselves apart. However, we need to be careful about how we apply these principles; we should resist the temptation to allow the application of our knowledge of these principles to become some sort of "one size fits all" solution to our different design problems. Such an approach could result in producing work that is simply formulaic.

I don't suppose for a moment that I am alone as a teacher of animation to have been asked by my new students, "How many drawings are needed for a walk cycle?" It may well be tempting to give them a short, definitive response that would send them away with a smile on their faces, having been given "the answer." It would also be completely misleading. Although it is perfectly possible to give very general answers about the principles involved in animating the rhythm of a walk, it is not at all helpful to claim a single set way of doing things or to give an answer claiming it to be *the* truth.

This book contains no truths. It contains plenty of observations, some evidence, and quite a lot of opinion, and hopefully somewhere along the line you will find it a useful guide. Hopefully it will also provide you with some practical and useful tools for research and analysis that help you develop your practice and improve your craft skills. But ultimately, success is down to individual readers and the practical efforts they make.

So, if it possible to make perfectly acceptable animation without the need for action analysis, why should we bother with such analysis at all? What is in it for us as animators, and how will the analysis of action be of any practical benefit and repay our efforts? The most obvious answer is that we undertake such study in order to improve our own understanding, and through that improved understanding we are likely to improve our own performance as animators.

As I say, that is the obvious answer, but what about the specifics? In other words, *why* should we bother? We should bother because there are benefits to be had that will be applicable and will have *direct* relevance to your work, immediately and in the long term, regardless of the techniques you use or the animation discipline you work in. The more you know about the issues that underpin your craft (not just action analysis), the more highly developed your craft skills will be. A deeper understanding of the principles will leave you better placed to engage in further creative explorations and open up other possibilities for you.

What *are* the benefits likely to be? Once you have gained observational and analytical skills through study and practice, you will be able to more easily differentiate between actions ostensibly of a similar nature but in actual fact rather distinctive. As a result it is likely that you will then be able to create distinctive animated actions. It is in the use of very subtle and distinctive actions that give personality to characters that are most appealing to an audience, and the more appeal a character has, the more likely an audience is to empathize with that character. It's through the development of these critical skills that you will be able to recognize (in your own work and that of others) any errors and more quickly establish what corrections are needed and how to make them.

Finally, *how* will all this work repay our efforts? Given that you will be able to make keener observations on action and that your critical eye will now allow you to recognize and identify errors, it would seem reasonable that the results you should be able expect are of a higher standard. You will have more tools in your toolbox to use when and on what you like. This will make you more efficient, effective, and economical in the production of your animation. You will be able to make it more quickly, and it will be of a higher standard. It follows that you should be able to make your animation in less time and for lower costs. It should not be too much to expect that advanced skills and knowledge will broaden employment opportunities. In short, you are likely to be able to earn more money and be more successful in your chosen field.

What I am suggesting here is that the study of animation through action analysis is not just an interesting activity in its own right; it has very real and practical applications and may offer very tangible results, enhancing both your animation and your broader professional practice.

It was never my intention that this particular study would replace any existing approaches to the study of motion and animation, but simply that it would supplement what was already out there. Hopefully it will make a useful contribution to the body of work and assist in the development of a deeper understanding of movement that helps the craft of animation and assists readers in exploiting and developing their creativity through animation. This will take effort, and as with most things in life, there are *no* shortcuts. The benefits you will accrue will be proportional to the effort *you* put in.

The scope of this text covers the analysis of action and dynamics and is primarily designed for and aimed at animators and those involved in creating or studying the naturalistic movement of organic and nonorganic subjects. In addition to animators, there may well be others that find the material and topics in the text interesting and a valuable resource for their own practice. It is my own very modest attempt to follow on, in all humility, the studies and work of Eadweard Muybridge and Étienne-Jules Marey. Muybridge's original work pointed the way by influencing a generation of photographers, artists, filmmakers, and designers. It is too much to expect that this book could possibly have the same impact as that groundbreaking work, though it would be nice to think that it adds *something* to the field of study, if only by encouraging the next generation of animators to engage more fully in the analysis of movement.

This book and accompanying Web site contain a collection of diagrams, illustrations, photographs, and movies, all intended to provide a collection of reference material; but more important, it is a guide to the analysis of action. Hopefully you will start to make and collect your own material that is more directly relevant to your practice.

Action Analysis for Animation can be used as a standalone resource for the study of dynamics, but it was always my intention that it be used in conjunction with other texts that deal with aspects of animation timing, performance, acting, design, and production. I have put together a list of recommended material, texts, and videos to help with this goal, but it must be said that this collection is far from complete and represents my own views. I am sure that you will discover your own suggestions and alternatives.

The study of motion and the analysis of action are undertaken by scientists, engineers, designers, physicists, physicians, biologists, naturalists, and artists, and among their numbers are filmmakers and animators. All of these people and many, many more use the observation and analysis of movement to benefit their particular field of activity. Much of this work has very practical applications that are of immense use to us all and affect our daily lives in so many ways— from the cars we drive to the aircraft over our heads, the buildings we live and work in, and even the clothes we wear. The creators of all these goods may be looking at movement and dynamics for different reasons, but the one thing they share is the desire to understand more about these phenomena.

It is unrealistic to expect animators to undertake an in-depth study of fluid dynamics or have a sound knowledge of engineering principles; this would be quite unnecessary unless, of course, one has a desire to know these things out of a sense of inquisitiveness. However, it may be beneficial for animators to gain some rudimentary knowledge of anatomy. Anatomical study will not only assist animators in gaining an understanding of how humans and animals are structured but also how they *move*. In addition to helping with animation, this knowledge may also help in designing and creating other, more fantastical creatures. If one understands how a heavy animal such as an elephant is structured and moves, it stands to reason that one is more likely to have a better understanding of how dinosaurs *may* have moved. There is an old design adage that form follows function; we only have to look at nature to see how accurate this statement is. Birds do not fly because they have wings; birds developed wings in order to fly.

In reading the text students will see that learning how to analyze action will improve their understanding of movement, but I would go further and suggest that we may also be taking a far more fundamental step: We will be learning to *see* and not simply to look.

Finally, I hope that this text encourages readers to study and pass on their findings to others, sharing knowledge and experience in the spirit of collegiate support for our fellow animators. It is my most earnest desire for this work to be of some *practical* use to readers in the development of their craft and the extension of their knowledge and understanding. I also hope it provides something that others will then add to and build on. If it does that, then I'll be a happy man.

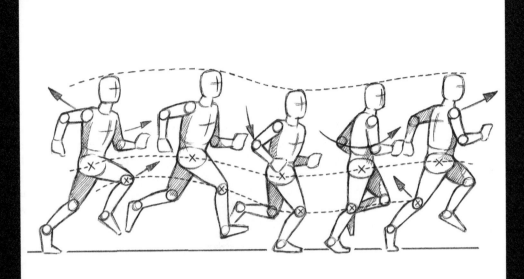

CHAPTER 1

The Study of Motion

Asking Ourselves Some Key Questions

Let's begin by asking ourselves a few questions regarding the study of motion.

We should start with the question, *Why should animators undertake the study of motion?*

It would seem perfectly feasible to argue that animators can produce work of a good standard and that is more than acceptable for all manner of productions without the need for such study. There are plenty of examples of self-taught artists who have gone on to become masters of their craft, not only leading the way for others to follow but creating seismic shifts in art and design and in the process becoming towering figures of genius within art history. Such remarkable individuals should be celebrated for their contributions and be seen for what they are: remarkable.

But such people are in the minority. The vast majority of people who work as creative artists within various traditions developed their talents along more conventional roads, studying at schools, colleges, or universities; a few fortunate ones have had the opportunity to study in the studios of established practitioners.

During a lecture and screening given by Richard Williams, the animation director of *Who Framed Roger Rabbit* (1988), at the Bristol School of Animation at the University of the West of England, he spoke of how the old masters of animation influenced him in the development of his craft and how the study of movement had helped him better understand the nature of performance-based animation. Although he was not apprenticed to the likes of Ken Harris, Art Babbitt, Grim Natwick, or Milt Kahl, he did have the opportunity to work closely with them. He studied their methods and processes and took what they had learned and applied it to his own work. He also made a systematic study of human movement; in doing so, he made his own major contribution to the art form. The way I see it, if this level of study is good enough for Richard Williams, it is good enough for me and my own students.

The one thing that none of these great animators depended on was the use of simple tricks or formulas. Don't get me wrong; tricks, tips, and dodges have their place and allow an animator to develop his or her animation skills to a certain degree. They will even allow a student to imitate the work of others. However, if this approach is taken as the *sole* way of learning and creating animation, it can only lead to students developing their craft by rote, creating little other than formulaic animation. Through in-depth study of the craft, serious students will be able to gain real understanding of the underpinning principles of timing and dynamics. Ultimately this study will allow them to create for themselves a path toward making performance-based animation with originality. Without a doubt, a good grounding in processes, techniques, and methodologies, coupled with intense study of an art form, will enable animation students to make progress toward their goals.

However, neither the tricks of the trade nor rigorous study are a substitute for talent. Talent is something we are all born with to different degrees. Although the potential we possess for anything from playing football or singing to animating varies from person to person, we all have some potential in all these areas. Our job is therefore to develop our talents to their full potential. Perhaps it is fortunate that we do not all have the same capacities, since there would then be no giants among us—no Picassos, no Mozarts, no Pelés, no Hemingways, and no Winsor McCays or Tex Averys.

I have often heard people claim that they can't draw. They can, it's just that they haven't yet learned how to do it or haven't developed their full potential for drawing. The same is true for animation. Of course, natural talent will take you so far, but through study, talent can be further developed through patience, practice, and the systematic application of what you have learned.

That brings us to the next question: *How should an animator undertake the study of motion?*

We need to establish from the outset that there is no one process that will provide animators with all the answers they need for the study of motion.

They must identify and then use the most appropriate methods for their particular needs. Often this will be simply referencing a text such as this one; occasionally it will involve other very specific processes.

Gaining an in-depth understanding of motion is clearly best done through actually making animation; this is experiential learning. As with most things in life, having a good instructor or mentor will ensure that you learn at a faster rate and at a deeper level. When I first began animating in the early 1980s, I had absolutely no idea what I was doing, and I knew it. The one thing I was sure of was that to progress within the industry, I had to learn my craft. Learning the principles of animation and the mechanics of the production process was difficult enough, but compared to learning the intricacies and subtleties of human movement, these things were a breeze. When it came to mastering performance and acting, I am still learning after 20-odd years. In this regard I firmly believe that we never stop learning.

I was lucky enough to study under two first-rate but little-known animators, Chris Fenna and Les Orton, within a studio environment. For the best part of two years I studied their drawings, their animation timings, and the way they handled dynamics, which gave me a great start in developing my own understanding. It also enlightened me to the fact that different animators are suited to different kinds of performance. This level of first-hand experience is invaluable to the trainee animator who wants to come to grips with the demands of animation and the importance of the study of motion.

A collection of reference material is absolutely *vital* to the animator who wants to develop her craft. These days there is so much material available to the serious student of motion and animation as to be a little confusing; books, DVDs, animation, live-action film, Web sites, and online learning material all have their parts to play. Much of this material was unavailable to me as a young animator, though there were some good texts. One of the very best was the classic *Timing for Animation*, by Harold Whitaker and John Halas. I couldn't afford my own copy, so I made copies of nearly the entire book using the studio photocopier; then, with my first paycheck, I bought my own copy, which I still treasure *and use* to this day. Now there are plenty of texts that provide good insight into processes of animation, and the Focal Press catalogue provides perhaps the greatest range of texts on all manner of topics from major contributors.

Watching and studying animation, not simply as a member of the audience being entertained but as part of your serious study of animation, will bring major rewards. You will find that going through parts of an animated sequence that is of interest to you a single frame at a time will help you analyze the movement. Begin by looking at the overall results in real time, then slowly focus your attention on the individual elements of the movement. Then, by single-framing the action, you will find that you gain a deeper insight into the separate actions and the way they interrelate. You will need to do this over and over again, checking each part of the motion in turn. This kind of analysis will enable you to gain insight into the way the master animators achieved those great performances. This idea is covered in more detail in the chapter on methodologies for analysis.

I began my own studies in action analysis by looking at the Disney classics *Snow White*, *Bambi*, and *Pinocchio*. I then moved on to studying the work of Tex Avery and Chuck Jones to gain an understanding of their particular brand of *cartoon* animation. Studying animated movement in this way does not necessarily help the student develop her directing skills or understanding of cinematography, but it does help a young animator in dealing with movement and timing.

As I began to study other animators, it became clear that all the great ones had their own distinctive approach to dynamics. Some concentrated on subtle actions; others had a broad approach to cartoon timing; some specialized in naturalistic animation. One only has to look at the differing approaches of Disney's "nine old men" to appreciate these variations in approach. It is important for the student of animation to remember that the benefits of studying movement are *not* limited to the methods by which the animation has been made. Studying classical 2D animation is just as useful to those making computer graphics (CG) animation as it is for any other animator, as long as you remember that you are studying *movement*, not *drawings*. The important thing here is to choose only the very best examples of animation for your study.

Although it is interesting and rewarding to study the work of the great animators to achieve a deep understanding of motion, one often needs to go directly to the source: live action. Studying live-action footage of a range of subjects will provide the student of animation with a wealth of material to analyze. Studying the action of humans and animals first-hand is very informative, but this is not always practical nor possible. Animals cannot be expected to perform on cue, and there are some animals to which most of us do not have easy access. It is arguable whether it is better to study the action of humans and animals by direct observation or if video footage provides a better opportunity for more systematic study. Both approaches have their positive points. Rapid and complex movements are perhaps better understood by repeated viewing than live action offers. You can also freeze-frame video footage, but you can't freeze frame live actions. The performance of live actors may also provide worthwhile reference, particularly if a distinctive dynamic action is sought. We may be familiar with the distinctive walks of both Charlie Chaplin and Groucho Marx and think that we have an understanding of the nature of these movements, but to *accurately* replicate such movements through animation, it would be as well to study the real thing. A wealth of wildlife documentaries is available to provide the animator with an excellent source for animal locomotion. There should be no need for the budding animator to visit the Arctic or keep a polar bear of his own in order to study them.

In the course of their work at some point or another, animators will probably find themselves dealing with two very distinct types of motion: *naturalistic action* and *abstract action*. Each of these types of motion presents its own range of possibilities and, as one might expect, its own particular difficulties.

For our purposes we can define naturalistic animation as any motion that is associated with realistic and recognizable movements, organic or nonorganic, undertaken in a completely believable manner. Although creating motion of this kind could present difficulties that are not easily overcome, at least identifying and studying the *nature* of movement is easy. Animators—and more important, audience members—are able to compare naturalistic animation against their own understanding of the real thing. Most of us know how horses run, how children walk, how the surface of water ripples in a breeze, and how smoke behaves; the list is almost endless. Because the audience can easily recognize the *actual* motion of each of these things, the demands placed on the animator are rather substantial; anything deviating from the audience's first-hand experience will be instantly identifiable as erroneous and the suspension of disbelief will fail. The study of naturalistic movement for this kind of naturalistic animation may be a simple matter of accessing the appropriate research material, including, of course, first-hand experience.

Abstract motion, on the other hand, *may* be open to interpretation. This could provide some leeway in the animation because it can't easily be measured against any "real" equivalent. Abstract motion may take on a wide range of actions, from cartoon characters designed in an abstract manner to actual abstract shapes. Subjects for this approach to animation could appear somewhere on a continuum ranging from the completely abstract movement of abstract shapes, movement that relates to nothing in nature, to movements more associated with cartoon animated motion. These may be recognizable inasmuch as they represent familiar things (cat, mouse, dog) though they do not move in ways that relate to that real-life thing.

At one end of that continuum we have the work of Oskar Fischinger, who specialized in abstract shapes interacting with one another and synchronized to sound. There is no motion within such work that we can measure against our own first-hand experience of these things. At the other end of the spectrum we have the work of animators such as Tex Avery, whose characters often fail to behave in the manner of the things they represent. However, as difficult as it may seem, animators working at either end of this continuum are able to make animation if not "believable," then at least convincing.

Study of this type of abstract animation may be more problematic, though it is not impossible. Believability in this instance may be the attribution of such qualities as the weight attributed to an object. Momentum and inertia may still be applied to abstract animation, and in these cases the study of momentum and inertia in nonabstract forms may be of value. The manner in which birds fly or fish swim or the mechanical motion of machinery may provide adequate reference and a good starting point for creating abstract motion.

Then there are the types of actions that the animator might want to appear to be naturalistic, even though by their nature they are abstract or at least completely unknown. Take, for example, the animation of dinosaurs or dragons. Although the first type of creature did actually exist on earth, we are left with no first-hand account of their movements, even though we can glean a good deal of information about the way they *probably* moved by examining what does remain of them. The second example, the dragon, is completely fictitious; as such the study of dragons becomes difficult. However, we are able to apply what we have learned from other sources. The study of large land animals such as elephants, rhinoceros, and hippopotamus may help with both examples; the study of snakes may assist the animator in getting to grips with the animation of a dragon's tail.

Early in my career I learned the value of using my own body to study and analyze action. I had to animate a number of rather difficult characters to a standard I had not previously worked to. This task was far more challenging than anything I had experienced before, and I was struggling. Then, on the advice of the project's director, I began to act out the scenes for myself, not *as* myself but in a way that my characters would move. Ideally I would have used direct reference material, but this was not practical, so I used the next best thing: myself. I spent the next few weeks walking around the studio in both the aspect of a young, powerful, and power-crazed princess and as one of her short and very overweight courtiers. Believe me, this activity helped a great deal. I not only learned through direct visual observation of my own movements as seen in a full-length mirror, but I was able to *feel* how my body moves in a particular way when undertaking a specific action. This exercise gave me insight into where the weight in my body was at any particular moment, where the center of gravity was, and how the figure balanced, and I was able to locate all the stresses and tensions within my muscles.

Years later some of my graduate students, who were then working for a studio in London making CG animation involving dinosaurs, were doing exactly the same thing as they too struggled with the animation of creatures they had no direct reference for. To get a better idea of how a wounded pterodactyl might have hobbled across a Jurassic beach, they took to hauling themselves along using crutches as makeshift wings and filmed the results. This technique worked very well, and the animation was very successful.

As a young animator I had far less technology at my disposal for creating my own reference material. Motion capture, digital photography (including stills), and video capabilities in mobile phones were not available to animators in the 1980s the way they are today. These are wonderful tools that can be used to great effect as long as they are used appropriately. Animators should not depend on any single source of referencing but rather should use a range of resources: textbooks, film (animation and live action), photography (your own and that of others), first-hand animation material (observation and sketchbook work), the first-hand experience of others through mentorship (one of the most useful techniques), and motion capture. We will look in more detail into each of these approaches later in the text.

The next question we should then ask is, *Who are the practitioners for whom such a study is relevant?*

All artists, designers, and creative individuals of various kinds take the study of their particular craft very seriously. This applies equally to those working within the creative industries and those engaged in more independent or less commercially oriented practices. Naturally, artists of all types deal with the particular aspects of their craft relevant to their art or creative process in their own way. In addition to a wide and varied range of practical and aesthetic issues, each artist will have an understanding of aspects particular to his or her craft: Painters will probably have a deep understanding of color theory; sculptors may have a profound understanding of form, space, and materials. Photographers have an understanding of light; musicians and composers have an understanding of the intricacies of sound; and graphic designers understand letterforms and typefaces, layout, and the relationship between text and image. In the same way, it is clear that animators need to study and gain an in-depth understanding of the nature of movement and dynamics. The pursuit of relevant knowledge through in-depth study, together with craft skills, underpins an artist's creativity.

Not all animators have the same requirements for study. Many factors dictate the areas of study and the depth to which one's study will be undertaken. The genre of animation, the production process, the animation format; features, commercials, games, and the like—each present the animator with particular demands and constraints. The exact nature of the study will invariably depend on the work being undertaken at any given time.

The need for study may also depend on the production pipeline. For animators working in a large creative team, many of the issues of animation production will normally be dealt with by other specialists on that production team. This may free up the animators to deal exclusively with movement, dynamics, and, most important of all, performance. In large production teams it may be possible and even desirable for individual animators to deal with particular characters. The study of motion may then be further focused and applied to a single subject or range of subjects. Such a focused approach to action analysis may provide the animation with a distinctive quality and give it consistency throughout an extended format, such as feature film work.

Animators working on smaller productions with fewer people on the creative team or auteur animators who may work largely on their own may often find themselves dealing with many aspects of the production, not just animation—such as story, design, editing, sound recording and editing, film language, and animation dynamics. Movement and animation timing are among the most important of these. All animators, regardless of process or technique, need to have an understanding of time and timing and how to use both in a creative manner. Such an understanding can only be gained from the systematic and long-term study of motion and dynamics and, more important, by practicing their craft that involves the application of timing.

After a time and with practice, the study of motion will become second nature and will result in a very different way of observing the world and understanding movement. This will result in the animator *seeing*, not just looking. We have all watched people as they walk down the street; we might have looked at how they swing their arms and lift their legs, but how many of us have *seen* those same people walking? Here's an example: For a number of years I have taught classes to first-year animation students looking at the principles of animation and action analysis. As part of these classes, students undertake a series of exercises involving figurative movement, walk cycles, lifting, throwing, carrying, pushing, and the like. During these exercises I encourage them to use their own bodies as reference material. They are encouraged to walk, lift, push, and so on. Many of these students start out by getting the basics of even the simplest walk cycle wrong. This should come as no surprise, really, since we are very good at taking things for granted—simply *looking* at things and events and assuming that we then understand them without ever questioning in any detail how things actually work. My students have *looked* at people walking; they even undertake these actions themselves as part of these exercises; but it quickly becomes clear that up until this point they have been engaged in *looking* at a walking figure and not *seeing* how the figure walks.

One of the first lessons in the study of motion is how to begin to *see*.

Pioneers of Action Analysis

The study of motion has been a serious endeavor for man for many thousands of years. Cave paintings offer evidence that early man had an understanding of the motion of a range of animals that can only have come about through intense observation. We can only speculate as to how or even if such an understanding had a practical benefit to those early hunters. Perhaps it helped their field craft and assisted in the success of their hunting efforts; we shall never know. We do have evidence as to how the study of motion in ancient times has had practical application: The study of the motion of the sun and the stars enabled early seafarers to travel the globe, even before the true nature of the solar system was known or understood, and in doing so give us an understanding of the planet on which we live.

Great scientists make great discoveries of which we lesser mortals may understand little, though from their findings we may be able to undertake a study from which we can then draw and apply knowledge. Isaac Newton put forward his theories on the laws of motion in his great work, the *Principia Mathematica* (1687), in which he set out the three laws of motion and described universal gravitation. These ideas underpin all our understanding of motion. For animators, the study of these laws will pay dividends, even though the math may be beyond many of us (it is certainly beyond me).

The pioneers of action analysis who are perhaps of most interest to the animator are Eadweard Muybridge and the less well-known but equally important Étienne-Jules Marey.

One of the most famous individuals engaged in action analysis was the English photographer Eadweard Muybridge. Born in 1830 at Kingston-on-Thames and the son of a successful businessman, Muybridge moved to San Francisco in his early twenties. There he began to dabble in photography. Losing interest in his own business career, he became a professional photographer around 1865. His initial interest was in a conventional approach to photography, which brought him a degree of success. Although his early images of the Yukon and Yellowstone landscapes are worthy of note, it was as a portrait photographer that he made his living. However, he eventually became famous for his work recording the motion of animals and humans; these studies would ensure that his name lived on as one of the founding fathers of animation.

It is said that Muybridge's investigation into recording animals in motion was the result of a wager between the wealthy businessman Leland Stanford and the financier James R. Keene. They disagreed over the idea of whether all four hooves of a running horse were actually off the ground together at some point during the run. The validity of this story, as colorful as it is, remains doubtful. Whatever the truth, Stanford did employ Muybridge to provide the evidence for further research into equine dynamics. The work began in 1872, but it wasn't until 1877 that the first of Muybridge's famous photographs was published. Using Occident, one of Stanford's famous horses, Muybridge made the first image that did indeed prove that a horse at gallop had all four hooves suspended off the ground. Later, this first photograph provided reference material for a painting by the artist John Koch, commissioned by Stanford and now in the Stanford University Museum in California. Perhaps this is the very first example of an artist engaged in action analysis and using photography as a research tool.

This work marked the start of an extended study of the movement of animals and humans that would last for the rest of Muybridge's life. His early studies of the motion of horses were conducted at Stanford's stock farm at Palo Alto, California. His first photographs were made in a traditional manner as individual images, though he quickly opted for the use of multiple images in series. He used a series of tripwires, each one triggering the shutter of a single camera within a whole bank of cameras located in a shed that was set on one side of the horses' trotting track. However, this process also proved to be unsatisfactory, so Muybridge went on to create a synchronized system in which each of the cameras was triggered by electricity.

Following a successful series of lectures based on these early sequences of Occident and other horses, Muybridge's work progressed within the Veterinary Department at the University of Pennsylvania. There Muybridge's extensive exploration into the movement of humans and animals would provide the world with the first substantial photographic body of work on action analysis.

Although Muybridge published his work in extensive, and rather expensive, portfolios, he never reaped the great financial rewards his ground-breaking work deserved. A mark of the importance of Muybridge's work is that it has remained in print to this day. His influence on artists, animators, and filmmakers is difficult to overstate, and although the poor quality of some of the images makes analysis rather difficult, they nonetheless continue to make a valuable contribution to the study of motion.

Étienne-Jules Marey was a contemporary of Muybridge. The work of this French physiologist also dealt with the analysis of motion, but it had very different roots. Born in 1830 in Beaune, Burgundy, Marey came from a purely scientific background. His early work was concerned with blood circulation and cardiovascular research. His first efforts into motion study were to record movement through the mechanical and graphic representation of that movement. The *sphygmograph* (pulse writer) of 1860 was a highly sensitive device that could register and record the pulse in the wrist of the person wearing it. The mechanical clockwork action of the sphygmograph, coupled to a stylus, provided a graphic readout of the pulse. From these early graphs Marey was able to analyze the heart condition of the patient on which it was used. His work in this field gained wide acceptance in clinical circles, and his research soon found practical applications.

Marey's work then progressed from cardiovascular research into the investigation of the movement of muscles and the measurement of fatigue. Once again, he created a number of instruments for recording through graphic means of movement within both the human body and those of animals. He also created a series of artificial animals and organs, including an artificial heart, lungs, and circulatory system; a mechanical insect; and a mechanical bird. As with his earlier devices, each registered the object's movements through graphic readouts.

As a result of seeing Muybridge's work, Marey began to explore the use of photography in his research. Unlike Muybridge, who used multiple cameras, Marey worked with a single camera and began to develop a single high-speed camera capable of capturing the motion of birds. This device became the now-famous *photographic gun*. The intricate mechanics of the gun provided by highly skilled watchmakers enabled him to capture the first high-speed photography of birds in flight.

Marey chose to use the process of *chronophotography* for the study of the dynamics of the human figure in motion. This process entails capturing multiple images on a single frame of film, creating the necessary sequence of motion. Although Marey's photography has an aesthetic quality to it and could be described as beautiful, these artistic aspects were not the purpose of the work. He returned again and again to the interpretation of movement. Placing high-visibility marks at strategic points on a figure or an animal and using chronophotography rather than a number of individual images, he was better able to trace the arcs of movement of specific parts of a figure in motion. This technique predates the use of such methods in motion-capture devices by almost a hundred years.

Marey's research and his scientific approach to recording, reproducing, and analyzing motion made a valuable contribution to both cardiology and aviation. His devices not only measured the movement in running figures—he studied wave patterns and the velocity of currents, and he created aquaria for the study of fish and fluids as well as wind tunnels for the study of air flow and turbulence over vanes and wings. Indeed, it was through his study of wings that the theory of flight and its application to early powered flight were better understood. Though Marey did not live to see man's first powered flight, the pioneering aviators the Wright brothers publicly acknowledged Marey's influence on their work.

Generally the producers of the early forms of animation needed little by way of reference material, since the animation was so simplistic. Demand for animation was very high from audiences that were intrigued by animation's novelty factor, which meant that audiences were satisfied with rather crude forms of cartoon animation. As funny or as charming as they may have been, these early films did not rely on the quality of the animation to sell them. This approach to animation production was perfectly suited to many studios that were happy to produce work quickly and cheaply with little regard to raising standards. Other studios and individual animators sought to make improvements to further the art form and, perhaps more important, to secure audience loyalty to particular characters and to ensure financial security.

The greatest of all these early animators was Winsor McCay. Although he wasn't engaged in formal study of action analysis, McCay clearly had a good understanding of dynamics and animation timing whereas others were struggling to simply make things move. He achieved believable action in his characters, including actions of which the audience had little or no first-hand experience. *How a Mosquito Operates* (1912) and *Gertie the Dinosaur* (1914) remain masterpieces of animation timing. They arrived at a time when many studios were struggling with the problem of creating enough animated product to satisfy the market. McCay's high-quality animation was not to be equaled until Walt Disney began work on *Snow White* almost 25 years later.

One pioneering studio that did much to employ action analysis as a way to improve the standard of the animation they produced was the Fleischer Brothers Studios. Based in New York, the studio was run by two brothers, Max and Dave Fleischer, who were contemporaries of Walt Disney. The studio became famous for producing many of the early stars of animation, including

Popeye the Sailor, Betty Boop, and, later, Superman. However, it was while they were producing an earlier series of films, *Out of the Inkwell*, featuring Koko the Clown, that they developed the *rotoscope*. Invented by Max Fleischer and patented in 1917, the rotoscope was a mechanical device and process for "capturing" realistic movement through the recording of live action and then utilizing the live-action footage as a template for making animated motion. The results were spectacular, with Koko moving across the screen in a completely naturalistic and realistic manner, something that no other animated character had done before. But although the work of Fleischer Studios was remarkable, they were simply not in the same league as the Disney Studios.

No text on the study of motion for animation would be complete without mentioning the work of Disney. From its earliest days, this studio did more than any other to develop and promote animation as an art form. Disney's approach to action analysis might not have been as in-depth as the scientific research of Marey or as extensive in its recording of movement as Muybridge, but Disney Studios were without doubt the most important contributors in terms of the development of action analysis and the study of motion specifically for animation. In this regard it could be argued that Disney made a more valuable contribution to the study of dynamics for animation.

During preparations for the studio's first feature, *Snow White*, audience demands for more naturalistic movement really began to grow. It was clear from the results of an earlier production, *The Goddess of Spring* (1934), that the animators still had some way to go before more naturalistic animation would become achievable more consistently. Although the *Goddess* film acted as a vehicle to develop more believable motion of human figures, it was necessary to go further.

In the early 1930s the studio's animators, led by Disney himself, started to regularly analyze the results of their pencil tests in meetings that became known as *sweatbox sessions*. The entire studio went to great lengths to improve the action and standards of animation, which would soon include direct observation of action. By 1936 Disney decided to employ the services of the art teacher Don Graham to improve his animators' drawing standards. They instigated regular life drawing classes and later would include the first-hand study of animals.

Disney was also determined that the studio address issues of more believable animation applied to all elements, not just the character-based work. This included such things as water, rain, reflections, smoke, and the like. The studio invested a great deal of time and money in technical developments and was responsible for advances in technologies that others would later pick up. One such development was in the area of *multiplane cameras*. In the film *The Old Mill* (1937), many of these technical issues were addressed, including the development of the multiplane camera, which allowed for more naturalistic effects, gave depth to a scene, and took animation special effects to a new, much higher level. This Academy Award-winning film was based on little more than a story of how a run-down old mill weathers a storm, but it demonstrated how the artistry and beauty of animation could enthrall an audience.

The Disney animators did not use the rotoscoping techniques developed by the Fleischer brothers to create their animation, but they did film performers for the action of a number of characters in *Snow White*. Mostly the live footage was used as reference material forming the basis for the animation. Although this was not the first occasion on which such referencing techniques had been used, the Disney studio did much to establish the tradition of recording live action and action analysis for animation, a tradition that many animation studios follow to this day.

The importance of art and animation training; the establishment of the principles of animation, acting, and performance; and, most of all, action analysis were uppermost in Walt Disney's thinking. To make the best possible animation, he clearly understood that the animators needed a deeper, more profound knowledge of anatomy, life drawing, and dynamics, and he set about putting this knowledge in place. We should all be thankful for that.

Books About Animation

A wide range of texts are now available on animation and are generally divided into books that deal with the historic context of animation production, theory, political economy of animation production, techniques, production processes from storyboarding to editing, and everything in between.

The first published text on the study of animation production was written by Edwin G. Lutz in 1920: *Animated Cartoons: How They Are Made, Their Origin and Development*. Lutz also wrote a number of books on other design-related areas: *Practical Graphic Figures*, *Practical Drawing*, *Practical Art Anatomy*, and *Drawing Made Easy*. Although *Animated Cartoons* isn't a text that concentrates on the study of dynamics or action analysis, it does provide notes on animals in motion and inanimate objects, which must have made it a very valuable early source of reference for animators. Disney Studios used this book as a reference in the early days of the studio, before they commenced their own far more in-depth study of motion. For that reason alone *Animated Cartoons* is worthy of note for its serious approach to the study of animation and holds a place in the history of the animation industry.

Naturally there are landmark texts covering animation, such as *Cartoon Animation*, by Preston Blair; *Timing for Animation*, by Harold Whitaker and John Halas; *The Animator's Survival Kit*, by Richard Williams, and perhaps best of all, *The Illusion of Life*, by Frank Thomas and Ollie Johnson. In addition, a great many texts dedicated to the creative and practical aspects of animation production are now available to the animator on the craft skills of cinema, directing, the principles of animation, texts related to narrative development and storytelling, design, storyboarding, editing, animation timing, drawing for animation, model making, lighting, and production, as well as a multitude of texts that deal with the use of specific software. To engage in the study of motion will invariably involve the use of a range of texts, this book being just one of many.

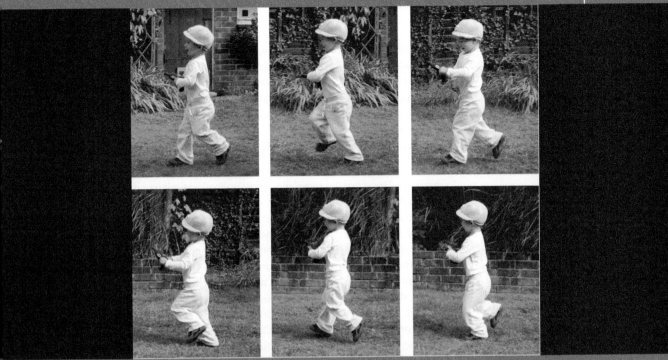

CHAPTER 2

Dynamics and the Laws of Motion

If you are to begin to study action and apply it to your work in animation, it can be useful to gain a little basic understanding of the laws that govern those actions you are aiming to analyze. Some understanding of such laws will improve the analysis of action and thereby improve your animation.

An Approach to Study: What You Need to Know

How do we go about using a knowledge of the laws of motion as part of your analysis and then apply this analysis to your practice as an animator? It would help at the outset to establish what level of knowledge and understanding you will need and that will be helpful. As interesting as this topic undoubtedly is, you may be relieved to hear that it will not be necessary to understand the underpinning mathematics behind the laws that govern the movement of objects. The study of the laws of physics and the nature and behavioral tendencies of materials under particular circumstances is, for some scientists, the work of a lifetime. Thankfully for the animator, such depth of knowledge is unnecessary, even though it may be of passing interest. It is completely unrealistic to consider that such laws must be fully understood to be successful as an animator who, for the most part, will be dealing with animation timing as it relates to performance-based animation. Such a deep understanding of the laws of motion and dynamics is not necessary for *most* animators. Bear in mind that you only need to know what you need to know.

Often the aim of the animator is to achieve *believable* animation timing and dynamics. This is not the same as *accurate* animation timing or dynamics. For the most part, animators are dealing with creating an illusion, one that fits in with other aims, such as entertainment. I have seen many young animators agonize over a piece of animation and the accuracy of the movement and timing when all the while their audience is almost completely unaware of their efforts and, perhaps more important, completely unaware of and maybe even uninterested in how the actual objects being animated behave in reality. More likely than not, the audience is interested in the *storyline*. Given this fact, you might want to keep at the forefront of your mind this idea: If the animation *looks* right, it *is* right. Obviously this is a somewhat simplistic approach and will not cover all situations, but it is a very useful little adage, one that has the potential to save you a lot of time—and money.

I cover this idea in much more detail in the chapter on animation principles, which discusses the various approaches to animation through simulation, interpretation and representation, hierarchies of animation, and my own categorization of the "Four As of Animation." Understanding each of these categories and approaches to animation will make your efforts more effective. Often the outcomes you are trying to achieve determine the approach you will take and indicate the level of knowledge of the laws of physics that you will need.

Regardless of what you are trying to achieve, you will, without doubt, gain great benefit from a basic understanding of dynamics and the laws of motion. We cover these concepts here. This study is intended to underpin the work of the animator; for our purposes at least, this study should not become the work itself. We need what we need as animators; we do not need to push the boundaries of our understanding of the world and everything in it.

Forces of Nature

We, along with everything else on earth, are governed by the laws of physics and by the forces of nature, though for the most part we might not be aware of these laws or forces. Indeed, it is not always possible for us to detect these forces, and it's only in recent times that we have gained a fuller understanding of them.

Understanding some of these universal laws of nature may prove useful for animators, not simply when making animation that is intended to illustrate movement in environments of which we have first-hand experience, but also by allowing us to make believable animation of all manner of alien and imagined worlds. Universal laws are exactly that—universal. They apply in the same way to objects and environments at the furthest reaches of our galaxy, and every other galaxy for that matter, in the same way as they do here on earth. Yes, there are places where conditions and circumstances mean that the laws of physics seem, if not to break down, then to stretch our understanding of them. For example, regions around black holes known as *event horizons* may be one such place.

By understanding a little about the forces of nature and the laws of physics and motion, we may be in a better position to make our animation, no matter how fantastical and alien, accurate or at least plausible. The same laws of motion that extend to all living things will also apply to alien life forms, if they exist. However weird and wonderful, these life forms will be required to comply with those same laws of physics that govern the ones found on earth.

A number of forces, objects, and matter are more familiar to physicists and cosmologists than the rest of us. Although we may know that these things exist, or at least we believe them to exist insofar as theories point to their existence, the possible impact on our everyday lives by such exotic concepts as dark matter, dark energy, and dark flow may not be of such urgent importance to us. On a day-to-day basis, these phenomena are not clearly evident to us; once again, though they may be of interest, they seem to have little impact on the way we live our lives or the manner in which we generally see that things behave.

Let's therefore concentrate for the time being on those four main forces that *do* impact our lives: gravity, electromagnetic force, weak nuclear force, and strong nuclear force. Of these four forces, it is only gravity that is clearly evident to us and impacts upon the way we live our lives. It is gravity that will determine the work we make as animators; so it is gravity on which we will concentrate in our study. For now it may be interesting to discuss, at least briefly, the other three forces and see how gravity sits alongside them.

The Weak Nuclear Force

The *weak nuclear force* is the weakest of the three other forces after gravity; its effects are swamped by both the electromagnetic force and the strong nuclear force. The range over which the weak nuclear force is effective is extremely limited and extends over only a very small region of space. It doesn't even work at a microscopic level but works at a subatomic level. The weak nuclear force enables the transmutation of subatomic particles that often results in these particles accelerating at very high speeds. It is not a force that is readily evident in our day-to-day lives, but when it does have an effect it has a big one. The weak nuclear force plays a role in supernova explosions, which generate such a burst of energy that they may even (temporarily at least) outshine an entire galaxy. In our work as animators we may, for the most part, safely ignore this force and its impact on the things we take for granted.

The Strong Nuclear Force

As the structure of the atom became more evident, researchers realized that there was a force that bonded the protons together, working against the force caused by their electronic charge. Physicists discovered that gravity was far too weak a force to be responsible for this phenomenon, so they had to find another very strong force capable of allowing this binding to occur. The *strong nuclear force* is the strongest of nature's forces; however, like the weak force, it has a very short range and is ineffective beyond the region of the proton or the neutron. Only the heavier atomic particles are influenced by this force; both protons and neutrons are subject to its influence, whereas electrons, photons, and neutrinos are not. The strong nuclear force is the source of great energy. Perhaps the best illustration of this concept can be found in sunlight. It is the strong nuclear force that controls the nuclear reactions in fusion reactors, examples of which are our own sun and other stars.

The Electromagnetic Force

By comparison to gravity, a *magnetic force* exerts a stronger force, though its effect is felt over a much shorter distance. If you hold even a very small magnet over a nail, you will see how the force from the magnet pulls the nail upward off the surface it sits on to snap onto the magnet. The force exerted by a magnet small enough to hold in your hand is greater than the gravitational force exerted by an object as large as the earth. Move the magnet just a couple of inches above the nail and the electromagnetic force is not strong enough to move the object, let alone lift it. It's only when the magnet is located very close to the nail that its force exerts any perceivable influence.

Electromagnetic force plays a major role in all the phenomena that we encounter in our daily lives. Electromagnetism provides the force that holds all the electrons and protons together in all matter. Without this force, matter would not bind together to form atoms, atoms could not form molecules, and the structures that form all the recognizable material could not exist. Still, as important as this force is to our very existence, its implications may be of relatively limited value to us as animators attempting to gain more insight into action and dynamics.

Gravity

Unlike the other forces of nature for which range is limited, the range of *gravity* is universal. Its effects can be felt across the universe. All objects in the universe exert a gravitational pull on all other objects in the universe. When an apple falls to the ground from a tree branch, its downward motion is due to the gravitational forces exerted on it by the earth. However, the apple also exerts a force (an infinitesimally smaller one) on the earth. Though we can detect the former (the falling apple), it is not possible to detect the latter. Large buildings may have an effect on us, however small, as we pass them, as evidenced in experiments that demonstrate the gravitational pull of mountains.

Gravitational forces are responsible for huge clouds of coalescing gases that then ultimately implode, ignite, and become stars. It is gravity that keeps our moon in orbit around the earth and the earth around the sun. It is gravity that gives the galaxies their shape. Without gravity, much of the matter within the universe would simply drift or fly off in all directions.

The Italian physicist and mathematician Galileo Galilei made experiments in the latter part of the 16th century that established the effect of gravity on objects of different weights, finding that they fell to earth at the same rate. Famously he

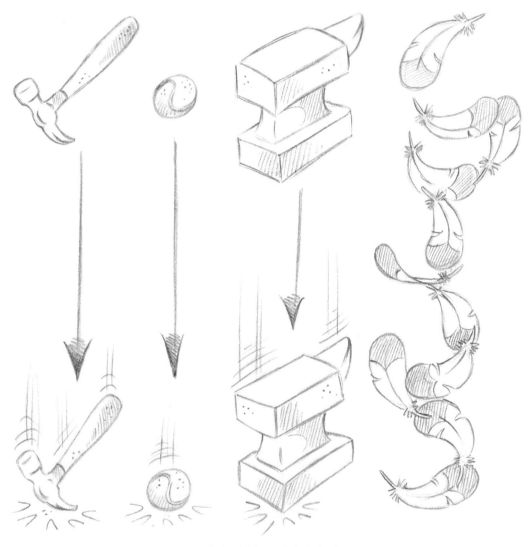

FIG 2.1 All objects fall at the same rate within a vacuum. Feathers fall slower only due to air resistance.

was supposed to have conducted these early experiments by dropping balls from the top of the Tower of Pisa. Unfortunately, this endearing story is more than likely apocryphal. However, the accounts of his experiments that entailed rolling a series of balls down slopes to demonstrate the effect of gravity aren't fiction. He demonstrated that through the effects of gravity, objects of varying weight fell and accelerated at the same rate, which supplanted the earlier belief, promoted by Aristotle, that heavier objects fell faster than lighter ones.

The difference that may be observed in the rate at which different objects fall to earth is due to air resistance. The air resistance on most objects is negligible, so a cannonball and a small marble released from the same height and at the same moment will hit the ground at the same time. A feather falls to earth at a slower rate than a hammer, not because the feather is lighter than the hammer but simply because of the different effects of air resistance on both objects. An experiment carried out by astronauts on the moon demonstrated that, when dropped at the same moment and from the same height, a hammer and a feather hit the moon's surface at the same time. Since there is no atmosphere on the moon, there can be no air resistance; therefore no friction acted on the falling objects.

Newton's Theory of Gravitation

In 1687 Sir Isaac Newton published his groundbreaking work, the *Principia*, in which he presented his theories on the principles of universal gravitation, meeting with immediate universal acclaim. Although there have been many further developments in the field since their publication, Newton's theories remain central to our understanding of the forces of gravity. In the *Principia* Newton set out the theories that explained the gravitational forces that accounted for the moon's orbit around the earth and the planets' orbit around the sun. Although some of the details of his theory have been replaced or superseded by the work of Albert Einstein and others, Newton's general theory still holds good to this day.

The general tenet of the theory states that every *point mass* (a theoretical point with mass assigned to it) exerts a force that attracts every other point mass that is oriented along a line intersecting both points. The theory goes on to state that every object within the universe attracts every other object with a force that is directly proportional to the objects' mass and inversely proportional to the square of the distance between the objects. The greater the mass of an object, the more force is exerted, and the closer the object, the more force is exerted.

Without the effect of gravitational forces, much of the material within the universe would simply fly off in all directions. Indeed, the universe as we know it could not have formed. Clouds of gas could not have coalesced and would then not have collapsed to form stars, and without the formation of stars, the heavier elements such as carbon (of which you and I are created) could not have formed.

Let's consider for a moment the effect of gravity on a cannonball shot from a cannon. Without the effect of gravitational forces or friction as a result of air resistance, the cannonball shot horizontally from a high place would simply travel in a straight line away from the earth and continue on its way into infinity, unless it encountered another object to stop or deflect it.

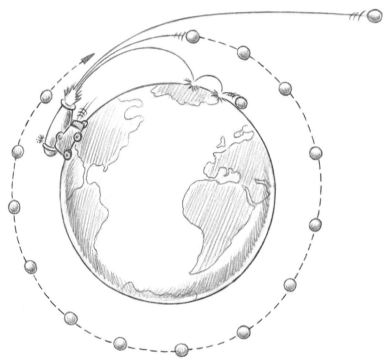

FIG 2.2 Escape velocity must be reached to send objects into orbit or beyond the gravitational pull of the earth.

However, gravitational forces *do* exist, and these forces determine that the cannonball will not continue to travel on and on but instead will fall back to earth. Where and when the cannonball falls to earth, or indeed *if* the ball falls to earth, is dependent on the different forces exerted and acting on the cannonball. The variations in these forces mean that different results will be achieved in each case.

At low speeds the cannonball will fall to earth; the lower the speed, the nearer it will fall to the cannon from which it was projected. At much higher speeds that are equal to a threshold velocity, the cannonball will not fall back to earth but will remain in orbit around the earth. This is a result of the balance among the velocity of the ball, the result of the explosion within the cannon that propels the ball *away* from the earth, and the gravitational pull of the earth that pulls the ball *toward* the earth. If these forces are in balance, a stable orbit is achieved.

At even higher speeds the cannonball will escape the earth's gravitational pull and will not fall back to earth nor be held in orbit around the earth; instead it will continue on its way and move away from the earth into space. It will continue in this manner until it encounters another object or the gravitational forces of another object, which will either stop it or deflect it.

Newtononian Laws of Motion

It is mostly very evident to the observer that animals and other animate beings have the ability to exert forces from within to create a whole range of movements that they have, for the most part, complete control over. They swim, they run, they jump, and they eat. There are many other things that we see around us that move, some of them in very dynamic ways that require external forces to create this dynamic motion: air pressure and wind create the waves on the ocean, tidal forces are responsible for moving vast quantities of material around, the flowing water in rivers is due to geographical and geological conditions—even the movement of clouds, the blowing of leaves on the trees, and the violent eruptions of volcanoes all are determined by a variety of external forces.

These laws describe the relationship between the forces acting on a body and the motion of that body. They are physical laws that form the basis for classical mechanics and are used to describe the motion of larger objects, whereas the motion of subatomic objects and material is described in terms of quantum mechanics. The laws that underpin classical mechanics are capable of producing highly accurate and predictable results; it is on this predictability that our engineering and technology are built and that provides us with a basis for our analysis of movement.

Newton outlined the laws of motion that, along with his work on universal gravitation, explained the findings of the German astronomer and mathematician Johannes Kepler with regard to Kepler's work on the motion of planets. Newton went on to use these laws to investigate the motion of many other subjects.

Newton asserted that all forces should not be seen as remote and divorced from objects and that any given force is dependent on the interactions between objects. As a result, there can be no unidirectional forces; they are all determined by the location of objects and their relationships to one another, as we shall see when we cover Newton's third law of motion.

Newton's three laws can be outlined as follows:

> *First law.* An object will remain at rest until a force acts on it.
> *Second law.* An object will accelerate proportionately to the force applied to it.
> *Third law.* For every action there is an opposite and equal reaction.

There should be no need for us to get bogged down with any formulas that fully explain these laws, but I think by adding a *little* more detail we would gain some benefit. So let's do that.

Newton's First Law of Motion

Newton's first law of motion simply reflects what others before him had already observed: An object at rest will remain at rest until a force acts on it. That idea would seem to be pretty straightforward and observable in our everyday experience. If we don't pick up the coffee cup, for example, it is likely to remain where we placed it. It is for this reason that Newton's first law of motion is also often referred to as the *law of inertia*. What is a little beyond our first-hand experience is the assertion that if an object is in motion, it will remain in motion in the same direction and at the same speed until it encounters a force to act on it. Under normal circumstances this is not what we experience. If we kick a ball, it will travel so far and no further. It will also travel in an arc and not in a straight line.

It was Galileo that established that a force acting on an object resulted in the *acceleration* of the object, not the object's speed. Newton's first law goes on to state that if there is no force acting on an object, there can be no acceleration of the object, and as a result the object will maintain its current velocity. If the velocity of the object is at zero, it follows that the object will remain at rest. Put very simply:

- An object at rest will remain at rest until a force acts on it.
- An object in motion will not change its velocity until a force acts on it.

It's this second point that seems to imply that an object will move and continue to move. We kick a ball and the reason we observe it slowing down is in fact

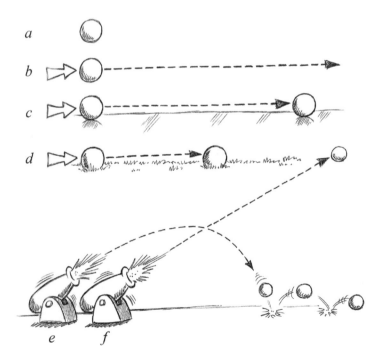

FIG 2.3 An object remains at rest. a: An object remains a rest if no force is applied. b: An object will move once a force is applied. c: The low friction of a smooth surface allows an object to move further than one moving along a rough surface with more friction. d: A high-friction surface. Constant velocity. e: The level of force applied to an object determines how far that object will travel. f: Greater forces applied to objects enable greater distances to be gained.

due to a force acting on that object; that force is friction. A rolling ball moving along a flat surface is seen to slow down regardless of how fast the ball was moving initially. Without any intervening force, the ball would roll on forever. The reason the ball slows down at all is that it encounters friction as it travels through the air and as it interacts with the surface it is rolling along. The smoother the surface, the less friction there will be and the further the ball will travel. The force acting on the ball changes its velocity and the ball slows down.

The direction of the force applied to an object will also determine the direction that the object will move it. Kicking a ball will apply a force along a given path, resulting in the ball moving in the direction of that path. Without any other force being applied to the ball, it will continue to move in the same

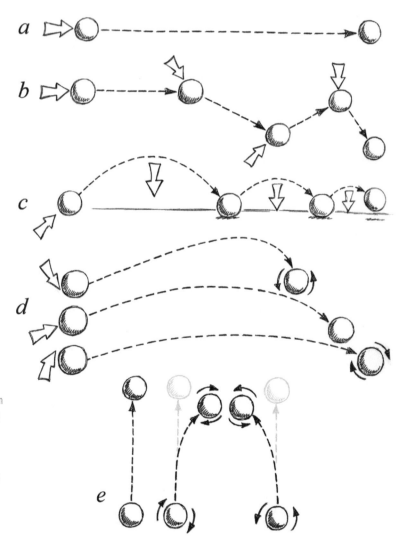

FIG 2.4 a: An object will move in the direction of the force applied. b: The object will change direction depending on the additional forces applied to it. c: An object will move in a way determined by the forces acting on it, in this instance a propelling force and the downward pull of gravity. d: The angle a force is applied to a sphere will create varying degrees of spin, which will determine its trajectory. e: The direction of spin will determine in which direction a ball will move.

direction in a straight line. Again, this is not what we generally experience. If we kick a ball into the air, it travels in the direction of the force, but it also describes an arc as it moves upward and then downward, back toward the ground, as a result of the gravitational pull of the earth. We may also see the ball swerve as it moves through the air, again due to other forces acting on it— perhaps asymmetry in the ball itself, either in its shape or its surface. Swerving may also be due to any spin we put on the ball. Spin creates differences in air pressure on one side of the ball to the other, and this difference creates lift in the direction in which there is more turbulence. The result is that a ball is seen to swing through the air. Many athletes use this principle to great effect when throwing, hitting, or kicking a ball toward a given target in order to deceive an opponent as to the trajectory of the ball.

Newton's Second Law of Motion

The second law of motion states that the greater the force applied to an object, the greater is the acceleration of that object, though this acceleration is also determined by and proportional to the mass of the object.

FIG 2.5 The greater a force applied to an object, the further it will move. Force is required to overcome the inertia within an object. The more mass an object has, the greater the force needed to move it.

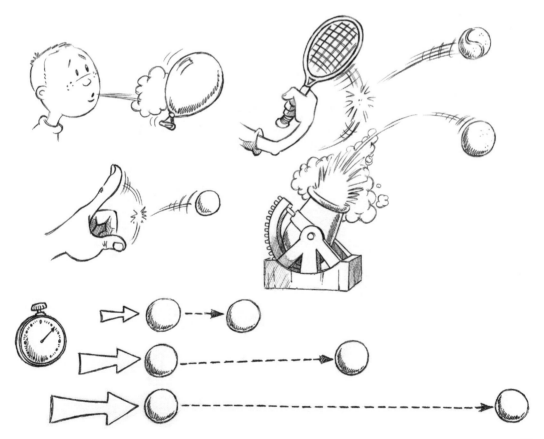

It is well within our everyday experience to observe that the greater the force applied to an object, the greater its acceleration. The harder you kick, throw, or hit a ball, the faster it will travel. We can also observe quite easily that the greater the mass an object possesses, the more force is required to move it. It is easier to set a ping-pong ball in motion by no more than blowing on it than to set a tennis ball moving, which would require more energy and force, or to set a cannonball in motion, which would require more force than either the ping-pong ball or the tennis ball. From this we can see that the more mass an object possesses, the more inertia it has.

This inertia needs to be overcome to create movement, and a higher degree of energy is required for objects of a greater mass to achieve a stated level of acceleration. In other words, it takes more energy to get a large truck moving at 20 miles an hour than it does to get a motor scooter up to the same speed.

Any increase in force will result in an increase in acceleration and the object will gain momentum. The increase in momentum will require a greater force to slow down or stop the object. This is also proportional to the mass of the object, so the greater mass an object has, the more momentum it possesses, and the more momentum it has, the greater force that is required to stop it.

FIG 2.6 The greater the momentum an object has, the more force required to bring the object to a standstill.

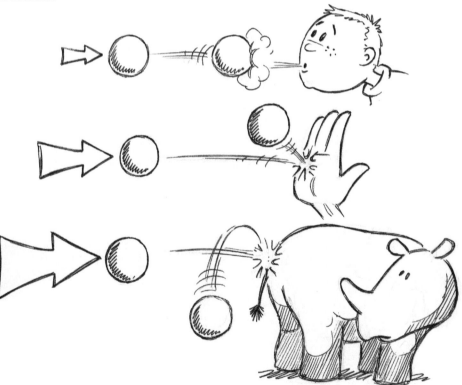

We have already seen that when a force is applied along a straight line, it determines the direction of the object, and if additional forces are applied, the direction of the object will change, determined by the direction in which the additional force is applied. The direction of this additional force will act in tandem with the force previously applied. If it is applied along the same orientation of the first force, it will result in the direction of the object remaining the same and the acceleration increasing proportionally. If the force is applied in the opposite direction, it will work against the existing force and cancel it, either in part or completely, depending on the strength of that force, resulting in the object either slowing down or stopping. If the additional force is greater than the original force, it will send the object in the opposite direction at a speed determined by the remaining force. Think of how a tennis ball is hit to and fro by opposing forces. If a force is applied obliquely to a moving object, it will create a change of direction in the object. This direction will be a result of both forces.

FIG 2.7 The direction and strength of additional forces will determine changes in the direction, speed, and spin of an object.

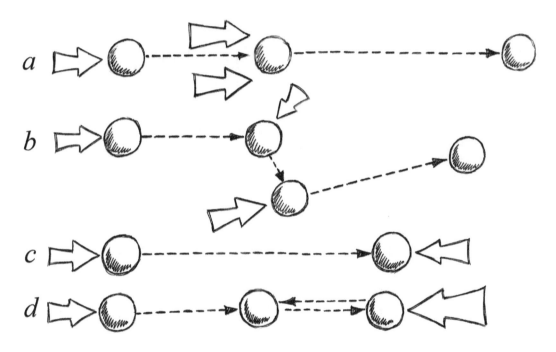

The application of a given force to an object results in the acceleration of the object to a constant speed. This works for a system in which the mass of the object remains constant. If the system is variable—if it gains or loses mass—the momentum of the object is increased or decreased. If the force is constant and the object within the system gains mass, the object will slow down. If the object loses mass while the force remains constant, the object will accelerate. This change in momentum is not a result of an additional external force but of mass either entering or leaving a variable mass system.

Consider a racing car being propelled by a given force. As it loses mass due to fuel consumption, the force applied, if constant, will result in an increase in speed.

Now consider a body in space as it moves through other material. The original object gains mass. Its collisions with other particles (however small) will slow down the object, but additional slowing will also occur due to the additional mass. A bus traveling down a street will slow down as more and more people climb aboard until it gains so much mass that the force is no longer sufficient to maintain the momentum, and it will stop.

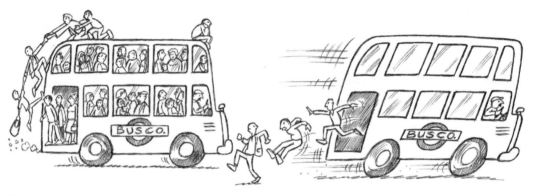

FIG 2.8 As mass is lost on a moving object, speed will increase if the force is maintained. If a body gains mass during motion, it will slow down.

Newton's Third Law of Motion

Newton's third law of motion states simply that every action has an equal and opposite action in direction and magnitude. The direction of both actions occurs along the same line, so when one object exerts a force on a second object, that second body exerts a reciprocal force on the first along that line.

When a horse is hauling a heavy cart, for example, the force the horse exerts on the load results in the load moving forward. However, the force that the horse exerts is reciprocated by the force that the load exerts on the horse. Although the actions and the forces are equal, the velocities of the individual objects

FIG 2.9 Every movement has an equal and opposite action. The horse pulling a load exerts forward movement, the load exerts backward forces.

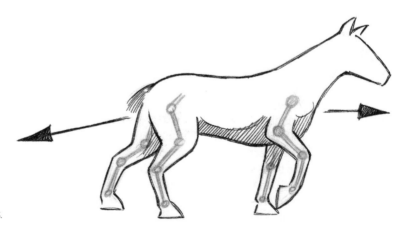

are not. The changes in velocities of each are proportionate to the separate bodies. As the horse continues to apply an increasing force, a point is arrived at whereby the inertia of the load is overcome and the cart moves forward.

The example of a cannonball being shot from a cannon is a good illustration of this concept. The forces on both cannon and cannonball are equal and result in equal actions, but as a result of the explosion within the cannon, the velocities of each object, cannon and cannonball, are different. The forward motion of the cannonball is far greater than the velocity of the backward motion of the cannon as a consequence of the difference in mass between the two. The cannon may move a few feet backward, whereas the cannonball will be projected over a much greater distance. If the mass of both objects were the same, the velocity would be the same for both objects.

FIG 2.10 A cannonball moves forward more quickly than the cannon only because it possesses less mass.

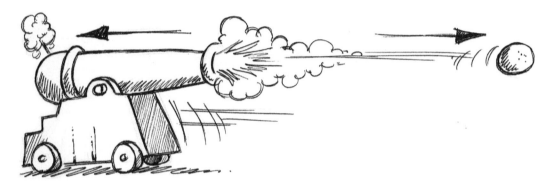

The velocity of a rocket ship's exhaust as it is expelled from the rear of the rocket during liftoff is far greater than the upward motion of the rocket, even though the forces on both the thrust and the rocket are the same. The velocities of each object are directly proportional to the object's mass, given that there are no other factors involved, such as friction acting on one object and not the other.

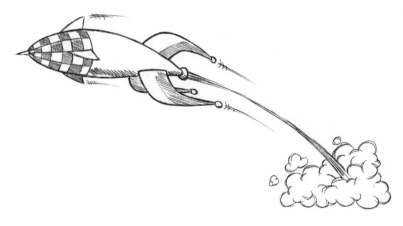

FIG 2.11 The gasses shooting out from a rocket move more quickly than the rocket because they possess less mass than the rocket.

Science is forever moving forward, expanding our understanding of the universe, and there are now many things that we take for granted that could not even have been dreamt of by Newton and his contemporaries. Einstein's theory of general relativity demonstrates that gravitational forces are not only capable of bending light, but when the gravitational forces are great enough they can even slow down time. Other theories and a deeper understanding of motion are constantly being developed that explore the nature of time, motion, and material. It is remarkable, then, that for our purposes we are still able to rely on the 17th-century findings of Newton.

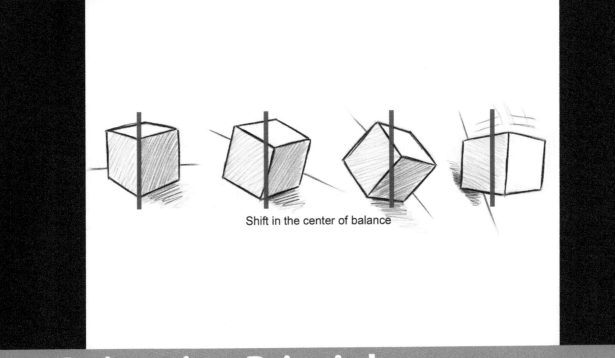

CHAPTER 3

Shift in the center of balance

Animation Principles

Animators face many difficulties in the creation of their art—difficulties that are not restricted to simply overcoming the technical challenges they face or the practical issues of managing a production. These challenges may indeed be considerable, as are the creative and conceptual issues of original productions. The difficulties animators face extend to the manipulation of models and objects, pixels, or drawings in their effort to interpret and replicate all kinds of movement.

A Little History

From a very early point in the history of animation, some practitioners began to analyze movement and started to formulate the basic principles of animation. This was done at least in part to accommodate the ever-increasing demand for more animation of a higher quality. As the popularity of animation increased significantly, driving demand for new product in turn meant that many more animation studios were created to meet that demand. However, the quality of the animation was somewhat variable, and unfortunately the majority of the work fell lamentably short of the standards reached by the likes of Winsor McCay.

Training soon became a vital part of the industrialization of the art form; establishing animation principles did much to enable individual animators' development and increase the studios' productivity. Since they were first formulated these animation principles have offered animators a system not only for the study of movement and dynamics but also for the creation of naturalistic and believable movement through animation.

During the first decade of the 20th century, simple animated movements of characters were usually enough to satisfy an audience, so naturally the studios were content to provide them with that. As competition for audiences became more intense, the demand for higher standards began to increase. Some studios rose to the challenge; others were content to continue producing what they had always done. No prizes for guessing which studios thrived and which ones began to struggle.

During my years as an animation teacher I have heard young aspiring animators utter many misconceptions. One of the greatest of these is the mistaken belief that the principles laid down by some of the pioneering animators no longer apply to modern-day techniques. These young animators couldn't be more wrong. Beyond a doubt, there have been some fantastic advances in production processes since those pioneering animators made the first animated films in the emerging studio system of the early 20th century. Indeed, there have been many changes since I first began animating in the early 1980s. But the principles hold as well now as they did way back then.

Approaches to Animation

Before we start to look in some detail at the animation principles themselves, we should look at three rather distinctive approaches to animation. These are not animation principles but rather guidelines that offer animators a way of looking at and classifying animation. We may find it useful to divide animated motion into three separate categories of movement: *simulation*, *representation*, and *interpretation*. Each one of these classifications provides a distinctive context in which the animation is seen by the audience. In addition, it may help to create a framework for the production of the animation.

Simulation

Animation that could be classified as *simulation* has a high degree of accuracy in its replication of naturalistic actions. Movement of this kind replicates exactly, or nearly as possible to exactly, the actual action or dynamics of objects and effects. It should be possible to test the results of simulated animation against real objects or events. Simulation is often used for highly naturalistic movement of objects and figures as well as effects such as water, flame, and smoke that appear in live-action films. The purpose of animation that simulates various effects in live-action films is to work seamlessly with the live-action elements.

To do that, the suspension of disbelief must be total. The film *The Perfect Storm* (2000) relied heavily on the accurate animation of the behavior of a hurricane and very heavy seas. To maintain believability, it was necessary to create the illusion of water in all its separate forms: the overall swell of the ocean, the giant wave that finally overturned the boat, individual waves that occurred on the surface of the giant wave, small wavelets, spray, and spume. All of these effects combined to create a magical but totally believable event. Many of the animated sequences were cut together with live-action shots of water, which placed extra emphasis on the accuracy of the simulated action.

The use of animation in most live-action films calls for this high degree of realism. It is this realism that is the key factor in audience acceptance. Computer-generated animation allows for a high degree of mathematical accuracy and occasionally even completely negates the hand of the animator.

Representation

Representational animation does not have the same constraints as simulation animation. It is usually made in a manner that demands less accurate movement than can strictly be evidenced in the actual behavior of the subject. Such a classification of animation may be extended to movements that may pass as "real," even if the actual movements themselves cannot be evidenced as such.

Consider the animated movement of dinosaurs. There is no doubting that these animals were real, but we have no hard evidence of how they moved. Therefore the animator is left with the option of making animation that is a representation of what we believe to be true. Animators may gather some insight into the way dinosaurs moved in life from the evidence offered by their fossilized remains, though even these remains may generate a degree of disagreement among paleontologists. Even so, we can make reasonable assumptions about dinosaurs' movements and very good or at least acceptable representations of their actions. We gather information about their size, an estimation of their weight, and theories about the articulation of their joints. All these pieces of information offer valuable clues for the animator.

It is possible that completely fictitious creatures may be represented in a "believable" manner if the animator uses reference material gathered from appropriate sources that allow for comparison with these subjects. Using animals and humans of a similar nature to the imagined creatures may offer a guide to the types of movement required if we look at each creature's shape and size, flexibility, and weight as a starting point. So, it is perfectly possible that unicorns, dragons, trolls, and hobgoblins—even the Devil himself—may all be represented by levels of believable motion. Some of the animated elements in *The Lord of the Rings* (2001–2003) integrated within the live-action footage are completely convincing. The evil Nazgul's dragon-like steeds are not only terrifying, they are totally believable.

Interpretation

Interpretive animation allows for a more creative use of animation and dynamics and leaves room for more personal expression that does not depend on either naturalistic or believable movement. Although the abstraction of movement and dynamics, and even the creation of completely abstract animation, falls into this area, interpretation is not limited to abstract forms. If we consider some of the best-known and well-loved cartoon animated characters, we can see that they are interpretations of the subjects they represent. Due to their very design, some human cartoon characters are destined to display movements that clearly do not reflect the actual movement of a human. Cartoon characters often have extraordinarily large heads, proportionally far larger than we would normally expect to see in real life. As a consequence they move in a manner we could consider cartoon-like. Indeed, cartoon characters of all kinds seem to obey the cartoon laws of motion rather than the laws of physics the audience experiences on a daily basis.

Striking a more abstract note, animated characters such as Daffy Duck and Bugs Bunny have few if any discernible qualities of either a duck or a rabbit. Yet we still accept them as representatives of their animal forms because, despite their abstraction, they possess the minimal requirements for recognition. Despite walking upright and looking more like a youth in a gray suit, Bugs has long ears, buck teeth, and a fluffy tail like a rabbit. Daffy has the same overall physiognomy as Bugs and he also walks upright, but he has a yellow bill and a small feathered tail like a duck. Other than these details there is little to commend them as either rabbit or duck. Instead, we recognize them not as their animal forms but as characters.

Other cartoon characters are even more abstract in nature. Ren and Stimpy, a cartoon cat and Chihuahua dog, barely resemble animals, let alone a cat or a dog. The artistic liberty animators and designers are able to take is extreme. These more abstract designs are open to interpretation because they are not being measured against anything that the audience has experience of, so they become acceptable as cartoon characters.

Four A's of Animation

Over the years I have considered the hierarchical nature of animated action, leading me to come up with an additional way of classifying animation to help us better understand and appreciate the nature of animated dynamics. These classifications are *not* an alternative to the principles of animation that are set out in this chapter; rather, they offer a useful addition to those principles. I call these concepts the *Four A's of Animation*.

There are four distinct levels of animated action that identify the nature of movement from the simplest to the most complex. The Four A's may best be considered in a sort of hierarchical fashion, with the most simple at the bottom and progressing upward to the most complex and sophisticated actions at the top. These categories of animation set out to differentiate between these levels. The categories are:

- Acting
- Animation
- Action
- Activity

These levels of animated action are appropriate to certain animated movements. They are not a ladder for the would-be animator to climb, nor are they meant to imply the ability of the animator. They identify the nature of movement in various subjects. The animator, regardless of the discipline he or she works in, the techniques used, the format of the production, or the intended audience, will at some point or another encounter all of these—sometimes all in a single shot.

Activity

The *activity* category describes the simplest of the four forms of movement and is at the bottom of the Four A's of Animation. Such movements are extremely basic and describe a type of dynamic that cannot easily be associated with any naturalistic movement. An object or image moving in this mode would not describe the behavior or movement that was recognizable as belonging to any given object. Activity is evident when an object or image appears at a particular point in space at a particular moment in time. This object or image would then be seen as either the same object or a different object at a second moment in time and point in space. The location in space and the place it appears on a timeline may be completely random, or it could follow a structured pattern but a pattern that does *not* conform to a movement the viewer would recognize as belonging to a subject in nature.

By way of illustration, let's consider for a moment the static "snow" on a television set that is not tuned in and receiving a clear signal. We witness a flurry of vigorous movement but not of a type that relates to any naturalistic movement. The individual sparkles move across time and space, though they do not represent the identifiable movement of any object. Sparkles on moving water, though not entirely random, could be said to represent simple activity.

Another example of animation that we may consider simply as activity is often evidenced in the credit sequences of nonanimated films. The moving text, whether scrolling down or across the screen, fading, flickering, or presented in a host of other ways, is clearly animated but has no form of movement that we can attribute to the image itself. The text in this instance is not represented

FIG 3.1 The movement within the neon lights in the examples shown top and bottom and the typography on the video screen in Tiananmen Square, Beijing, may be classified as activity within the four A's of animation.

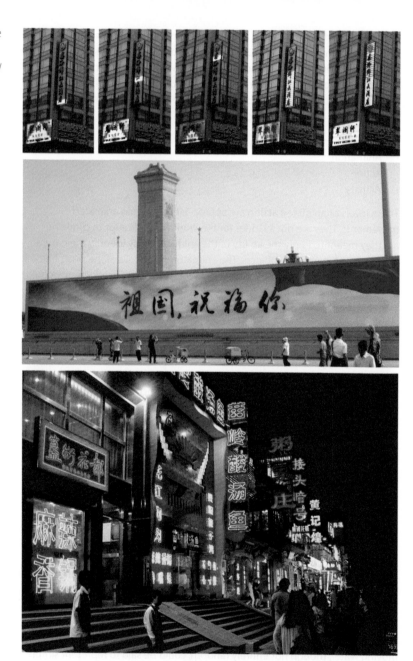

as a natural way of moving, since typography has no natural way of moving, though we still witness the movement. This is simple activity. It is possible for animators to create the illusion of a recognizable dynamic using typography as a subject, and through their skills they may make that type appear as heavy as stone, as light as a feather, or as fast as a hawk and then be recognized as having movement that relates to those things. In general terms, the movement of text on a screen usually conforms to simple activity. Movements that relate to and demonstrate such qualities as weight or balance come under the next category of animation: action.

Action

The *action* classification of animation relates to the identifiable movements of an object or image that are natural to that object. The nature of the animation that falls under this classification depends on a number of factors, principally the nature of the object itself. The material the object is made of will influence the action. The reason a tennis ball bounces more than a cannonball is due, at least in part, to the material of which it is made, which allows for more bounce; it is more flexible, being made of rubber rather than the metal of a cannonball. We can all easily recognize the flexible movement of wooden planks in a footbridge, though the flexibility is less evident in shorter and thicker pieces of wood; we understand how cloth flutters when made into a flag that hangs at the top of a flagpole and how it is less prone to flutter when made into garments. We know that flesh is soft and metal is hard, that concrete crumbles but does not do so as readily as biscuits.

Now consider the movement of the flame of a candle, smoke billowing up from a garden fire, waves on water, leaves on a tree blowing in the breeze, and thousands of other examples. All may be said to possess the kind of dynamic range that can be attributed to those known objects and that the actions are recognized by the viewer as belonging to those objects. There is even more to take into consideration in animating subjects with an attributed action. Objects not only demonstrate an action determined by their material or their shape and size; their actions are also demonstrated by the external forces that act on them. Gravity will impart an action; air resistance and wind power may

FIG 3.2 The movement of the candle flame, the flaring match, and the water droplets are classified as "action" within the four A's of animation.

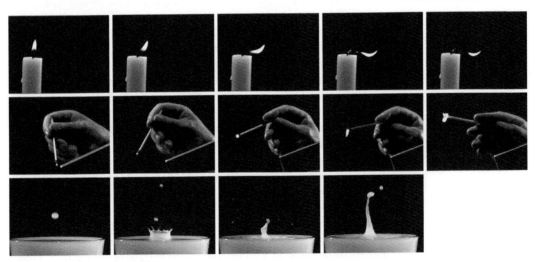

impart another kind of action, as will rain. The action of a bouncing ball on a street will be very different from a bouncing ball on the moon or the same ball at the bottom of the ocean. The one thing all of these "naturalistic" actions have in common is that they are all subject to the same laws of physics.

The nature of movement is inextricably linked to the nature of the subject. Boulders roll down a hill in the way they do because they are made of rock, they are heavy, and more often than not they are uneven in shape. Leaves fall to earth from a tree because they have been blown by the wind, but they do it in a particular way due to their weight, shape, and size as well as the material of which they are made. These characteristics give these objects a particular and recognizable action. The key point here is that all of the subjects we have covered move without the *intention* to move at all, let alone in any given way; it is simply in their nature to move the way they do. The movement that we witness demonstrates only those actions that are related to the object itself and the forces acting on it. The intention to move is the topic that takes us one step higher in the hierarchy of action.

Animation

The *animation* level of action classification describes all the movements, naturalistic or not, that are generated from within an object or image itself. Although these images or objects are still subject to external forces acting on them, the motivating factor behind this movement comes from within. A bouncing ball from our earlier example does not generate its own movement; external forces do that. The external force made the ball move in the first place; gravity causes it to fall, and the surface it hits and the material properties of the ball determine the bounce. In contrast, cats and dogs and mice all move as a result of their *intention* to move.

The complexity and range of dynamic possibilities of the various kinds of movement are almost endless. If we simply look at the various types of locomotion, we can see how they relate to the varying nature of the structures that undertake locomotion; fish swim, birds fly, frogs hop, and humans walk upright. The various types of physiognomy of the subjects— some with legs (of varying numbers), some with fins, some that are smaller than a pinhead, some larger than a London bus—determine the various types of movements they make. Not all fish swim in the same manner, and not all birds fly using the same flying technique. Some variations are down to the choices the animal makes; other differences are a result of physical and behavioral dissimilarities. These differences, along with the various influences (physical and psychological) by which the creatures are motivated, simply determine the type of action. Big or small, swimming or flying, living creatures and their various movements have one thing in common: They demonstrate a choice in their movement, and that is the key to animation in this context: *intention*. A flag does not intend to wave, it does so because of its nature and the forces that apply to it under any given circumstance. However, a spider does intend to crawl across the floor, a lion

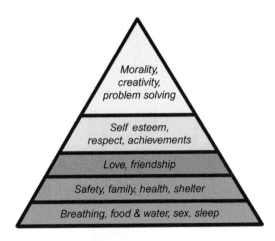

FIG 3.3 Maslow's hierarchy of needs.

does intend to drag down a zebra, and the zebra does intend to escape the lion's clutches.

Motivation is as varied as the forms of physiognomy. Psychologist Abraham Maslow's hierarchy of needs goes some way to classifying these motivations:

- *Self-actualization*. Morality, creativity, spontaneity, problem solving.
- *Esteem*. Confidence, achievements, respect.
- *Love/belonging*. Family grouping, sexual intimacy.
- *Safety*. Of body, of resources, of family, of health, of home.
- *Physiology*. Breathing, food and water, sex, homeostasis.

Clearly, not all living beings are motivated to respond to the same degree, and for some organisms these "rules" may not even apply at all. The epic journey that salmon undertake from the sea back up to the river in which they were born in order to spawn and then die is motivated by sex and the need to pass on their particular genes. The bounding action of a gazelle as it makes its way through the African bush demonstrates a survival tactic to avoid predators. The human commuter running to catch a train during the morning rush hour may not be doing so to guarantee his genetic heritage or in an effort to avoid predation, but nonetheless he may still be motivated by a factor of great concern: earning money. We are all motivated by different things.

The motivations that drive this vast and varied range of movements and actions we see within all living creatures are likely to shift and change, creating shifts and changes within the patterns of movement of the individual subjects. These changes may occur over various periods of time. External forces may motivate and trigger certain actions at different time scales. For example, every day the onset of evening brings about activities in moths and their hunters, bats. Every autumn the shortening day results in the mass gathering of martins and swallows for their annual migration from Europe to Africa. Some motivating factors are even longer: The periodical breeding cycle of some cicadas can be as long as 17 years.

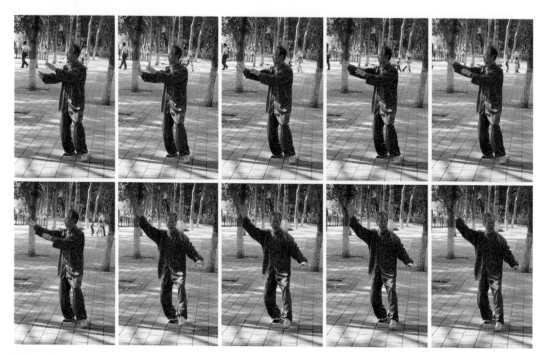

FIG 3.4 Gentleman practicing tai chi in a park in Changchun, China. The action is generated entirely from within the figure and as such may be classified as animation in the four A's of animation.

In most cases the shifts in behavior are brought about over very short periods of time. It is those internal psychological and emotional forces that motivate actions that we will look at in the next and highest *A* of animation: acting.

Acting

It is perfectly feasible for a student of animation to gain a grasp of animation timing very quickly. Understanding the principles of animation may take a little longer, but they can still be acquired over a reasonably short period. Acquiring the knowledge and expertise needed to create believable, naturalistic animation will almost certainly demand a more prolonged period of practice.

Then there is the task of mastering the art of performance-based animation. This is more akin to becoming an actor; it is likely to take a great deal of time and effort. It not only requires an understanding of the craft skills; it may also demand an understanding of the human condition, something that takes both time and experience to acquire. Acting is the highest form of action in animation. For the performance to be believable, it must transcend the manipulation of the physical and deal with mood, temperament, personality, and thought. Acting in animation deals in thoughts and feelings; the emotional range of the animated characters underpins all good performances. Without it we are left with moving manikins.

The characters in the animated film *The Incredibles* (2004) are some of the most well-defined and well-rounded personalities that have ever been seen in animation. They transcend their physical appearance and are emotionally complex. It is because they are so completely believable that the audience becomes emotionally engaged.

In the film we see the characters take on several guises. One of the main characters is Helen Parr; in her everyday role she is a typical young American woman, though in her role as superhero she is Elastigirl, doing her bit in the fight against crime. As Mrs. Incredible she is wife to Mr. Incredible and the mother of three children; she is the glue that keeps this family, with all its pressures and stresses, together. She is no simple superhero with special powers (however impressive those powers are); she is a real person and as such is completely believable and engaging. We see her, as a mother and housewife, trying to do the best for her family, balancing the different needs and demands of everyday experience—the school run, the trip to the market, feeding the baby, keeping a home, and being a loving wife to a loving husband. When she discovers evidence that she mistakenly reads as the infidelity of her husband, she reacts and behaves in ways based on her emotional responses. We feel her anxiety, disappointment, and anger. In the performance of this character we witness animation as acting. The complex emotions she exhibits are the motivating factor behind her actions.

These psychological and emotional motivations bring about the shifts in movement and action that determine the nature of an animation and a performance. For animators (actors), these psychological and emotional aspects of animation take the greatest time to master. Perhaps we never truly master the craft of acting for animation; perhaps we merely develop and refine our abilities. This is the height of our craft.

Even in the most humble of animated action, the psychological state of a character may be in evidence. The nature of a walking figure will vary depending on the mood and temperament of the character walking. According to the veteran animator Richard Williams, a regular walk cycle conforms to march time and is completed over 12 frames. Although this may provide a reasonable walk cycle, it is a little simplistic to suggest that *all* walk cycles will be of the same duration. A character that is unhappy or depressed may walk more slowly (certainly not in march time), taking shorter steps and completing the cycle over many more frames. A walk undertaken as a result of a character being elated, let's say at the news that the individual has just won the hand of a beautiful woman, would probably result in the figure walking rather faster than normal and with a lighter step, perhaps even quicker than march time. The point here is that these walk cycles, though still modes of locomotion, will all vary depending on the psychological and emotional state of the walker.

For the most part animators deal with the issue of animated movement that asks for action and animation in their subjects. The use of acting, certainly acting that demands the highest level of emotional engagement, is less frequent. Appreciating all these separate A's of animation and being able to differentiate between them, as well as seeing how they might work separately or in combination, will enable the animator to gain a better understanding of animation and develop toward becoming a master of his or her craft.

Timing for Animation

I have lost count of the number of times students have asked me, "What is good animation timing?" Like any teacher, I am always very eager to help and be as much use as I can to my students in their efforts to make the most of their education. So I strive to tell them and demonstrate to them what good animation timing is. The truth is: I can't. Well, that is not strictly true. What I always try to emphasize is not *good* animation timing but *appropriate* animation timing. What is appropriate timing for one type of animation may be completely wrong and inappropriate for another type of animation. Only once the animator has established the demands of the animated film can that animator make a judgment about what constitutes good or successful animation timing. Naturalistic animation timing is not the same as cartoon animation timing and may not necessarily be the same as comedy animation timing.

All good comedy is a matter of timing. In this regard it is easier to establish what is good timing or not. If the timing of a gag is wrong, it simply won't be funny. However, this is easy to say but a good deal harder to explain or teach. Good comic timing is not a simple matter of saying that a successful pratfall is funny if it's over 12 frames, whereas one over 16 frames is unfunny. Good comedy acting is a matter of experience, not a formulaic approach to timing. It is difficult to learn and takes a great deal of practice and experimentation.

The use of animation timing is the principle source of all naturalistic or abstract actions and all animated performances. Regardless of discipline, technique, or process, animation timing is central to all animation; regardless of discipline, animation timing takes a great deal of patience and practice to fully master.

Timing for animation can be divided into three very distinct types that describe the various aspects of animated film: *pacing, phrasing,* and *animation timing.* Let's look at each in turn.

Pacing

Pacing describes the variations in the dynamics of a film narrative and the animated film in its totality. This form of animation timing describes the manner in which a story is expressed within a specific timeframe. It determines how a film narrative develops, how the tension is built through a series of sequences, how mood is established, and how action is driven along. Fast action sequences work together and interweave with slower sequences in an elaborate pattern to build a varied narrative and cinematic dynamic. Building such a dynamic draws in the audience in order to build suspense, create tensions and stresses within the framework of the film, and develop a mood response in the audience. The result takes an audience on an emotional journey, one that is varied, exciting, interesting, and engaging. This is possible only if the pacing of the film changes over the timeframe.

Again, there are no hard and fast rules regarding structuring and pacing in a film, but in general, fast-paced sequences are used to create high drama and action, and slower sequences help develop gentle intimacy and the opportunity to establish mood, location, or characterization. Pacing is concerned with narrative and storytelling rather than the actual timing of objects moving across the screen. That is covered by both phrasing and timing.

Phrasing

Phrasing aims to describe the variation in the speed and dynamics of a *series* of movements over a short time period, often in a short sequence of shots and within a single scene. This classification of animation timing does not refer to the overall narrative of a film but rather the relationship between actions within a sequence. The key point to bear in mind here is *the relationship between a series of actions*. It may be very useful to consider phrasing as a form of animation choreography. This idea is not limited to dance; it applies to all forms of animation, though it is perhaps within figurative animation, particularly animation of multiple characters, that it is most clearly evident. Rather like most dances, phrasing of action consists of fast, medium, and slow actions that work together to create a series of movements that demonstrate meaning and shifts of mood within a sequence. The way these movements are made and the way they are timed create the animated performance. The variation of timing between the individual movements is essential. If every single action within the shot moved at the same speed, there would be no sense of either naturalist action or a performance. We would be left with just movement— movement that would be pointless and would generate no meaning or context for the performance.

Acting is a matter of thinking, and this thinking then leads to action. Thinking brings about change within movement, a change that is brought about by various motivating factors. The change in speed of the animation denotes the thinking process within a character and subsequently a change in behavior brought about by that thinking. Such phrasing is not limited to animated characters that have personality; such changes will also take place in animated creatures and animals that have no discernible personality but are still driven by psychological factors. Phrasing, when applied well, can even create personality in abstract animation. Chuck Jones's *The Dot and the Line* (1965) is an excellent illustration of this concept.

Animation Timing

The term *animation timing* aims to describe the speed of a single movement of a character, object, or animated effect. Animation timing does not deal with the overall narrative or the acting or performance within a narrative; instead, it deals with such issues as the speed of an object's actions. This covers all actions, everything from a bouncing ball to a man's hand reaching out to pick up a cup of tea, a bucket of water falling over and splashing its contents onto the floor, a child turning her head, or leaves blowing on a tree. Animation timing is not restricted to naturalistic animation; it also refers to cartoon-based animation and even completely abstract action. The wonderful animation created by Oskar Fischinger depends no less on a profound understanding and mastery of animation timing than does the figurative work by master animators such as Barry Purves, Hayao Miyazaki, or Glen Keane and Andreas Deja. Regardless of style or technique, format or audience, it is animation timing that gives meaning to motion.

The basics of animation timing are really very straightforward: The closer images appear to one another on subsequent frames, the slower the movement will be. The further apart the images appear on subsequent frames, the faster the animation appears. It is as simple as that. However, it is the complexity of the variations in the movements—fast and slow, acceleration, deceleration, and constant speed—that forms the basic currency of animated dynamics. Using this basic currency of timing, animators are able to construct all manner of sophisticated movement, making elaborate performances possible.

Things in nature seldom move at a constant speed. They have a tendency to accelerate and decelerate at different moments within an action. Movements begin and finish at different moments, actions instigate other actions, they overlap one another, they repeat and they cycle; actions reverse and they progress at different rates. Actions are immensely complex.

In all forms of animation, regardless of process, timing is the one thing they have in common, and the one thing that all students or practitioners of animation should bear in mind all the time is that *timing gives meaning to motion*.

The Hierarchy of Animated Actions

When we look at the nature of articulated movement—that is, movement in subjects that have constituent parts such as limbs or appendages and are not simple objects with no discrete and separate elements capable of independent animation or movement—we may witness a form of *hierarchy* of dynamics within the movement of the subject. More simplistic objects, such as rocks, planks of wood, tables and chairs, apples and pears, cups and saucers, and any single-celled creature that does not have articulated parts, would not possess the capacity for such a hierarchy of action. We may consider those subjects that do have articulation and are capable of using their different parts independently of one another as having the potential for a hierarchy of action. These I have divided into three areas: *primary action, secondary action,* and *tertiary action*. Each of the separate parts of a subject may possess its own range of movements, some of them capable of primary motion, others only having the ability to move as tertiary action. Arms are usually able to lift objects; the tails of some animals can't. Each of the different elements of an object or a living being may also demonstrate different kinds of movement as they react to the external forces that act on them. Consider the effect that a light breeze has on hair; this effect will be very different from the breeze's effect on the head on which the hair grows.

The hierarchy of actions that I set out here is not necessarily set or fixed; it can shift throughout a particular movement. During one phase the primary action may be located in one part of a figure. As the action progresses and changes, the source of the primary action may also shift and change.

Primary Action

The term primary action is an attempt to describe the types of actions and the sources of those actions that *drive* a particular movement. For some types of movement, the primary source of the action may be constant throughout the action; for other actions the primary action may change and shift throughout the movement.

Let's take a look at a couple of examples. First, consider a figure walking in a regular fashion on a flat and even surface. The primary action and the source of the movement in this walk are located in the figure's legs and hips. A human figure walking could be described as controlled falling. The balance of the figure is thrown forward (for forward motion) and each leg in turn is swung forward from the hip until the foot is placed on the floor, which prevents the figure from falling to the ground. Parts of the figure other than the legs may be in motion during a walk, but they are not the source of this form of locomotion. It is only the legs swinging forward and the hips rotating that provide the primary source of action. Certainly motion in other parts of the anatomy during the walk may be considered primary, but for the animator's purposes it might be useful to limit the attention to the legs. The primary source of action throughout a regular walk cycle is located in the hips and legs and for the most part will not change or shift throughout the action.

Now let's consider the action of a human figure lifting a heavy object from the floor. The principle action will shift throughout the animation of the lift. Initially it may be located in the legs and hips as the figure bends down to prepare for the lift. As the dynamics of the lift progress, this action will shift to the arms as the object is picked up. This action may then transfer back to the legs as the weight is lifted, though it may be transferred to the spine as

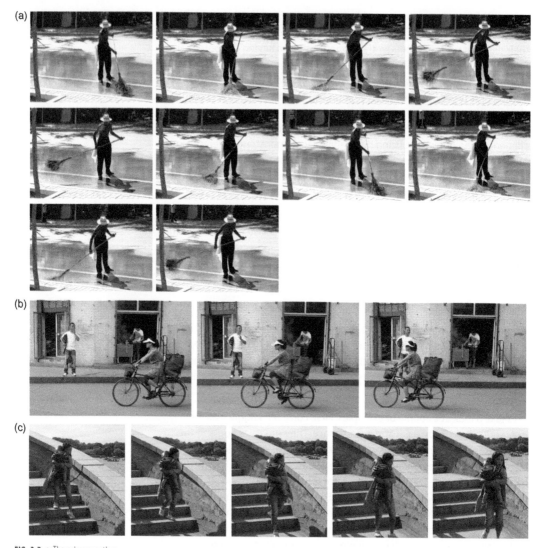

FIG 3.5 a: The primary action throughout this sweeping action is within the arms. b: The primary action in cycling is generated by the legs. c: The primary action during walking down steps is within the legs. Note how the arms play no part in assisting the action.

the action of the lift concludes. Some elements, such as the movement in the head, may remain constant throughout the action, though this movement would *not* be considered primary action. All three elements—legs, arms, and back—may be thought of as the primary action at certain points throughout the movement, whereas the movement in the head may not make a direct contribution to the lifting of the object.

Secondary Action

The kind of animation that we may consider as secondary action occurs as a *result* of the primary action and may even assist in the overall dynamic of a moving subject. However, even if these secondary actions help with

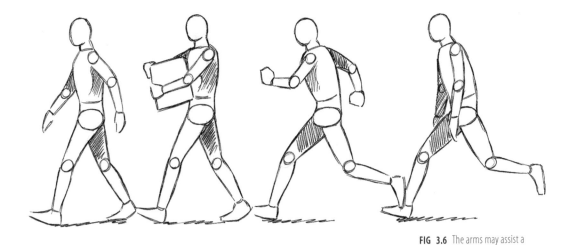

FIG 3.6 The arms may assist a
figure in locomotion but they are
not vital to the action. As such, they
demonstrate secondary action.

locomotion by creating balance or efficiency in movement, they do not *drive* the movement.

These secondary actions may often make for more effective, efficient, and economic movement in the figure as whole, but it may still be possible for the figure to move without the use of these secondary actions.

Secondary actions occur in all manner of movements. Although they might not be the focus of an animated movement, they will often provide the necessary element to make the animation appear believable. If they are omitted from an animated action, the results are at best rather ordinary and at worst lack naturalistic and convincing movement.

The action of the arms during a walk makes a contribution to the overall movement, providing a twist to the upper torso and a countermovement to the legs. However, the animation of the arms isn't critical or even necessary for that particular movement to be made. Although it might look a little unusual or even completely unnatural, it is perfectly feasible for a figure to walk without swinging its arms. The action of the arms during a run is more dynamic and more pronounced than in a walk; the role the arms play in assisting the overall dynamic of a run may be far greater than in a walk. Once again, it is still possible, if a little more awkward, for a running figure to keep its arms motionless and hanging by the side of the body throughout the action.

Tertiary Action

Finally, let's look at tertiary action. This action, like secondary action, is a result of movement brought about by primary action. Tertiary actions are those that are a result of the main movement or secondary actions and do not themselves assist or necessarily contribute to the effectiveness of the overall movement. In addition to being instigated by primary action, tertiary action may also be brought about by the less dynamic movement of secondary action. Tertiary action is usually associated with the appendages of a figure such as hair, mane, or tail. Because these appendages do not have the ability to generate movement of their own volition, tertiary action very seldom occurs in limbs or parts of the anatomy that are capable of independent movement.

Think about the different flowing actions of the mane and tail of a horse as it walks, canters, trots, or gallops. The mane and tail will stream out behind the horse to varying degrees as a direct result of the movement generated by the animal's running action. Now consider the action of the long, floppy ears of a dog as it runs. The ears may be animated with a very vigorous action, moving upward and downward because they are attached to the dog's head, but the dog's head is demonstrating secondary action. The head moves the way it does because the entire animal is being driven by the primary action of the

FIG 3.7 a: The tertiary action is evident in the movement of the garments worn by this running girl. b: The movement of the hair is tertiary action.

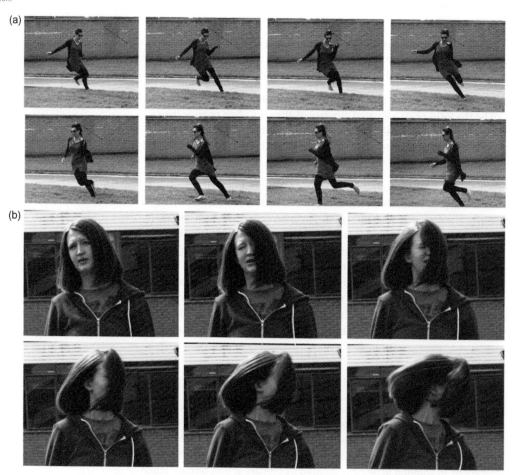

(a)

(b)

legs and the spine. In the process of this action the ears will demonstrate the animation principles of drag and overlapping action but will add nothing to the dog's running action.

Tertiary actions are also often associated with costumes and props. Take a look at the way the various fabrics of clothing move with a figure. The nature of the material itself will determine, in part, the manner of the movement. A very light silk will move more freely and readily than a heavy cotton or woolen garment. The movement of air across the clothing will perturb lighter fabrics more than heavier ones. The style of clothing will also generate different kinds of motion. Tight trousers may demonstrate very little tertiary action, whereas very baggy trousers or ones with flared legs will demonstrate more movement. Even very heavy objects may move quite freely, depending on how they are attached to the figure. A heavy sword hanging from a belt around the waist may swing and sway quite a lot, particularly if the figure begins to move at speed.

For animators to create naturalistic animation, it is important that they become aware of these different types of action and have a good understanding of how they relate to and interact with each other. Such understanding will then enable the animator to prioritize his or her efforts in the creation of believable animation.

Animators may choose to undertake the primary animation of a figure before attempting to deal with secondary or tertiary actions. This makes for a systematic approach to creating animation, one that often leads to a more effective and economical way of working. Clearly, however, this approach is not always possible, depending on the nature of the subject being animated, the techniques being used, and even the animation discipline, and it might not always be desirable. Each animator will find his or her own particular way of working; occasionally animators may find that they get better results by working with the separate elements of the animated figure all at once. Making straight-ahead animation often provides an additional vitality to the animation, something that keyframe animation may occasionally lack or even work against. Even when one has the option of keyframing it may not always be the best option. If the action is fast and chaotic and contains figures that have a lot of detail, with appendages and props and irregular movements that vary in timing and that change direction on a regular basis, straight-ahead animation may be the best way to deal with this action.

Of course, some animators need to consider primary, secondary, and tertiary actions all together. Stopframe animators face these constraints each time they animate, as straight-ahead animation is part and parcel of their craft skills. Straight ahead animation demands that all aspects of the animation must be completed at the same time, with each of these different types of action being made on each progressive frame of film. This clearly illustrates just how important it is for *all* animators but particularly those involved in stopframe animation to have a good understanding of the nature of the various types of action.

The Principles of Animation

The *principles of animation* came about through a perceived need to improve the standards in animation and animated performances. What started out as a way of defining animation and improving practical methods of production soon resulted in the establishment of certain working practices and processes. More important, it was a development in the *approach* to making animation. These working practices were found to have almost universal application to animation and as such became the principles of animation. Now, all these years later, through the use of the animation principles and an understanding of dynamics, animators are able to make the most believable and compelling animated sequences.

Of course, these principles apply to both naturalistic and abstract animation, even though abstract animation may not necessarily conform to the laws of physics. Via these principles, animators are able to apply types of movement that imbue objects, abstract shapes, and even simple marks with a quality and nature such as weight, articulation, inertia, and momentum that lend authenticity to the abstract form. Naturalistic animation also benefits from the application of these principles, since some of them relate directly to the qualities everyday objects possess, such as weight and balance.

One of the greatest challenges the animator faces is the creation of believable characters. This depends on many factors and is not simply limited to the way they move. However, for those characters to deliver a believable and engaging performance, it is important that they are convincing within the particular context of a given narrative or film. Therefore it is usually necessary that animated characters move in an appropriately believable manner. Understanding the notion of "appropriately believable" may be valuable at this stage.

Let's consider two very different productions with distinctive approaches to animation. In animation, feature film work has the highest production values and highest production budgets to match. TV series animation generally has lower production values and is far cheaper to produce. For our first example we will look at the Disney classic *Bambi*; the TV series category will be illustrated by *Ren and Stimpy*. The intention here is not to state that one form is better than the other; they are simply different. What they do have in common is that both are of the highest order within their particular format.

All the characters in *Bambi* represent real animals that for the most part undertake naturalistic action, though animal behaviorists might dispute that claim. For our purposes it is appropriate to call them naturalistic. On the other hand, neither Ren nor Stimpy behaves in any way like either a cat or a dog, which they represent. Their movements, as abstract and cartoony as they are, still owe a lot to the application of the same principles of animation as the characters in *Bambi*. It is the level to which these principles are used that differs. The limited use of squash and stretch in naturalistic animation may enhance the dynamics of the character and create more engaging and, in the context of entertainment, more believable animation. It is not important here for the movement to be correct but to *appear* to be correct and therefore acceptable. The extreme use of this same principle, squash and stretch in cartoon-based animation, does not simply enhance the movement in an effort to make the action realistic; it creates a distinctive form of movement all its own. We no longer compare the action to our own knowledge or preconceived ideas of movement; we are more than content to accept the action as appropriate to the form. Clearly what is appropriate usage for one may be inappropriate for the other. If the animation used for *Bambi* were expressed in the same manner as *Ren and Stimpy*, with shifts in volume, unnatural timing, and lack of perceptible weight, the bounds of believability would be broken. Conversely, if the animation of Ren and Stimpy conformed to an accurate illustration of weight and balance, timing, and the use of volume, it would lose much of its appeal and almost all its humor. It is the appropriate level of animated movement that creates a relevant and appropriate performance for individual productions. The point here is: If it looks right, it is right.

These principles, applied to animated actions, are not limited to character-based animation. They apply equally to animated effects such as water, fire, smoke, wave actions, and the animation of materials such as fabrics, metal, and wood.

It is my intention in this chapter to cover each of these principles in some detail. The principles of animation that were set out by the early Disney animators are a good starting point in covering this topic. Those principles are:

- Timing
- Secondary action
- Slow in and slow out
- Straight-ahead action and pose-to-pose
- Squash and stretch
- Anticipation
- Staging
- Follow-through and overlapping action
- Arcs
- Exaggeration
- Solid drawing
- Appeal

Although these principles may have been useful to animators in the 1930s and 1940s who were striving to improve not only their own work but to raise the level of craft skills and in doing so develop the art form, they do not necessarily reflect all forms of modern animation. Since those early pioneers of animation first struggled with creating animated performances, the craft of animation has moved forward a good deal, and it may be that today's principles of animation are slightly different from those identified in the Disney studio. At least there may be additional identifiable principles to be added to the original list as a result of those developments. The majority of these principles clearly remain relevant to animators working in any discipline, despite the fact that these were established before any form of digital animation was available. In those days 3D animation simply referred to what is now termed *stopframe animation*. There was only one form of 3D animation; it involved using actual objects moving in the real three-dimensional space. Now when we think of 3D animation we understand it to mean geometry-based computer animation.

If one original principle laid down by these pioneer animators might not have made the transition to universal relevancy for all forms of animation, it is *solid drawing*. This is a principle clearly more appropriate to animators who work in 2D classical animation. Solid drawing is still relevant and very useful for drawn animation, but it generally applies to drawn animation of a particular type—one that depends on a more academic approach to form, the understanding of form often gained through observational drawing and academic life drawing.

Though I see the relevance of *all* these principles, I would like to suggest a couple of additions to them, in part as a response to more recent developments in animation production processes:

- Drag
- Balance and weight
- Solid modeling
- Energy flow

I will go on to deal with these topics and leave it to the reader to assess whether they are worthy of being called additional principles of animation. We'll discuss the details in good time, after we've examined the original list.

Timing, Secondary Action, and Slow In and Slow Out

I have grouped these three principles together because they were already covered separately earlier in the chapter. In doing that I hoped to link these topics with other aspects of animation and animation timing. I think there is little point covering them separately here as well. Let's move on to cover in detail those other animation principles laid down by Disney animators during what became known as their Golden Age.

Straight-Ahead Action and Pose-to-Pose

I am choosing to deal with the principle of straight-ahead action next because it relates directly to animation timing and the mechanics of timing and animation production more than some of the other principles do. The two main modes of creating animation, *straight-ahead animation* and *pose-to-pose animation* (also known as *keyframing*), offer animators an opportunity to approach making animation in different ways. These different approaches each have their benefits and drawbacks and are very useful tools in creating vibrant and believable animation effectively and economically.

Straight-ahead animation is called that because the animation is made by creating one image after another in sequence, starting at the beginning of an action and moving progressively forward—that is, straight ahead—toward the end of the action. Image one is made, followed by images two, three, four, and so on. All stopframe animation is made using straight-ahead animation. It is in the nature of the discipline and as yet there is no alternative method available to animators who manipulate actual objects within a real space to create their animations. The process for Stopframe animation using straight-ahead techniques is deceptively simple: A model is positioned and then filmed for a given number of frames; it is then repositioned and filmed again. The process is repeated again and again until the action or shot is completed. The discipline needed to undertake this kind of animation calls for a high level of concentrated effort, particularly if the animator is using multiple characters in a shot. The process of straight-ahead animation is not the sole prerogative of stopframe; animators working in 2D classical animation or digital animation may find benefits to working this way.

If the action required is a fast one and the animation has a high degree of complexity to it, with plenty of separate elements all requiring animation with their own discrete timings, it may be more effective and economical to use straight-ahead animation to deal with all the elements at once. Trying to work out the keyframes for all these separate elements may be far too laborious and restrictive.

One disadvantage for the 2D classical animator working in this way is that the drawn figures may appear to shrink as the animation progresses. This is a result of very minor differences between subsequent drawings. The individual variation may be only the width of a pencil mark, but over the duration of 50 or 60 drawings, this will be a considerable difference. Care must then be taken to ensure that shrinkage does not occur.

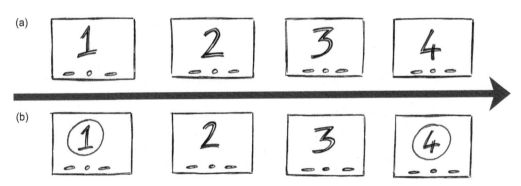

FIG 3.8 a: Straight-ahead action. b: Pose-to-pose animation, images 1 and 4 being keyframe.

Animation made using the straight-ahead method often has more liveliness to it, a vivacity that may not be easily achieved using the pose-to-pose approach, but the latter does allow for more control. The term *pose-to-pose* comes from the way animators make individual drawings of the key poses with an action or sequence of movements, with the intention of then animating from one pose to the next—thereby pose to pose. Using such poses allows the animator to identify the key moments in the action—hence the name of these drawings: *keyframes*. This technique, developed for use with 2D classical animation long before the availability of computers for animation, is now standard practice for animators working in *computer-generated imagery* (CGI). Making such drawings (or positioning models and images on a timeline in digital animation processes) allows the animator to plan, in some detail, the exact movement of either a single figure or object to multiple characters. The positioning of these keyframes along a timeline allows action to shift either backward or forward in time by the addition of frames or the reduction of frames. This helps ensure that an action takes place on exactly the frame on which the animator requires it to happen, allowing for a great deal of control. It may be a useful method, but used clumsily, it can result in actions looking a little wooden.

Consistency of drawing is much easier to achieve using pose-to-pose animation because comparison can easily be made between keyframes, ensuring that scale is maintained throughout the action. Using keyframes as a guide, the inbetweens are far less likely to vary in size.

Many animators regularly use a combination of the two methods, straight-ahead and pose-to-pose animation, within a single action or sequence. This approach to using the technique most relevant to the demands of the animation can result in more believable and fluid movements, an added level of control allowing well-structured phrasing throughout the animation, and complexity of movement and timing, and finally, it gives the animation a liveliness that it might otherwise not possess.

Squash and Stretch

The term *squash and stretch* describes the action of an object put under certain pressures. Push down on a rubber ball and it will squash; pull a sheet of rubber and it will stretch. However, squash and stretch does not simply apply to rubber balls or rubber sheets; it can apply to everything, or almost everything.

Most things in life possess a certain degree of flexibility. Certainly living flesh has a great deal of flexibility, no matter how bony the underpinning structure. The use of squash and stretch in animation allows for a degree of flexibility in all animated objects and figures. When a person smiles broadly, it isn't just the mouth that moves—the whole face animates and demonstrates a high degree of flexibility. Everything from flexing an arm as it lifts a heavy

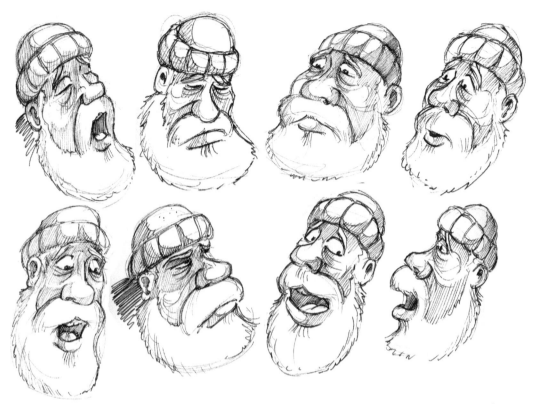

FIG 3.9 Squash and stretch is evident in the cheeks and chin of the figure. The use of squash and stretch can also help generate the illusion of weight.

object to a figure running or jumping will express varying levels of squash and stretch.

Let's consider the movement of a very heavy character such as a giant ogre as he takes a stride. The entire figure may squash down slightly on impact, making him look heavy and cumbersome. Lighter characters, such as fairies, may need to demonstrate less squash, since they are infinitely lighter than giants.

Before animators began using this technique, animation was rather wooden, stiff, and awkward. When used clumsily, squash and stretch may result in all the animation flexing and bending with no real objective and to no real effect. Some of the early animators tended to flex all aspects of a figure almost indiscriminately, resulting in what became known as *rubber-hose animation*. This was because characters ended up with limbs with little or no structure—no shoulders, elbows, or knees, just bendy tubes rather like … well, rubber hose.

The use of squash and stretch may enhance movement, whereas in nature no such action would be evident. A bouncing ball on impact with the ground would clearly flex and squash downward, but as the ball begins its fall, its shape will remain spherical. However, if the animator chooses to add a little stretch to the ball on the beginning of the fall, the action of the fall is enhanced. Squash and stretch may even be used to good effect in animating objects where no squash and stretch could be possible. A little squash and stretch may be applied to quite rigid material such as glass or ceramic—material that would not normally be subject to squash and stretch. If this is done subtly, it will enhance the action. If it is overdone, which can easily happen, it will make the material look like rubber and will destroy the illusion. One of the key things to bear in mind in using squash and stretch is that although the object may deform in shape, it retains volume. In this regard it neither grows nor shrinks—it merely changes shape.

When taken to extremes, squash and stretch creates very cartoon-like animation, which may be very good for comedy effect but is less useful for naturalistic actions. The master animator Tex Avery regularly used squash and stretch in his animation to such extreme levels that the movement looked completely abstract. His almost unique approach to the animation principles makes his work distinctive and almost instantly recognizable.

Anticipation

Most actions undertaken by most living creatures capable of independent thought and motion are anticipated in some way or another. Though the anticipation of a movement often begins as a thought process, sometimes conscious but on other occasions completely instinctive, it instigates a form of physical anticipatory movement quite separate from (but not independent of) the main movement itself. Reflexive movement brought about by unanticipated external forces such as receiving an electric shock, a physical impact, and steady pressure from something like a high wind or the ocean's wave action will not be accompanied by anticipatory actions. The preparation for an action varies depending upon the nature of the action and may be very slight or rather extreme. A human figure making a simple upward jump does not simply entail the upward movement of the figure; it is preceded by a downward movement by bending the knees in order for the figure to contract muscle and limbs, very much like a compressed spring. This is done so that the figure can then push off against the floor, flexing muscle and stretching limbs quickly to create the jumping action. The movement of an athlete making a jump may be far more exaggerated in the anticipation of the jump itself because more energy needs to be expended early to fuel the greatest jump possible.

An anticipated action does not have to be undertaken by the entire body; it may be limited to a part of the anatomy such as the arms, the legs, the head. To throw a punch, for example, it is necessary to draw the arm backward, again rather like compressing a spring, before releasing it with a high level of energy. A punch may entail the movement of the entire figure, but it need not. If we consider a fisherman about to cast his line into the river, he must raise the rod tip over his shoulder and move it backward. This action will more than likely entail not only the movement of both arms but also a

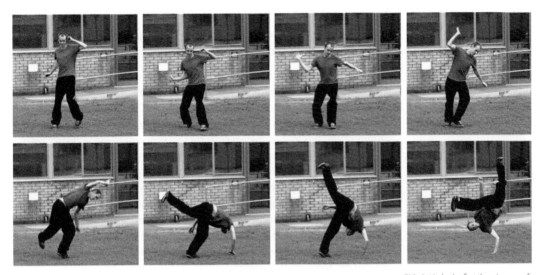

FIG 3.10 In the first three images of this sequence, we can see the figure anticipating the action that follows.

rotation of the upper torso and, depending on the nature of the cast, maybe even movement in the legs and feet. These movements, probably quite slow ones, are in anticipation of the very rapid forward and downward movements that constitute the cast itself. The first movement is not the actual cast but an anticipation of the cast; the cast is an action that would not be possible without this first anticipatory action.

In cartoon-based animation, the sharp, rapid turn of a head in reaction to something happening or said, termed a *take,* relies heavily on anticipation. Although this anticipation is generated in the mind as a reaction to some external stimuli, it is made visible to the observer by a distinct movement of its own. Without this anticipation the take becomes a simple turn of the head.

Anticipation leads one action into another and flags to the audience what is about to happen. It is a useful device in guiding an audience's attention, though if it's taken to extremes the action will look artificial and cartoon-like.

Staging

The animation principle of *staging* refers to the manner in which the action is presented in order for it to be read and understood by the audience. Action is generally presented in such a manner that enables the character to be recognizable and so that the individual actions that make up content of the individual shot or sequence of shots is clear. Staging is all about presenting the work in such a way as to create or enhance the mood within the narrative and to present only those aspects of the narrative that the director intends. Staging clarifies the action, the action supports acting, and the acting delivers the story.

The same action may be presented in hundreds of different ways; each one of them will present different outcomes offering differing levels of clarity, drama, and audience interpretation. The key point here is communication.

There is a wonderful shot in Disney's *Hunchback of Notre Dame* (1996) where the harlequin leads the parade of fools into the square at the front of the cathedral. There is action everywhere in the scene. Crowds of onlookers are making merry, waving flags and cheering, while a procession made up of various characters in their festive costumes all show off to the audience with their own distinctive movements. While all of this is going on, the harlequin leads the festival attendees into the square as he performs his song. Over the top of this background, multicolored pieces of paper gently rain down on the whole scene. It sounds completely chaotic, but it isn't. It *is* very busy and it *is* very lively, but because of the way it is staged, the action is very clear. The audience's attention is drawn to exactly the point where the animators intended; they see only what the animator wants them to see and in exactly the manner the animator intends.

The way an action is staged for clarity not only allows the audience to focus on any given action; it may also offer a nuance in the script, allowing for subtlety of characterization and relationships—relationships that may shift during the shot. Any such shift of emphasis throughout a scene is often determined by the way it is staged and is not at all random. A shot or sequence is usually planned well before the animation begins through storyboarding and the use of animatics and character layouts. Each of these tools provides a level of staging for the action. *Storyboarding,* or blocking out an action within an individual shot by positioning the characters or objects in a shot along a timeline, provides a very good indication of what is happening and when, and more important, what the audience will see. Blocking out the action this way gives the animator a clear indication of how the action may shift throughout a shot or a sequence, enabling the animator to make decisions about the performance before committing to animation. Clear communication is the key to good staging.

Follow-through and Overlapping Action

In the early days of animation, animators would either move a character or leave it at rest, regardless of its design or any detail it had. Seldom do we experience in nature all actions beginning and ending at the same time or moving at the same rate. Actions of a single figure will generally overlap one another; the actions begin at different points in time, depending on their nature and the inertia they possess, and they end at different times, again depending on their nature. This, logically, is called *overlapping action*.

The action of an object made up of a number of parts, often from different materials or at least of a different nature—the hair on a young woman's head, a dog's floppy ears, the fabric of a long garment, a sword hanging at a knight's side—all demonstrate overlapping action and follow-through as the figure moves. Consider a dog with long, floppy ears. The dog does not have the ability to control the ears independently of the rest of its body (apart perhaps from twitching the base of the ear by flexing the attached muscle). The ears do not possess the potential for independent movement. When this dog begins a very fast run, the head moves up and down. As the head moves

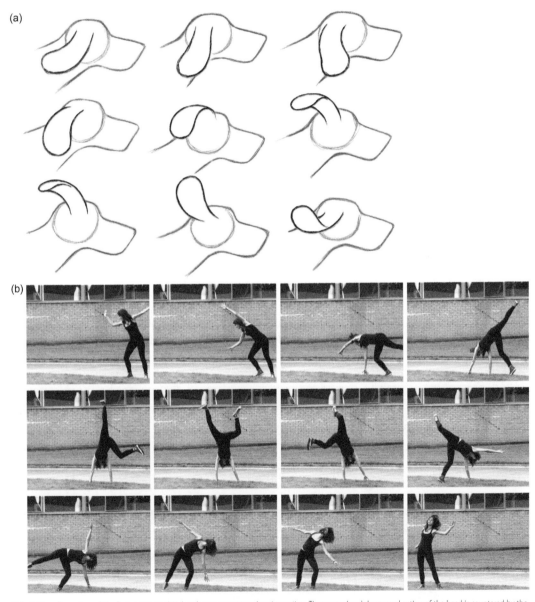

(a)

(b)

FIG 3.11 a: The action of the floppy ears on this dog demonstrates overlapping action. The upward and downward action of the head is countered by the ears. b: Overlapping action occurs in the legs and arms during this cartwheel action.

upward, the ears trail behind, facing downward. As the head begins to move downward, the action of the ears continues to move upward—in other words, the action *follows through*. When the dog comes to a halt, the ears will once again continue to move forward until the action is arrested, because of the ears' attachment to the head. One action stops, the second continues to move in the direction of the force. The action has *followed through*.

Overlapping action describes how various parts of a figure in motion move at different rates and at different times. As a standing figure turns to walk away, the action may start with a slow turn of the head followed by the upper torso, the hips, and then the legs. There are often no hard and fast rules as to how a figure will behave or the exact sequence in which the separate elements will move; it is enough to state that these separate parts of a figure will almost always move at different times. The actions will overlap one another.

Arcs

In nature, objects seldom move in straight lines. This kind of action is more associated with mechanical actions like those of human-made objects such as machines, engines, and robots. Linear actions may be exactly the right ones for abstract actions, but such movements will look very unnatural in more organic subjects. If you look at the arm action of a human figure throwing a ball using an overarm motion, you will see that the hand describes a very large arc, starting from behind the figure and progressing to a position directly over the figure before extending in front of the body, then finally moving downward, then back toward the body.

However, arcs are seen in all manner of movements, not just the more extreme actions such as a throw. Consider the hand action in a walk cycle. The main action is obviously with the legs and the swinging arms, but through

FIG 3.12 The arc of the movement of the ribbon is clearly seen in this example.

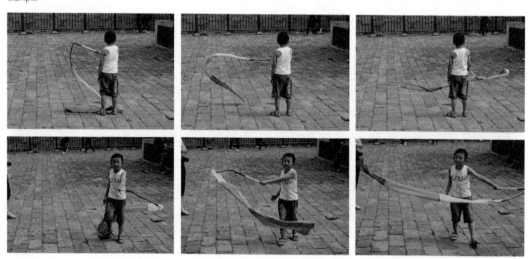

observation you will see that there is a slight backward and forward motion of the hands. Even this very slight action describes an arc. One of the biggest mistakes inexperienced animators make is to put inbetween drawings exactly between two points on the key drawings when what is needed is for the inbetween to be slightly offset, to create a more believable arc within the action. It is attention to this level of detail that turns simple motion into true animation and makes movements convincing.

Exaggeration

One could easily mistake the reason for using exaggerated movements as to simply make exaggerated animation. There are indeed plenty of examples that use such exaggeration to create cartoon animation that has an abstract dynamic resembling nothing in nature but that is more about design than it is about naturalistic movement. The fantastic animation created by Chuck Jones used exaggerated action and timing to great effect. Though this technique was completely convincing for the movement of such wonderful characters as the Road Runner or Wile E. Coyote, the actions never attempted to describe the real movements of either creature.

FIG 3.13 The drawings are an exaggeration of the photographed action.

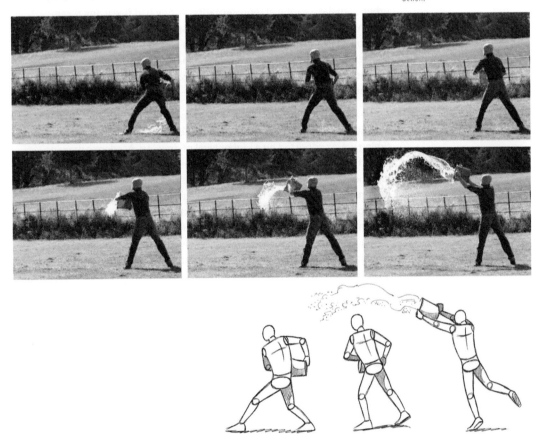

It would be a mistake to think that there is no place for exaggeration in more naturalistic actions. The important point here is that the use of a little exaggerated motion will make the animation *appear* to be naturalistic. A little bit of squash and stretch on a falling object may just add that touch more spark to the action and give it a little more snap. When used well, this level of exaggeration is *felt* within the action rather than seen. Without it the movement may seem a little flat.

Animators will exaggerate the action either for obvious visual effect or simply to make an action a little more readable and apparent to the audience. The first may be cartoon-like and stylized, the second may be less obvious but have no less impact for all that. Used with intelligence, appropriately exaggerated action will enhance almost all animation.

Solid Drawing

The term *solid drawing* refers to an approach to making drawings that deals with form, volume, weight, balance, space, and surface values. Many of the pioneers of animation dealt with a much simpler form of animation drawing that didn't have to demonstrate that the characters were anything other than flat, graphical representations. They had few if any three-dimensional qualities, and the use of perspective drawing was minimal. The volume and shape of early characters would often change in even the shortest of animated sequences, which may well have suited the stylistic fashions of the day but did little to address more naturalistic drawing or animation.

As the art form began to develop and a more naturalistic approach to animation began to emerge, animators became aware that movement and timing were supported by a higher level of drawing. Academic drawing skills that could encapsulate intricate forms capable of suspension of disbelief were needed if the animation was to imitate nature. Character design, then, needs to be undertaken in such a way as to allow a character or a figure to make naturalistic actions. Heavily stylized designs may be very interesting and attractive, but they offer far less potential for natural action. Consideration must therefore be given to the possibility of animated movements when we're designing characters, and an understanding of basic anatomy will certainly help in this regard. The ability to draw well is an obvious advantage in making 2D classical animation that uses naturalistic figures and characters.

Appeal

The principle of *appeal* deals with the relationship the animation creates between an audience and the characters on screen. This is not a mere matter of design, though it is with character design that the process begins. Through good design, appropriate animation, good staging, and believable performances, animators are able to make characters attractive to the audience. As a result, the audience will find the characters interesting and engaging and ultimately more able to carry and develop a complex storyline. Appeal in a character should not be misinterpreted as meaning that all characters with appeal are cute and cuddly—far from it. Some of the most memorable characters are villains, who often have more interesting personalities than the "good guys." Appeal is at the heart of all good character-based animation; without it the work is reduced to movement and the characters become simple manikins.

The script is the source of the emotional engagement, but the acting and performance are what develop characters to a point where they possess appeal. This should not be considered necessarily as being dependent on naturalistic movement; simple actions or exaggerated movements can do much to enhance a character's appeal. For example, the very simple animation of the characters in *South Park* is very much part of their appeal, whereas the extreme gymnastic display by *Spider-Man* is as much a part of his persona as is his distinctive costume design. Both types have appeal but for very different reasons.

I think that the additional topics I cover in the rest of this chapter are worthy of consideration separately from the principles set out in the earlier portion—not that they necessarily occur separately from any of the principles, it is just that they are such important factors in animated movement.

Drag

We will cover the issue of *drag* in more detail later, when we look at animal locomotion. For this chapter's discussion it might be enough to say that drag acts on an object as it moves through a gas or a fluid. Resistance is encountered on the surface of the object as it moves through the fluid or gas, creating drag on the surfaces and trailing edges of the moving object and resulting in turbulence.

For the purposes of this discussion we can see how an object will move; as a result of drag, part of that object will be delayed in its movement. A figure wearing a coat with very long sleeves might illustrate the point well. If the outstretched arm in the long sleeve makes a rapid sideways movement, the inertia in the arm is overcome before the inertia in the long sleeve that hangs limply down. When the sleeve does move, the area nearest to the arm moves first as it is drawn through space with the arm. The cloth that hangs farthest from the arm moves at a later time and trails behind the action of the arm. As a result of drag on the trailing edge of the sleeve, a curve occurs in the flowing material.

We may see evidence of drag in all manner of objects. Though it applies to all moving objects (it is only the amount of drag that varies), it is particularly evident in things such as long hair and fabric.

Balance and Weight

One of the greatest difficulties animators face is creating the illusion of weight in an object or character. This is such an important aspect of animation that it is worth linking with the principles of animation. The balance of an object or a figure depends on both its weight and its shape. As a figure moves, shifting its weight to adjust its balance, it undergoes a shift around its center of gravity. Identifying and working with this center of gravity and the shifting of the weight around it are central to creating believable dynamics in a figure. An object's weight may be illustrated in a number of ways, and the timing of the action will illustrate the amount of inertia a figure, or a part of a figure, possesses. Timing also illustrates momentum of a figure, with both inertia and momentum directly linked to the mass an object possesses.

It is the illusion of weight and balance that gives drawings, models, and images of other kinds a level of believability in their movement. This illusion may be achieved through the use of squash and stretch, overlapping action, follow-through, and drag. Balance and weight are among the basic currencies of animation; if they are not achieved in an animation, more elaborate aspects of movement linked with acting and performance will become difficult, if not impossible.

Solid Modeling

As with solid drawing, *solid modeling* deals with aspects of form, volume, space, and surface values that impact the animation of any character. Solid modeling can also give a character a good deal of appeal. The transition from design to build is a very important one, and retaining the qualities of the concept art or the character design is important but often presents difficulties when translated into three dimensions. The practicalities of articulating a figure, particularly one that needs to demonstrate naturalistic and believable qualities, are substantial. Poor modeling will not only restrict the way a figure moves and behaves; this restriction in turn will definitely impede performance. Lack of solid modeling may also mean that the character not only lacks any kind of appeal but appears "dead" and incapable of expressing the spark of life that all characters must have if they are to be believable and capable of expressing emotion.

It is important that any figure be built in such a way that the animator is capable of using it to create the animation necessary for the narrative. If movement is restricted at all, it is doubtful that the animator will get the best from the model, regardless of that animator's skills.

Energy Flow

With a figure in motion it is possible to track the way energy is directed through the body as an action progresses. This capability may prove very useful in thinking about how the body shifts and rotates and how the various tensions and stresses within the figure contribute to an action or how they counter weights or stresses applied to the figure.

If we consider the action of a figure throwing a javelin, we can see how the action of the throw progresses through the figure and how the energy of the throw flows through the body. If the figure is throwing the javelin from a standing position—that is, not running—we may see how the movement starts from the ankle. The entire body will begin by moving forward and slightly pivoting at the ankles. The energy quickly moves on to a movement in the legs and progresses to a twist in the hips. This creates a rotation in the upper torso. At this point there is considerable momentum in the throw, which is increased as the shoulders continue to rotate around. The energy of the throw is evident through the progressive movement of the upper arm, which moves rapidly forward, an action taken up by the forearm, then the hand, and finally the fingers, before the javelin is released. In this model we can see how the energy flows from the ankles right through the fingertips to complete the throw.

Not all actions are as extreme as a javelin throw, and the flow of energy will be different in each case, but if the animator understands this flow of energy, it will invariably make for more fluid motion and naturalistic animation in the animator's work.

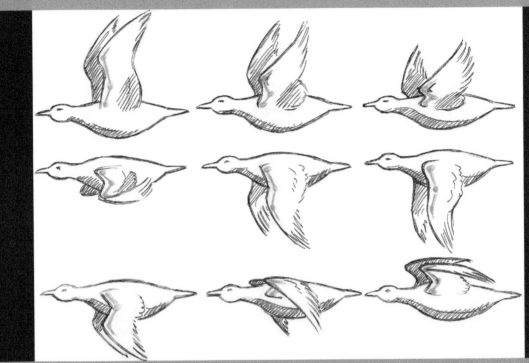

CHAPTER 4

Animals in Motion

The Richness of Life on Earth

The variety of life on earth is staggering in its enormity. There are an estimated 8,000 species of mammals, over 6,000 species of reptiles, 9,000 species of birds, and 25,000 species of fish, all either swimming, walking, flying, or crawling over our planet. The number of individual species of insects, which make up over 90% of all life forms on earth, is estimated at anywhere between 6 million and 10 million. That's a lot of bugs. I say these are estimated figures because, though we live in an increasingly crowded world, much of it still remains almost completely unexplored. The simple truth is that no one knows exactly how many undiscovered species exist in the deeper seas or the remote jungles and forests, even if these last two are diminishing environments. The number of species that have been lost to the world, and continue to be lost at an alarmingly high rate, is beyond imagining.

It is well beyond the scope of this text, or I suspect any other single text, to cover the dynamics and locomotion of all the different forms of animal life on earth. To cover the entire animal kingdom would clearly be impractical for this rather modest project and would possibly take the effort of many lifetimes, even though the result would undoubtedly be an invaluable resource. This single chapter doesn't even try to cover all that is of value in even a single category of the animal kingdom. With these kinds of numbers, how could it? For the sake of space I have limited this chapter on animal locomotion to quadrupeds, birds, and fish; within these categories I have had to further limit the subjects while trying to present a useful range. To work in a limited space I have had to omit the entire insect world along with much else that would no doubt be of interest and value to animators and others. So be it.

The three classifications I concentrate on here represent a huge range of life forms. Therefore I have had to limit even the range of samples from each of these three categories. The ones I have included from within each of the separate classifications have been chosen to usefully represent the broadest range of animals within that classification. It is also important to remember that this study does not set out to be a substitute for other, more scientific texts that exist to deal with a narrower group of subjects but to a much deeper level. This is not a scientific zoological or biological study, but it does perhaps provide a starting point for a more in-depth study. The depth to which I have covered the various examples does not extend to providing the relevant mathematical equations or formulas that underpin or illustrate the performance of muscle, animal locomotion, drag coefficients, or anything else related to animal dynamics. A number of texts cover these topics already and provide a seriously in-depth study of the samples I cover. These may perhaps be of interest only to other specialists in that particular field and are certainly beyond my experience and expertise as an animator, but I have recommended a number of texts that the reader may find useful for further study. I must remind the reader that this text is intended only to assist animators and others working in related areas and disciplines in analyzing movement.

Some of the individual examples of animals here should offer a reasonable and useful substitute for other animals of similar species. I have tried to choose examples that offer the animator not only direct reference but also an indication of locomotion of the broadest range of other related subjects. It should then be possible to use the example of a particular subject and, in a very general sense, apply the results of that study to other subjects of a similar type, size, and shape. For example, in making a study of the flight of a carrion crow, it is reasonable that we would be able to gain an appreciation of how other types of crows, rooks, ravens, and even other unrelated birds of a similar shape and size are *likely* to move.

It might be useful to begin the chapter by looking at few principles of animal physiognomy and the way that environmental and other conditions have helped shape and determine their physicality and behavior, as well as the way we have gained insight into and deeper knowledge of the natural world.

Human Understanding of the Animal Kingdom

Humans have always had an intimate relationship with the rest of the animal kingdom—hardly surprising since the human is, after all, just another animal. Animals' evolution and our own evolution are not dissimilar. We have depended on them for food and for clothing. They have a political, economic, religious, and cultural significance for us. We have domesticated them and developed an intricate emotional relationship with them. Just look at the way we treat our pets today. And in all of this we have steadily gained an in-depth understanding of the animal kingdom—and we are still learning.

Perhaps one of the greatest single developments in our understanding of the natural world is due to the work of the British naturalist Charles Darwin. Darwin, born in Shrewsbury, Shropshire, in 1809, showed an interested in natural history from childhood, though it was while studying medicine at Edinburgh that he began to study natural history. While there he increasingly neglected his studies in medicine in favor of natural history, and while he was studying at Christ's College, Cambridge, he became more serious and this long-time interest began to bear fruit. In 1851 Darwin embarked on the now famous venture that would later make his name as a leading proponent of evolutionary theory: He joined the ship *HMS Beagle* on its around-the-world journey to survey and chart coastlines. He did have some experience and expertise in geology and entomology, though at this stage he still had much to discover and his work had just begun.

Darwin was 50 when he finally published his great work, *On the Origin of Species*, in 1859. The work was based on his extensive studies of the animal world, including those made during his epic journey of almost five years on the *H.M.S. Beagle*. *On the Origin of Species* created an immediate stir in the scientific world and among the general public alike; the original print run of 1,250 copies sold out as soon as it left the printing press. The work not only went on to have a profound impact on our understanding of the natural world; it also placed evolutionary theory at the forefront of scientific and religious debate. The issue of evolution, and in particular the implications for the origin of man, struck at the heart of religious sensibilities of the time. So far-reaching were his theories that they continue to be the cause of controversy to this day.

The natural selection of species and theories of evolutionary development that apply to all living creatures as first expounded by Charles Darwin explain how the diversity of life on earth has adapted and changed over time. Darwin went on to suggest that these developments occurred in order for species to fill the various niches that opened to them within a broad range of natural environments. Darwinian theories assist us in understanding not only how animals have exploited their particular niche in the natural world but also how they have developed physical and behavioral traits to either avoid competition (by exploiting new and untapped resources) or to gain an advantage over their competitors. The physical and behavioral differences between species distinguish them from other, similar species. Indeed, it was the need for animals to take advantage of different resources that led to the diversification of species. Darwin's study of finches from the Galapagos Islands, specifically the birds' beak shapes and sizes, did much to demonstrate the ongoing changes that occur through evolutionary development. Through his research Darwin concluded that different beak shapes were linked to the particular diet of each finch; to avoid competition, the species had exploited different food sources. The heavier beaks are able to crush large seeds, whereas smaller beaks are more suited to a mixed diet that includes smaller seeds and insects. Finches with more delicate beaks are more suited to a diet composed almost entirely of insects. The crossbill has a beak design that is unique among finches, specifically suited to prying open pinecones to reach the nutritious seeds held within.

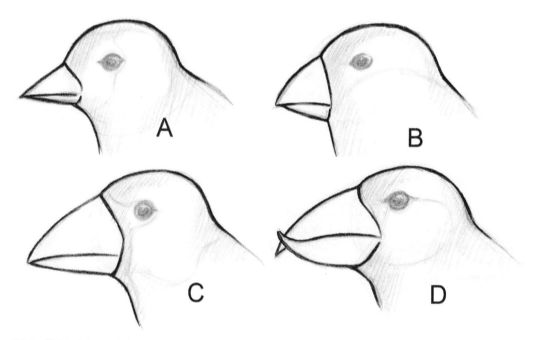

FIG 4.1 Finch beaks have evolved to deal with different food sources. A: Goldfinch. B: Bullfinch. C: Hawfinch. D: Crossbill.

The shape and size of a bird's beak are good indicators of its diet and its mode of feeding. The sharp, curved beak of a bird of prey is the ideal design for ripping and tearing at flesh; the upward curve of the slender bill of the avocet allows it to filter out the miniscule shrimps and marine worms it feeds on in shallow waters. A hummingbird's beak and the length of its tongue have developed that way due to its specialist diet of nectar and the particular flowers it chooses to feed from. The refinements of physiognomy and differences in beak shapes are not limited to extreme differences in diet

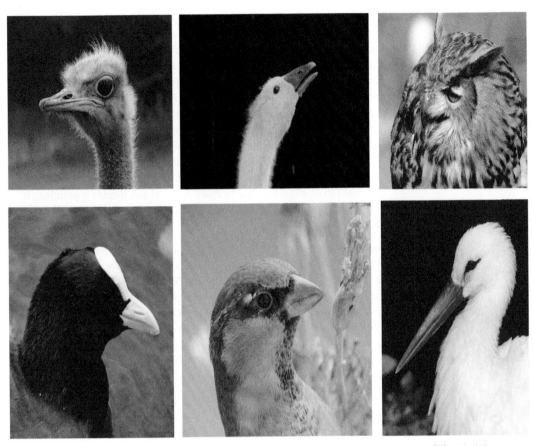

FIG 4.2 Different beak shapes are suited to different tasks and diets.

such as meat, water insects, seeds, or nectar. The differences may be much more subtle than that, but they are no less marked. Certain hummingbirds have beaks of a particular length to reach and exploit the nectar that can be found deep inside the flowers of specific plants. One species of hummingbird has evolved a beak so long it is no longer able to reach its own preen glands with its beak, as most birds do, and has had to develop an alternative way of reaching backward with its feet to get at the valuable oil from the preen gland to keep its feathers in tip-top condition.

Evolutionary development is not limited to the size and shape of an animal but also extends to the animal's movement, though size and shape certainly affect and enable specific types of movement. The evolution of the cheetah, for example, has resulted in a physiognomy that provides both strength and agility, enabling the cat to achieve the fantastic speed and extreme level of maneuverability needed to catch the very agile prey on which it feeds.

Evolutionary forces apply to every detail of animal physiognomy. Teeth needed to tear flesh have become strong, long, and sharp. Ears needed to locate moths in the night have become extremely sensitive, and coats needed to insulate against intense cold have become long and thick. It looks like nature provides the best illustration of the old design adage that *form follows function*. Behavior is also shaped by those same evolutionary forces that determine animals' physical aspects. Birds of paradise demonstrate a wonderful array of displays and have developed a particularly spectacular range of specialist feathers to enhance the effect. Along with dancing, hopping, display flights, and swinging upside-down from branches, the male birds have also evolved a range of distinctive calls and songs to turn the head of any discerning female. The lyrebird has even taken to presenting its collection of iridescent beetle-wing casings, flowers, and seeds in its effort to attract a mate. None of this display is pointless; it indicates in one way or another the suitability of a particular mate for the passing on of genes.

The variety of forms these animals take is just as staggering as the variety of life on earth. From the enormous blue whale, the largest animal ever to have lived, to the smallest known insect, *Dicopomorpha echmepterygis*, a parasitic wasp smaller than the head of a pin, all are subject to generational development. They are the way they are due to an evolutionary response to the environment they live in—their need to feed, to reproduce, and perhaps above all else, to avoid falling prey to other animals. Nature has provided rather elegant solutions to all these problems in a huge variety of ways.

If you need to navigate around your environment so you know where you are going, then eyes that provide clear color vision seem to be one of the best options, but they're certainly not the only one. If you need to get around in a watery medium, swimming with fins is perhaps your best bet, though even this strategy might not be the only solution. Some insects and mammals use limbs to row themselves through the water; the nautilus propels itself through the oceans by jet propulsion. If you need to fly, wings would seem to fit the bill perfectly, but once again these are not the only solution that nature provides. Some spiders spin long, slender webs that they use to catch the breeze, which lifts them from the ground and transports them great distances over land or water. Admittedly, the web doesn't offer the same level of control as a bird's wings, which means that the spider doesn't have a great deal of choice over where it ends up, but it is undoubtedly a strategy that works. If you need to get along on the ground, a whole range of options is open to you. You can walk, run, slither, wriggle, hop, jump, burrow, and even swing, though you will probably need access to a tree or two for that particular mode of locomotion.

In considering effective and efficient modes of locomotion, size really does matter, as with many other things in life. Because of their large body mass, elephants do not have the ability to undertake the same scurrying action as a rodent. Only much smaller animals are capable of such rapid movement. The inertia inherent in the heavy legs of the elephant would demand the release of huge amounts of energy in a very short period of time for scurrying to take place. The level of energy required for scurrying would therefore demand much larger muscles, which in turn would increase the weight of the leg and as a consequence the demand for more power. Likewise, when very large legs are in motion, they gain a great deal of momentum, which becomes difficult to shed very quickly in order to come to rest. Legs the size of an elephant's could not do this at a speed quick enough to constitute a scurrying motion; the strain on the skeletal structure would be too great. Small dinosaurs may have been able to turn their heads with the speed of a bird, but this would have been impossible for the larger dinosaurs such as the brontosaurus or the tyrannosaurus. Obviously, the study of these now extinct animals is limited to the study of their fossilized remains, so there is a degree of conjecture and not a little controversy among paleontologists regarding the details of these creatures. However, it is possible to make reasonable assumptions about their movements based on their skeletal structures, their size, and the comparative study of animals that exist today; they are, after all, subject to the same natural laws as those extinct creatures.

Flying as a mode of locomotion also has its limitations. Birds are limited in their size due to the power-to-size ratio. Muscles needed to provide the power for flight have an upper limit on their effectiveness. Size may also limit the type of movement possible. Because of the manner in which they fly the hummingbird has natural limits to the size it is able to achieve: about the size of a blackbird. Any larger than that and a hummingbird will not be capable of flapping its wings sufficiently quickly to create the necessary lift. Nature really is the supreme designer.

The Principles of Locomotion

The methods of locomotion that various creatures use to get around vary greatly from species to species, but despite these differences there are some common features of locomotion, such as maneuverability, that they all share. All creatures also have to deal with and operate within the same laws of physics.

What is interesting is the way that different types of animals approach the problem of getting around in very similar environments. For example, it's not only fish that swim. Some birds, mammals, insects, spiders, and reptiles have taken to the water too. Likewise, there are fish that quite regularly take to the air. All these animals have one other thing in common: They have all evolved modes of movement through need.

Speed

The importance of speed to an animal is not simply a choice of movement based on a whim; it may be a matter of life or death. It has become necessary for some animals to be able to move at high speeds to catch their food, and conversely it has become important for other animals to be able to achieve equally high speeds in order not to end up as lunch for an even faster animal. For other, more sedentary animals, speed is less important. Herbivores may not need to be able to travel quickly to gain a meal, but they might need to move rapidly in order not to become a meal. Plants are not going anywhere, at least not very quickly, and so animals that depend on plants for their food may take their time. Not all animals need to be fast; the fast ones do not need to be fast all the time. Many of them spend a good deal of their time at rest. It is only when a predator turns up that they might need to be able to turn on the speed as and when necessary.

Many predators use speed as a way of hunting their prey, though the acceleration of a predator is often more important than its top speed to its success in hunting. The critical factor to the outcome of a hunting chase is distance between predator and prey at the time the chase commences. If the predator manages to get close enough to its prey, it will have enough time to accelerate to a speed that is higher than the prey. If the chase begins with the predator too far from the prey, the predator will not be able to sustain its speed to catch it. This is of course if the predator and prey engage in a straight chase, which is often not the case; swerving and turning usually contribute to the success or failure of the prey's efforts to escape. Interestingly enough, very fast animals that depend on high speed to catch a prey animal often also depend on very slow speeds for their success as they try to position themselves to close the gap between themselves and their prey. They do this by stealth, and to be stealthy an animal needs to be slow and silent.

In very general terms, larger animals are more capable of higher speeds than smaller ones. There are obvious exceptions, of course; the giant tortoise and the elephant are two. There are differences, however, some of them great, in terms of the speed of animals of similar sizes.

Maneuverability

An animal's physiognomy determines how maneuverable it is, which does not simply make it easier for the animal to get around but rather like speed maneuverability may be an issue of life or death. Animals often depend on their maneuverability to escape the clutches of a predator. The ability of the hunted to swerve sharply at speed is a tactic that compensates for a top speed that may be slower than that of the hunter. A gazelle might not be able to outrun a cheetah in a straight race; to elude a predator the gazelle needs to depend on its maneuverability and the speed with which it can make these maneuvers. The ability to execute very tight turns at speed has therefore become an evolutionary imperative for the survival of some species.

The point in the chase at which an animal executes its evasive maneuver is critical to its successful escape. If the acceleration of the prey's swerve

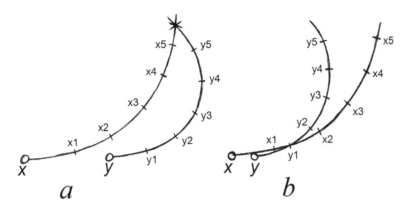

FIG 4.3 The distance between a predator and its prey is critical. a: The differences in swerving action of the predator x results in the interception with the prey y. b: The sharper swerving action of the prey y allows it to avoid the predator x that cannot turn as quickly.

is higher than the speed achieved by the predator and the timing of the maneuver is right, the prey will escape. The later a prey animal leaves the swerving action and the closer the predator to it when the action is executed, the more successful the prey is likely to be in the maneuver. However, if the swerve is instigated too early in the chase, the turn is more likely to be matched by the hunter and valuable distance between hunter and prey may be lost. If the maneuver is executed too late, the prey animal will be caught. Furthermore, if the swerve is made too early but the distance between prey and predator is great enough, the swerve will be matched by the hunter and will result in the two animals' paths converging. Lunchtime.

Endurance and Economy of Energy

As some readers might know first-hand, running a marathon is very different from running a sprint, placing very different demands on a body. Although it may be possible for some animals to run great distances and on other occasions to run at speed, most animals are more suited to either one or the other. For some, their physical constraints make it possible to do only one or the other well; it could be very difficult or even impossible to do both. Some animals might be able to bring on a turn of speed if necessary, but they might not have the potential to execute high-speed performance to the same degree as others. For example, the cheetah is considered the fastest land animal and can reach speeds of 29 meters a second at full stretch, but it can maintain this speed for only a relatively short period of time. In contrast, African hunting dogs are not capable of such speeds but are capable of sustaining a hunt over very long distances and over considerable time; indeed, they depend on stamina rather than acceleration for their success as hunters. For the hunting dogs, shorter bursts of high speed are achievable but are far more difficult to sustain.

Predators and prey are often fairly evenly matched in their performances; if this wasn't so, prey animals would soon become extinct due to excessive

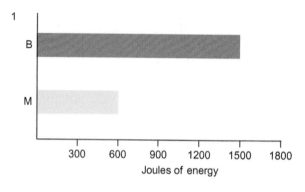

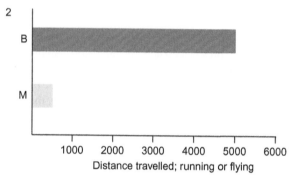

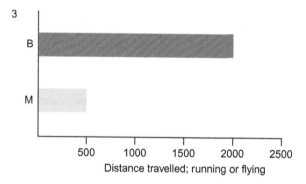

FIG 4.4 Comparisons of energy consumption between birds (B) and mammals (M). 1. The amount of energy used during 10 minutes of locomotion. 2. The distance covered during 10 minutes of flying or running. 3. The distance of travel for a given amount of energy (500 joules).

predation. Conversely, if they consistently outperformed the predators, hunters would starve to death due to lack of success. It would seem that nature has ensured an interdependent balance between species in which stamina and speed are important factors in the survival of both prey and predators.

For a number of animals, endurance plays an important part beyond hunting. Migration is a periodic movement that sometimes entails travel across great distances, requiring a great deal of energy and therefore energy consumption. Wildebeests and zebras cross huge distances on their annual migrations, which demands continuous energy consumption. Smaller mammals do not undertake such epic journeys, but small birds do. Swallows, swifts, and martins regularly travel from their summer homes in northern Europe to their winter homes in South Africa. Albatross cover even greater distances. Flying is a far more economic mode of travel than travel by land, which is why even small birds such as the reed warbler, weighing in at around 13 grams, are able to migrate from northern Europe to North Africa each year.

The use of energy and the demands for energy usage can differ by species within the same animal family group. A racehorse is clearly built to travel at high speeds; a shire horse is built for strength in pulling power and endurance. I'm not a gambling man, but if both of these horses were entered in the Grand National, I think my money would be on the racehorse.

For a few animals, a combination of endurance and speed is the norm. Swifts spend the vast majority of their lives flying and only return to land again to nest; they even sleep on the wing. For them a sustained period of movement, much of it at speed, is the normal condition.

The nature of movement has an impact on the energy intake of the animal, the frequency with which it feeds, and its diet. The very nature of flight in hummingbirds entails a rapid action that burns energy quickly, in turn demanding regular high-energy intake. We will look at this phenomenon a little more closely later in the chapter.

Stability and Gait

Stability in an object is achieved when it is either at rest or moving at a constant speed when the forces acting on it are balanced. An object is most stable when it is balanced across a broad base with the center of gravity supported across that base. Stability is less easy to achieve when the center of gravity is over a single point located directly below the center of gravity. A pyramid is most stable if supported by its base; invert it and the support on the point becomes very much less stable.

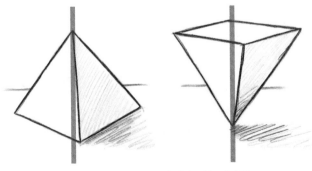

Center of balance is linked to stability

FIG 4.5 The pyramid on the left is a stable structure due to its wide "footprint" and distribution of weight. The inverted pyramid on the right represents a far more unstable structure with a much smaller "footprint."

Animal structure has evolved to provide them with the level of stability most suited to each animal and its particular mode of locomotion. Gazelles have four slender legs with minimal contact with the ground over a relatively small area. This allows for agility and the ability to move very quickly. The giant tortoise also has four legs, relatively far fatter than those of the gazelle and extended well beyond the body, providing a broader support base. They move much more slowly and are far less agile. This structure provides more stability when the tortoise lifts one of its legs during a walk cycle.

When supported by a broad base (four legs spread wide apart), a figure may maintain its balance, even with a relatively high degree of displacement. A mass supported at a single narrow point has less tolerance to resist forces that may displace it; therefore balance becomes more difficult to achieve. The larger the area covered by the supporting structure, the greater stability an animal has and the more displacement it can resist. Spiders supported on eight splayed legs well away from their bodies have more stability than a horse that is supported on four legs across a relatively lower supporting area. Displacement is more an issue with the spider than the horse because of their relative sizes and the relative position of their bodies to the ground. Spiders are much more likely to be blown over by the wind than a horse is. Crabs also have a large spread of support with their legs splayed well out and their bodies very close to the ground; this structure provides the necessary stability against displacement, which may occur due to water currents. The body placed nearer the ground in the case of spiders and crabs also offers additional stability. Heavier animals are able to have the bulk of their weight supported further from the ground.

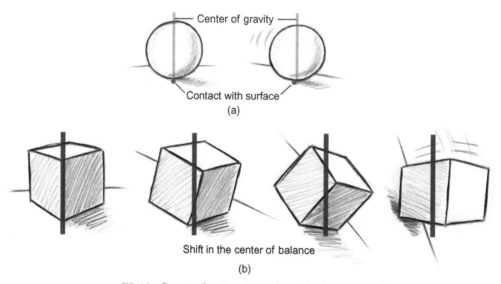

FIG 4.6 a: The center of gravity on the ball is located directly over its point of contact with the ground; when this shifts, the ball rolls. b: The stability of the cube is maintained until the point where the center of gravity goes beyond the point of contact with the surface it sits on.

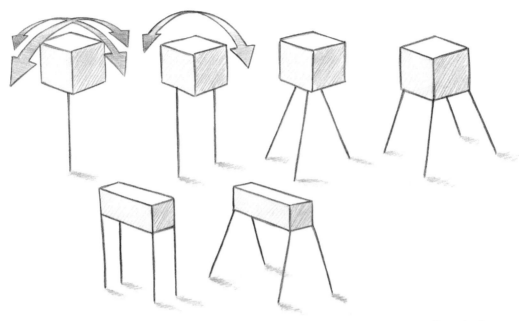

FIG 4.7 The number of supports and the spread between those supports determines the stability of the object.

The center of gravity of a figure at rest may be maintained if supported by an adequate number of supports over a wide enough area. However, for the figure to move, the center of gravity must be shifted to ensure that balance is maintained. An animal supporting its mass on four legs does so by even distribution of the weight across the area defined by the point at which the four legs touch the ground. If one of the legs is then lifted, a shift of the center of gravity is necessary if stability is to be maintained. Then for the mass of the body to be supported by the triangular configuration of the supporting legs, the center of gravity must be relocated over the center of this triangle.

The point at which contact is made with the ground is also important. A gazelle has relatively small contact points with the ground, but because it has *four* such contact points, it is able to maintain its balance well. Humans are also able to balance well, but they manage this on two legs and can even manage reasonably well on one leg due to their relatively large feet, which spread the contact with the ground over a larger surface area.

So far we have looked at how agility, speed, maneuverability, and stability offer benefits to various animals. There is a balance to be struck between these factors, and as so often is the case, a compromise in the design of the animal is the result. The results are completely based on the suitability of one or another animal to the individual species. The design solution, and therefore an animal's agility, speed, or stability, is determined by the niche it has found in nature. Sloths do not need to move quickly, but sparrow hawks do. Snakes do not need to have high levels of stamina, but wildebeests do. A giant tortoise does not require great agility; a squirrel does.

Along with an animal's physical attributes, natural selection has also ensured the most appropriate gait that reflects the demands placed on that animal. Walking and running are probably the two modes of locomotion that we are most familiar with as humans because we do them on a regular basis, but there are many more modes of locomotion using legs. Horses not only walk and run, they trot, canter, and gallop. Even more modes of locomotion than that are open to legged animals. And it is not only animals that have legs that possess the ability to use different gaits. Swimming, flying, hopping, jumping, crawling, climbing, burrowing—all have their uses. The ways in which different animals choose to do any one of these varies a great deal. All creatures that swim don't choose to use the same gait, and the gaits they do choose may vary due to circumstance.

We will be taking a closer look at some of these movements later on in the chapter. A very useful starting point is the definition of a gait that is offered by Alexander (1989):

> A gait is a pattern of locomotion characteristic of a limited range of speeds, described by quantities of which one or more change discontinuously at transitions to other gaits.

A particular gait or adjustment of a gait may depend on a number of factors such as requirements for speed, economy of energy, or stability. The transition from one gait to another can be a gradual process taking place over an extended period of time; however, the actual change made from one gait to another is usually a rather sudden process. The transition from a walk to a run is usually a response to the efficiency of motion based on the energy costs of one mode of locomotion over another one. Once the top speed of walking is reached, it becomes more effective for the gait to be altered and another gait to be adopted. The metabolic rate increases with the workload and it becomes more efficient to make changes in the gait or mode of locomotion in order to become more efficient.

Let's take a brief look at two very different case studies to illustrate the way gaits may change throughout an action. First we consider a human walking along a reasonably flat beach into the sea.

A human walking along a flat surface such as a firm, sandy beach will look like the regular walk most of us do on a daily basis. The figure will remain upright throughout the walk, with the length of the stride being fairly wide and the knees lifted just enough for the feet to be raised clear of the flat ground. This gait will be maintained even as the person steps into the very shallow water on the shoreline. Then, as the figure continues to walk and the water becomes deeper, the water will splash around the ankles and shins, though the gait will remain the same. As the walk continues and the water gets deeper still to around halfway up the shin, the walk will begin to change. First the knees will be lifted higher so that the feet leave the water. The figure at this point is stepping in and out of the water. A similar

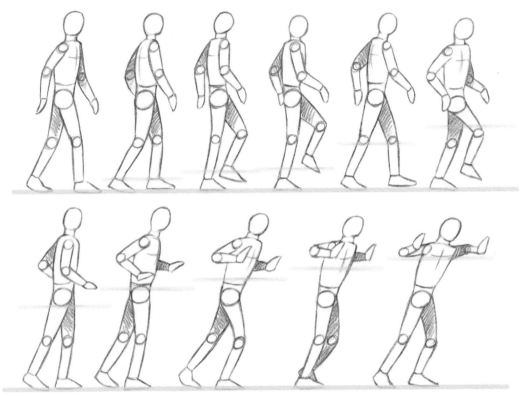

FIG 4.8 A figure will change its gait to suit the environment it is moving in.

gait is used when we walk through snow over a few inches deep. This is a more efficient mode of locomotion, stepping in and out of the water rather than trying to push through it. As the water gets even deeper, it becomes increasingly difficult and awkward for the figure to lift the feet out of the water. At some point it becomes impossible to lift the feet clear of the water. Before that moment, the walker reaches the decision to stop lifting the legs as high and returns to swinging the legs forward in the same manner as the regular walk. However, the water resistance on the legs is such that the forward movement of the legs is more difficult to achieve and requires more effort. The stride length may be slightly increased to become more efficient; in order to increase the power to the legs, the rotation of the upper body will increase and become more pronounced than in a regular walking gait. As the water becomes even deeper to a level around the hips, the arms will be lifted clear of the water, and the rotation of the upper torso will also continue to become increasingly pronounced. As the water gets deeper still, to about the level of the stomach, the figure will no longer walk upright but will tend to lean forward slightly, allowing the figure's weight to be slightly supported by the water. The arms will be raised even higher and the rotation of the shoulders, no longer providing the additional assistance to the movement, will be much reduced. Of course, if the figure continues in this way it becomes more effective to change the mode of locomotion altogether from walking to swimming.

As we can see, the progressive movement of this walk involved a number of alterations to the gait that were driven by the need to maintain efficiency of movement in response to different environmental conditions.

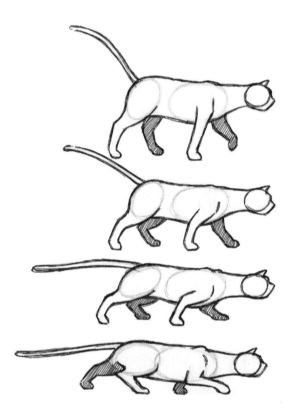

FIG 4.9 The change of gait of a cat from walking to prowling.

Our second example is that of a domestic cat prowling after its prey. Initially the cat is sitting at rest in a fairly upright stance with its forelegs straight and hind legs bent, enabling it to sit back on its haunches. On seeing its prey, the attitude of the cat changes; it begins to prepare for the attack by stalking the prey animal in anticipation of a rapid movement forward. The cat's front legs bend, allowing its body to move downward, making a lower and far less pronounced profile. As it does this its head pivots to maintain its view of the prey. The front legs move forward in a single step; the rear legs stretch, lifting the pelvic girdle upward. The cat's body now assumes a more horizontal attitude. With its knees bent, the cat's shoulders are located almost directly over its front feet. It has lowered its profile to remain out of sight of its prey. Keeping low and moving slowly, the cat's movement is restricted to the legs, with very little upward motion of the body. As the cat moves forward, the shoulder blades become prominent as they rotate. The cat proceeds to stalk its prey, keeping its profile low and head steady before coming to a halt at a position where it judges the distance from its prey to be such that will enable a successful chase. In anticipation of the next move, the cat bends its front legs and draws the hind legs forward in readiness for a thrust of power that will come from the hind legs to achieve high levels of acceleration in which to begin the chase. At this stage the cat often twitches its shoulders and the tip of its tail in anticipation of the chase. A sudden burst of energy takes the cat from its slow, anticipatory movements into a full run in an instant.

Our two examples demonstrate how the change from one gait to another may be gradual process or a sudden transformation.

The speed of a walk is determined by the length of the stride (its amplitude) and how regularly the stride is made (its frequency). To walk more quickly, an animal increases the frequency of the stride. Once this change has provided the maximum return and to increase the speed even further, it is then necessary to increase stride length. Once both the length and the speed of stride are at their maximum, it then becomes necessary to change the gait from a walk into a trot. To create an additional increase in speed then requires a further change in gait to a run.

Quadrupeds

When we think of quadrupeds, we naturally imagine such animals as cats, dogs, and horses, but it is accurate to say that not all animals with four limbs are strictly quadrupeds. Some animals have developed forelimbs that through evolution have become fins, wings, or arms with hands used for manipulation or for locomotion. Those animals that have four limbs are classed as *tetrapods*, and quadrupeds are just one of the groups that fall within this classification. The term *quadruped* has its root in Latin, meaning *four feet*, and is used to denote land animals that use four legs as a mode of locomotion. Mostly it applies to mammals and reptiles.

Legs provide a very effective and efficient way of getting around on the land, though it is not the only method. However, legs are so effective that most land animals with legs are capable of faster travel than animals without legs, and in very general terms those animals that have four legs are capable of higher speeds than comparable animals with two legs.

Quadruped Anatomy

The anatomical structure of various animals serves them in different ways, though the complexity of forms, from the simplest animal to the most advanced, share common features based on the common needs for locomotion, feeding, breathing, and procreation. The detailed design solutions for all these actions are wide ranging, but they serve the common purpose. Here we take a look at some of the structures that relate to locomotion.

Bones

The structures of many animals, though by no means all, are supported by a complex skeletal framework of rigid bones. Internal skeletal structures, known as *endoskeletons*, enclose and protect the vital organs and soft tissue while providing a network of connected bones to which the various muscles are attached. *Exoskeletons* provide an external support for an animal and are typical of invertebrates, forming a shell that almost entirely encloses the animal's internal organs. By necessity such animals undergo the periodic shedding and subsequent growing of their exoskeleton in order for them to grow.

Bones are widely varied in their shape and size, depending on their role in the skeleton, though all of them are generally strong and light. They are linked and articulated in such a manner to allow for a range of movements that is suited to serving the needs of various animals.

Muscle

Muscles can be classified as cardiac, smooth, or skeletal. Cardiac muscle, as the name suggests, is located in the heart. Smooth muscle can be found in internal organs such as the stomach. Skeletal muscles, at least for most animals, provide the power for locomotion. For the purposes of this text we will only be looking at skeletal muscle.

Skeletal muscles have the properties of *extensibility, elasticity*, and *contractility*. The first two allow the muscle to be stretched, much in the same way as an elastic band, returning to their rest position once the force creating the stretch has been discontinued. Muscle's ability to contract allows that muscle to produce tension. On average, muscle fibers can shorten and stretch to about half as long (or short) again as their position at rest. The difference between the maximum stretch and contraction of a muscle is called the *amplitude* of its action.

Skeletal muscle may be classified as either fast-twitch muscle or slow-twitch muscle. *Fast-twitch muscle* fibers are larger, are paler in color, and have a less elaborate blood supply than slow-twitch muscle. They are capable of very fast responses but are not able to sustain the activity over extended periods and tire quickly. These properties make them highly suited to fast actions such as sprint activities and lifting heavy weights. These muscle fibers are powered through anaerobic metabolism, which involves the release of energy by the conversion of glucose to lactic acid. Anaerobic metabolism releases far less energy from a given mass of food than does aerobic metabolism.

Slow-twitch muscle fibers are smaller and are red in appearance as a consequence of their richer blood supply. They carry more oxygen than the fast-twitch white muscle. Slow-twitch muscle fibers are much slower to react than white muscle fibers; they are highly efficient and tire much less quickly, making them ideal for endurance events and posturing actions. The lower speeds generated by slow-twitch muscles are powered by aerobic metabolism, which involves the release of energy by oxidizing food to carbon dioxide and water. The rate at which the power is able to be released depends on the speed with which the respiratory and circulatory systems can supply the muscle fibers with oxygen.

In short, anaerobic metabolism powers short-sprint activities; aerobic metabolism provides the power for sustained locomotion. Athletes who exert maximum effort for 10 seconds derive around 85% of the energy to do so from anaerobic metabolism. In 10 minutes of maximum effort, 10% to 15% of energy is derived from anaerobic metabolism. In two hours of maximum effort, around 1% of energy is gained in this manner.

Fast-twitch anaerobic and slow-twitch aerobic fibers generally appear alongside one another in the limb muscles of mammals. However, in fish these different muscle types are segregated, with the red slow-twitch aerobic muscles running along the body on the outer surface and the white fast-twitch anaerobic muscles on the inner.

For some animals it has not become important to move at anything other than very slow speeds. This has resulted in the animals using their slow-twitch muscles for much of the time. Slow muscles are much more economical in the way they burn energy and they require less energy intake. This may be very useful if the food supply is not very plentiful or if the animal lives on a very poor diet consisting of material with a low calorie content. A giant tortoise that is capable of eating large quantities of food when available is also able to go for long periods without food or drink.

A cheetah is highly dependent on speed for its survival and has developed thigh muscles that are 50% heavier than those of a typical quadruped of the same body mass. Anaerobic metabolism plays a far more important role for this animal than for the more sedentary tortoise.

Energy consumption is a vital part of an animal's existence. The more efficient animals are at locomotion, the more energy they are able to conserve, and in so doing they are able to turn energy from food into growth, fitness maintenance, or reproduction.

Tendons

It was originally thought that the only purpose of tendons was to connect muscle to bone. However, it is now realized that the elastic properties of tendons enable them to behave like a spring, allowing them to both store and release energy and thereby making a contribution to locomotion. As tendons are stretched or compressed, they store energy, and then on recoiling they release that stored energy and assist the related muscle in generating locomotive power. Working in conjunction with the muscle, the tendon enables the muscle to generate a greater force; in doing so it makes a contribution to the conservation of energy.

Anatomy

A huge variety of animals are classified as quadrupeds. Here we'll examine some of the most common quadruped forms in an attempt to provide a wide base for study. We covered the general issues of bones, muscles, and tendons in the previous section, so we concentrate here on the distinctive skeletal structures, movements, and other topics related to selected animals.

Unlike humans, quadrupeds, when in an upright position, usually have a spine that is oriented along a more or less horizontal plane, which means that the angles between spine, neck, and skull are more pronounced than for animals that move with a more upright gait.

Quadrupeds may be divided into further classifications of *cursorial animals* and *noncursorial animals*. These terms denote the distinctive way in which the legs of the animals in each classification are oriented. *Cursorial* is a biological term that describes animals that are adapted to running. It is also a term that is sometimes linked to animals' feeding habits; a zebra would therefore be classed as a cursorial grazer, whereas a lion would be classed as a cursorial predator.

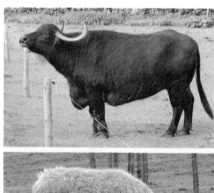

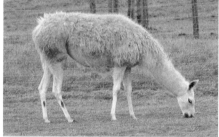

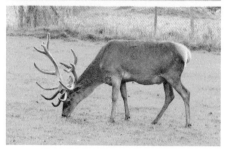

FIG 4.10 Cursorial quadrupeds stand on upright legs with their weight supported directly over them.

This distinction between cursorial and noncursorial is made to describe the manner in which animals in each classification stand and use their legs to aid in locomotion. Cursorial animals are those that stand and move with their legs held straight and the femur and humerus inclined toward the vertical. Horses, cows, and sheep fall into this category.

Noncursorial animals have strongly bent legs with the femur and humerus held at an angle to one another and both of them more closely aligned to the horizontal than the vertical. Animals such as rodents and small carnivores like stoats fall into this category.

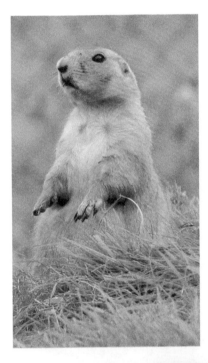
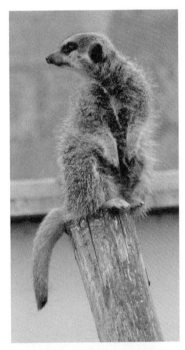
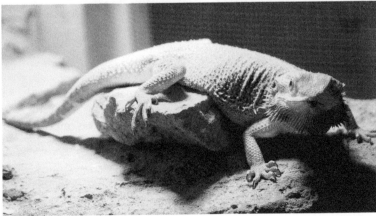

FIG 4.11 Noncursorial quadrupeds have legs that are held away from the body with a more horizontal orientation.

Legs that are upright are able to more efficiently support heavier weights and result in most small mammals being noncursorial whereas larger mammals over 3kg are cursorial.

As with other elements of animal anatomy, feet have evolved in different forms to meet animals' needs. The shape of a foot, the number of toes, and the manner in which the feet are used have all developed to aid locomotion, often at speed. This has led to a further classification of animals that applies to quadrupeds and others based on the way the foot is used to support the animal and to aid locomotion. Let's look at these classifications now.

Ungulate is a general term that describes mammals that have developed either paws or hooves, with most of them standing on the tips of their toes, such as horses, zebra, cattle, goats, pigs, moose, deer, gazelles, and giraffes.

There are three separate classifications of animals that describe the manner in which they use their feet to stand: plantigrade, digitigrade, and unguligrade.

FIG 4.12 Different foot types: a: Unguligrade. b: Plantigrade. c: Digitigrade.

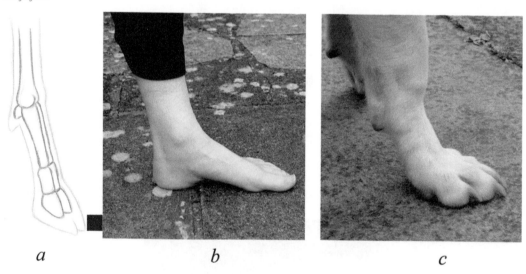

a *b* *c*

Plantigrade describes animals that stand with the whole of the foot, from the toes to the heel, placed flat down on the ground. Humans and bears both fall into this category. The greater surface area that makes contact with the ground allows for increased balance. Amphibians and reptiles are also plantigrades.

Digitigrade denotes animals that stand and walk only on their toes, with the heel lifted completely off the ground. Cats and dogs fall into this classification.

Animals that are digitigrades are capable of a much greater stride length than plantigrades, allowing for far greater speeds. Walking on the toes also gives such animals the capability of moving with much more stealth and far more quietly, which is clearly of great benefit to predators. Birds are also digitigrades and walk, hop, and stand on their toes.

Unguligrade is a classification of animals that have developed a mode of walking on the very tips of the toes. This provides an even greater stride length and as a consequence even higher speeds, which proves useful since most of these animals are prey animals hunted by digitigrade predators. Animals such as zebras, deer, and gazelles all fall into this category.

Horses

There is a broad range of horse breeds, from the small Shetland pony to the large shire horses. There is only one single truly wild horse species alive today: the Mongolian wild horse, *Equus ferus przewalskii*. In the same manner as dogs, horses have been bred in response to man's needs. Some have been bred as riding horses, some more suited to travel at speed, others more suited to dressage. Some, like the shire horse, have been bred to undertake heavy work, such as hauling loads or pulling a plough.

The Horse Skeleton
A horse's body is suspended relatively high off the ground on long, thin legs. The length of the leg is important for long distance travel and the ability to

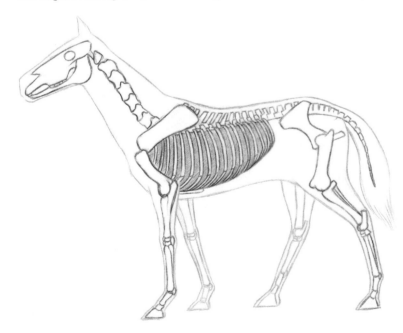

FIG 4.13 Horse skeletal structure.

sustain travel at speed. Animals such as horses that have become specialist runners have legs designed to deliver power. The bones in the upper leg are short and strong, providing a support structure for the powerful muscles. The bones in both the lower front and hind legs are fused together and have no need for the rotation of the forelimbs.

The close location of the leg muscles to the horse's body means that only relatively short contraction of the muscles provides maximum movement and power for locomotion. This makes for very economical use of energy in providing movement to the slender lower legs. There are no muscles in the lower front legs below the carpal joints or the lower hind legs below the tarsal joints.

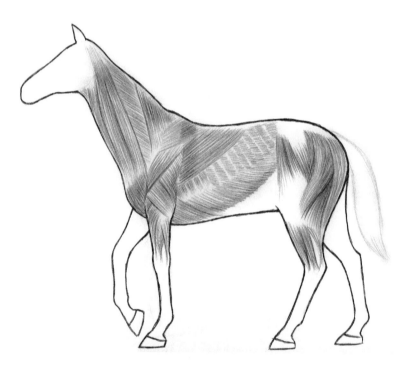

FIG 4.14 Horse musculature.

The neck is relatively long, and as with all quadrupeds the length has to do with its access to food.

Cats

From the domestic cat to the tiger, the variants in felines are less extreme than with dogs. They have developed in size, coloration, and density of coat according to their environment, but largely they have not been subject to man's intervention in terms of purposely cross-breeding changes into their physiognomy. Perhaps this is because humans saw less potential in using cats in a domestic environment or for herding sheep or hunting prey. There are some color variations among domestic cats, but they are not as marked as those among domestic dogs.

The length of the legs of predatory quadrupeds that depend on stealth, surprise attack, and short periods of chase are generally shorter than those of predators that depend on more sustained chases, such as dogs. Hunters that lie in wait for their prey, such as lions, tigers, and the humble domestic cat, differ from those that pursue their prey. Cats have proportionately shorter legs than those of dogs and a far less upright stance. The shorter legs are far more substantial, with larger bones and more muscle. The forearms of a cat need great strength to bring down another animal—often an animal larger than itself.

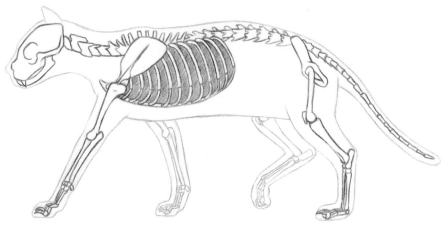

FIG 4.15 Cat skeletal structure.

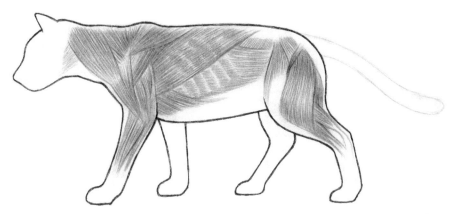

FIG 4.16 Cat musculature.

The shape of the cat's skull is somewhat flattened; the neck is short and the body heavy. With quadrupeds there is a direct correlation between the length of the neck and that of the legs. As a result the cat's neck is short but very powerful. Coupled with large muscles in the shoulder, this feature makes it ideal for subduing prey and then tearing flesh from bone. The cat's retractable claws help to ensure that they remain sharp.

Despite their rather squat shape, cats are very agile and are capable of jumping to considerable heights, balancing on very narrow surfaces such as the branches of trees or garden fences and, when falling from a height, they have the ability to right themselves to land on their feet. They possess an ability to climb and cling to the trunks of trees or branches using their paws. To do this they have a quite free use of their forelimbs, and they are able to rotate their paws as a result of the radius's ability to turn around the ulna.

Dogs

There is a huge range of modern dog species, thanks largely to the intervention of man, who has, through selective breeding, enhanced certain qualities in each breed. Originally these qualities were chosen for the practical purposes of hunting and controlling livestock, but more recently characteristics have been bred simply for aesthetic purposes. Dogs' distinct qualities continue to offer practical benefits to humans; some are favored for their particular physical attributes, others for their temperament. Working dogs have been bred specifically to undertake certain specialist activities, from the hunting qualities adapted to help in herding sheep to the fearless and aggressive temperaments of guard dogs and war dogs. Others have a more even temperament suited to becoming guide dogs for the blind; still other dogs with an extremely sensitive sense of smell are trained to sniff out all manner of things, from drugs and explosives to missing people.

Dog species range from the large, such as Great Danes and St. Bernards, to what have become known as toy dogs, such as the Chihuahua and the Pekinese. Some of man's selective breeding has developed conditions that have become problematic for the health of dogs.

These breeds may be very different from one another, but they all share certain physical traits and a common ancestor: the wolf. If we look at a wolf-like dog—that is, one retaining a similar body shape—we can see that the body is positioned much higher from the ground than a cat, on legs that are long and slender and most suited to running at speed over extended periods. The dog's head has a considerably long snout and is held in a more upright position on a relatively longer neck than a cat. The ears are held upward. The tail, although capable of a sideways wagging action, is far less maneuverable than a cat's. Unlike cat claws, dog claws are not retractable.

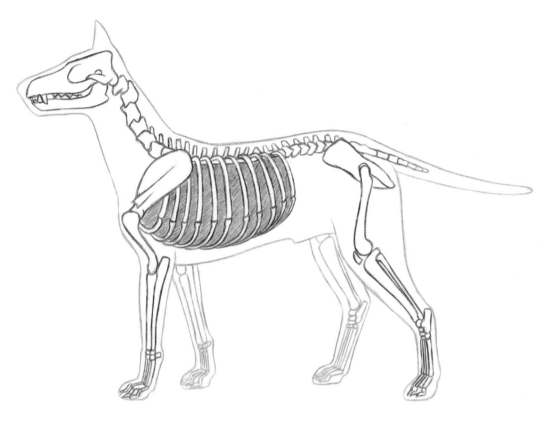

FIG 4.17 Dog skeletal structure.

Cows

First domesticated around 9,000 years ago, cattle were bred not just for meat and milk production but for their hides, bones, and horns. The cow's physiognomy reflects its nature; it is a digitigrade that walks on its toes. The cow is capable of walking and galloping, but compared with the horse it is limited in its locomotion due to its size and weight. A cow's legs are long but much heavier than that of a horse to enable it to support its massive frame.

The cow's musculature is well developed; the neck is rather shorter than that of a horse, though is particularly strong and supports a large and heavy skull. The thickset cow body is located closer to the ground than that of a horse.

Cows have several stomachs that enable them to undertake a second chewing of the grass on which they feed. A large stomach is required in any animal that depends on a diet of grass so that they can process the cellulose in the grass. Higher mammals are incapable of such digestion. Such a system allows more nutrients to be extracted from a relatively poor food source.

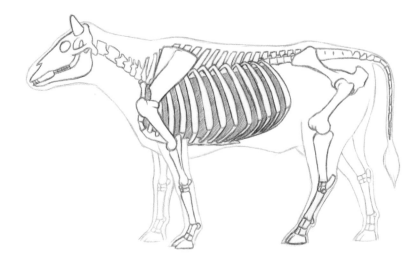

FIG 4.18 Cow skeletal structure.

Other Quadrupeds

A large number of animals have developed a highly specialized and almost unique physiognomy that calls for a distinctive mode of locomotion. Their evolutionary development has been shaped by the particular demands and constraints placed on them, in much the same way as all other animals.

Camels have developed a very a particular type of dynamic when running, which is known as *pacing*. This is an action during which the legs on the same side of the animal move in unison, with the right front and right hind legs and the left front and left hind legs working as pairs. This is achievable only at moderately high speeds, during which there is a suspension phase. At the lower speed of a walk, the camel moves in much the same way as other quadrupeds, using the same sequence of leg movements.

Giraffes also have a distinctive action that's very similar to that of the pacing camel. A giraffe's legs are so long that its mode of locomotion demonstrates a kind of loping action that gives the body a forward and backward rocking appearance. Again, this action happens only at increased speeds. When a giraffe walks, the general quadruped sequence holds. To keep the head relatively still, there is a more noticeable movement in the giraffe neck as it pivots. This tendency to keep the head on an even keel is seen in most animal locomotion. Extremes in animal movement, such as stretching and flexing actions of a cheetah as it runs at full tilt, are in contrast to the stability of the head. This can also be seen in particular with animals with long necks, such as horses, giraffes, geese, and swans.

A walking kangaroo demonstrates a shuffling gait, a kind of rocking action that constitutes low-speed locomotion. Kangaroos move both hind feet together in unison, placing their front paws on the ground to support their

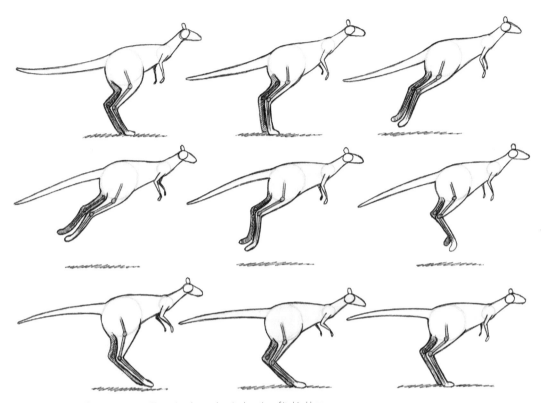

FIG 4.19 Kangaroo hopping sequence illustrating the synchronized motion of its hind legs.

weight as the rear legs are swung quickly forward. Once on the ground the legs, along with the tail, create a balanced platform that then enables the front legs to be swung forward. The kangaroo's strong tail offers a third point of support when it is moving at slow speeds and provides a firm base of support when the kangaroo is standing upright. When moving at great speed, the kangaroo hops, using its tail to act as a counterbalance to the body. The front legs play a very small part in the locomotion. The front legs terminate in paws rather than feet and are far more suited to delicate manipulation than propulsion.

Crocodiles

The crocodile is fairly typical of reptilian quadrupeds in that it holds it legs splayed away from its body. When at rest, a crocodile's body and long tail are supported on the ground and then lifted during the walk. To what degree they are lifted depends on the speed of the walk. At low speeds the body is barely lifted clear of the ground and the tail may drag. At higher speeds the crocodile will often lift its body much higher off the ground. The lateral rotation of the body of quadrupeds that have splayed legs is far

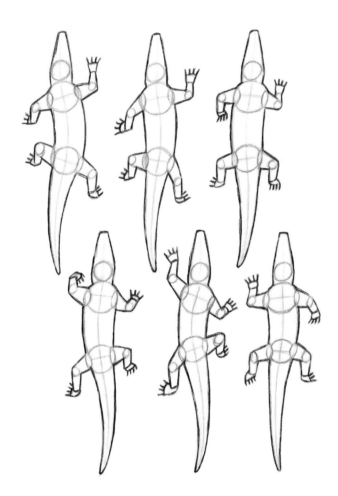

FIG 4.20 Body rotation in a crocodile walk sequence.

more pronounced during a walk than for quadrupeds that walk with a more upright gait and without splayed legs. When moving at speed this rotation of the body is increased to fairly extreme levels and is far more evident. The crocodile is quite capable of moving at high speeds both on land and in the water. When swimming, the crocodile depends in part on the undulating action of the body, though the principle source of locomotion comes from the undulating action of its very long and strong tail. The legs may make some contribution to swimming, but they are generally restricted to assisting in the creature's maneuverability.

Squirrels

The squirrel's physiognomy gives it quite remarkable agility. Squirrels are capable of very rapid actions demonstrating extremes of acceleration and deceleration. When running they seem capable of stopping instantly with no deceleration at all. Their lack of mass and relatively large muscles enable

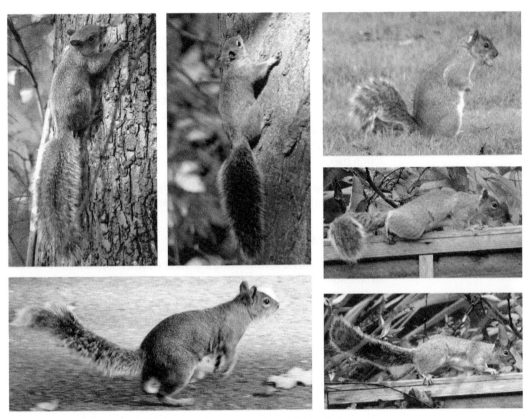

FIG 4.21 The squirrel stance with its widely spread front legs and the squat aspect of its hind legs coupled with sharp claws allows it to cling easily to vertical surfaces.

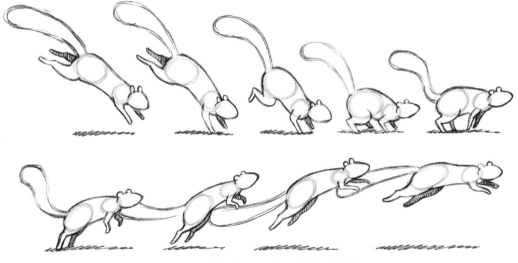

FIG 4.22 The cursorial nature of the squirrel gives its motion a bounding aspect. The animal is so light that there is very little evidence of acceleration or deceleration when it starts and stops running.

them to accelerate very quickly and shed momentum with equal rapidity. These features provide the squirrel with its most distinctive, bounding action, which is emphasized by its long and flexible tail. Its ability to climb vertical surfaces almost as quickly as it moves along the ground adds to this very distinctive action. This action is perhaps best typified by very fast movements with sudden stops followed by periods of almost complete stillness. The splayed legs of this noncursorial animal allow it to get its body very close to a tree. Coupled with its broadly splayed fingers and long, sharp claws, this characteristic allows the squirrel to gain a firm grip on rough bark.

When running on the ground, a squirrel's body is held well off the ground; when clinging to a tree, the body is held closer to the surface of the tree.

Quadruped Animation

There are definite benefits to being a quadruped when it comes to locomotion. Four legs allow for greater speed and provide a more stable base and better balance.

To get along in their normal mode of locomotion, different quadrupeds may choose to scurry, walk, trot, run, or hop, depending on their physiognomy and, of course, the urgency of their journey. To get over obstacles, some of them may hop or jump. A more extended action of small jumps can be undertaken, resulting in the animal bounding. Some quadrupeds can also climb, many swim, others dig and burrow; there are even one or two that fly. Well, actually, they glide, and that's the next best thing to flying.

For most quadrupeds the sequences of actions that constitute a walk are very similar. Although there may be slight variations in the timing of the individual legs, the order in which they are moved is the same. However, there are more differences than similarities between the running actions of various quadrupeds. Some of them incorporate other actions, such as a leaping, as part of the run. Some smaller animals moving at high speeds use a scurrying action; others gallop. So, the action of moving at speed (running) may vary from animal to animal, but they do share some common traits.

It is not necessary nor even possible for an animal to maintain equilibrium at every point in its locomotion. During a walk cycle, for instance, the forward momentum, the shifting weight, and the lifting of alternate legs create what could be considered little more than a controlled fall. However, though there may be lack of balance during the stride, in fact this lack of balance is often central to such motion. It is important that equilibrium is maintained throughout the action in its entirety.

During a run, unlike a walk, the subject undergoes a suspended phase when all four feet are lifted off the ground. Clearly it would not be possible to consider that the subject is balanced at this point in the action.

Quadruped Walks

We can study the details of a typical quadruped walk, but even taking into account the movement of the individual legs, the sequencing of the leg movements, the rotation at the shoulders and hips, the spine movement, and the subtle actions of the head and tail, the study will still be a very general one. There are many variations for individual species. However, this initial investigation will still provide us with a reasonable starting point. Later in the text and in the images we'll see other examples that could provide a useful comparison.

At this point it might be worthwhile to briefly revisit the classifications of action we've covered elsewhere, to help us analyze the action. As we discussed in Chapter 3, we can break down most movements into three quite distinct classifications: primary actions, secondary actions, and tertiary actions. Having an understanding of how these classifications apply to any given movement may provide a better understanding of that movement.

- Primary action: Cause
- Secondary action: Supplement
- Tertiary action: Effect

Primary actions are those that provide the main source of any given movement and without which the movement would not be possible. The movement of the legs in a walk cycle is one such action.

Secondary actions are those that assist in a movement and make a contribution to the movement, though they are not necessary for the movement to take place. Swinging arms in a walk may help with the walk but are not vital to it.

Tertiary actions describe those movements that occur as a result of other movements and are affected by primary and secondary actions. Consider the action of the tail of a horse as it runs. The tail's wave action is a result of the run; it does not contribute to it. A tertiary action makes little or no contribution to locomotion.

There are many aspects to even the most basic of walks. We must first consider the part of an action that creates locomotion. *Duty factor* is a term used to describe the part of a given action that contributes to the effort within that movement. When applied to a walking action, the term describes the period during which the individual feet are placed on the ground, providing support and the power for forward locomotion.

When an animal wants to increase its speed during a walk, it naturally lengthens the stride of each leg. It also increases the frequency of the step, thereby reducing the duration of the duty factor of each step. Stride length is determined by a number of factors, varies among animals, and varies by motivating factors within individual animals. There are physical constraints on the stride length, the main one being the actual length of the animal's leg and the manner in which the legs are held (cursorial or nonecursorial). The

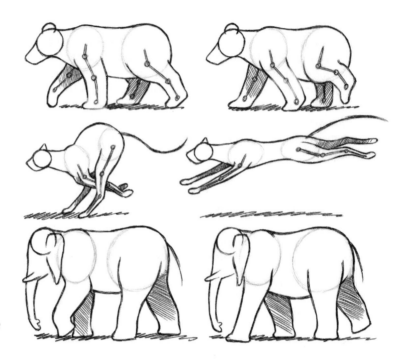

FIG 4.23 The different stride length of quadrupeds depends on the physiognomy of the animal and the speed at which it travels. Elephants are incapable of a true run and have a limited stride length. The anatomy of the cheetah makes it capable of achieving great speeds due to its flexibility, which results in a very wide stride length when in full gallop.

stride length will also vary a great deal depending on the motivation factors for the movement. Grazing animals moving slowly across a meadow may take very short strides, whereas animals moving in a more continuous and purposeful manner, such as migrating wildebeest, will demonstrate a longer stride length that will increase even further if there is an element of urgency in the action.

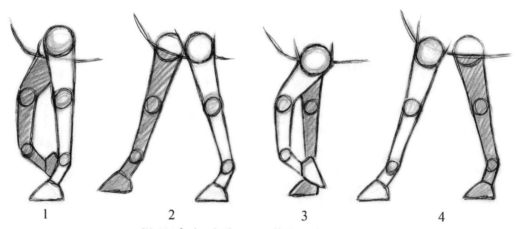

1 2 3 4

FIG 4.24 Quadruped walk sequence of forelegs. 1: Passing position. 2: Stride. 3: Passing position. 4: Stride.

Before considering the sequence of leg movements for a quadruped, let's look at the action of an individual leg. This movement of a single leg during a walk cycle may be divided into different phases. Because this movement is part of a cycle, there is no distinct starting position, just a given point within the cycle. I have chosen the front leg of a horse as an illustration for this action, though the principle holds for other quadrupeds.

The two main positions of a leg during a walk cycle are the stride and the passing position. *Passing position* is a term used for a phase within the walk cycle when the paired legs are positioned alongside one another. One leg is held rigid and straight and supports the weight of the animal (or person); the other leg is held bent as it swings forward and passes the supporting leg. Cursorial mammals and birds move their legs along parasagittal planes. That is, they move them parallel to the length of the animal's body. In this example of a passing position, the feet are located directly below the position of the animal's shoulder or hips. Noncursorial animals move with their legs held at an angle away from the body; as a consequence the foot is not located directly beneath the shoulder or hip during the passing position.

Stride describes the moment within the walk cycle when the paired legs are outstretched in opposite directions, one facing forward in anticipation of taking on part of the duty factor of the walk while the other is held backward, having just completed its contribution to the duty factor.

The sequence of a complete walk cycle is much more complex and involves the transition from one position, the passing position, to the other, the stride. Let's examine this scenario more fully.

Phase One

This phase begins with the leg stretched backward to its furthest extent. From this position the leg begins to move forward from its backwardly extended position and moves with the foot lifting clear from the ground and a bend at the elbow and at the wrist. As the foot is lifted, the shoulder is also lifted to assist in raising the foot clear off the ground. This leg finishes this phase with the elbow located almost directly beneath the shoulder as it passes the now upright supporting leg on the opposite side of the body. The leg is no longer straight and the angle between radius and the third metacarpal bone is at its most acute.

Phase Two

The front leg begins this phase as it passes the supporting leg (the passing position). It has gained momentum and continues to swing forward, and as it does so the leg begins to straighten at the elbow and the wrist. As the leg reaches its forwardmost position, the foot is located well ahead of the shoulder. The foot has swung forward to present the underside parallel to the ground and ready for it to be placed flat on the ground. During this phase the shoulder starts to drop again as it assists in extending the reach of the leg. The forward momentum continues and the foot is finally planted on the ground. The animal's weight is then supported by this leg, which also begins to assist in the animal's balance.

Phase Three

At the beginning of this phase the foot is planted flat on the ground and placed well ahead of the body, with the leg being held straight at the elbow and the wrist. As the animal continues to move forward, the leg now enters a supporting phase and increasingly takes the weight of the animal. The leg remains locked throughout this phase as it rotates at the wrist to an upright position. The shoulder rises again to its highest position as the foot passes directly beneath it. For the first time in the cycle, force is applied by this leg, which makes this phase the first part of the duty factor for this leg. The leg at this stage uses a pulling action to provide forward motion. The leg completes this phase of the movement with the shoulder located directly above the foot. The opposite front leg is now in the passing position.

Phase Four

This phase starts with the leg locked and completely upright. There is a rotation at the wrist and the shoulder is moving forward and dropping slightly

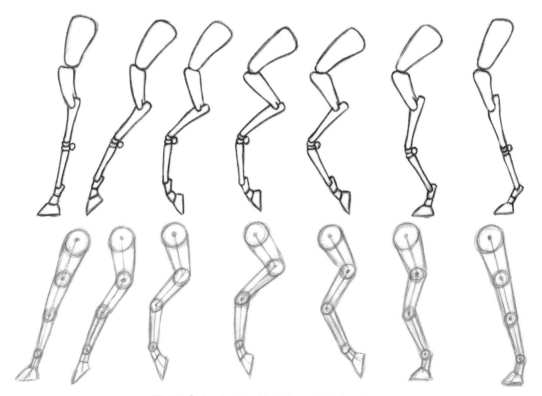

FIG 4.25 Foreleg of quadruped during forward stride of a walk cycle.

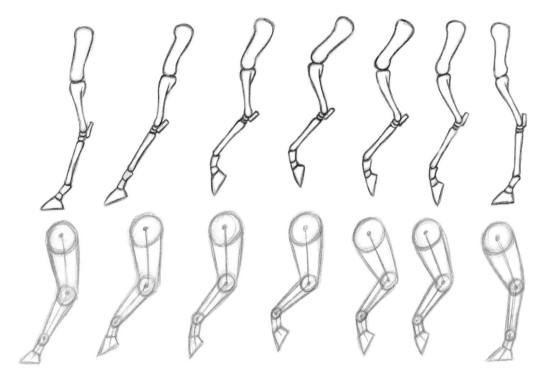

FIG 4.26 Hind leg of quadruped during forward stride of a walk cycle.

as the angle of the leg declines from the upright. This phase represents a continuation of the duty factor for this leg, though at this stage the leg begins to push the animal forward. The phase is completed as the foot is extended backward to the point where the foot is located at its furthest point behind the animal, well behind the shoulder of the same leg. This phase is concluded when the leg reaches the point at the beginning of Phase One and the cycle begins again.

The Cursorial Walk

The walking gait of a quadruped is a symmetrical action. There is no strict starting point, though the cycle has a clear structure and operates within a regular sequence of leg movements. The sequence is as follows: left fore, right hind, right fore, left hind, then left fore again and so on. Once again, establishing a starting point for this cycle is problematic because the starting point for a walk depends on the animal's rest mode. Different animals may use slight variants of this quadrupedal walk, though the differences are more likely to be in the periods between each of the legs moving and where they plant their hind feet in relation to their front ones. This varies from animal to animal, as does the speed at which they are moving.

The following phases of this walk sequence form a cycle, and as such there is no natural start or end position to this sequence. However, the sequential order still holds.

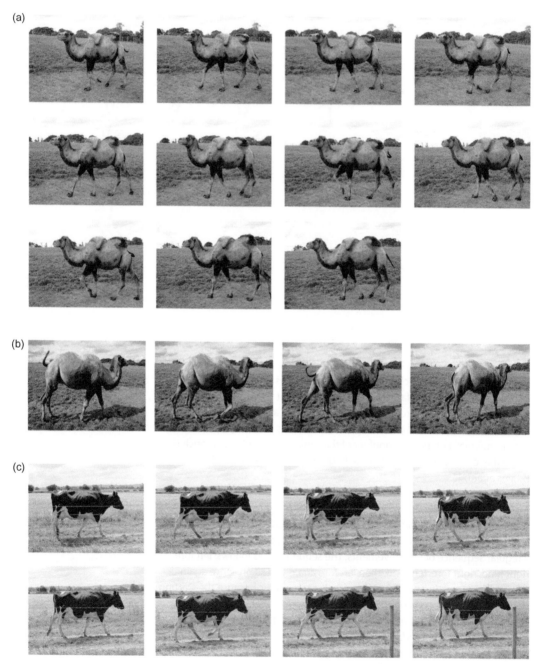

(a)

(b)

(c)

FIG 4.27 Continued

(d)

(e)

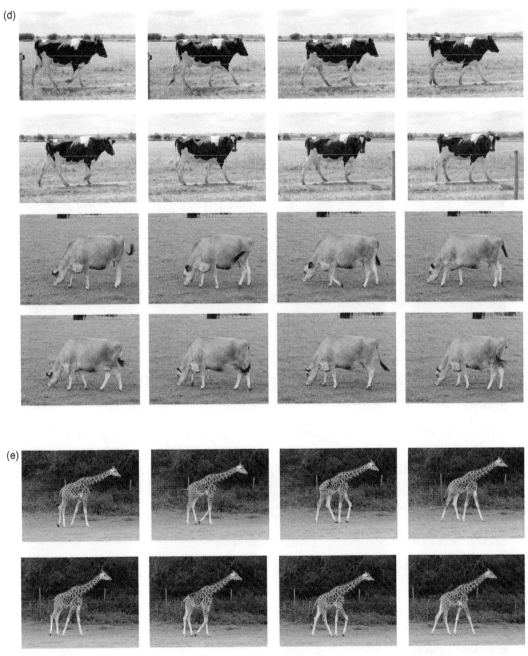

FIG 4.27 Continued

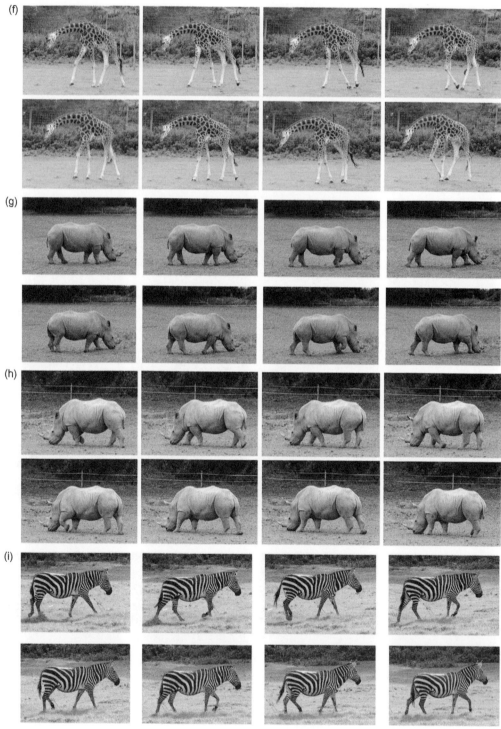

FIG 4.27 Continued

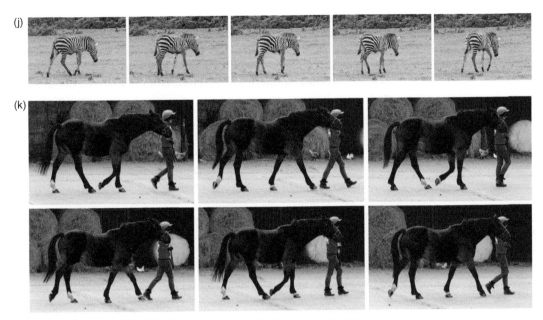

FIG 4.27 (a–k) Cursorial quadriped walk cycle. Notice how, when the front legs are in the passing position, the hind legs are in the stride position and vice versa.

Phase One

We start the sequence by establishing this phase with three of the four feet on the ground. Note that while the hind legs are in the stride position, the front legs are in the passing position.

- Front right leg is held straight and upright and supports the front of the animal. It is halfway through its duty factor.
- Front left leg is swinging forward.
- Hind left leg is extended forward and has just been placed on the ground. It is about to start its duty factor.
- Hind right leg is extended backward and has just completed the duty factor. Both back legs are supporting the horse at this stage. Balance is spread over the three legs, providing a triangular configuration.

Phase Two

The front legs have now moved into the stride position while the hind legs have moved into the passing position. The horse is supported on only two legs, forming a diagonal support of left front and right hind.

- Front right leg is extended backward and takes the weight of the horse's front end.
- Front left leg has swung forward with the foot located well ahead of the shoulder, poised to be placed on the ground.
- Hind left leg has moved backward and is in a near-upright position.
- Hind right foot has lifted from the ground and begins to swing forward.

Phase Three

The support of the quadruped is now maintained by two legs on the same side of the animal: front left and hind left. The balance is shifted slightly as the center of gravity is located more closely to the supporting legs. The front legs have moved once again into the passing position and the hind legs are in the stride.

- Front right leg is swinging forward and neither supports the animal nor contributes to the duty factor.
- Front left leg is held straight, rigid, and upright. It is halfway through this stride duty factor cycle. This leg is supporting the animal's front end.
- Hind left leg is now extended fully backward at the end of its contribution to the duty factor.
- Hind right leg is extended fully forward with the foot held flat as it anticipates being placed on the ground.

Phase Four

The balance is shifted as the support moves from two feet on the same side of the animal to the front left and hind right feet creating a support structure diagonally across the body.

- Front right leg is extended forward, but the foot is not yet placed on the ground.
- Front left leg is now extended fully backward, thereby creating a stride position with the other front leg.
- Hind left leg has just lifted off the ground and begins to swing forward.
- Hind right leg has its foot placed on the ground, is supporting the rear end of the animal, and is beginning to move backward.

Phase Five

Three of the feet are now placed on the ground, creating a triangular configuration of the supporting legs. The front legs are now in the stride position and the rear legs are entering the passing position phase.

- Front right leg is fully extended with the foot placed on the ground.
- Front left leg is extended backward with the foot preparing to be lifted from the ground.
- Hind left leg has lifted and has swung forward and is located half way through the passing position.
- Hind right leg is now in its upright position and supports the rear end of the animal.

Phase Six

This is the final phase of the cycle. Once again the animal is supported by the two legs on one side of the animal, this time by the front right and hind right.

- Front right leg is moving backward and is almost in the upright position.
- Front left leg has been lifted from the ground and swings forward.

- Hind left leg is now swinging forward of the halfway position.
- Hind right leg continues to support the animal's rear end and has moved backward of the upright position.

The sequence is now complete and the movement progresses from Phase Six back to Phase One, thereby completing the cycle.

During a walk, a quadruped is supported on either two or three legs at any one time. Unlike a run cycle, at no point are both front legs and both hind legs off the ground at the same time.

The Noncursorial Walk
The walking gait of a noncursorial animal is due to the manner in which the legs are held away from the body. Noncursorial animals demonstrate greater lateral movement of the spine, creating distinct and exaggerated curves during the walk. The twist in both the upper body at the shoulders and the lower body at the hips in noncursorial animals is much more pronounced than that of cursorial animals. While the shoulders are oriented in one direction, there is a twist in the orientation of the pelvis in the opposite orientation, creating a bend in the spine.

Trotting
Trotting is a gait in which the animal is moving at a moderate speed—faster than a walk and slower than a full gallop. This gait is sometimes used as a transitional stage between walking and running if the transition is not a rapid one and is extended over time. During a trot diagonally opposite legs are synchronized and moved in phase with one another; the front left leg and hind right leg form one pair, and the front right and hind left form the other pair. Once again, there is no particular starting point in this sequence that works as a cycle.

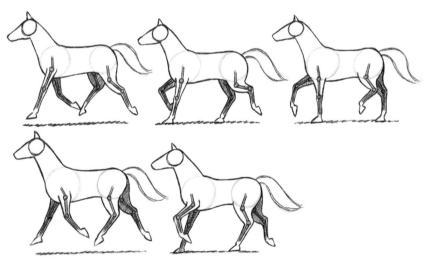

FIG 4.28 A quadruped trot cycle that illustrates the suspension phase in which all four feet are off the ground.

I have broken the trotting action into four main phases that describe only *half* the cycle. For a full cycle, the phases would be repeated using the opposing legs. These four phases are:

1. The extended stride: backward
2. The suspension phase
3. The extended stride: forward
4. The passing position

Phase One

The body is supported on two legs and is in an *extended stride backward* position.

- Front left leg is held off the ground and is extended and thrown forward.
- Front right leg is extended fully backward and at the end of its duty phase.
- Hind right leg is off the ground and bent and swinging forward.
- Hind left leg is extended backward and supports the animal.

Phase Two

The animal has now entered the *suspension phase*, during which all four feet are held off the ground. The entire body is at its highest point away from the ground than at any other stage during the trot.

- Front left leg is now fully extended in preparation for the foot to be placed on the ground.
- Front right leg is still extended backward and has just lifted from the ground in readiness to be swung forward.
- Hind right leg remains bent and is advanced of the passing position.
- Hind left leg has just been lifted clear of the ground and is held backward.

Phase Three

The animal has now made contact with the ground again. The body is supported on two diagonally opposed legs and is in an *extended stride forward* position.

- Front left foot is now firmly on the ground, though still extended forward.
- Front right leg is raised off the ground and is swinging forward.
- Hind right leg is extended forward with the foot on the ground.
- Hind left leg is now bent as it begins to swing forward.

Phase Four

The animal has now entered the *passing position* with the supporting legs about to undertake their highest levels of duty factor.

- Front left leg is straight and locked and now supports the animal.
- Front right leg is heavily bent and swings forward past the supporting leg.
- Hind right leg has taken the shock of landing on the ground and is now held straight and vertical, supporting the animal's weight.
- Hind left leg is halfway through its swing forward and is located alongside the hind supporting leg.

The passing position of Phase Four leads to an extended backward stride phase that resembles Phase One but with opposite legs. During the transition between these two phases, the supporting legs provide the highest levels of thrust, creating forward locomotion. In the phases that follow, what was undertaken by the front left leg is now undertaken by the front right leg until the cycle is completed.

The Gallop

The transition from a standing repose position or a walking gait into a running one may be abrupt. Galloping occurs when walking or trotting is no longer the most effective and efficient gait. Rather like the trot, the galloping gait is distinguished from a walking gait by the inclusion of a suspension phase, a part of the action when all legs are suspended off the ground.

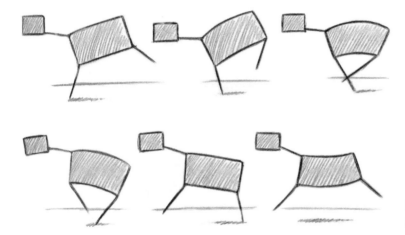

FIG 4.29 A much simplified galloping action of a quadruped.

Unlike the walk cycle, galloping for a quadruped presents an asymmetrical action of the legs, and as a result the sequence of leg movements changes from a walk to a run. In addition to the suspension phase, there are two distinct points in the gallop when the animal is supported on only a single foot: as it lands from the suspension phase and again as it jumps.

By compressing and flexing its spine, the animal is able to increase the reach of its legs and therefore increase its stride length. In a gallop it is normal for hind legs to land in a position forward of the point where the hind legs left the ground. This is most noticeable in the cheetah, where the extreme flexibility of its spine allows its hind legs to reach well forward of the front ones.

The highly simplified illustration demonstrates how the hind legs and forelegs cross and the spine compresses and arches. It also indicates that the rotation of the body mass imparts a kind of forward and backward rocking action in the animal. Throughout this action the head is held relatively still.

The five phases described in the following sections are intended to represent a full gallop cycle in a little more detail, illustrating the sequence of all four legs and the use of the individual joints and pivotal points.

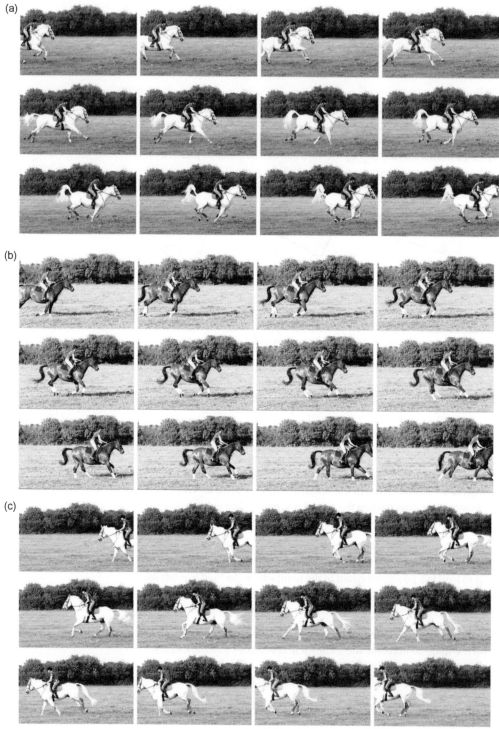

FIG 4.30 (a–c) Horse gallop sequence.

Phase One

We start with this sequence as the animal is supported on three legs. The body is held slightly higher at the rear.

- Front right leg is planted firmly on the ground and extended forward.
- Front left leg is held off the ground and heavily bent at the carpal joint and has swung to a forward position.
- Hind left leg is extended forward and planted on the ground.
- Hind right leg is extended fully backward but has not yet left the ground.

Phase Two

The animal is suspended on two legs at this point.

- Front right leg has now pushed to a backward position, providing thrust.
- Front left leg is fully extended forward and held straight in preparation for placing the foot on the ground.
- Hind left leg supports the animal and is held in a vertical position.
- Hind right leg has been lifted from the ground but is still extended backward.

Phase Three

It is at this phase that the animal pushes off the ground and is supported by only a front foot. The body is supported at the front end only; as a result the body is angled upward toward the rear.

- Front right foot is held off the ground and swings quickly forward.
- Front left foot is the only foot that remains on the ground.
- Hind left foot has left the ground and swings forward.
- Hind right leg moves together with the left one; they are both still extended slightly backward.

Phase Four

This is the suspension phase of the sequence during which the animal is completely suspended from the ground. At this point the animal is at its highest point off the ground during the sequence. The body is held level horizontally.

- Front right leg is extended furthest forward but at this stage is still bent.
- Front left leg is still trailing backward slightly. Both front legs are bent at the elbow and carpal joints.
- Hind left leg is has reached the upright position and is moving with the hind right leg.
- Hind right leg is extended slightly in front of the hind left leg.

Phase Five

At this point the animal is supported by a single hind leg as it lands from the suspended phase. The body is tilted upward toward the front end and the hips are lower than the shoulders.

- Front right leg continues to swing forward.
- Front left leg is extended forward in anticipation of contact with the ground.
- Hind left leg is extended fully forward and will be the next foot to make contact with the ground.
- Hind right leg has made contact with the ground and bends slightly as it cushions the impact. This is the only point on which the animal is supported.

The next stage of the run is a transition period between what was described in Phase Five and the subsequent position outlined in Phase One.

Many animals (mostly those that are the prey of predators) incorporate a leap within their running action, though such a leap does not normally form a part of the sequence that is repeated at regular intervals and at a specific moment within the action. Rather, the leap forms an occasional part of the run as part of a flight response. The irregular timing of the leap within the run probably assists the animal in evading capture. However, when an animal is being pursued by a predator, an exaggerated leap may actually be a disadvantage if it is not timed properly, because it may actually slow down the run. Gazelles will often leap high in the air as a response to the presence of a predator prior to the chase commencing. This kind of leaping may be done in part to demonstrate the animal's agility to the predator with a view to dissuading it from the chase.

Pacing

The transition from a walking gait to pacing involves a change to the sequence of leg movements. Walking camels demonstrate the same sequence

(a)

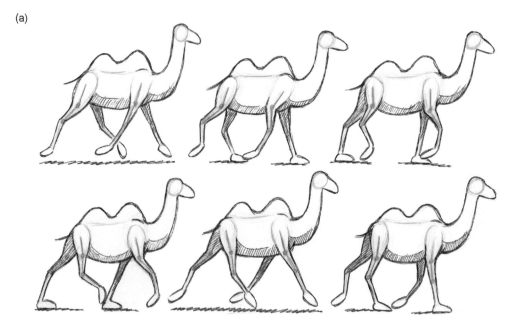

FIG 4.31 Continued

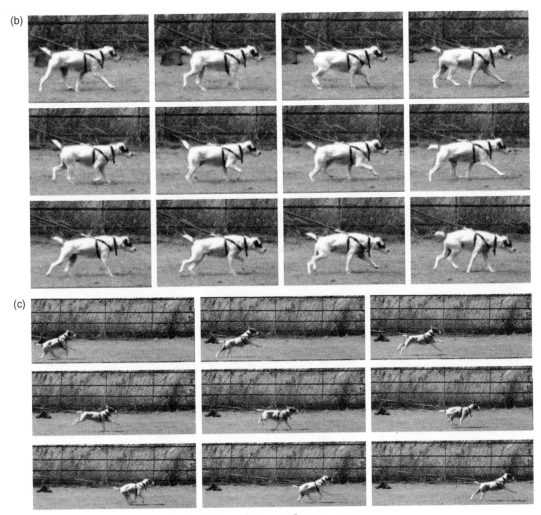

FIG 4.31 a: The pacing action of a camel moving at speed. b: Dog walk sequence. c: Dog run sequence.

of leg actions as a horse does. Pacing occurs when the animal needs to move faster; it is an action that is possible only at higher speed because it involves lateral pairing of legs—that is, legs on the same side of the body moving together in phase and being lifted at the same time. The action alternates from the left and right sides of the body with the right fore and right hinds moving in unison, followed by left front and left hind.

If this were done at slow speeds, it would probably be impossible to maintain balance. This pacing kind of action is suited to animals with very long legs and is also occasionally used by giraffes.

Jumping

The ability for any given animal to jump, as with all forms of locomotion, is synonymous with that animal's need to jump. For a few heavier animals such as elephants and hippopotamus, jumping may be very difficult or even impossible. Other animals may jump only very infrequently; still others depend heavily on jumping and integrate it into other actions such as running or climbing. Mountain goats often jump to traverse difficult terrain; antelope and deer often leap as part of their running action, possibly to evade predation.

In anticipation of leaping over an obstacle, a jumping horse plants both its hind legs firmly on the ground together, squashing down slightly in preparation for providing the necessary upward thrust. The head is held upright during the first part of the jump, with the neck stretched forward and downward in a counter-movement as the body rises. As the horse leaves the ground, the hind legs are extended fully backward together while the forelegs are bent and tucked tightly into the body to avoid contact with the obstacle. As the horse is positioned over the obstacle, the hind legs are bent and tucked in while the forelegs are extended fully forward in anticipation of making contact with the ground. As the horse's body rotates with the front end dropping the neck is pivoted and the head is once again lifted.

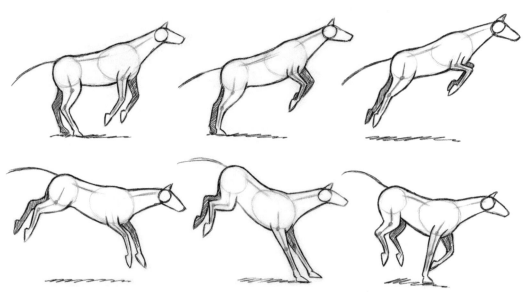

FIG 4.32 Horse jumping sequence.

Deer and antelope use a kind of bounding jump in their run actions. During this action both front and hind legs become tucked into the body at the same time and may be extended downward together, or at least much closer together than when the animal is leaping over an object such as a fence.

116

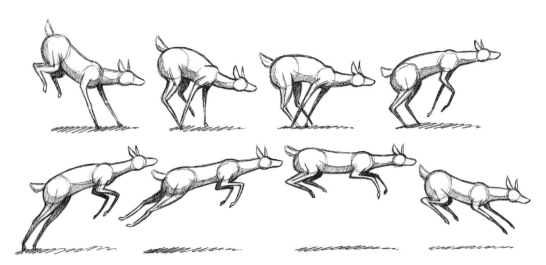

FIG 4.33 The bounding action of a deer.

Cats often hold their tails erect when they walk, though as they begin to stalk prey, the tail is lowered, as is their entire profile. When a cat runs at a full gallop, the spine is flexed on the contact point of the run and then fully stretched with the forelegs extending fully forward and the hind legs extended backward during the suspension phase. Cats are capable of demonstrating great agility and balance, as the feat of jumping onto a fence many times higher than their height clearly demonstrates. Other quadrupeds such as dogs find more difficulty in such actions.

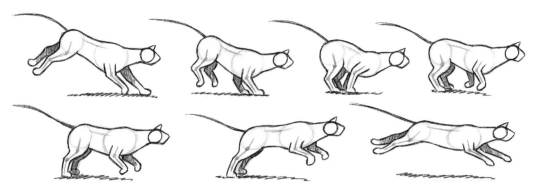

FIG 4.34 Cat gallop sequence.

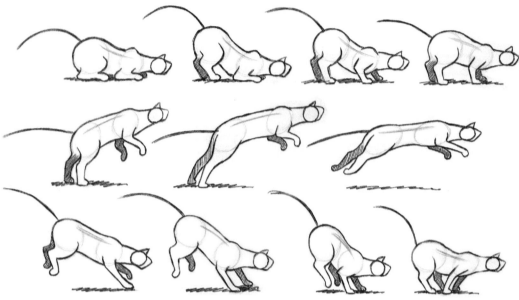

FIG 4.35 Cat pounce sequence.

Hauling Loads

Animals carrying loads suffer a general increase in energy cost of locomotion. Although there may be some noticeable differences in gait, such as a head held lower than in a normal walk, the upright stance is maintained. However, when an animal is hauling a load, the change in stance may be more noticeable. Horses that pull carts may maintain a very similar posture to a normal walk, particularly once the inertia of the load is overcome and forward momentum of the load achieved. The differences are more noticeable with heavier loads or when the animal is pulling against pressure that is constant, such as in plowing. In this instance a horse can be seen to be holding its head less upright; it is generally extended either forward or downward. The forward reach of the horse's legs may be shortened slightly while the backward thrust is extended. This gives the appearance of the body being angled forward, an effect enhanced by the hips being held lower than in an ordinary walk. This stance enables the horse to deliver more power to the hind legs, which are providing the main source of thrust for forward locomotion.

Group Action

Many animals gather together in herds, flocks, shoals, or crowds. Such group actions have benefits in protection from predators, as is the case with the flocking of starlings as they go to roost or the bait-balling behavior of sardines in the presence of predators such as dolphins, seals, or larger fish. Animal groupings obviously offer benefits to those animals; group bonding is one such benefit. Some animals choose to live in extended family groups or larger troupes of various sizes throughout their lives; others come together more periodically, often for migratory or mating purposes. Some groups have distinct hierarchies, and certain actions such as a pecking order in birds are undertaken to establish and maintain social order. Grooming among primates establishes very elaborate family and group dynamics. Similar bonding activities and hierarchies can be seen in large cats such as lions and wild dogs. Seasonal group behavior is not uncommon among animals; stags will gather to fight over female deer, and black grouse regularly gather together in the spring at the same communal display area known as a *lek*. When mating instigates group activities, normal modes of behavior are sometimes abandoned for other, often more violent conduct. Some animals even change their physical appearance—for instance, growing brighter plumage or long, sharp horns.

Birds

Birds are not the only animals that have taken to the air and developed the ability to fly. Many insects and some mammals also find it useful to get around in this way. In the greater evolutionary time scale, birds have taken to the air relatively recently. The earliest fossilized record of what is considered to be a modern bird, Archaeopteryx, shows that it flew around 145 million years ago. The fossil shows clear evidence of the asymmetrical nature of its feathers. This is a very significant factor because it is the asymmetrical nature of the feather that is needed to form a seamless wing, which in turn is essential for powered flight. The wings of Archaeopteryx also show the vestiges of three fingers, complete with hooked claws that would be ideal for clinging to branches and assisting climbing and perching. Its jaw, while extended like a modern bird's beak, is full of short, sharp teeth; this jaw, combined with a spine that extends into a bony tail, demonstrates the reptilian ancestry of Archaeopteryx.

Most modern birds have lost all these traits, but the Hoatzin *Opisthocomus hoazin* is a modern bird living in the forests of South America that has retained very similar small claws on its wings. These claws enable it to move around in the trees, much as its earlier ancestors did in order to feed on a diet of leaves.

Long before Archaeopteryx took to flying, insects ruled the skies, first colonizing the air around 350 million years ago. With no airborne competitors, they grew to sizes much larger than their modern-day equivalents. There is evidence of dragonflies with a wingspan of a meter plus. Dinosaurs also had their representatives that took to flying as a preferred mode of locomotion. The earliest pterosaurs are thought to have existed around 200 million years ago, though there is a great deal of conjecture as to why they developed in order to take to the air. The largest of the earliest flying dinosaurs were around the size of a modern seagull. The size and shape of the dinosaur wing suggests that the mode of flight was largely dependant on soaring, in much the same way as modern gulls soar over the ocean waves. There is even some evidence that supports the notion that these creatures existed, also rather like modern seagulls, on a diet of fish. Later, pterosaurs developed and became much larger. The largest of these is *Quetzalcoatlus northropi*, which had an estimated wingspan of between 11 and 12 meters. Such immense size would make it difficult for such a creature to undertake powered flight. Other than taking off or landing, it probably depended largely on soaring. Apparently this specimen lived nowhere near either the ocean or large bodies of water, so, unlike the earlier pterosaurs, it probably depended on something other than fish for its diet.

The one thing that all pterosaurs had in common was the manner in which the wings of stretched skin were held between their arms and legs to form the smooth surface of a wing.

There is a fair degree of uncertainty as to exactly how and when the pterosaurs took to flying, but today's flying lizard of Borneo may offer us some indication. These small lizards climb trees, as do many lizards, but these use flaps of skin connected between the front and hind legs that, when stretched, form a wing that enables them to glide great distances from tree to tree.

The first bird flew around 145 million years ago. Then, by around 60 million years ago, all the modern species of birds had established themselves. By that stage they had become, much as they are now, the modern masters of the air. Evolution has seen birds develop into a huge variety of species that has allowed them to colonize the entire earth, from the tropics to the poles, and in doing so exploit all possible environments. It is as a direct result of the development of the wing and powered flight that has allowed this colonization and made birds capable of undertaking the most remarkable of journeys.

Just as flight is an evolution response to conditions, most probably to avoid predation, becoming flightless is also an evolutionary response to conditions. If birds couldn't fly, they wouldn't last long against their natural predators. Desire for safety from these predators was probably the reason they took to the air in the first place. Without such ground predators, one group of birds has found much less need to fly; as a result they have lost the power of flight, some of them having no feathers that are even suitable for flight. Birds that have gone down this evolutionary route of flightlessness find themselves either having to find other ways of avoiding predation or suffering the consequence of potential extinction. Such was the fate of the dodo. Only a small minority of birds have become flightless; they are generally ones that live in island communities with no ground predators or they occupy the more isolated parts of the world.

Penguins are one of the best-known examples of the flightless bird. These birds are not much better at walking than they are at flying. They no longer have any need to fly because they have no ground predator to escape from. Coupled with other environmental factors, this fact has resulted in penguins developing a highly specialized and very distinctive physiognomy. They may no longer be able to fly, but they have become one of the world's greatest swimmers, capable of achieving very high speeds with great maneuverability.

This not only helps them catch their chosen prey; it also helps them evade their oceangoing predators. Being flightless clearly doesn't mean being completely safe.

Birds have also evolved into different sizes and shapes, ranging from the large, now flightless ostrich to the smallest hummingbird. Birds have evolved in response to specific evolutionary forces and opportunities. A number of birds have developed to occupy those evolutionary niches that are usually occupied by land mammals, such places where mammals are absent and don't compete for that niche. In New Zealand a number of species exploit situations usually dominated by such mammals. The kiwi forages among the debris of the forest floor and along the tideline of beaches, where it rummages and grubs for insects and worms. It has become nocturnal and lives in burrows. In short, it behaves in much the same way as a badger would do.

Bird Anatomy

Birds are varied in size and shape in response to different environmental circumstances and their place in the natural order of things. Bird behavior differs between species and their diets are as varied as their plumage. The shape and size of body and beak are determined by a bird's diet, but much of a bird's anatomy is determined by its need to fly, and to that end the majority of birds share one common feature: the wing.

Birds' process of reproduction—gestating their young in eggs laid externally—has allowed them to develop flying as a mode of locomotion. The demands of powered flight make it difficult if not impossible for birds to gestate their young in their bodies in the same manner as mammals. Carrying the additional weight of unborn young would probably make flight impossible for them.

A bird's diet is also restricted in part due to its need to fly. Geese eat grass but have a particular way of dealing with this difficult-to-process food. Grass does not provide a meal in which the calories are easily extracted, and it requires a great deal of digesting. Cows manage this through the use of several stomachs that enable them to take on large quantities of grass for extended periods and then chew the grass for a second time to extract the maximum nutrition. Geese use a different system based on their need to keep their weight down in order to fly. As a result they are only able to extract a little nutrition from the grass as it passes quickly through their system. This in turn requires them to graze at a much higher rate than cows. The demands of flying mean that geese have to process the grass at a high speed, resulting in excreting on a very regular basis, maintaining a lower body weight, and thereby retaining their flying capabilities.

As with all animals, different birds have developed different physiognomies in a response to the environmental niches they exploit. Some birds have long legs in order to wade in water. Others have short legs so as not to restrict flying in dense undergrowth. There are birds that have webbed feet to assist in swimming; others have large, splayed feet that enable them to spread their weight over a large area so that they can walk over soft ground or across beds of delicate lily pads.

The Bird Skeleton

Although the size and shape of different species of birds may vary a great deal from each other, birds, unlike mammals, are in a very general sense all very similar to each other in their basic skeletal structure. Weight is a major factor in most birds, and in most cases the bird skeleton reflects the need to keep weight as low as possible. The bone structure of birds differs from bone structure of mammals; birds have far fewer bones and although, as in mammals, the bones are very strong, enabling them to deal with the stresses and rigors of flight, they are much lighter than mammalian bones. Birds' bones are honeycombed and filled with air cavities that make them less dense while retaining great strength. The demands of flight have resulted in the development of large muscles in the bird's breast that provide power to the wings. This in turn has resulted in the development of a very pronounced keel on the breastbone that anchors these muscles to the skeletal frame. The feathers that cover the bird are also very light, making birds much lighter than mammals of a comparative size.

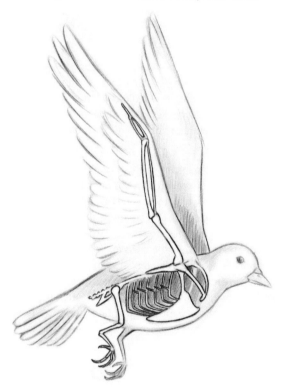

FIG 4.36 Bird skeletal structure.

There are exceptions to all cases, however. A kiwi's bones, for example, have adapted to the bird's flightless lifestyle. No longer restricted by weight, the kiwi's skeleton has lost the keel on the breastbone that in other birds provides an anchor for the strong wing muscles, and their bones are no longer honeycombed but are more solid and filled with marrow, much in the same way as mammal bones.

Beaks

The beak is a very versatile tool, one that is shaped and determined by the nature of the bird's diet. For example, the curved and sharp beak of a raptor is ideal for ripping flesh from bone.

Some beaks, thin, short, and pointed, are suited to a diet of insects; blunter and stronger ones are suited to a diet of seeds; fish are best hunted with a spear-like bill. Some beaks act as tools. The sturdy beak of the woodpecker allows it to hammer holes in wood to reach insects or, in the case of a sapsucker, to chisel out shallow wells in the bark of pine trees to tap the supply of sap rising through a tree in spring. A sturdy beak is also useful in excavating nest sites. The length of a beak may be also be critical and determined by a particular kind of diet. A curlew's beak is long and curved, allowing it to reach food deep under the sand, and nectar is best probed for from the depths of flowers by very long and slender beaks like that of the hummingbird.

Not all beaks that are intended to do similar tasks exhibit the same design solutions or the same shapes. Filter feeders such as flamingos, shoveler ducks, and avocets have different-shaped beaks that reflect the manner in which they gather their food by filtering. They all sort out very small crustaceans and other material from the water, but shovelers do it by filtering from the surface of the water with their broad, flat bill as they swim along. Flamingos, being tall, hold their heads down on the ends of their long necks and seem to filter the water from an inverted position with their large, curved beaks. Avocets have a far more slender and delicate upturned beak that they sweep through the water in a sideways motion, gathering any food particles that the beak strikes on its passage through the water.

As we have already seen, the shapes and sizes of finches' beaks are good indicators of their specialist diets, even for birds within a single family. The crossbill is one such finch; it is the only bird that has developed the ability to achieve lateral movement in the beak by twisting the upper and lower parts to access the seeds inside pinecones, on which it feeds.

Legs and Feet

The variety in bird leg length and the nature of the bird foot reflect environmental and behavioral changes and adaptations. They provide support, perching, walking and running, climbing and clinging, swimming, grasping, hunting—even the manipulation of primitive tools. Birds with long legs are able to wade into water, giving them access to other environments to exploit for food sources. Short legs are ideal for birds used to living among dense hedgerows, as are feet that have developed gripping

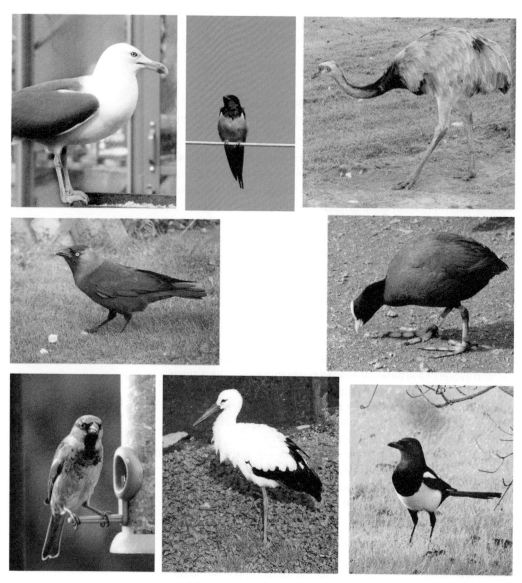

FIG 4.37 Different types of bird leg allow for different kinds of locomotion. Some are small and made for gripping small branches, others are long and allow for wading, walking, or running at speed.

toes for perching. At first glance it would appear that the leg of a bird has a reverse angle to that of a human leg, but what we see here is not the knee joint but the ankle.

The manner of a bird's locomotion other than its manner of flight bears a direct relation to the size and shape of its feet. The feet determine such actions as hopping, walking, running, swimming, climbing, and clinging. The largest group of birds known as *passerines* are those described as capable of

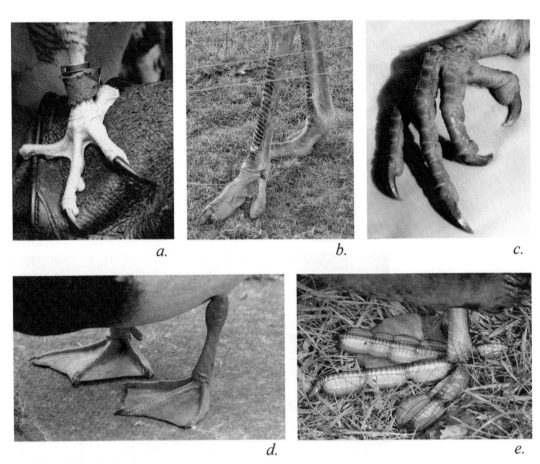

FIG 4.38 Bird feet have evolved to meet a wide range of conditions and behavior. a: Talons for hunting and killing prey. b: Powerful feet for running at speed. c: Gripping claws for perching on branches. d: Webbed feet for swimming. e: Feet with wide fleshy extensions to support the bird on soft wet ground.

perching. These are usually small, with four flexible toes and long sharp claws capable of gaining a grip on a range of surfaces.

Birds with splayed toes capable of supporting them on soft surfaces are generally water birds that inhabit the marginal area between land and water. Water birds that have taken to the water more fully have webbed feet that provide the necessary tool to propel them either on the water's surface with a paddling action or underneath the water with more high-powered swimming action. Birds such as divers have their webbed feet located much further toward their back end than others, making for increased speed and maneuverability, though this skill comes at a cost: On land such a configuration makes walking very difficult.

Birds of prey have highly developed feet and very long and strong toes with sharp, curved talons. They are so long and strong that they can dispatch prey in an instant and make grabbing and holding onto a flopping fish a feasible hunting tactic.

The ostrich foot has evolved into two large, strong toes, neither capable of perching or holding onto prey but highly efficient for incredibly high running speeds.

Feathers

Birds' reptilian ancestry can still be seen in the feathers that cover all modern birds' bodies. Feathers are made of the same substance as the scales that birds have on their legs, which is *keratin*, the same material that makes up the scales that modern reptiles have all over their bodies. Feathers are simply modified scales that have evolved into a more filamentous form; in so doing they have enabled birds to achieve powered flight.

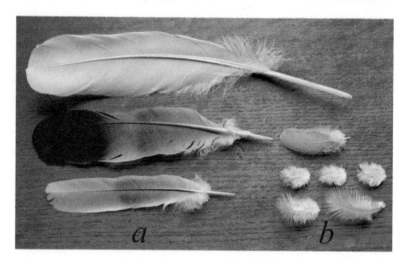

FIG 4.39 Different types of bird feathers. a: Flight feathers (pennae). b: Down feathers (plumulae).

There are two main types of feathers: the outer feathers (*pennae*) that define a bird's shape and provide insulation, and an inner layer of down feathers (*plumulae*) that provide additional insulation.

Feathers have become such a vital part of powered flight because they provide the wing with the necessary smooth and even surface. Feathers possess a series of interlocking barbs that enable them to form a single smooth surface, their asymmetric shape providing the necessary shape for flight. The nature of flight feathers remains the same for all birds, but some have been modified depending on the birds' modes of flight. Owls have a rather fluffy edge to the feathers that cuts down the noise of the wing beat—a valuable development for a predator that depends on silence for its success as a hunter. This silence is not necessary so that the prey can't hear the owl's approach; it is to allow the owl to hear the sound of the prey over the noise of its own wing beats.

Feathers are essential not only for flight; they also provide insulation, helping to keep birds warm or cool, depending on their circumstances. Because of feathers' thermal properties, penguins are able to withstand all that the Antarctic winter can throw at them, surviving months of extremely low temperatures. At the other end of the scale, ostriches are able to keep cool under extreme high temperatures due to the nature of their feathers. Although they have become completely useless for flight, the filaments having lost their barbs, making ostrich feathers incapable of being zipped together and forming an interlocking, smooth, seamless edge for an aerodynamic wing, they offer protection both from the midday heat and from the cold at night.

Feathers also play an important role in providing plumage designed to both hide and attract. Feathers have become an essential aspect of camouflage, particularly for the vulnerable nesting female, and they have become an essential part of the male's display when trying to attract a mate. There are some feathers that have become so modified and specialized that they actually *impede* flight. It could be argued that the beautiful display feathers of some birds, rather than contributing to their success as a species, have in part endangered their very existence by drawing attention not only from prospective mates but also from prospective predators. Man has hunted some birds to near extinction for the aesthetic qualities of their plumage. Despite these examples, feathers are an important part of a bird's survival strategy.

Wings

If one feature distinguishes birds from any other animal, it must be the feather. The second and perhaps more obvious feature is the wing. The majority of birds share both of these features: They all have feathers and most have wings, or at least vestiges of wings.

A bird's wing has three distinct bands of feathers covering it. The largest flight feathers, located on the outer edge of the wing, can be broken into primary, secondary, and tertiary feathers. The primary feathers are the longest and deliver the maximum power to propel the bird forward. The secondary feathers, located on the forearm, create a large surface area, providing lift. The tertiary feathers are attached to the upper arm and ensure a seamless surface between the body and the outer wing. These feathers are covered by two other rows of feathers, called *coverts*. These are aligned in such a manner that enables them to slide over one another during flight and thereby maintain the aerodynamic shape necessary to reduce drag and turbulence and for continued stability in the air. The *alua*, a group of feathers attached to the bird's thumb, is normally held flat against the bird's wing. During slow-speed flying, the alua is extended to redirect and increase air flow over the wing, to prevent stalling.

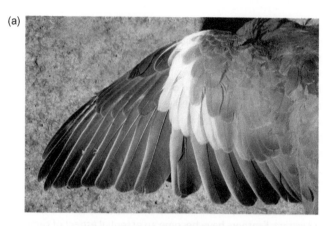

(a)

(b)

FIG 4.40 Bird wing. a: Top side.
b: Underside.

As we have already seen, flying is a remarkable and very efficient way of traveling that enables birds to travel over thousands of miles without ever having to land. Some birds are capable of flying at altitudes of around 25,000 feet. The peregrine falcon, *Falco peregrinus*, is capable of reaching speeds of around 200 miles an hour, making it the fastest animal on earth. The swift spends the majority of its life on the wing, coming to earth only to lay eggs and feed its young. Swifts even mate on the wing. All of these achievements are a result of the development of the wing.

FIG 4.41 Different wing profiles result in different types of flying. A: These wings are suitable for regular flapping during the powered flight of passerines. B: More rounded wings are suitable for the slow silent flying of owls. C: Large wings with splayed out primary feathers are suitable for the soaring of eagles. D: Long, slender crescent shaped wings are suitable for the high speeds of swifts and swallows. E: Shorter, broader wings allow for the maneuverability within undergrowth, as seen in birds such as pheasants. F: Large ratio wings allow for gliding with very little need for powered flight, as seen in the albatrosses.

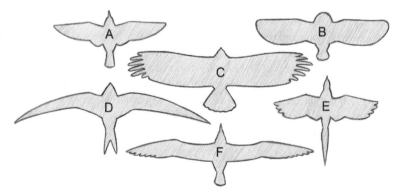

We will take a more detailed look at wings and how they work later in the text in the section covering the principles of flight and types of flying.

Small Birds

For the purposes of our discussion I include here only those birds that range in size from the wren to the blackbird. Small birds such as hummingbirds, swifts, swallows, and martins, which I have grouped together, have been covered elsewhere.

It is easier for smaller birds to hover, but it's harder for them to fly at faster speeds. Their wing-to-body ratio is more suited to sustained, powered flight. Although their size and wingspan make them less suited to soaring or gliding over long distances in the way larger birds do, their particular mode of flying does allow them to glide over shorter distances during a flight. For some small birds this results in a rather undulating flight pattern.

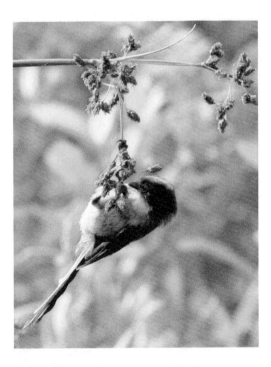

FIG 4.42 Small birds are capable of hanging from the lightest and most slender of branches and reed stems.

A bird's size affects the type of flight the bird is capable of, but it does not affect its ability to travel over great distances. Many very small birds undertake migration, some of them over huge distances. Metabolic rate in small birds is higher than in larger birds, the extreme example being hummingbirds. During cold weather smaller birds are far more susceptible to hypothermia, and in particularly harsh winters mortality rates can be very high. Size also allows birds to exploit different food sources. Many birds, such as the long-tailed tit,

Aegithalos caudatus, feed almost exclusively on small insects and spiders. They move around in large groups, traveling from tree to tree and hanging from branches in their search for insects and at night huddling together for warmth.

Medium-Sized and Large Land-Based Birds

Birds around the size of a pigeon and larger often move in different ways from smaller birds. When on the ground they have a tendency to walk or run rather than hop, though some use a combination of all three methods of locomotion. As we have already seen, an increase in a bird's size means that flapping a wing requires more energy in larger birds; therefore flapping is generally much slower in birds such as a pigeon or crow. However, the increase in wing size makes these birds more capable of gliding over greater distances and even of exploiting thermal uplift to achieve a soaring mode of flight.

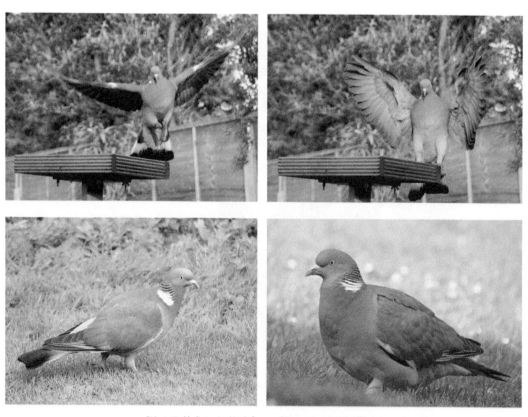

FIG 4.43 Medium-sized birds favor walking on the ground to hopping.

Some large birds still choose to move around in large groups, but they are far less susceptible to the changes in weather and are therefore less likely to huddle together for warmth during cold spells. The obvious exception to this rule can be seen in the behavior of penguins, which do exactly that during the long Antarctic winters.

Water Birds

A great number of birds other than specialist seabirds have taken to life on and in the water. Many of these exhibit adaptations to this way of life. Perhaps the most obvious one is the development of the webbed foot that allows for propulsion on both the water's surface and underwater. The body shape of water birds is generally elongated and broad; they have long necks and their legs are set well back on their bodies to aid swimming. The position of the legs gives these birds their distinctive walk: a waddling gait.

Buoyancy for all water birds is a critical factor and the care of plumage to retain waterproofing is essential. Without proper preening the feathers would become waterlogged, making it impossible to retain the necessary buoyancy. Some water birds have evolved to exploit and feed at different levels on and in the water, thereby avoiding unnecessary competition. The shoveler *Spatual clypeata*

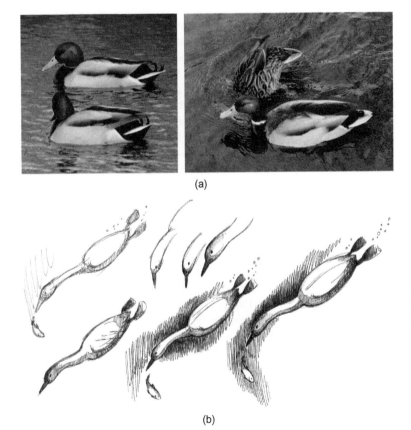

(a)

(b)

FIG 4.44 a: The waterproof properties of their plumage give the ducks great buoyancy and they ride high in the water, unlike those that dive to catch fish such as the great northern diver. b: The divers' lack of buoyancy enables them to remain underwater for greater periods of time to catch their prey, fish.

feeds by grazing on the surface of the water; some ducks such as the mallard *Anas platyrhynchos* and swans may also feed below the water by extending their necks underwater and dabbling, even occasionally upending, to feed at greater depths. A number of ducks dive to exploit deeper water. For ducks that live on a diet of fish, such as the goosander *Mergus merganser*, the ability to dive and swim has become an essential part of life. To do this efficiently, loons and divers such as the black-throated diver *Gavia arctica* have developed legs located much further toward the rear of the body. Though this structure makes for great difficulties on land, it is a great aid in swimming, enabling these birds to swim at great speed and dive to depths of 200 feet.

We have already seen how webbed feet are of immense use in swimming, but their use as paddles is not the only method of propulsion. Though not water birds in the same way as ducks, geese, or swans, the dipper *Cinclus cinclus* manages to catch its meals by swimming below the surface of fast-flowing mountain streams and rivers. In appearance it is not unlike many birds one finds in gardens; its unwebbed feet with four long toes terminating in curved claws are more suited to perching than paddling. Perhaps it is more correct to say that the dipper *flies* under water rather than swims, for instead of using its feet for propulsion it uses its wings much in the same way it uses them to fly.

Similarly, kingfishers—though hardly classified as water birds—do depend on water for their existence and spend a great deal of time in and around it. They don't swim on the water's surface the same way waterfowl do, nor do they swim underwater as dippers do, but they are expert divers. Using an overhanging branch of a tree, kingfishers perch overlooking the water in which they hunt their prey, fish. They dive in head first to grab a fish with their long and rather thick, straight beak, turn, and then launch themselves from the water's surface to return to their branch. They are adept at handling a fish once out of the water; with a flick of their heads they stun the fish against the branch before quickly turning it to swallow it head first so that the fish's scales do not catch in its throat.

Wading Birds

Even though the birds that fall into the category of waders may vary a great deal in size and habits, I have separated them out for special attention because of the common solutions that nature has come up with to assist them in exploiting the environment. Waders are birds that have developed long legs, often coupled with long necks and long beaks, to exploit the shallow water at the edge of the ocean or still water. There is even a good deal of variation in the designs of wading birds that allow them to exploit the various aspects of the shoreline and inland waterways and avoid any unnecessary competition for food.

The differences in some instances, though not large, are enough to ensure suitability for collecting particular foodstuffs from a particular place on the

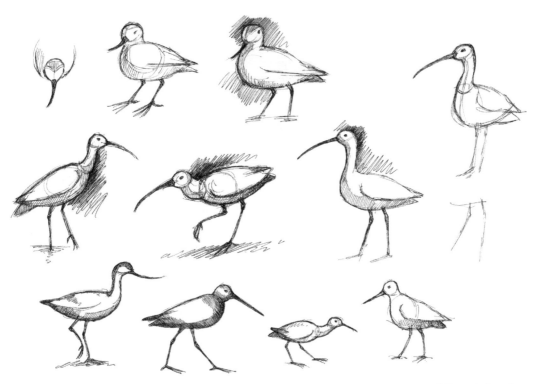

FIG 4.45 Differences in the wading birds' length of leg and beak help them exploit different food sources.

shoreline. Consequently one may see a variety of species at any one time foraging along the shoreline. The strong, straight bill of the oystercatcher makes it ideal for gathering mussels and other mollusks and crustaceans; the curlew has a longer curved beak that it can use to probe mud flats for worms and small mollusks. At half the size of the curlew, the redshank uses its shorter beak mainly to collect insects, free-swimming shrimps, and lugworms.

One small bird, the wrybill *Anarhynchus frontalis* of New Zealand, has developed a unique feature to assist in getting food from under small stones. It is the only bird in the world with a sideways bend in its beak. This bend allows the bird the leverage with which it turns over small stones and pebbles on the shoreline to reach small crustaceans, insects, and worms. Interestingly, all wrybill beaks bend to the right.

The black heron *Egretta ardesiaca*, found in Africa, has a particularly neat trick called *canopy feeding* to catch its prey of small fish. By extending its wings to cover its head as a kind of umbrella, it effectively shades part of a body of water from the glare of the sun, enabling the bird to see more clearly into the water. This shading of the water also attracts small fish, providing them with what they perceive as shelter and safety.

Hummingbirds

The consequence of living on a diet of nectar means an almost constant feeding pattern to meet the high energy demands of the hummingbird's particular flying techniques. Hummingbirds have become such specialist feeders that their location is limited to places where a ready supply of nectar is constantly available. To access nectar, they have developed the ability to hover using high-speed wing beats and beaks that are modified in both length and shape to allow them to access nectar deep within flowers of various kinds. Some have become such specialists that they are dependent on a single species of flower. The beak of the sword-billed hummingbird *Ensifera ensifera* is actually longer than the rest of its body, making it necessary to use its legs to preen itself. Its beak is simply too long to reach the preen gland while the bird is balancing on one leg.

Birds of Prey

The category of birds of prey covers a broad range of birds that are present all over the world. Although they all depend on hunting live prey, they have developed different diets that depend on availability. Some of them have developed a highly specialized diet; others will take a far broader range of prey animals—small mammals, other birds, fish, carrion. Many birds will take live prey as part of a diet but fall outside the classification of raptor. Carrion crows, as their name suggests, enjoy the delights of eating previously killed animals; however, other birds—the vulture family—have become more specialist in this regard. The diet of a meat eater allows for long periods between hunting.

Birds that have become specialist meat eaters have developed physical features such as sharp beaks and talons to deal with it. Shrikes have neither the talons to catch their prey nor curved beaks to tear them apart; instead they use the large thorns on bushes to assist in dismembering the lizards on which they feed. Vultures have developed featherless heads and necks as a result of the way they shove their heads into the bloody carcasses of dead animals.

The methods of finding and hunting down their prey also vary. In some cases the modes of flight have become an important aspect of predators' success. The hobby is capable of great speed, allowing it to catch very fast birds such as swifts, swallows, and martins; sparrowhawks' speed and agility allow them to hunt small passerines through rather dense hedgerows and woodland. For many raptors eyesight is a critical factor. Forward-facing eyes allow for binocular vision, enabling distances to be judged better; the large eyes of owls allow more light to fall onto the retina, enabling them to hunt in low-light conditions. Although owls don't distinguish color well, they are very sensitive to shape and movement; luckily color is not a critical factor for nighttime hunting. Daytime hunters are able to distinguish color and to locate their prey at great distances.

Some owls depend on their acute sense of hearing for success in hunting. This has resulted in the rounded shape of the barn owl's wing and the way its the feathers are arranged to enable the bird to fly in almost complete silence—as mentioned earlier, not so the prey is unable to hear the approach of the owl but rather for the owl to hear the movement of the small mammals on which they prey.

Seabirds

Seabirds exist mostly on a diet of fish and have developed a number of techniques to catch them: They dive, they swim, and some skim the surface. This has resulted in different physiognomies among seabirds. With its short wings and fat, rounded body, the puffin is not an elegant flyer, but it swims superbly. Gannets are more elongated and streamlined, making them more suited to diving, which they do from a great height in order to catch fish. Some seabirds fish on or just below the water's surface; others manage to go a little deeper, a few meters; still others are capable of diving to greater depths. Gannets begin their dive from high above the water; turning downward, they power toward the surface before folding their wings fully back a split second before plummeting into the water. This action reduces drag and therefore allows them to dive to greater depths. What enables them to dive so effectively hampers them underwater, however, and these birds at least cannot swim to any great extent.

Other Birds

It would seem that design solutions in nature are always something of a compromise when two or more conflicting needs must be satisfied; the need for some birds to both swim and fly throws up some interesting results. The prioritization of needs within individual species has determined aspects of locomotion and subsequent changes to bird physiognomy that reflect this prioritization. Extreme cases where swimming has become the priority over the need to fly have resulted in the bird becoming entirely flightless, the price paid to become a consummate swimmer. The penguin is perhaps the prime example here; it's hardly capable of walking on the ground, but once in the water it is capable of great turns of speed and maneuverability. Other species retain the capacity for flying, though they are perhaps less well suited to swimming. The puffin *Fratercula arctica* is perhaps a good example of the way there is a balanced compromise between the two driving factors. Retaining the ability to fly very well, the puffin has a body shape and wing size that also make it very suited to swimming underwater to catch the sand eels it feeds on.

Other birds have made less of a compromise. Ostriches have become entirely flightless and have developed into grazers, rather like the quadrupeds with which they often share their environment. The number of toes on the ostrich has been reduced to two very powerful ones that are incapable of perching but are highly suited to assisting in walking and running at great speeds. Being flightless, the ostrich needs other tactics to avoid predators; its long legs, powerful muscles, and strong toes enable it to sprint at speeds in excess of 40 miles an hour, higher speeds than many quadrupeds can achieve.

Bird Animation

One typical feature of birds—in addition to their main feature, feathers—is their ability to fly. The large majority of bird species do this very well. Many of them use flight as the main mode of locomotion, but they also walk, run, hop, jump, swim, climb, and even burrow with varying degrees of expertise. Bird dynamics are determined in part by each bird's size as well as its physiognomy.

Some birds, like the South American rhea, run very well; others seem to have difficulty even walking. Emperor penguins are an example of the compromise in design often seen in nature. Each year they walk, in large columns, long distances from their breeding grounds on the mainland of Antarctica back to the sea to feed. As they do so, at times they drop down onto their bellies and slide along on the ice and snow, propelling themselves by their feet. On the downward slopes this seems to be a more efficient and effective way of locomotion. A different physiognomy would no doubt prepare them better for this journey. Longer legs would clearly be better suited for it, though given the distances involved, flight would be the best mode of travel. However, once the penguins arrive at the coast and slip into the water through the gaps of sea ice and begin to hunt for their diet of fish, they demonstrate that they are more than suited to life underwater. There is a compromise here, and it is clear that the most important factor in their survival is their capacity for swimming at speed.

Principles of Flight

Several forces are associated with flight: *weight, lift, drag*, and *thrust*. Two of these forces impede flight; the other two counter those impediments. Weight is a vertical downward force experienced as a result of gravity that must be overcome for a bird to become airborne. Any forward movement is a result of thrust, which in turn induces drag. Drag is a horizontal force that comes into play as an object moves through a particular medium such as air or liquid. Flight becomes possible only if these forces are balanced appropriately, with the force of lift being greater than the force of weight and thrust being greater than drag. The amount of drag induced is a direct result of the size and shape of the object; the more streamlined a shape, the more efficiently it will travel through a medium.

Wings alone will provide lift only if there is forward motion or if the air moves across the wing. Wings vary in length, width, thickness, and shape, with most wings being asymmetrical and having a rounded, leading edge that tapers

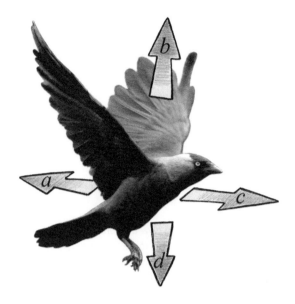

FIG 4.46 A number of forces are associated with flight. a: Drag. b: Lift. c: Thrust. d: Gravity.

toward a very thin rear edge. Most wings demonstrate a curve or camber throughout their width. The cross-section of the wing, known as the airfoil, and its curve are critical to the wing's performance, with different-shaped airfoils producing different aerodynamic characteristics. The distance from the leading edge to the trailing edge is known as the *chord*.

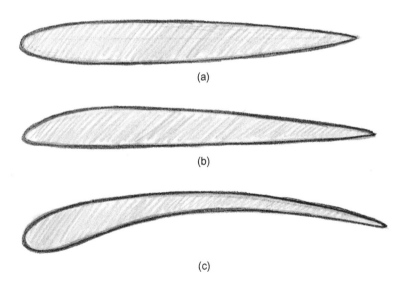

(a)

(b)

(c)

FIG 4.47 Different airfoil shapes provide different lift dynamics. a: Symmetrical shape provides more speed. b: Asymmetric cross-section provides additional lift. c: Extreme curve within the profile makes for slower speeds but additional lift potential.

Air moving across a wing produces lift due to the airfoil's profile. The wing's upper edge deflects air across the upper surface of the airfoil, increasing the airspeed and lowering the air pressure. The airfoil deflects less air on the underside of

137

the wing, making for a slower airspeed and critically higher air pressure. The differences between the low pressure on the upper side of the wing and the lower face of the wing, although slight at times, are enough to create lift.

Fast air speed - low air pressure

Left

FIG 4.48 The asymmetric profile of a wing produces lift through the differences in air pressure.

Slow air speed - high air pressure

This basic model is useful to explain how the force of lift works for asymmetrical airfoils, though bats and some airplanes use symmetrical wings. The orientation of the wing in relation to the direction of movement is the angle of attack. It is the adjustment of this angle that enables an increase or decrease in lift. The shape of the cambered airfoil creates lift even when the angle of attack is at zero. As the angle of the airfoil's leading edge moves upward from the horizontal, more air is deflected across the upper surface of

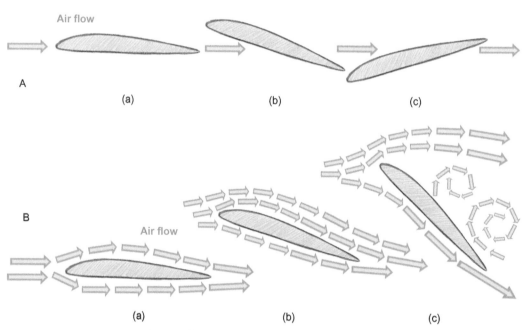

Air flow

A

(a)   (b)   (c)

B

Air flow

(a)   (b)   (c)

FIG 4.49 A: The angle of attack of the wing determines flight behavior. a: Level flight. b: Upward angle of the leading edge creates lift for a climb. c: Downward angle of leading edge creates downward lift for a dive. B: As the upward angle of attack increases, the flight behavior changes. a: Level flight. b: Climb. c: The increase in angle creates an increase in drag and turbulence on the trailing edge of the airfoil. This will slow down the flight to a point where all lift is lost and the flight will stall.

the wing, lowering the air pressure on the upper surface, and additional lift occurs. However, there are limits. As the angle increases, the air moves less smoothly across the airfoil's surface and there is an increase in turbulence on the trailing edge of the wing's upper surface. Along with the increase comes an increase in drag. Once the angle of attack reaches a critical state, the drag factor equals the thrust and a stall is the result. Stalling may generally be seen as a negative factor in general flight and something to be avoided, but it can be beneficial during landing as a bird attempts to shed air speed.

Symmetrical airfoils are more unusual than asymmetrical ones but are still able to produce lift, though this is achieved by the angle of attack. Asymmetrical airfoils are capable of producing lift with a zero angle of attack and can produce more lift than symmetrical ones. Lift during inverted flying is achieved by increasing the angle of attack, thereby making what would generate negative lift into positive lift. In this way aircraft flying upside down do not fall out of the sky; instead they demonstrate an elevation of the front end to create the increase in the angle of attack.

We might consider flight to be the most noticeable feature of bird locomotion, but not all birds fly, and though all birds have wings or vestiges of wings, wings are not restricted to birds. Many insects, a few animals, and even a number of plants have developed flight as a solution to their particular needs. To do this they have each developed wings of one sort or another. Some of them allow for gliding, as in the winged seeds, called *samaras*, of certain plants like the sycamore *Acer pseudoplatanus*, the ash *Fraxinus excelsior*, or the field maple *Acer campestre*. Other flyers have more sophisticated design solutions that allow for powered flight.

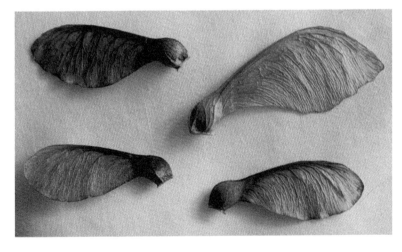

FIG 4.50 Seed wings.

Nature developed the wing and in so doing created different shapes and sizes relative to the body that enable different kinds of flight.

Large numbers of insects are consummate flyers, and along with the birds, bats have developed the strong, powerful, and light wings needed for powered flight so they can exploit insects as a food source. However, bats have no feathers and their wings are fleshy membranes held taught by long, slender bones. Bats' mode of flight differs from a bird's because they do not fold the wing on the upbeat. Folding a wing that does not have the benefit of feathers to ensure a seamlessly smooth surface continuously throughout flying would result in the membrane becoming wrinkled and folded, which would in turn cause a great increase in turbulence, the loss of lift, and a resulting stall.

The shape of a bird's wings and the size of the wing relative to the size of the body are key factors in the nature of flight and are critical in enabling a specific mode of flight. Flying is a varied mode of locomotion with a number of very distinctive "gaits." The most obvious classifications are those of powered flight, made possible by flapping wings, gliding, hovering, and soaring.

Wings play such an important part in bird locomotion that, even now, flightless birds retain the vestige of wings, a reminder of an ancestry that once depended on flight as a mode of locomotion.

Types of Wings

The shapes and proportion of wings have different properties and offer opportunities for different kinds of flight suited to different environments and the needs of different bird species. Energy efficiency, maneuverability, and speed are all factors that have determined the general shape of the wing. All engineering, including natural engineering, involves a compromise, and there is no ideal, one-size-fits-all shape for a wing.

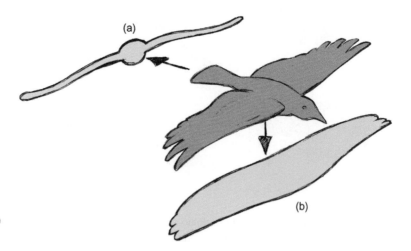

FIG 4.51 a: The frontal area of a wing. b: The platform area of a wing indicates the surface area available to create lift.

140

Broad, short wings create more drag than do long thin wings. An albatross's wings are long and slender and are more suited to efficient flying over very long distances. The greater the area of wing, the greater the amount of lift it provides. There are a large number of wing designs as solutions to the problem of flight, though these generally fall into a few basic types:

- Elliptical wings
- High-speed wings
- High-aspect-ratio wings
- Soaring wings

Whether the wing is slotted, the degree to which the wing curves, the aspect ratio of the wing—that is, the proportion between wing length and breadth—and finally, the wing loading (the total surface area of the wing compared with the weight of the bird) are all factors that must be considered when we talk about wings.

Elliptical Wings

Elliptical wings are short, broad, rounded wings that have a low aspect ratio and are suited to birds living in dense vegetation or woodland. Many of the small, common garden birds have wings that fit in this category. They provide great maneuverability and a high takeoff speed, both characteristics that are well suited to birds that need to evade predators. Birds such as crows and pheasants have such wings.

High-Speed Wings

Birds that have wings designed for high speed are capable of a high wing beat rate, though such an approach to flying is generally rather more expensive in terms of energy consumption. *High-speed wings* lack any of the slots found in other wing types; these slots tend to increase drag and therefore slow the bird down. The world's fastest birds, the peregrine falcon and the swift, both have this type of wing. The swift has a very distinctive highly curved, streamlined, and very smooth wing that makes it capable of the high-speed maneuvers it needs to catch insects in midflight.

High-Aspect-Ratio Wings

Wings with this type of design, far longer than they are broad, are very useful for flying at slower speeds. They are most suited for gliding; not surprisingly, many seabirds have this type of wing. Terns have this design, making them capable of a flying at such slow speeds that when they face into a headwind the action almost resembles hovering. The albatross also uses this design that demands very little by way of flapping but makes it able to exploit the very minimal levels of lift generated from the wave actions at sea. These wings are able to make the most of the little updraft that exists just above the waves. Such wings prove to be rather cumbersome during takeoff and landing, however. Birds with this type of wing often need to taxi to gain enough airspeed and the required lift to take off.

Soaring Wings

Wings that are suited to soaring are large, with deep slots at their tips. They are shorter and broader than the high-aspect-ratio wings and, rather like elliptical wings, they provide valuable assistance during takeoff. Many larger raptors, such as buzzards, eagles, and vultures, have such wings. Soaring is a mode of flying suited to those larger species that fly over land. The heat from the land provides plenty of thermal lift, and these large broad wings are capable of exploiting the maximum lift such thermals provide. Birds with this wing design also often have broad tails that provide additional maneuverability and lift.

Taking Off

Takeoff is a very demanding part of flying that often requires a great deal of energy, particularly for birds that are restricted to taking off from the land or water. Launching from a perch or an elevated position aids the process. Birds have developed many different ways of becoming airborne, but they all have one thing in common: All birds need to have air traveling over the wing at sufficient speed to create the necessary lift. So, gaining momentum to get the air moving across the wing is a critical factor. Some of them simply fall into space from a cliff face or a high perch. For some other land-based birds this may not be possible; they are faced with the option of jumping to take to the air, but jumping takes a lot more energy. Small birds may achieve

FIG 4.52 Takeoff sequence of a pigeon jumping into the air.

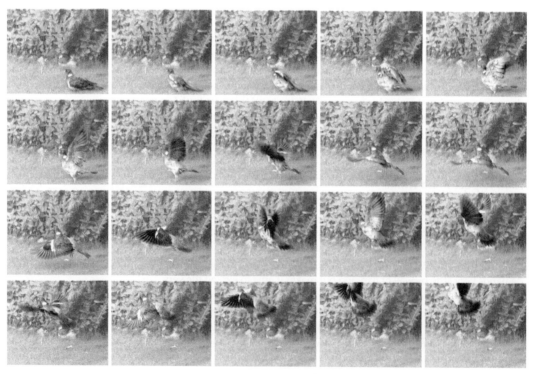

takeoff simply by leaping from the ground into the air to gain the necessary momentum because they require less initial thrust to get airborne. Clearly, jumping to become airborne works well only if the bird is below a certain size. Birds a little bigger than a pigeon find that the huge wing beats required for this kind of takeoff are very difficult; larger birds find it impossible and have had to develop other ways of becoming airborne.

Taking off from the branch of a tree or other kind of perches may require nothing more from the bird than simply allowing itself to fall away from its perch. Pigeons and seabirds regularly take off from a cliff face or the side of a building by simply dropping or pushing away from the surface. The momentum from the fall alone is enough to create sufficient air speed over the surface of the wing to gather the necessary lift.

FIG 4.53 Small passerine (starling) taking off from a perch.

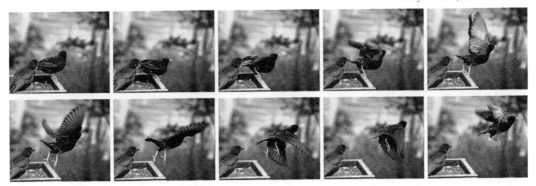

Larger birds might need to run or taxi to generate sufficient airflow over the wing to become airborne, or they get airborne from an elevated position such as a cliff face. Facing into the wind helps with takeoff because the airspeed provided by the wind brings with it a degree of lift. In some exposed positions such as at the top of high buildings or cliffs, takeoff may simply be a matter of a bird extending its wings and allowing the breeze to provide all the lift that's required.

Taxiing is a method of takeoff that's more suited to large birds with large wings. They run along the ground or water with outstretched wings, much the same way that aircraft travel along a runway gathering speed. Swans provide

FIG 4.54 Large water birds take off by taxiing.

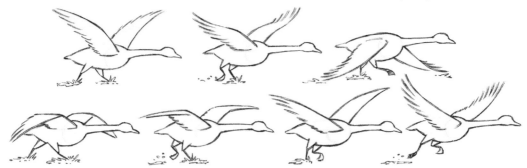

a perfect illustration of this method used on water; albatrosses do a very similar thing but they run along the ground, preferably into a headwind.

Landing

Getting airborne is one thing, but landing demands a very different approach to flying. The need in this instance is for a bird to shed speed in a very controlled manner so that it can land safely. Landing requires a lot less energy than taking off, but it also demands a good deal more control. Accuracy is critical if the bird is to avoid injury and come to rest exactly where it intends. Some birds find this process more straightforward than others. The ease of landing often depends on the surface on which the bird needs or prefers for landing. The timing of landing is critical; birds need to arrive at the required landing spot at the very moment they have ensured that their airspeed is zero.

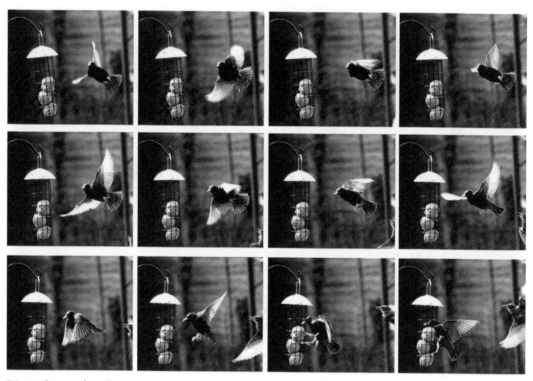

FIG 4.55 Sequence of a small passerine (starling) landing on a feeder.

Landing on the ground is the only option for some birds. Large birds find this more difficult than smaller ones because they have more momentum that is difficult to shed. In coming in to land geese often undertake a steeply angled, high-speed descent by executing a maneuver called *whiffling* that involves a rapid series of alternating sideslips in which they twist their bodies to extreme angles, shedding any lift on the wings. This enables the geese to shed height at a high rate.

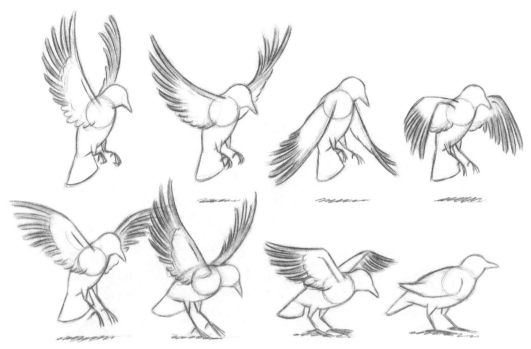

FIG 4.56 Sequence of a bird landing on the ground.

As a bird approaches the ground, its body is held upright with the legs extended downward in preparation for contact with the ground. The downbeats of the wings become rapid and are intended to reduce the speed of the fall. Once the bird is on the ground, the legs bend at the joints, the wings are quickly folded, and the body moves to a more horizontal angle.

Landing on water offers a simpler and somewhat less critical solution, though one that is not available to all birds. Swans use a body of water to land on with their feet thrust forward, rather like water skiers, to take the remaining energy out of the forward momentum. Albatrosses land on the ground in a rather less elegant manner that resembles something akin to a crash landing.

FIG 4.57 Large water birds use the qualities of water to assist in landing.

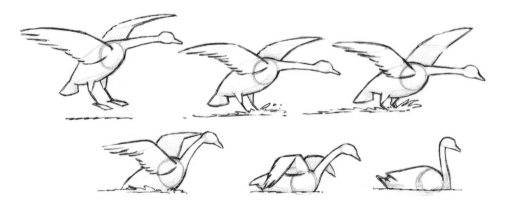

Divers and loons land on water, but their legs are located so far back on their bodies that they skim along the surface with their bellies rather than using their feet until they finally come to a stop—a somewhat less elegant and more ungainly action than the swan.

Precision landing on branches or cliff faces is a more demanding process. Landing into the wind helps maintain lift and assists in control throughout the maneuver. A bird landing on a cliff face flies toward the cliff, aiming for a spot below the landing site. As it nears the landing site it begins to climb upward, losing momentum as it goes. Using gravity to help shed speed, it arrives at the exact spot it chose, with a forward air speed of zero.

FIG 4.58 Landing on a cliff face often entails flying below the landing point and moving upward at the last moment before touchdown.

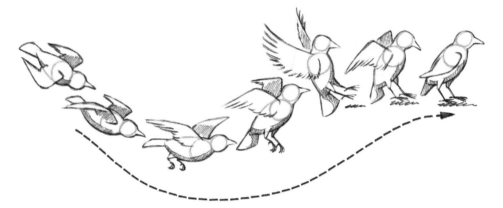

Types of Flight

Birds have developed many different types of flight that frequently depend on the reason for flight: hunting, chasing prey, avoiding predation, migration, preparation for migration, flocking, display, courtship, group or partner bonding, developing flying skills, or defense of nest sites or young. Birds that are suited to hunting various kinds of prey use various kinds of flying. Gannets that dive for fish have a different-shaped wing than the kestrel, which hovers as it hunts for small rodents and beetles.

Powered flight, gliding, hovering, or soaring—whatever the type of flying a bird undertakes, it is suited to its particular circumstances and needs. The demands that these different gaits place on the bird and the purposes of each mode of flying vary from species to species. Some are capable of a range of flight types; others use a limited range of actions. The physiognomy of each bird intrinsically links it to a particular form of flying.

The upward and downward movement of a flapping wing results in the countermovement of a bird's body. This is particularly noticeable in larger and heavier birds. As the wing moves upward, the body drops slightly, countering that action. Then as the wings are thrust downward, the body rises a little, countering the action. The bigger is the wing beat, the more up or down action on the bird's body.

Efficiency is critical in all forms of locomotion; flying is no different. When carrying a load a bird will even attempt to adjust the load to reduce drag and make flying more efficient. Osprey have been observed to shift their grip on a fish they've plucked from water and position it in such a way so the fish is facing forward, presenting a more streamlined profile and thereby reducing wind resistance. Flying isn't always just about getting from points A to B.

If the act of flying wasn't difficult enough, birds have to face the additional demands and modes of taking off and landing, which are just as varied as flying.

Powered Flight

Most birds, having taken to the air, drive themselves forward by the action of flapping their wings. The wing changes shape through the flapping action,

(a)

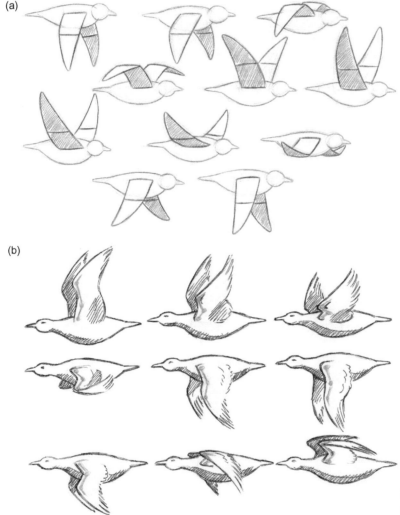

(b)

FIG 4.59 (a–b) Simplified flight cycle of a small bird.

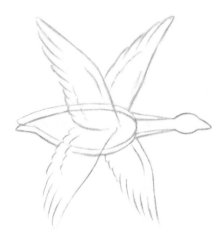

FIG 4.60 The upward and downward actions of the body of a large bird during flight.

but the feathers slide across one another to maintain a perfectly smooth and streamlined wing surface that keeps drag to a minimum. The action of flapping is often rather like a human rowing a boat: The wings are stretched forward in preparation for the downward motion, and as the wing moves upward it is half folded to reduce surface area and resistance.

The cost of flying in terms of energy consumed is very high; a bird's streamlining is very effective in keeping this energy consumption to a minimum. Flying requires more energy than walking, yet overall there is a lower cost for flying than in ground-based travel. If a small mammal and a bird of a comparable size were to travel for the same amount of time, the mammal would use a great deal less energy than the bird—around three times less. However, the mammal would travel around 10 times more slowly than the bird. If each were to be limited in the consumption of energy, the bird would cover around four times the distance as the mammal for the same amount of energy. Flying does cost a lot of energy, but it requires less total energy than walking over distances.

The speed of powered flight varies a great deal from species to species. A peregrine falcon can fly at 200 miles an hour; it sweeps downward on its preferred natural prey of pigeon, using gravity to assist in its speed, folding back its wings to achieve a more aerodynamic shape and then powering forward with powerful wing beats. Owls, on the other hand, hunt very slowly. The shape of an owl's wing is broad and rounded to increase lift, but the feathers have developed in such a way as to reduce noise.

Gliding

Gliding is perhaps the simplest form of flight and probably the earliest form of flight in birds. Most mammals that use flight as part of their locomotion depend on gliding. Indeed, the only mammals to have developed a mode of powered flight are bats. Gliding is a simple process of ensuring that the upward forces are great enough to oppose the downward force of weight, which is all well and good if the air moves across the wing at a sufficient speed to create higher pressure on its underside and lower pressure on the upper surface, thereby creating lift. When the air speed is too low, powered flight (using wing beats) is the solution. Gliding is undertaken by all birds to a lesser or greater extent and is particularly useful during the approach to landing as the bird adjusts its weight and assesses its distance from its final landing site. Gliding is often interspersed between periods of powered flight and used in order to save energy. This is most evident when birds fly in flocks.

Soaring

Soaring is perhaps the most efficient way of flying. Depending on the thermals from the earth requires little more than slight shifts in the wing to catch the updraft. This requires large surface areas on the wing. The length of wing on a gliding bird gives some indication of the ratio of surface area of body to wing. Using the lift from thermals, birds are capable of achieving altitudes of 18,000 feet and more. The greatest demand on birds using soaring as a mode of flight is during takeoff, but once the bird is up, if the lift from thermals can be maintained, very little energy is required.

Over land, thermals are generated by the nature of the geography. Rocky outcrops warmed by the sun's rays are often a strong source of lift. At sea the thermals are far less strong and are created by the waves deflecting wind upward. Although minimal, this deflected air movement enables the albatross to remain airborne with hardly a wing beat. It is often necessary for it to fly very close to the waves to catch these very slight updrafts.

Hovering

Hovering is maintained by striking a fine balance between lift and gravitational forces. Birds need to create just enough air movement across the wings and the position in the air will be maintained, though how this is done may vary. Hummingbirds maintain a hover through very high-speed powered flight. An animal's energy output per kilogram of body mass decreases as the body size goes up, and the energy demand is greater for hovering than for forward motion. This puts size limits on animals that hover. Small animals such as insects and the smaller of the hummingbirds can hover for extended periods of time, small birds can hover for shorter periods, medium-sized birds may hover very briefly, and large birds are totally incapable of hovering. Smaller wings are easier to flap, requiring less energy, though the smaller the wing becomes, the faster it must move to create the necessary downward thrust. The fastest wing beat of any bird is achieved by the purple-collared woodstar with a wingspan of around 2 inches at 75 beats a second.

The hummingbird's very particular way of flying by moving its wings at very high speed also places limitations on the size that such birds can achieve; the largest is around the size of a European blackbird. Birds larger than this are incapable of moving their wings at the speeds required for this type of hovering.

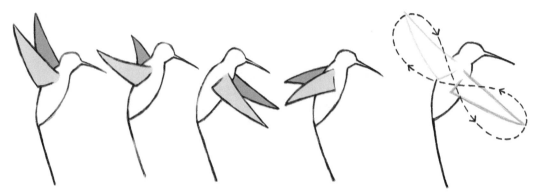

FIG 4.61 The wing action of a hummingbird describes a figure of eight, creating lift on both the forward and backward thrusts.

Hummingbirds need to hover to reach their food supply and therefore maintain lift in calm conditions by their particular way of flying. Instead of the simple upward and downward actions demonstrated by most birds, they also use forward and backward strokes in a figure-eight configuration, generating lift on both the downbeat and upbeat of the wings.

Some birds such as kestrels achieve a hovering gait by facing into the wind and, through very delicate wing movements, simply allow the wind itself to create the necessary lift.

Groups, Flocking, and Formation Flying

Flocking and living in groups present birds with some very distinct advantages for species in which competition for food is not an issue. Starlings gather together in huge numbers to roost, a tactic that offers greater safety against predation. Flocks may vary from small family groups to large flocks, often made up of mixed species. This is often seen on the shoreline of estuaries, mudflats, and beaches and can be seen in European winters as small passerines gather to forage for food. Other birds group together for warmth. African sparrows build large communal nests not just for breeding purposes but for protection against the cold night air. Penguins form huge colonies that huddle together for protection against the extreme conditions of Antarctica, each taking a turn on the outer edge of the flock to take the brunt of the weather while those in the center of the group enjoy the higher temperatures afforded by the bodies of their fellow penguins.

The general rules for a flocking model involve alignment, separation, and cohesion. These three rules work together to ensure that collisions are avoided. *Separation* ensures that overcrowding is avoided, *alignment* ensures that the bird and its immediate neighbors face in the same direction, and *cohesion* ensures that any change in movement, direction, or speed is coordinated throughout the flock. The alignment, movement, and synchronization of flight in a flock of birds are known as *alilomimasis*.

Shifting masses of birds do not have a leader in the flock; though they often seem to be moving in a rather haphazard way, the individuals in the flock seldom collide. The shifting of the flock is a result of a bird mimicking a shift in movement to another bird in the flock; the slight delay in movement sends a wave through the flock. Studies of flocks using high-speed cameras have suggested that individual members of a flock are influenced by the nearest 5 to 10 of the bird's neighbors, with the emphasis being placed on neighbors to either side of the bird rather than those either in front or behind. This may have something to do with the field of vision of the kinds of birds that tend to flock. Studies using humans identified that shifts in the direction of groups that have very similar patterns to flocking birds are determined by the movement of around 5% of the group, at which point the remainder of the group will follow.

Some groups of birds such as crows and rooks form clans. Other birds form bonds that last a lifetime; for example, swans are said to mate for life, though for some birds multiple breeding partners offers a better solution. The female hedge sparrow or dunnock is one such that chooses to mate with a number of males.

Bird flocking is also very useful during migration. Martins and sparrows gather together in northern Europe around the end of September to mid-October each year. This gathering might assist with navigational aspects of long-distance travel, though for some animals flying together offers energy-efficiency gains.

It has been observed that swarming locusts will fly in loose formations and synchronize their wing beats to reduce turbulence and assist in their flight. Flying in more formal formations may also produce increased efficiencies. For a bird flying behind and slightly to one side of the lead bird, the turbulence created during flight may offer additional lift because the greatest turbulence

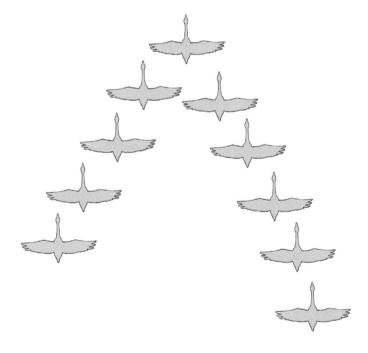

FIG 4.62 Geese flying in formation minimizes the drag on the birds flying in the wake of the leading birds.

151

occurs just behind the wing tip. Some birds mix gliding with flapping to achieve even greater energy efficiencies. Coordinating their gaits increases that efficiency even further. So, when a lead bird in a group of birds decides to glide, the rest will follow. When the lead bird decides to begin flapping again, the rest do likewise. Synchronization in both position and timing make for the most efficient and economical way of group flying and is particularly useful for birds migrating over long distances.

Walking, Hopping, and Running

Flying is obviously of great importance to most birds, but a lot of birds depend on being able to get along on the ground to forage for food, to find a mate, or to build a nest. They may choose to walk, run, or hop. Some birds get along on the ground by doing only one of these; others engage in more than one such behavior. Size once again plays a part in determining which one is best suited to the bird. The ostrich may be capable of jumping—that is, leaping off the ground with both feet at once or slightly out of synch—though it doesn't do this as a regular mode of locomotion and this movement could hardly be described as hopping. Most small birds hop as a way of getting around on the ground. They are light, so the effort involved in hopping is comparatively low. For larger birds hopping becomes a very inefficient way of getting around; they are heavier and the energy required to hop is much greater. In small birds hopping is usually a symmetrical action, with both feet leaving and returning to the ground at the same time. Some larger birds such as small crows may demonstrate an asymmetrical hopping action during which one foot leaves the ground and subsequently returns to the ground slightly in advance of the other.

Pied wagtails, although not a great deal bigger than those birds that favor hopping such as the house sparrow, opt to run rather than hop. It is perhaps true to say that rather than run they walk at very high speeds. A run is distinguished from a walk by the inclusion of a suspension phase during which

FIG 4.63 Bird hopping sequence.

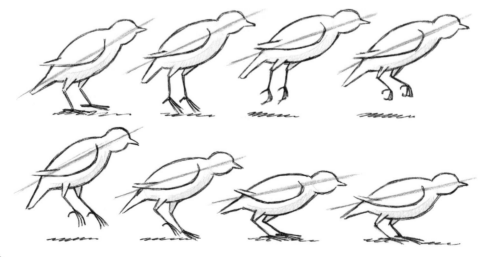

all the feet are off the ground. The wagtail running gait is very distinctive. They drop their body to the near horizontal and undertake very rapid movement of the legs with sudden acceleration and deceleration. Blackbirds also use a running gait to get around under hedgerows and parkland. They too drop their bodies into a more horizontal position before beginning their fast forward run, though this is far slower than the small wagtail's.

For the most part, birds as large as the wood pigeon tend to walk, though a number of birds utilize mixed modes of locomotion to increase efficiency.

FIG 4.64 The run sequence of (a) an ostrich, (b) the walk sequence of a goose.

(a)

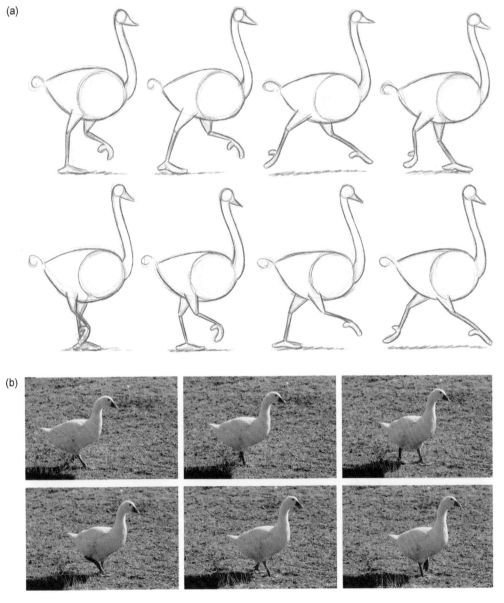

(b)

Members of the crow family, such as magpies, rooks, and jays, get around on the ground by walking, though they will often hop in both a symmetrical and asymmetrical fashion when faster speeds are called for. During an asymmetrical hop it can be clearly seen that the feet are out of phase with each other but by less than half a stride. The slow walk of a large bird with short legs results in a noticeable sideways motion coupled with a sharp forward and backward movement of the head. Larger birds with long legs tend not to demonstrate this level of waddle. This waddling action is much more pronounced if the legs are located toward the rear of the body, as in ducks, geese, and swans.

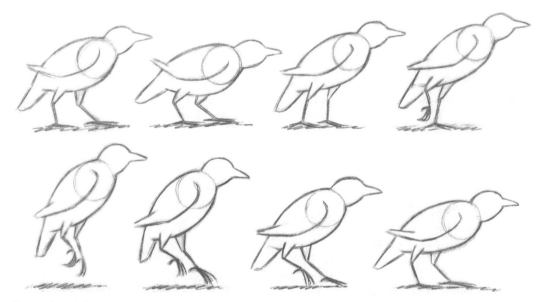

FIG 4.65 Larger birds often mix modes of locomotion between walking and hopping.

Flightless birds have to take other action if they are to avoid predation. Larger birds run in a more upright fashion than the smaller passerines. Emus, rheas, and ostriches all have long, powerful legs and rounded bodies with small heads on the end of long, slender necks. For the most part these birds walk upright; when need arises they run with long, powerful strides. The reduction of the number of toes to two on the foot of the ostrich enables it to generate increased thrust during the duty phase of the stride.

Fish

Fish might not be as advanced as either birds or mammals in that they do not display the same levels of intelligence, highly developed social bonding, or complex patterns of behavior, but they do form a unique part of the animal kingdom, occupying the largest part of our planet—water. They are uniquely adapted for life across a broad range of environments.

Fish may not demonstrate the same level of bonding or create distinct community identities or individual identities within a community as some mammals and birds, but they do often live in large groups and are interdependent on one another and occasionally on other species. Most species of fish do not possess the tendencies to bond as pairs in the same way many birds do. Swans not only select a mate, a common process in birds, but this pairing often lasts for life. Furthermore, some fish species go to some lengths to attract females. Male sticklebacks are territorial, selecting the sites most favored by females to build nests made from filamentous algae and water plants to entice the female to lay her eggs. The male alone then carefully tends the eggs by wafting his tail, creating a flow of oxygenated water over the surface of the eggs.

There is a selection process of sorts during the mating of salmon. Cock salmon demonstrate aggressive behavior toward other males as they jostle for position alongside the hen salmon as she deposits her eggs in a depression in the gravel bed (known as a *redd*), though this more often than not still results in a group mating activity.

Despite the exceptions to the rule, fish often tend to breed en masse, with many males gathering together in an attempt to fertilize the eggs of the females. The majority of fish fertilize their eggs externally, but sharks and rays are among the fish that fertilize eggs internally—a strategy that results in the laying of egg capsules or the female bearing living fish. The external fertilization of eggs is a process that for some species has led to a tendency toward hybridization. For those fish capable of hybridization, and indeed in some waters this has become a tendency to hybridize, the process may present some danger for the preservation of original fish stocks.

Such a strategy negates the need for males to compete for a mate in the same way as birds and mammals do.

Fish seldom demonstrate the same tendency as animals to live in identifiable family groups with hierarchies, nor do they tend to have a capacity for the use rudimentary tools, like some mammals and some birds. However, unlike birds, some fish regularly eat smaller fish, including the young of the same species, which may even include their own young. Despite the odd exception, once fish are born there is very little aftercare; they are on their own.

The diversity, distribution, and morphology of fish are hugely varied, with the greatest range of diversity found in sea fish. The wide variety of morphology found in fish is very different from that of birds. Birds share, in a very general way, a common physiognomy, but fish vary a great deal in both size and shape.

The classification of fish is a rather complex matter and has been subject to many modifications since this branch of science began. It continues to offer ichthyologists a challenge. For the purposes of this text we can safely ignore many of these complications, though it might be useful for us to recognize that fish seem to share a common ancestry. Some of the earliest fossil records of early fish-like creatures come from China and show small fish-like chordates, *Cathaymyrus*, and *Myllokunmingia*, which swam earth's waters around 530 million years ago. These ancient fish are distinguished by a notochord (a hollow dorsal nerve chord), a post-anal tail, and myotomal muscles to accommodate an oscillatory swimming action.

Modern fish have now developed a range of design solutions to occupy many different environments. There are freshwater fish and saltwater fish and some fish that spend considerable parts of their lives in both types of environments. Others have developed a tolerance for life in brackish waters. Some fish are suited to acid conditions; others prefer alkaline environments. Some can tolerate low oxygen levels, and others demand highly oxygenated water to thrive. There are even fish that have the ability to breathe air and spend extended periods of time out of water.

Water temperature, water pressure, and light levels are also major factors in fish location and distribution. The Atlantic cod is one of many species that thrives in extremely cold water; there are a good many more thousands of fish species that prefer warmer tropical waters. Some fish are very widely distributed and can be found around the globe; others migrate huge distances throughout the oceans. Bluefin tuna, *Thunnus alalunga*, migrate from Florida to Norway; others are restricted to a single, very small location and have evolved into a distinct and unique form through isolation. The northern cavefish, *Amblyopsis spelea*, is a species of fish that has colonized submerged caves with no access to daylight and as a result they have lost their pigmentation along with their eyesight.

Fish also occupy and thrive at different levels within a body of water, some preferring to swim in shallow waters or living close to the surface and others living at greater depths. The free-swimming fish are called *pelagic*; fish that live on or close to the bottom are termed *benthic*. There are fish capable of living at great depths and to survive immense pressures that would be fatal to most fish. The *Abyssobrotula galatheae*, a species of cusk-eel, was discovered in the Puerto Rican Trench at a depth of 8,372 meters. Still others can survive at very high altitudes, such as the Tibetan stone loach, *Triplophysa stoicczkai*, which occupies lakes at over 5,000 meters in the Himalayas.

As a general rule sea fish are able to reach larger sizes than their stillwater relatives, though some fish, such as the arapaima *Osteoglossum*, found in the rivers of Brazilian rainforests, and the mahseer that swim in the rivers of India, can achieve rather impressive sizes.

Fish Anatomy

Fish can be divided into two very broad groups: bony fish (*osteichthyes*) and cartilaginous fish (*chondrichthyes*). Bony fish possess bony skeletons; cartilaginous fish have structures made of cartilage. Bony fish lay eggs that are fertilized outside the body by milt (semen); in contrast, the eggs of cartilaginous fish are fertilized inside the female's body. Most fish lay eggs, but there are some that are known as live bearers, for which fish fry emerge from the female. Unlike bony fish, the cartilaginous fish have no swim bladder; as a result they must swim continuously to maintain their vertical positions in the water. All the sharks and rays fall into the cartilaginous classification of fish.

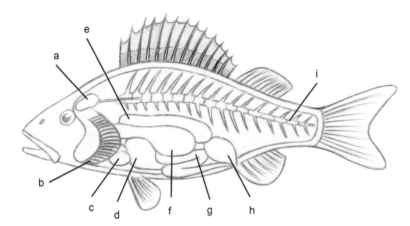

FIG 4.66 Basic fish anatomy. a: Brain. b: Gills. c: Heart. d: Liver. e: Kidney. f: Stomach. g: Intestine. h: Gonad. i: Spinal column.

Bony Fish

A typical osteichthyes has two sets of paired fins (the pectoral and pelvic fins) in addition to the dorsal, caudal, and anal fins. Their gills are protected by a bony structure located below and behind the eye sockets and known as the *gill cover* or *operculum*. These fish possess swim a bladder that enables them to maintain buoyancy by altering the amount of gas they hold in this chamber and thereby maintain their depth with the water column.

Cartilaginous Fish

Unlike bony fish, chondrichthyes have no rigid skeletal structure that includes spines radiating from the spinal column. Fish with no swim bladders are forced to keep swimming to maintain their depth within the water. Failure to continue swimming results in the fish sinking. Sharks' elongated and rigid pectoral fins act as wings that create lift as their tails propel them forward.

Rays have mouths located on their undersides. Their fins are adapted into wings that they use in a manner very similar to birds. The undulating action creates both lift and forward thrust on the upstroke as well as the downstroke. The dorsal fin has become a single thin extended spine that seems to serve little purpose in either propulsion or stability.

Many modern fish have retained the basic streamlined kind of shape of their early ancestors built around the axial notochord, though this has still resulted in a great deal of variation in body shape: globular, elongated, some are compressed dorsoventrally (rays), some (such as the ocean sunfish *Mola mola*) are compressed laterally. Still, within all this diversity, the general trend is for fish to remain streamlined in shape. There are, as ever, some exceptions to the rule. Some fish do not conform to a streamlined shape. Perhaps there are no better examples of nonconformity than the seahorse and the sea dragon. Some fish have very flexible bodies that enable them to turn in very confined spaces; other have rather stiff and rigid bodies. The variations in body shape along with fin configuration, as well as the number and shape of fins, affect a fish's behavior, maneuverability, and speed. The diversity of body shape is most evident among the numerous inhabitants of tropical reefs and in large tropical rivers, though these variations are not restricted to one particular environment.

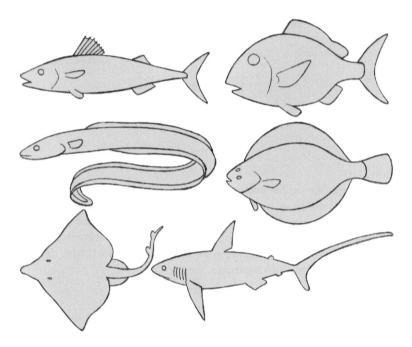

FIG 4.67 Fish have different body shapes, resulting in different swimming gaits.

The bream *Bramis brahma* has a very deep body shape though it is rather narrow. Its fins are suited to maneuverability rather than high speeds. Its overall shape illustrates its preference to group together in large numbers and graze along the bottom of lakes, ponds, or slow-flowing rivers and streams.

The trout *Salmo trutta* is long, thin, and very streamlined and perhaps represents a stereotypical image of a fish. It has a shape that makes it much more suited to colonizing fast-flowing water. The large fins and streamlined profile enable it to hold station in the faster flow of small upland streams.

The eel *Anguila anguila* is elongated with one continuous fin extending halfway along the top of the body. The eel's unique shape allows for an undulating action, providing an ability to swim equally well both forward and backward.

Flat fish such as the European plaice *Pleuronectes platessa* have their fins located around their outer edges, with the caudal fin remaining distinct but flattened.

The manta ray *Manta birostris* has a flattened body and pectoral fins that have developed into extended wings. The anal fin is completely absent.

In addition to the overall variations in body shape among fish, there are three distinctive mouth shapes in most of the fish that have jaws:

- Terminal
- Superior
- Subterminal

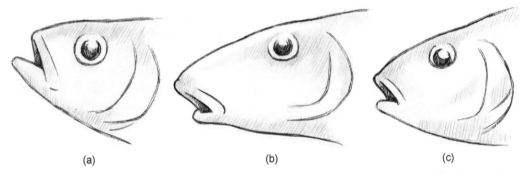

(a)   (b)   (c)

FIG 4.68 The different mouth configurations of fish. a: Superior. b: Subterminal (inferior). c: Terminal.

Terminal Mouth
A mouth that is located at the very tip of the head is known as *terminal*. This is illustrated clearly in the wrasse *Labridaea*, a family of fishes of around 500 separate species. They have protractile mouths that reveal their short, sharp teeth, which enable them to feed by dislodging limpets and mussels from rocks or, as in the cleaner wrasse, enabling a symbiotic relationship with other fish feeding on dead tissues and the scales and parasites that infect their partner species.

Superior Mouth
Mouths that are upturned with the lower jaw protruding beyond the upper jaw are known as *superior*. The rudd *Scardinius ertythropthalmus* is one such fish. The orientation of the mouth makes the fish supremely suited to feeding from the surface and upper layers of the water. However, not all fish that feed from the surface have this kind of mouth.

Subterminal Mouth
A mouth that is located on the underside of the fish's head, as with the tench *Tinca tinca*, is termed *subterminal* or *inferior*. Fish with such mouths are more suited to feeding on the bottom; though this does not prevent them from feeding higher in the water column or taking food from the surface, it is less likely they will do so.

A number of fish also possess fleshy extensions on their mouths, known as barbels. These soft, fleshy extensions of the mouth enable fish to locate food through taste. The barbs vary in number: The tench *Tinca tinca* has two, the barbel *Barbus barbus* has four, and the stone loach *Noemacheilus barbatulus* has six. Some fish that have these barbels are very small; others are longer and more substantial.

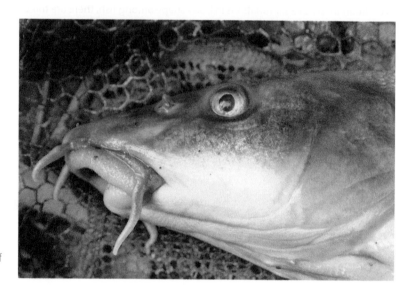

FIG 4.69 The fish in this example has a subterminal mouth and a set of four barbels.

A fish's nostrils are known as *nares*. Unlike birds' and mammals' nostrils, these are not used to breathe; they are used for a sense of smell, detecting food, and detecting pheromones and thereby assisting in the mating process. They may even play a part in salmon being able to locate the exact place at which they were spawned after a journey of several thousand miles.

Fish Movement

FIG 4.70 The direction of the movement of an object through space (in this instance a fish) is denoted by three terms. a: Pitch. b: Roll. c: Yaw. The same terms are applied to birds and aircraft in flight.

The stability of fish, their orientation, and their movement are not at all dissimilar to those of birds, boats, and airplanes and are described in the

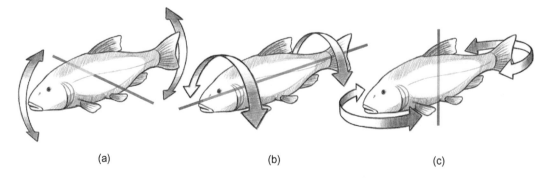

(a)   (b)   (c) very same terms. The various types and orientations of movement may be described as roll, yaw, and pitch, depending on the axis along which the rotation takes place.

Roll
A *roll* describes a rotation along the length of the body longitudinally along the anteroposterior axis, creating alternate upward and downward movement of each flank of the fish.

Yaw
Yaw describes a rotation at the center of the fish along the dorsoventral axis, creating a sideways action of the fish moving laterally from left to right.

Pitch
Pitch describes a rotation at the center of the body along the lateral, left/right, axis, creating an alternating rising and falling movement of the fish's head and tail.

Fish vary a great deal in shape, but they do share common features such as the notochord, gills for the extraction of oxygen from water, scales (though not all fish are scaled or fully scaled), and fins.

Fins are perhaps the single most defining feature of fish. Fish possess a number of different types of fins, varied in shape and size from one species to another. Though some fins have become highly specialized, they all by and large serve the same purpose: to provide the fish with stability, lift, and the means of locomotion.

There are paired fins that are capable of providing extreme maneuverability and allow fish to undertake very precise and delicate actions. Sharks have very stiffened paired pectoral fins made from cartilage; they are incapable of being furled but provide the necessary lift to help sharks maintain their depth in the water. Marlin pectoral fins are also stiff and strong and more than capable of resisting the stresses that swimming at high speeds induces on the fin. As with the shark, the marlin is not able to furl its fin, though unlike the shark the marlin is able to fold the pectoral fins tight against the body to assist in streamlining and reduce drag at very high speeds or when not in use. Flying fish have developed especially long pectoral fins that, once unfurled and extended, have an aerodynamic profile similar to that of a bird's wing that enables the fish to glide over the water's surface.

The pike *Esox lucius* has developed fins located at the extreme end of its streamlined body, allowing for high acceleration from the weed beds where it spends much of its time in hiding, waiting for its prey to come within range.

The ways that body shape and fin configuration have developed in fish provide them with a morphology that allows them to thrive in the environments in which they live.

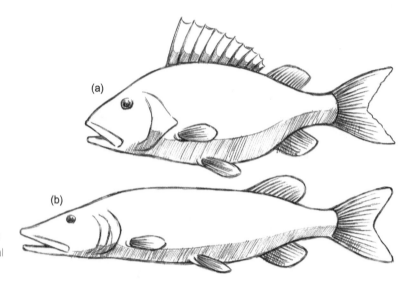

FIG **4.71** a: The perch has a large centrally placed dorsal fin that gives it great maneuvrability. b: The pike has a dorsal fin located much further back in the body, providing additional thrust for higher speeds.

The Dorsal Fin

The dorsal fin is located on the back of the fish and varies in number from one to three. These fins also vary a great deal in size and shape. Dorsal fins are mostly used to assist in maneuverability and in the prevention of a rolling action, but some of them incorporate sharp spines that not only aid rigidity, they afford some protection against predation. In most fish the dorsal fin does not contribute directly to providing power for locomotion, though in seahorses the dorsal fin provides the main propulsion through its undulating action.

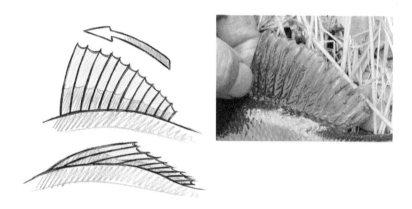

FIG **4.72** Dorsal fins.

The Caudal Fin

The caudal fin is most commonly known as the tail and is attached to the body by the caudal peduncle, through which the power for locomotion is provided to the tail. Though other fins make a contribution to powering locomotion, it is through the caudal fin that the power for high speed and sustained swimming are transmitted.

There are various shapes of caudal fin. Asymmetrical caudal fins that have vertebrae extending into the larger lobe are known as *heterocercal*. In sharks the upper lobe is longer, or *epicercal*, while the tails of fish that have longer lower lobes are known as *hypocercal*.

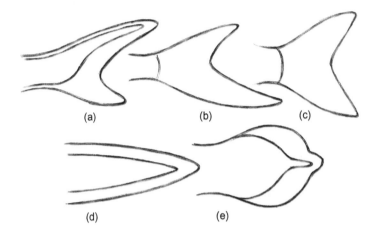

FIG 4.73 The tail or cordal fins vary from species to species. a: Heterocercal. b: Hypocercal.
c: Homocercal. d: Protocercal.
e: Diphycercal.

However, most fish have tails in which the vertebrae do not extend into a lobe and the tail fins are more or less symmetrical; these are termed *homocercal*. There is still a good deal of variation in the shape of caudal fins that conform to this homocercal structure.

Rounded caudal fins are almost completely rounded at the end as in the barramundi *Lates calcarifer*. Truncated caudal fins have an almost vertical edge, as can be seen in the Atlantic salmon *Salmo salar*. Forked caudal fins may end in two prongs of roughly equal lengths, as in the roach *Rutilus rutilus*. *Emarginate*

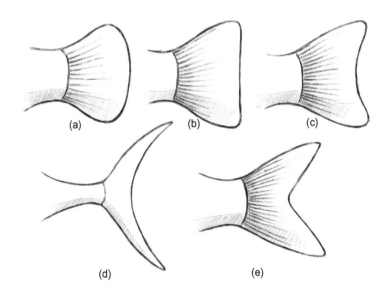

FIG 4.74 The different shapes of caudal fins. a: Rounded. b: Truncated.
c: Emarginate. d: Lunate. e: Forked.

163

describes a caudal fin that has a slightly inward curve, as in the European perch *Perca fluviatilis*. Lunate caudal fins are highly curved and form a crescent shape, as in the albacore *Thunnus alalunga* and the wahoo *Acanthocybium solanderi*.

Members of the *Scombidae* family, which include tuna, albacore, wahoo, and mackerel, have very slender caudal peduncles and sickle-shaped tails. The mass of myotomal muscle transmitting power to a huge tail through the tendons in slender caudal peduncle enables high-speed tail beats, making these fish capable of sustained swimming with occasional bursts of very high speeds of up to 64 mph.

The Pectoral Fins
Pectoral fins are paired fins that are located on either side of the fish, just behind the gill cover or operculum. These fins are capable of generating dynamic lift. In sharks these are rigid and assist in maintaining depth. In some fish these fins are modified to support their bodies and assist them in "walking" along the bottom. Many fish have spines on the pectoral fins that provide protection from predators. Mud skippers use their pectoral fins rather like arms to drag themselves across the soft mud on which they spend much of their lives.

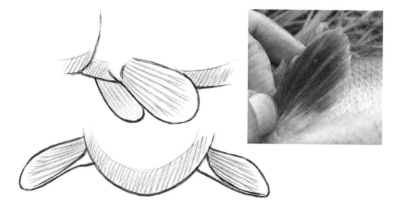

FIG 4.75 Pectoral fins provide propulsion at low speeds, maneuverability, and stability.

The Pelvic Fins
The pelvic fins are also paired fins, sometimes known as ventral fins, that are located on the underside of the fish, behind the pectoral fins and in front of

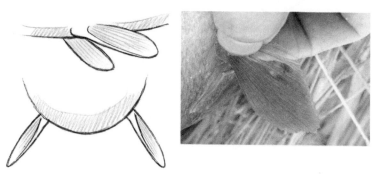

FIG 4.76 Pelvic fins provide the fish with stability.

the anal fin. These fins are also used to stabilize the fish during swimming, preventing roll and allowing a high degree of control, enabling slight movements and delicate maneuverability.

The Anal Fin

The anal fin is located on the underside of the fish, just behind the vent or anus, and is used to prevent roll and thereby ensures stability while the fish is swimming forward. Fish will often furl their fins, reducing their profile and allowing for a more streamlined shape, thereby reducing drag and increasing speed—a very useful tactic when acceleration over short distances is required.

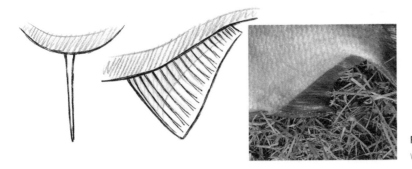

FIG 4.77 Anal fins provide the fish with stability and aid maneuverability.

The Adipose Fin

A number of fish possess a small fleshy fin located on the back behind the dorsal fin and in front of the caudal fin. The adipose fin is absent in most fish, though all salmonids, trout, salmon, grayling, and char have them. The purpose of this fin is uncertain since it has no rays and doesn't seem to provide or assist in either maneuverability or locomotion.

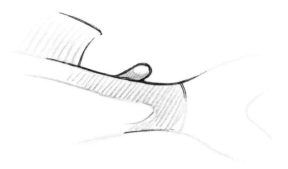

FIG 4.78 The adipose fin is a small, fleshy fin located behind the dorsal fin.

Some species of fish possess *finlets*, which are rows of small, rigid fins located on the upper and lower sides of the fish along the caudal peduncle, between the dorsal and anal fins and the caudal fin. These finlets are hard and not retractable.

Not all fish have the same kind of scales. Some are covered in very large numbers of small scales; others have smaller numbers of large scales. There are some species that appear to have no scales at all but are instead covered in what is termed an *enameloid* tissue. Many fish have bodies covered in protective mucus; some, such as eels, catfish, and bream, have large amounts of this mucus. In the case of eels this outer coating makes the scales all but undetectable.

Fish have a lateral line that runs along the length of the fish and is part of their central nervous system, allowing them to detect movement, vibrations, and changes in current. The lateral line is also instrumental in assisting fish to locate prey and in schooling behavior.

Muscle, as in other forms of animals, provides the power for locomotion in fish. The muscles that move the pectoral fins that do much to assist with maneuverability are located at the base of the fin; the muscles that provide the power for swimming are located along the flanks of the fish. These, known as myotomal muscles, are the source of the majority of power behind the undulating action in swimming. The myotomal muscles are placed in various triangular configurations along the flanks of the body and consist of two different types of muscle: slow-muscle fiber and fast-muscle fiber, though these remain distinct and are not intermingled. The greater mass of myotomal muscle is made of red fast-muscle fiber that allows for short periods of high-speed swimming. The rest is made up of white slow-muscle fiber, used in sustained swimming at slower speeds.

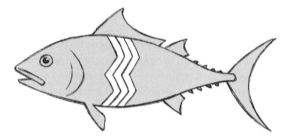

FIG 4.79 Myotomal muscle is arranged in a zigzag configuration down the flank of the fish.

A number of fish do not fall comfortably into the simple classifications I have set out in this chapter. Though they may share some of the common features

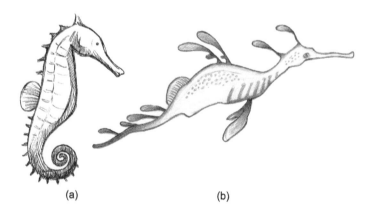

FIG 4.80 Some fish have unusual placing of the fins. (a) The seahorse and (b) the sea dragon swim not with the undulating action of a cordal fin on the rear of the fish but by a gentle and constant wafting of a fin located on the back of the fish.

(a)   (b)

of more "typical" fish, they are so distinctive as to be worthy of separate study. However, to describe them fully and appreciate their peculiarities would take more space than is available here. Fish such as hagfish, lampreys, seahorses, and sea dragons are perhaps among the most exotic of these.

Fish Animation

Fish may be more primitive animals than either birds or mammals, but though the range of actions for fish may be more limited than either those of birds or mammals, they do possess the ability to undertake a range of actions, including a number of different modes of swimming. These various swimming actions may be determined by a range of stimuli: feeding, migration, mating, display, and defense. The different forms of movement are generated through the use of different parts of the fish. These may be similar across a broad spectrum of species, but there are variations between species. Eels depend more largely on an undulating action; rays use their elongated pectoral fins that have developed into wing shapes in a similar undulating fashion that creates lift and forward momentum.

Maneuverability is achieved by the use of a series of fins in combination to create the most delicate of actions that enable some fish to rotate their bodies, pivoting around their center of gravity and creating a turn so tight that they are able to maintain their overall position within the water. Some fish are even capable of fin actions that enable them to swim directly backward without the need to turn; other fish, such as sharks with their rigid pectoral fins, are incapable of such actions.

In general, powered locomotion may be generated from the caudal fin (the tail), groups of paired fins, and the undulating action of the body. Other than swimming to get from A to B, fish move to in particular ways to undertake particular activities such as feeding or courtship.

Fish that root in the silt to get to the food that lives there often use their pectoral fins to make fine adjustments in their forward and backward movement and to create a downward tilt. Archer fish use the pectoral fins in a similar manner to create an upward tilt as they position themselves to hunt insects from overhanging branches by spitting out a column of water. Female salmon use their paired fins to roll on their sides while using their large, powerful caudal fin to excavate depressions in the gravel of streams in which they lay their eggs. They then rapidly oscillate their bodies, creating very powerful downward forces that clear the gravel while only slightly moving the fish forward.

The mouth movements of fish also vary a great deal depending on the species of fish. Predators feeding on other fish and that use speed to catch their prey tend to use a snapping action, grabbing a fish as they lunge forward. Fish that use ambush instead of chase, such as catfish, quickly open their large mouths, thereby creating a strong current that helps them gulp down any unsuspecting prey. Some fish have extending mouth parts that enable them to sift food from silt, to reveal teeth, or to remove food items from a variety of surfaces, including other fish.

Fish often engage in the behavior of leaping out of the water. For some this could be a tactic to avoid predation, but for the salmon and migratory trout it is a way of leaping obstacles such as waterfalls to access breading grounds. Some fish may use leaping to get rid of parasites such as lice and ticks.

Swimming

As you would expect, animals have developed different ways of propelling themselves on or through the water, and moving on the surface of water is a very different matter from moving in it.

Slow-speed swimming, sustained swimming, and high-speed swimming demand different approaches, and often the generation of thrust is created by different processes (oscillation, rowing) and from different parts of the anatomy (caudal fin, pectoral fins), though all forms of swimming must overcome issues such as inertia and drag.

On the face of it, swimming and flying seem not too dissimilar. Neither flying birds nor swimming fish are supported by the ground; both seem suspended within their particular medium, air or water. However, the forces needed for swimming vary considerably from those needed to fly. Animals that get around by flying need to overcome strong vertical forces (gravity) to support themselves in the air. This requires a great deal of effort on the part of the animal in countering those forces with forces generated by their own actions (lift). By comparison, animals moving in liquid are not subject to the same degree of vertical forces. Animals that live in water are much closer in density to that of their environment; as a result they need to exert far less effort in creating vertical forces to counter those that impact on them. Fish and other water-dwelling animals expend far less energy to maintain their position in their medium than birds do in theirs.

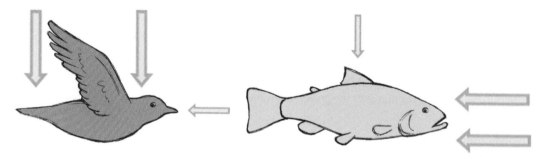

FIG 4.81 The forces acting on animals moving through air and water differ in the effects they have on the animal. Gravitational effects are felt more strongly by birds than by fish. However, the force required for locomotion through water is greater than that required for motion through air.

By contrast, the horizontal forces needed for propulsion through air are far lower than those needed for horizontal movement through water. Air is less dense than water, so there is far less friction in moving through the air than there is in moving through water and therefore the energy costs are considerably lower. The denser the medium, the higher are the energy costs to an animal moving through that medium. The more streamlined the profile an animal presents, the less drag its movement will incur and the less effort it will need to propel it forward. Fish such as sailfish and tuna are very streamlined, thereby making them capable of very high speeds. When carrying a fish in its talons, an osprey will maneuver the fish to face forward, creating a more streamlined profile, reducing drag, and therefore reducing the effort needed to fly while carrying its prey.

Some animals other than fish manage to get around in and on water. Ducks and other water birds manage to swim on water's surface due to buoyancy, but some animals use the natural surface tension of water to support them. Liquids do allow animals to travel along their surface in this manner, but due to the limitations of the forces that the surface tension exerts on objects, this practice is limited to very small animals. Once again we find that size really does matter. A large fisher spider (*Dolomedes*) weighing in at around 1g can easily get around on the surface of water by distributing its weight over a wide circumference on legs that are around 50mm in length. Each leg makes contact with the water around 15mm. To put this in some kind of perspective, if a spider weighing in at around 1kg chose to walk on water in the same way, its legs would have to form a perimeter of 140m.

Swimming on the surface of water also requires more energy than submerged swimming due to wave drag effects. Measurements of energy expenditure in sea otters showed that 70% more energy was required to swim on the surface than swimming at the same speed when completely submerged. Boats traveling at very high speeds along the water's surface experience *hydroplaning*. This results in hydrodynamic lift, which greatly reduces wave drag effects and makes energy consumption far more efficient.

Swimming with Hydrofoils

Many animals, including fish, have adapted to use their limbs, paired fins, and tails as hydrofoils to propel themselves through the water. Sea lions, dolphins, turtles, and penguins as well as fish all use various parts of their anatomy to propel themselves in this way. The difference between a hydrofoil action and a rowing action is that during a rowing action, the oar moves more or less at a right angle to the body, whereas in a hydrofoil action the limb or fin moves at a much shallower angle to the body. Lift may be generated on either the up- or downstroke and is determined by the angle of attack. A steep angle provides the thrust; a shallower angle prepares for the next power stroke. Penguins and marine turtles use their wings and their fore flippers, respectively, as hydrofoils and gain lift on both the up- and the downstroke. To achieve this effect, the angle of attack for both up- and downstrokes are

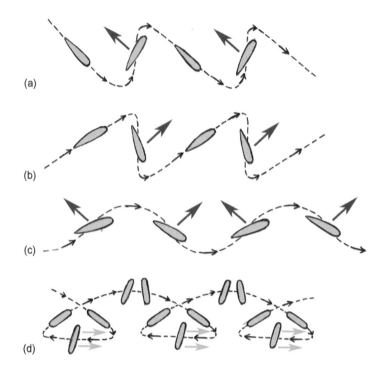

FIG 4.82 Swimming with hydrofoils and oars. a: Demonstrates lift on the upstroke. b: Demonstrates lift created on the downstroke. c: Creates lift on the downstroke and the upstroke. The red arrows denote the direction of lift. d: Illustrates propulsion by a rowing action. The green arrows denote drag.

much shallower than in the former examples. During the downbeats, the wing creates both an upward lift and forward thrust; during the upbeats, the wing creates downward lift and forward thrust. To achieve a steady horizontal movement, the upward and downward lift must cancel each other out, leaving the forward thrust to propel the bird through the water.

Unlike with the use of limbs or fins as oars, whereby they are required to be furled or bent on the forward recovery stroke to reduce drag, the use of hydrofoils depends only on the adjustment of the angle of attack of the limb or fin. The shallower angle of the recovery stroke in the hydrofoil action has the same effect of reducing drag.

The net result of movement with oars or hydrofoils with regard to acceleration is the same: On the power stroke the animal achieves greater acceleration, and on the recovery stroke the effect of drag reduces acceleration. For very small animals this may result in deceleration. Those animals that use a hydrofoil action by paired fins or limbs to create lift on the up- and downstroke achieve a more consistent acceleration throughout the sequence.

Hydrofoils are not just used in pairs, as in turtles and penguins. Whales and dolphins use single hydrofoils. Nor is it necessary for hydrofoils to be limited to a horizontal orientation; tuna and other fish use their caudal fins as vertically oriented hydrofoils in much the same way as a dolphin uses its tail flukes. There is no significant difference between the way a whale uses its flukes to generate thrust and the way a tuna swims. They both drive the hydrofoil through a relatively slender caudal peduncle, the whale beating its flukes up and down while the tuna beats its tail from side to side.

Whales, dolphin, and tuna all use their hydrofoils in the same manner with a relatively rigid body. The model that describes an action achieving equal thrust on the up- and the downstroke holds true in these cases.

There is some evidence that swimming with limbs as hydrofoils may provide a more efficient mode of locomotion than swimming with limbs as oars. However, research has demonstrated that thrust with oars offers better acceleration and enables better turning and breaking, and though hydrofoils may be more efficient in power output, oars offer better maneuverability. Many fish tend to use a mixed economy when it comes to the use of their paired pectoral fins, sometimes using them as oars and at other times opting for a hydrofoil action. In slower actions it may be possible to distinguish an oar-like dynamic, but it is not always clearly evident when fish choose to use their fins as oars or hydrofoils.

Swimming with Tails

As we have seen, the power for swimming comes from two distinctly different kinds of muscle: fast red muscle fiber capable of generating short periods of very high speed and slow white muscle fiber capable of maintain cruising speeds over extended periods. The process of swimming with tails may use both sets of muscles.

Swimming powered by the use of a tail is perhaps the most typical of all gaits for fish locomotion. In very general terms, fish that use their tails for power swimming keep their bodies fairly rigid, though this does not mean that they are inflexible. Tuna have exceptionally rigid bodies and they depend on being driven forward by their tails via the strong tendons within their very slender and highly flexible caudal peduncles. The amplitude of the tail beat in swimming fish, except at very low speeds, during which it may drop significantly or stop altogether, remains fairly consistent, but this does vary from species to species. At much slower speeds some fish drive themselves forward by the use of pectoral fins, as we'll see in a moment.

To achieve swimming speeds from a standing start to a cruising speed, a fish will increase the size of its tail beat. As swimming speeds continue to increase, the size (amplitude) of the tail beat does not continue beyond a certain point. Instead the increase of speed is achieved by increasing the frequency of the tail beats. The tail does not move a greater distance; the fish simply moves it faster and more often.

Swimming by Undulation

As we have already seen, fish that use their tails to swim generally maintain a fairly rigid body posture. The tuna provides us with an illustration of a fairly typical fish that depends principally on its tail action for swimming.

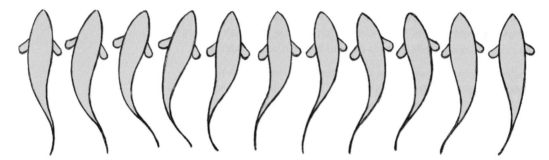

FIG 4.83 The behavior pattern of a fish swimming by undulation.

However, many fish and some snakes create their swimming action to propel themselves through water using an undulating motion of their entire bodies.

Of course, unlike fish, snakes have the ability to swim both on the surface of the water and submerged using this kind of undulating action.

We know that different fish have slightly different patterns of undulating action and the level of movement varies from species to species, but they all share some common traits within such actions. The action begins at the head of the fish and progressively makes its way along the body length. For most fish the amplitude of the wavelength created by undulation increases as it progresses from the tip of the nose toward the tail. Eels of all types have the most extreme undulating action, and their particular form of undulating swimming makes them quite capable of swimming both forward and backward with equal maneuverability and strength. The pectoral fins have become rather small and ineffectual, while the dorsal, caudal, anal, and ventral fins have become a single continuous fin that aids the body's undulating action.

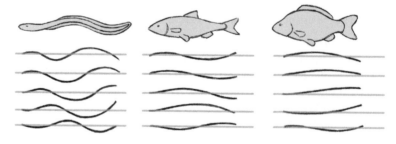

FIG 4.84 The amount of undulation within a swimming action varies within types of fishes depending on their individual physiognomy.

The distance a fish travels during a single cycle of undulation is known as its stride length, which varies from species to species.

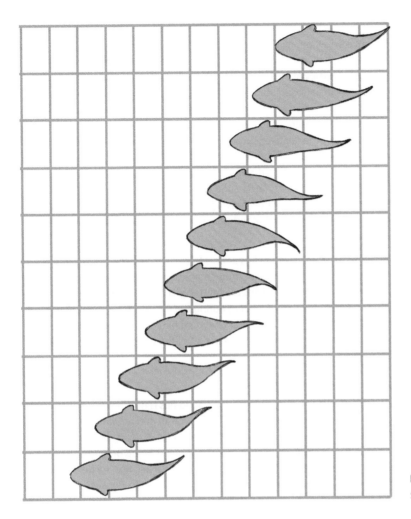

FIG 4.85 The stride length of a fish swimming by undulation.

Swimming with a Rowing Action

Occasionally fish swimming at very slow speeds choose to propel themselves forward with the use of their pectoral fins rather than using their entire body to propel the caudal fin. Using their pectoral fins as oars, they are capable of creating a rowing type of action.

During this kind of action the fins or limbs of the animal may act as an oar, with the surface of the limb or fin moving more or less at a right angle to the body, creating thrust on the power stroke. On the return stroke the fin or limb moves at a far shallower angle of attack, thereby reducing drag. The power stroke of the rowing action is generally a more rapid action than the animal's swimming speed. Human swimming uses this kind of drag action on the arms because they are used as either horizontally or vertically oriented oars. Propulsion by some species of water beetles is more akin to the rowing action of a figure in a boat than swimming by oscillation, as most commonly seen in the powered swimming of fish. The water boatman (*Sigara striata*)—no prizes for guessing how it got its name—uses its legs to make a backward stoke, during which they are then propelled forward. As the legs are drawn forward again to make a subsequent stroke, the legs are furled or bent to reduce the amount of drag. Even so during this process the animal clearly decelerates at this point. The amount to which deceleration occurs is to some degree determined by the relative size of the animal and the viscosity of the water. Larger animals such as fully adult tuna will decelerate at a slower rate than very small animals such as the water flea, though the surface area of the tuna is far greater than that of the flea and thereby subject to higher drag. The momentum of a larger animal moving at speed, particularly an animal with a more streamlined profile that reduces drag, will be maintained over greater relative distances.

Some fish use their pectoral fins as oars to create the same rowing action. They push the fins backward at right angles to the body, thereby powering the fish forward. The paired fins are then angled and furled into a position with a lower profile to reduce drag during the forward movement that completes the cycle. The forward movement of the fins also produces a degree of drag, but this is far less than that of the backward power stroke of the action.

Swimming by Lift on Paired Fins

Swimming with a rowing action using paired fins is not the only option open to fish. Paired fins can also be used to produce lift and forward thrust, perhaps best illustrated in sharks. Many sharks have rather large, rigid pectoral fins of cartilage that are not veined nor capable of being furled or backward motion, as with many of the species of bony fish. Instead these fins are held rigidly out from the body and act in the same way as wings do. Because sharks are heavier than water, they sink if they are not continuously swimming forward, so the large pectoral fins assist them in maintaining their position in the water and in forward motion. Their large caudal fin and extended caudal peduncle provide the power to ensure that water passes over the pectoral fins to create the necessary lift. The degree of lift varies depending on the angle of attack of the pectoral fins in exactly the same manner as discussed when we looked at bird wings. These large pectoral fins allow for a very efficient form of locomotion because they use the strong currents to create the necessary lift.

Flying fish have another and rather unique use for their pectoral fins. As with many other fish, the flying fish uses its tail to provide the power for the majority of its locomotion, but occasionally it uses its pectoral fin as a principle source of locomotion. These fish spend much of their time swimming close to the ocean's surface and, as with most fish that are prey to larger predators, they leap from the water to escape becoming a meal. As a result of this regular behavior, over thousands of years the flying fish's fins have evolved to become almost as long as their bodies and, once unfurled, can be used as wings. Their fins, once held out at right angles to the body and flayed out to the full, provide a large surface area that acts much like the wing of a bird and provides enough lift to create their distinctive flying action. As a result the usual short periods above water that leaping provides have now become extended periods of flying over considerable distances to escape predators.

Porpoising

A number of animals engage in a "porpoising" action that forms only a part of the locomotion that makes up swimming. During this action the animal leaps periodically out of the water while swimming at speed. Both dolphins and penguins do this on a fairly regular basis, simply as part of their swimming action, though some fish do this as a strategy to avoid predators.

The benefit of porpoising is difficult to assess in terms of efficiency of locomotion and economy of energy consumption. Some experts think that it does indeed show an efficiency benefit for animals that travel at high speeds. For penguins one of the possible benefits of porpoising is the frequency with which it allows them to breathe. The speed at which they are able to travel underwater is much greater than they can travel on the water's surface. Underwater they are able to propel themselves using their wings as hydrofoils; on top of the water they are restricted to using their feet, a far less powerful tool. As with other forms of locomotion, the option of porpoising is available only to animals under a certain size. The energy required for such a gait is within reach of dolphins, but it would seem to be beyond larger animals such as whales.

A number of animals propel themselves through the water by jet propulsion. Water is drawn in at the front of the animal and driven out under pressure from the rear end. Animals that use this mode of locomotion experience fluctuating velocity; they accelerate quickly as the water is expelled under pressure and decelerate as water is taken in. In some animals the frequency at which the water is taken in and then expelled is so high that any fluctuations in speed are negligible.

Shoaling

Rather like birds, fish gather together in large numbers for a variety of reasons, the main one being for safety against predation, with individual fish in a large group being far less likely to fall prey to a predator. Some predators have become capable of exploiting the defensive shoaling trait of prey fish when they form large bait balls. Sailfish, tuna, seals, dolphins, and many others round up small prey fish such as sardines for ease of feeding.

Other fish shoal together in large numbers during spawning. Shoaling also forms part of a migratory pattern in some fish. Salmon return to the rivers of their birth in large numbers to spawn; elvers (small eels) swim in huge numbers from the Sargasso Sea to rivers in Europe. Unlike their journey as elvers, their return to the Sargasso Sea as adults to breed is a solitary activity, with each animal making its own way there.

Some fish migrate only a couple of times in their lifetimes, but other migrations occur on a more regular annual basis, and some animals migrate daily, driven by the day length. Some fish living at depths in the ocean make an upward journey toward the surface as the light begins to fade so that they can feed in the upper layers. They then return to the relative safety of the deeper, darker water during daylight hours. Though not all fish that migrate vertically do so to reach the surface, they may simply move upward to exploit different feeding levels in the water column.

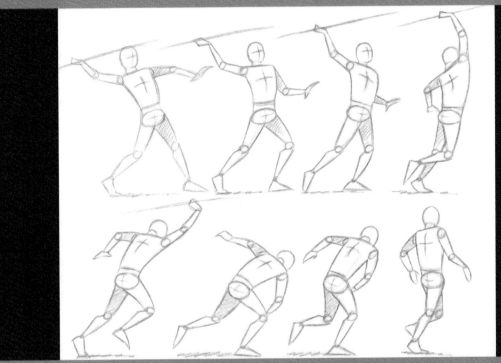

CHAPTER 5

Figures in Motion

The controversy Charles Darwin created in 1859 with the publication of his groundbreaking work *On the Origin of Species*, in which he inferred the evolution of different species from common ancestors, including man's own descent from the apes, has still not entirely disappeared. There are still people who completely refute any suggestion that humans evolved from the primates, even though the prevalent scientific opinion is to the contrary. Whatever the truth regarding the development of modern humans, one thing we know for certain is that we are now the only bipedal mammal that has learned to walk with a consistently upright gait.

Although the manner in which we get around is really rather unique, it is not this alone that marks us out from the rest of nature. Instead it is man's capability to create, advance, and use technology. It is this and our capacity for the development of cultures and (I almost hesitate to use the term) civilizations that truly differentiates us from other animals. A number of other animals use rudimentary tools, but only humans have the capacity to create a broad range of advanced technologies for specific purposes. And although many animals group together socially as families, groups of families or clans, and wider communities, none do so with the same complex level of cultural identification and differentiation as humans.

All animals have developed the ability to communicate with others of their kind and with other species. There are even a number of species that have developed their communication skills into what may be considered a more advanced language of one sort or another. Furthermore, research has shown that some birds of the same species have developed songs that demonstrate regional accents.

Language is a central element of any culture, and it is likely that humans have the most complex system and wide-ranging verbal language of any animal. In addition to vocalization and in common with many other animals, we regularly use nonverbal visual methods of communicating with one another. This form of communication is a more ancient one and transcends any language barriers that arise due to geographical distribution or cultural differences.

The distribution of humans across the globe from our original home located somewhere in what is now Africa has resulted in local variations as a response to local environmental conditions. In this regard we are no different from any other animal. The human body has simply developed and changed to meet these conditions.

Physical variations may be evident in different races of humans, but we all share a common trait: that the human body improves with use, provided this use remains within certain limits, and we become fitter and more capable of a broader range of actions with repeated use and practice. Not only do we see an increase in strength and stamina, but through practice and repetition we also become increasingly capable of undertaking very intricate and delicate actions and manage to acquire increased dexterity. We may acquire more highly developed skills and the physical attributes to execute these skills that allow us, with practice, to become better at, say, football, open heart surgery, or weightlifting. Naturally, practice alone will not suffice; individual attributes such as spatial awareness, dexterity, and a physiognomy allowing for strength are important factors in enabling us to be football players, surgeons, or weightlifters.

Human Anatomy

There are very many aspects of human anatomy that this chapter does not and cannot cover, given the limited space. The context of this study is animation. The book is intended for animators, so we will look at human anatomy to a degree that we hope will be of some use to animators. However, I have made a number of suggestions for further reading, including texts that will assist you with the study of anatomy and that you might want to explore if you require more detailed and specialized information. For the purposes of this text I have limited the subject of anatomy to the human musculoskeletal system that enables movement.

There can be no doubt that there are many cultural, religious, and political differences between humans; however, other than slight variations in our body physiognomy, we are all pretty much the same. Those physical variations that do occur between some races of people are of an environmental and geographic nature. Differences can be found between people that are indigenous to mountainous regions and those living at sea level. Due to the lack of oxygen at higher altitudes, people living in high mountainous regions have developed a greater capacity to breathe much thinner air than people living at sea level. For this reason, athletes from low-lying countries need to acclimatize themselves to conditions at high altitude before they can compete at their optimum performance in such regions.

Unlike the babies of many mammals, the human baby remains vulnerable and dependent on its mother for care and nourishment for an extended period after birth. Some quadrupeds are up on their feet and running within the hour. Human babies take much longer to get around under their own steam. Human babies generally begin to crawl at somewhere between six and seven months old, and it takes them around a year before they begin to walk. To walk steadily and with confidence may take many months more.

The physiognomy of the human body changes throughout our lives. Initially the body lacks strength and does not have the capacity to support itself, though it is very flexible. We have all seen with what ease a baby can place its toes in its mouth. We are born with very large heads compared with the size of our bodies, but as we grow through childhood and into adulthood the proportion of the head to body size changes.

Having gained confidence with walking, children continue to develop and learn to run, jump, and hop, along with a variety of other modes of locomotion. As we grow we also become increasingly dexterous and we develop a capability to use tools.

Growth continues until a point between 20 and 25 years, when we complete the process that replaces with bone any of the parts of our skeletal structure that began as cartilaginous and are destined to become ossified. Once this process stops, no more growth occurs.

It is normal for individuals to physically deteriorate as the body begins to age. As we grow older we experience a loss of calcium, which results in our bones becoming porous and brittle. Some of this loss is due to the aging process and is perfectly natural. However, serious loss of calcium may occur as a result of a condition known as *osteoporosis*. For people that have this condition, it can become a serious issue, particularly if it affects weight-bearing bones or bones used in muscle pull actions. It is not uncommon for brittle bones to result in falls and injury. As an individual becomes increasingly frail and less strong, through either the natural aging process or illness, the impact on mobility increases. Osteoporosis occurs in women more often than men.

Physical differences in individuals clearly make a difference in the performance of certain tasks, and of course there are obvious differences between the genders. Women have larger hips and narrower shoulders than men, and in very general terms men are stronger than women.

Cultural, religious, and political differences may result in certain behavioral variations in people, but it is less certain that differences between ethnic groups may be as easily identified. The idea that certain ethnic groups are more able or more suited to certain physical activities than others remains controversial.

Human Skeletal Structure

The skeletal structure offers strength for support and protecting soft tissues and organs and is a system for the distribution of power. The skeleton works

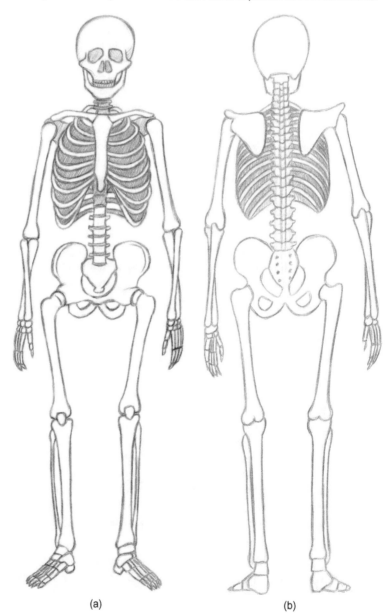

FIG 5.1 Human skeletal structure, a: anterior, b: posterior.

(a)

(b)

as system of articulated levers through a series of joints. In this structure there is a degree of compromise between strength and flexibility. The rigidity of the structure allows for greater strength, stability, and protection, whereas the structure's articulation allows for more flexibility and a greater range of movement. The cost of achieving flexibility is that joints do not have the same degree of strength as the rest of the bones.

The number of bones in the adult human skeleton is 206 (which may vary slightly from individual to individual), but at birth a newborn baby has approximately 300 bones. The difference between the two numbers is a result of the fusing together of a number of the smaller bones during growth. In a healthy adult, the skeleton accounts for around 14% of the total body weight.

The skeleton is complex structure of a wide variety of bones, which can be classified into four major groups:

- Long bones
- Short bones
- Flat bones
- Irregular bones

Long Bones
Long bones are generally cylindrical in shape and broaden out to become knobbier at each end. Bones in this category are found in the arms (humerus, ulna, and radius) and the legs (femur, tibia, and fibula). They are also to be found in the hand (metacarpals and phalanges) and the feet (metatarsals and phalanges).

Short Bones
Short bones are generally solid and thickset and are typified by bones in the wrist (carpals) and in the ankle (tarsals).

Flat Bones
The pelvic bones, sternum, and scapula fall into the category of flat bones.

Irregular Bones
The 24 vertebrae that make up the spinal column fall into the category of irregular bones, as do the sacrum and the coccyx.

The necessary articulation in the skeleton is achieved through a series of joints that interconnect the separate bones. These joints allow the bones to be moved in relation to each other by the transmission of force through the connected muscle. All joints are not the same, and they vary in both their stability and flexibility. A joint's stability relates to its resistance to displacement and has a direct impact on the amount of flexibility it provides;

the more stable they are, the less flexible they are. The differences in the structure of the joints can be attributed to the different roles that each joint plays within the skeleton. The shoulder and hip joints are the most flexible and are of the ball-and-socket type. The shoulder joint has a shallower coupling than the hip joint and provides a greater degree of flexibility. However, the hip joint is less prone to displacement. The role of the hip is to be load bearing; the shoulder's function is to provide flexibility in order to enable manipulation such as lifting. Stability in this case comes at the expense of flexibility.

A number of different types of joints in the skeleton allow for various levels of articulation and movement:

- Plane joint
- Hinge joint
- Pivot joint
- Condyloid joint
- Saddle joint
- Ball-and-socket joint

Plane Joint

Plane joints are quite irregular in shape though usually flat or slightly curved; they only allow movement of a sliding action. These joints are to be found between the carpal bones in the hand.

Hinge Joint

Hinge joints allow movement in one plane around a single axis. The joint found at the elbow is a hinge joint. This type of joint only allows for movement along a single axis. This is known as a *uniaxial* joint.

Pivot Joint

Pivot joints allow bones to roll around one another in a rotation movement, as can be found in the radius and the ulna. A pivot joint is also a uniaxial joint.

Condyloid Joint

Condyloid joints are oval or egg shaped and fit into a concave shape. These joints allow movement through two axes: forward and backward and from side to side. Such a joint is found at the junction between the metacarpal and phalangeal bones.

Saddle Joint

Saddle joints are a modification of the condyloid joint and allow for more freedom of movement. They are another example of a biaxial joint. A saddle joint is located in the thumb.

Ball-and-Socket Joint

Ball-and-socket joints are triaxial joints that allow movement through three axes. These joints comprise a spherically shaped bone that fits into a reciprocal cup shape within the adjoining bone, enabling a swivel type of action. Such joints are to be found at the hip and the shoulder.

There are other joints that are cartilaginous, fibrous, or ligamentus in nature that unite two bones by means of interconnecting cartilage or fibrous tissue. The most important of these as far as movement and mobility are concerned are those that make up the vertebral column. The thickness of the vertebral disks allow for a degree of movement that is not dissimilar to that achieved with a ball-and-socket joint.

The Skull

The skull's role is to provide protection for the brain. Made up of 22 bones, the skull is joined together by ossified material that only occurs in the skull. Part of the skull is composed of air-filled sinus cavities that offer strength and reduce the skull's weight.

The jaw is held in place by the temporomandibular joint, which is composed of fibro-cartilaginous tissue that offers a great deal of flexibility.

The Spine and the Rib Cage

The spine is a remarkable structure that provides support, strength, and a degree of flexibility to the entire body. It is primarily a mechanism for maintaining our upright position and permitting a range of movements for the head, neck, and trunk. The spine's flexible action allows the entire figure to maintain balance throughout many actions. The level of flexibility also allows for the transmission through the body of forces that enable locomotion. It is often the position and orientation of the spine that animators use to identify the "line of action" within the figure.

The normal human spine consists of around 33 different and irregularly shaped vertebrae. These are grouped in four regions, from top to bottom: cervical, thoracic, lumbar, and sacrum, as follows:

- Seven cervical vertebrae
- Twelve thoracic vertebrae
- Five lumbar vertebrae
- Five fused sacrum vertebrae
- Three to five fused vertebrae that make up the coccyx, which forms part of the sacrum region of the spine

The vertebrae of the spine are classified as irregularly shaped bones, the spaces between which are filled with a cartilaginous material. This material provides a form of lubrication that enable humans' high degree of flexible movement.

The rib cage provides protection for vital organs, the heart and lungs; although the rib cage is a rigid structure, it too offers a degree of flexibility. However, the rib cage plays no part in the generation of movement, nor does it play any major part in enabling movement.

A couple of fairly common abnormalities in the spine may have an impact on the movement and gait of individuals and so could be worth mentioning at this point. A forward curve of the upper spine may be due to kyphosis. In the young this abnormality is often described as a slouch; in the elderly it may be known as a dowager's hump.

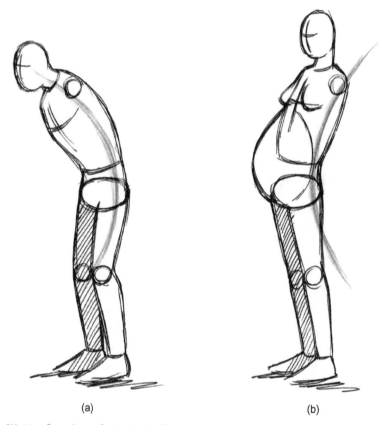

(a)   (b)

FIG 5.2 a: Forward curve of spine, slouch. b: Backwards curve, swayback.

A curve in the opposite direction—that is, backward—may be due to lordosis, a condition also known as hollow back or swayback. In quadruped animals this may also be known as saddleback. This backward curve of the spine located at the lumbar region is a fairly common temporary condition in pregnant women who adjust their gait to account for the additional weight.

Human Musculature

In humans, most limb muscle contains a roughly equal amount of slow-twitch and fast-twitch fibers, though they are not evenly distributed. The muscles of the back contain far more slow-twitch fibers than fast-twitch fibers. The average adult male body is made up of 42% skeletal muscle; the average adult female is made up of 36% skeletal muscle as a percentage of total body mass.

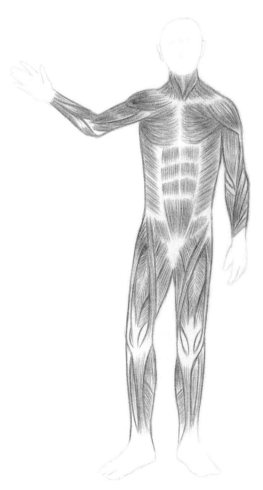

FIG 5.3 Human musculature.

Neck and Shoulders

Both the neck and shoulder are capable of independent movement, but they often work in tandem in a given action. In addition to movement along the sagittal and transverse planes, the neck is capable of a degree of rotational movement. Rotation of the head to around 180 degrees can be achieved by the horizontal rotation of the neck, facilitated by the flexibility of the vertebrae in the cervical region of the spine.

There are a number of muscles that form parts of the shoulder and are connected to a series of bones and joints to accommodate movement. The illustration shows how these muscles are connected to the ribs, the sternum, the scapula, the clavicle, the spinal column, and the humerus. The movement of both the shoulder girdle and the shoulder joint allows for movements of the arm. It is this structure that allows for combined and cooperative actions of both the shoulder and the arms; this in turn enables the range of arm movement to be extensive.

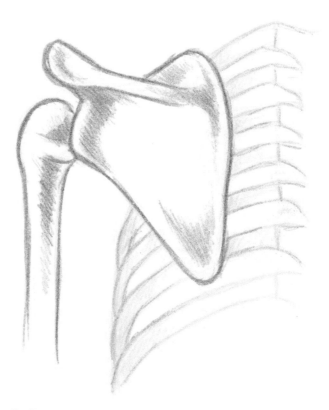

FIG 5.4 Shoulder construction.

Arms

The upper arm bone is the humerus, which is long and strong and allows for the transmission of power through leverage. The lower arm is supported by a two-bone structure: the ulna and the radius. These bones allow for rotation of the lower arm at the elbow joint. The biceps are the primary muscles that allow for flexion of the forearm and provide power for lifting actions involving movement within the arms.

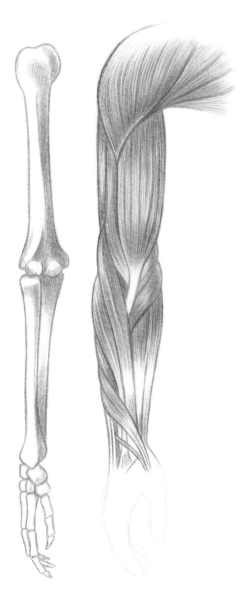

FIG 5.5 Arm skeletal structure and musculature.

The Elbow

The elbow is a complex joint. Though it may be considered a hinge joint, the two bones of the forearm, the ulna and the radius, are attached to the humerus in different ways. The connection between the humerus and the ulna is a hinge joint; the connection between the humerus and the radius is a restricted ball-and-socket joint, a kind of gliding joint. The structure allows for the flexion, extension, and rotation of the forearm.

187

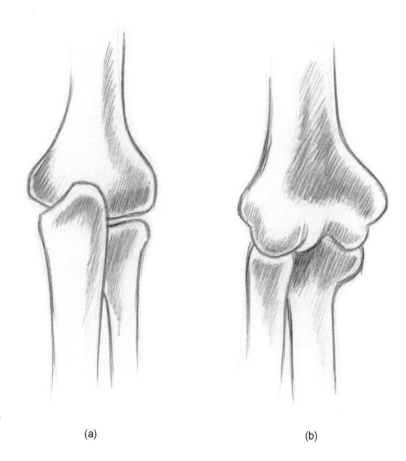

FIG 5.6 The elbow joint. a: Posterior view. b: Anterior view.

(a)

(b)

The Wrist and the Hand

The most dexterous part of the human body, one capable of the widest and most complex movements, is located within the wrists and hands. This dexterity is a result of the number and complexity of individual bones and joints that make up the hand and wrist. This complicated structure not only allows for dexterous movement; it also provides strength and allows for a high degree of shock absorption. The structure may look delicate and fragile, but the hands are extremely strong and are capable of taking high levels of stress and sustaining heavy impacts. This combination of dexterity and strength makes us capable of using a wide range of tools.

The radius and the ulna are attached to the wrist joint, which is made up of two rows of four carpal bones. This structure provides a degree of articulation between the separate bones as well as between the two rows of bones.

The lower row of bones connects with the separate metacarpals. These in turn connect with the phalanges.

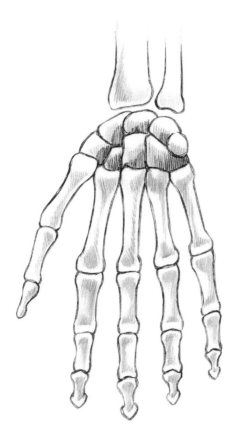

FIG 5.7 Skeletal structure of the human hand and wrist.

The Hip Region

The pelvic girdle consists of two separate pelvic bones that provide a rigid structure and a link between the torso and the legs. Each of the pelvic bones is made up of three separate bones: the ilium, the ischium, and the pubis, which become fused together around the age of puberty to form a single entity. The sacrum region of the spine is firmly connected to the pelvic girdle at the iliac bones by sacroiliac ligaments.

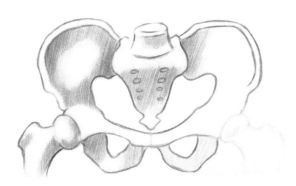

FIG 5.8 Pelvis, anterior view.

The position of the pelvis shifts through movement of the spine and the hip joints. Other than slight movements during childbirth, there is considered to be little or no movement within the pelvic girdle itself under normal conditions. The position of the pelvis at these joints allows for a tilt forward, backward, and sideward. Rotation at the hips is provided through the movement of the torso via the spine and the legs via the hip joints.

Hip Joints

The hip joints are typical ball-and-socket joints that connect the pelvic girdle to the femur. The femur terminates in a spherical ball at an angle of around 45 degrees of the upright, the head of which fits into a cup-shaped recess, the acetabulum, located at the juncture of the ilium, ischium, and the pubis. The acetabulum is lined with a cartilaginous material that serves as a protection between the two bony structures and provides a degree cushioning against impacts or stresses. It also allows for a smooth movement within the joint. The hip joints provide for a range of movements—forward and backward, sideways and rotational.

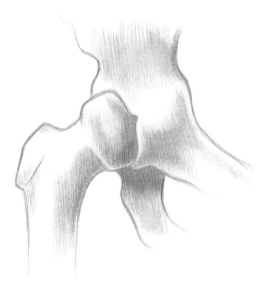

FIG 5.9 Hip joints.

The Legs

The femur is a long weight-bearing bone that is angled inward slightly from the upper end, where it joins the hips, to its juncture with the tibia. However, this angle is not really evident by looking at our bodies and is only evident once the skeleton is revealed. At the upper end of the femur the bone has a ball that fits into a recess inside the hip. At the lower end the femur sits on top of the tibia, with two ball-like protuberances called *condyle* that sit side by side. The condyle rest within two depressions on the upper extremity of the tibia; these depressions are separated by a roughened area called the *intercondyloid eminence*.

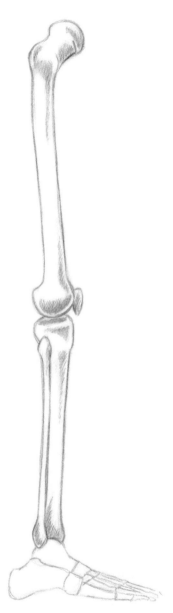

FIG 5.10 Skeletal structure of leg, side view.

The body is supported at the lower leg by the larger tibia and the more slender fibula that runs down the outer edge of the lower leg.

The Knee
The femur and the tibia meet at the knee joint, the largest and most complex joint in the body. It is subject to the greatest stresses and strains

of any joint, and because it is a necessary part in facilitating locomotion, it needs to be strong enough to support the entire weight of the figure and flexible enough to accommodate a wide range of movements. It also needs to be able to provide stability to the figure throughout these movements, some of which—running, jumping, hopping, lifting, and swimming—can exert considerable strain on the joint. To assist in these movements, the knee is protected by ligaments of great strength and attached to a musculature capable of transmitting immense power. The knee joint is classified as a hinge joint, though it looks like two condyloid joints sitting alongside one another that fit with the two condyle joints of the femur.

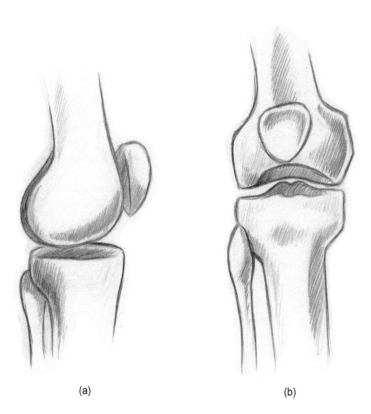

FIG 5.11 Knee joint. a: Side view. b: Anterior view.

(a)

(b)

The Foot

The foot provides the stable platform on which the entire figure is supported and plays a vitally important role in locomotion. Because of these roles there is a need for great flexibility and strength and a capacity to tolerate considerable stresses and sustain heavy and regular impacts.

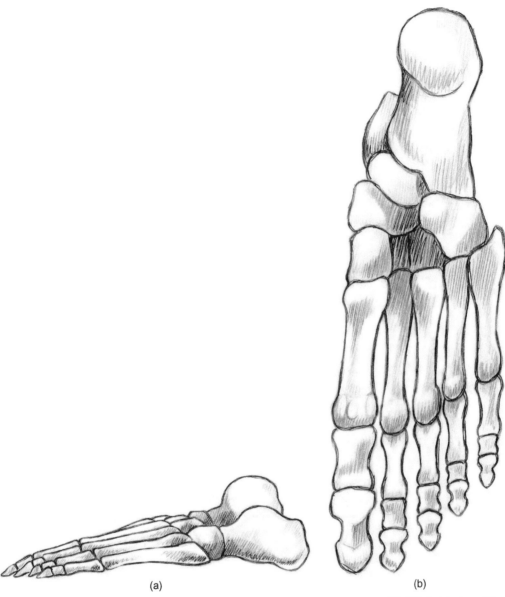

(a)

(b)

FIG 5.12 Foot structure. a: Side view. b: Top view.

The foot is connected to the leg at the juncture of the tibia and fibula with the ankle joint, the talus.

The foot itself is a complex structure that may be considered in two parts: the inner and the outer. The inner part of the foot is made up of a number of bones: the talus (this connects the leg to the foot), the calcaneus (the heel), the navicular, the cuboid, and three cuneiforms. This combination of bones provides the shock absorption during locomotion.

The outer part of the foot consists of five metatarsals connected to the three cuneiforms and the cuboid. The metatarsals are in turn joined to the bones at the extremities of the foot—the structure that makes up the toes, the phalanges.

Human Animation

The human body is a remarkable piece of engineering capable of undertaking some extreme movements and dynamic possibilities. A person with a healthy body will possess a fair degree of stamina and considerable strength and will have a capacity to demonstrate a high degree of dexterity as well as being capable of using and manipulating tools to undertake the most delicate of actions or exert quite substantial forces.

As we have seen, the human figure comprises a series of articulated joints powered by strong muscles forming strong levers that are capable of flexing, pivoting, stretching, and compressing, all achieved by the use of the musculoskeletal structure. Muscles provide the power and the skeleton provides the framework of bones that act as supports and levers that enable actions requiring strength, sustained effort, and extreme dexterity, giving the human body the capacity for moving at high speed and with high levels of maneuverability.

When at rest the human body is designed to be well balanced and energy efficient in maintaining its stability. This is a condition that is shared by all living creatures capable of independent locomotion. Nature has seen fit to design them all to be as energy efficient as possible. The design for economic energy consumption while our bodies are at rest or in motion is also something that is in-built in all animals. Providing a full range of movements necessary for the animal and its particular needs while running, flying, or swimming is done in the most energy-efficient manner possible. If we are to gain a full appreciation of the figure and its various modes of locomotion and gaits, we must consider the figure both at rest and in action and the way in which both of these states work together to create an animated dynamic.

Stillness, or more accurately a figure at rest, should be our starting point from which we consider one of the major factors in all animal movement: balance. Let's first take a look at the orientation of a figure standing at rest and by doing that establish a center of gravity. The center of gravity is a shifting point within a body, around which all parts balance each other—if not exactly, then sufficiently to create stability.

To understand the direction in which a figure moves, we should start by establishing the separate planes along which the figure is oriented and the

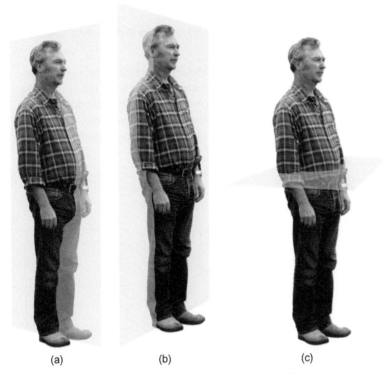

| (a) | (b) | (c) |

FIG 5.13 Orientation of a figure along planes. a: Sagittal plane b: Lateral plane. c: Transverse plane.

axes of motion within a figure that stands at rest. There are three planes along which a figure or an object can be oriented and positioned:

- The sagittal plane
- The coronal plane
- The transverse plane

The Sagittal or Median Plane

The *sagittal* or *median plane* divides the figure in half vertically and from front to back, dividing the figure into left and right sides.

The Frontal or Coronal Plane

The *frontal* or *coronal plane* divides the figure in half vertically from side to side, dividing the figure into anterior and posterior halves.

The Transverse or Horizontal Plane

The *transverse* or *horizontal* plane divides the figure in half horizontally into upper and lower halves.

Each of these separate planes passes through the center of gravity at some point. The point at which these three planes intersect is the center of gravity in the figure. However, although this center of gravity representing the point of balance in any object may be easily located in a figure at rest, this point will shift as the object or figure shifts and moves its position throughout any given action.

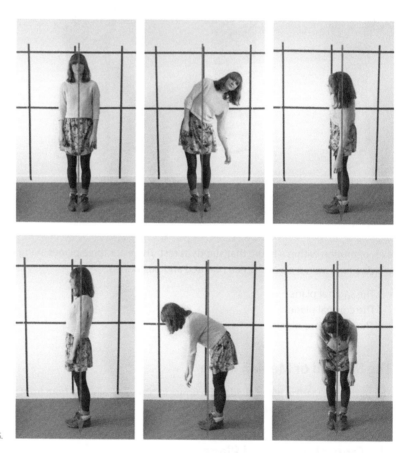

FIG 5.14 Center of gravity within a figure at rest with different orientations.

As we can see in our series of images of a figure at rest with different orientations along the three different planes, the center of gravity is clearly located in different regions of the figure. Balance is achieved in the figure at rest by the offsetting of body mass to ensure that equal amounts of body mass are located equally on either side of the planes.

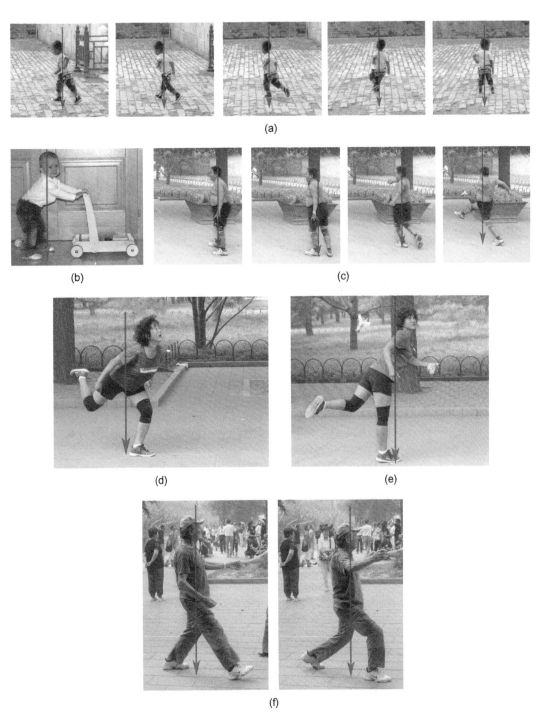

(a)

(b)

(c)

(d)

(e)

(f)

FIG 5.15 Center of gravity within a moving figure. a: A child playing. b: A baby holding on to an object for support. c: The shift in the center of gravity during a kick. d and e: A woman running. f: The shift in the center of gravity during a rocking forward motion.

Objectives of Movement

We have seen how it may be necessary to readjust the position of the body at rest to achieve balance. Before we look in some detail at the various aspects of movement, it may be useful to look at a very simplified set of classifications of the objectives of movement. This study can go some way to identifying these different drivers that instigate movement and may help us gain a deeper understanding of the nature of those movements. To understand movement, it is helpful to understand why a particular movement or set of movements is undertaken. The *objectives of movement* fall into five separate categories:

- Balance
- Locomotion
- Projection
- Manipulation
- Effort

Balance

One of the primary objectives in movement is for the figure to maintain stability during an action. This applies during both fast and slow movements, though achieving stability is determined in part by the nature of the movement. For example, it may be easier for a figure to maintain balance on a bicycle moving at speed rather than one moving at very low speeds.

Balance is the state of a figure that has achieved a degree of stability either during motion or at rest. Balance may be the objective of an action in order for a figure to gain, maintain, or regain this stability. Balance may be gained as a result of an action or at the end of an action, or it could be necessary as part of the preparation for an action.

Locomotion

The objective of *locomotion* may simply be for the figure to move from point A to point B or for it to travel a given distance. Locomotion may describe movement in a particular manner or mode: running, walking, swimming, hopping, jumping, or a combination of these. The manner of locomotion will be determined by a range of internal and external factors. Walking may conserve energy; running may result in shorter travel times; and swimming is clearly the preferred method of locomotion through water.

Projection

The *projection* of an object through space via a throwing action will also be determined by the outcome required. It may be necessary to use maximum force and for the object to describe a particular trajectory in order for an object to achieve the maximum height. To achieve maximum distance the force required may be similar in that used to achieve maximum height, though the trajectory may be very different. The throwing action required to achieve these different projections will, in all likelihood, be very different from each other. To achieve accuracy in a projection, using such actions as throwing or kicking may require far less force than a more controlled action. For maximum speed of projection, perhaps as part of executing multiple projections that require neither maximum distance nor accuracy, the action will naturally be faster than an action suited for maximum accuracy and less powerful than one aimed to achieve maximum distance or height.

Manipulation

Other than locomotion, it is perhaps *manipulation* that determines most actions, particularly human actions. We learn from a very early age how to manipulate objects, then quickly go on to learn how to use a wide range of tools, from knives and forks to automobiles. Naturally we manipulate our own bodies, just as all animals do, to move and undertake a wide range of actions such as dance, communication, and exercise. We have the ability to manipulate ourselves and objects to create patterns of action as part of a production process used to make things: knitting, baking, drawing, or manipulating tools in sequence. Communicating through a visual language such as sign language may be considered manipulating one's own body to make patterns. We are also capable of manipulating an external resistance or force—pulling or pushing objects, controlling weights, or directing external dynamic forces.

Effort

The *effort* that goes into any given movement will also vary depending on the nature of the movement and will naturally vary from individual to individual and from activity to activity. The amount of effort and type of effort will also vary and depend on whether maximum speed, power, or force is required. Effort may be seen as a physical attribute but be defined by the individual's physical and mental attributes.

Clearly these separate categories will overlap and several of the objectives may be involved in undertaking a single action. An archer shooting an arrow at a target will undertake a complex series of movements within a single action, each of which may involve a number of these classifications: balance to achieve stability of the figure so that the arrow may be aimed with accuracy, skillful manipulation of the bow and string, strength and effort to provide the power to achieve maximum distance, and a great deal of control, required to hit a target.

Our discussion should progress now to the body in motion by looking at the different classifications of movement a figure or parts of a figure may undertake and the terminology for some of these movements. All these classifications may apply to different parts of the anatomy and are not limited to the examples I give here. You will find examples of these classifications in all the case studies given throughout the book; once you read them, you will be able to then go on to identify the different classifications of movements within your own animation research.

For clarity, the movements illustrated here are viewed from different angles:

- *Flexion*. Flexion describes a motion occurring when a part of the body is bent from its normally straight position. In the arm flexion occurs when the elbow joint is bent and the angle of the joint between forearm and upper arm is decreasing. A fully flexed arm is a position in which the arm is

FIG 5.16 Flexion, extension, hyperflexion, hyperextension.

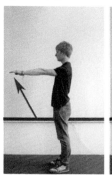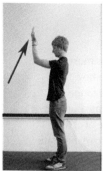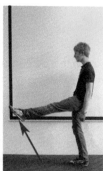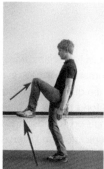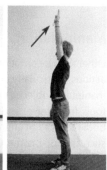

Flexion

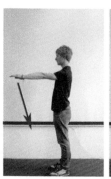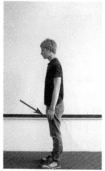

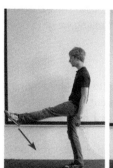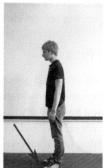

Extension

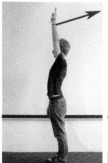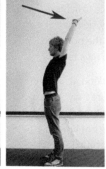

Hyperflexion

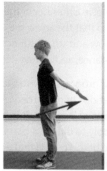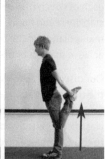

Hyperextension

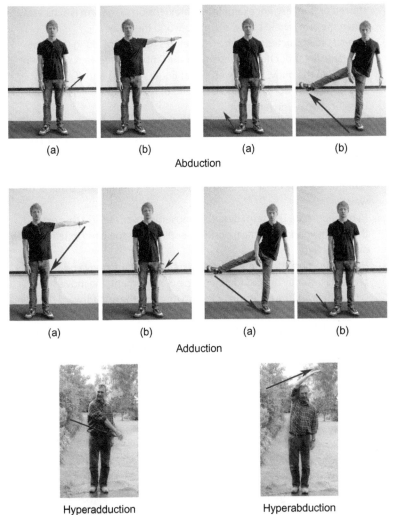

(a)   (b)   (a)   (b)

Abduction

(a)   (b)   (a)   (b)

Adduction

Hyperadduction   Hyperabduction

FIG 5.17 Abduction, adduction, hyperabduction, hyperadduction.

held straight at the elbow and the entire arm is fully elevated into a vertical position, with the hand held above the head and the humerus aligned with the femur.

- *Extension*. Extension describes the action of a flexed joint returning to its straight position after it has been flexed.
- *Hyperflexion*. Hyperflexion refers only to the movement of the upper arm and is achieved when the arm is extended beyond the vertical. In other joints, the flexion action is physically limited by the contact of one part of the body with another. The forearm may be flexed only to a point whereby the lower arm comes into contact with the upper arm; likewise, when moving backward, the lower leg is restricted by its contact with the upper leg.
- *Hyperextension*. Hyperextension describes the position of a part of the body that is moved to a point beyond the straight position at which it

started or is at rest. For example, hyperextension in the arm is achieved when the arm is held backward, out beyond the body.

- *Abduction*. Abduction describes a sideways movement along the sagittal plane. An abduction movement of the limbs is a sideways movement away from the body. The movement of fingers of the hand, if splayed sideways, away from the middle or palm of the hand, also falls into this classification of movement.

- *Adduction*. Adduction describes the movement that results in the return action of a part of the body, a limb or the fingers of the hand, from a position of abduction.

- *Lateral flexion*. This refers to a sideways or lateral bending action from the upright; this may be of the head at the neck or a bend in the trunk at the waist.

- *Hyperabduction*. This term describes movements of the arm that extend the arm beyond the vertical position, ending with the hand extended well over the head.

- *Hyperadduction*. Although the relative position of the body and the arm prevents a strictly hyperadduction type of movement, the movement is possible with the inclusion of flexion (moving the arm forward slightly). In this way the arms can move in front of the body.

- *Rotation left and right*. Rotations may be applied to the head and neck, the torso, the pelvis, the legs, and the arms. The rotations of the legs and arms are termed outward (*lateral*) rotations when the limb is twisted away

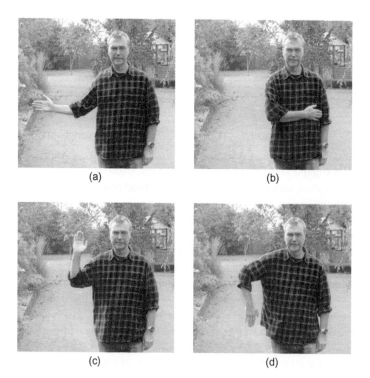

(a) (b)

(c) (d)

FIG 5.18 a and b: Outward and inward rotation. c: Supination. d: Pronation.

from the body, inward (*medial*) rotation when the limb is twisted toward the body. The rotation of the forearm is described as *supination* (outward rotation) and *pronation* (inward rotation).

- *Circumduction*. This term describes a type of rotational movement that occurs through three planes. The movement of the part of the body being moved in this manner (the trunk, arm, or leg) describes a cone shape, with the point of the cone located at the pivot point of the movement.

FIG 5.19 Circumduction of the arm, front view and side view.

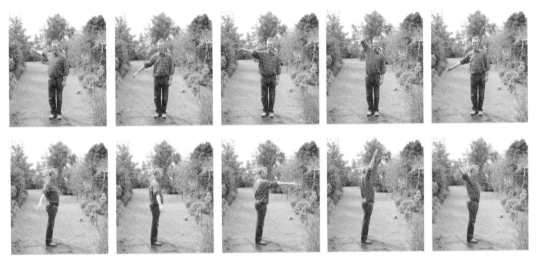

FIG 5.20 Circumduction of the leg, front view and side view.

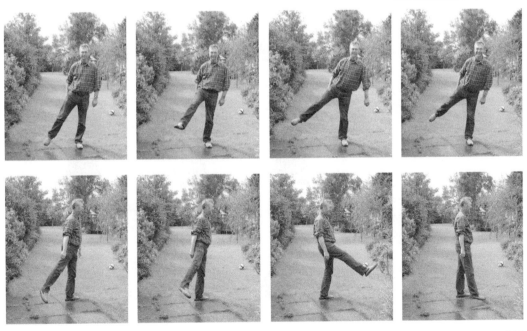

- *Shoulder movement.* Movement of the shoulders may be made independently or the two in tandem. *Elevation* describes the upward movement of the scapula with the rotation of the clavicle from the horizontal. An upward rotation is achieved when the arms are held outward to the side. An upward rotation with a lateral tilt is achieved when the arms are extended to the horizontal position and forward of the figure.

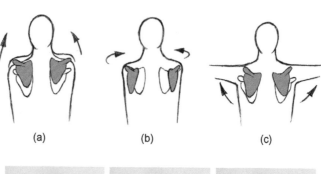

(a) (b) (c)

FIG 5.21 Shoulder action. a: Elevation. b: Abduction. c: Upward rotation.

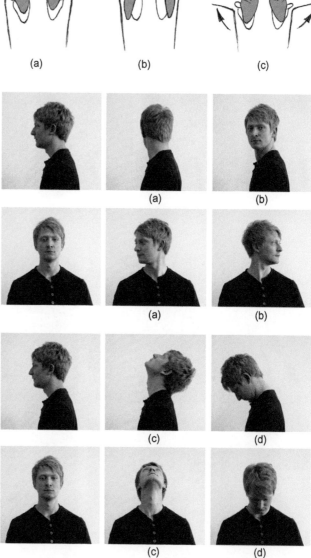

FIG 5.22 Head actions. a: Rotation right. b: Rotation left. c: Hyperextension. d: Flexion.

If we are to undertake further exploration of human movement to include the analysis of locomotion and other actions and activities, it may prove useful to start by taking a look at motor skills and identifying their various aspects.

Motor skills may be described as those movements that support the primary purpose of any given action. Without a rudimentary understanding of the reason an action is being undertaken, it might be difficult to fully evaluate the nature of the movement and the effectiveness of that movement. If we take, for example, a human's use of a hammer, we may establish that the principle *reason* for this action is to knock nails into a piece of wood. The *purpose* is to transmit sufficient power from the blow to the nail to drive it home. It may follow that such an action calls for a degree of accuracy (to hit the nail) and to hit the nail with sufficient power to send it deeper into the wood (force) while avoiding splitting the wood (control). To drive a panel pin into a thin strip of wood may require a similar action but a far more subtle blow.

The manner in which an action is undertaken and the various ways in which a tool is manipulated are both determined by the reasons behind the action. We can use a knife in different ways, depending on what is being cut. The action of butchering an animal carcass is very different from slicing a steak, which will probably be very different from making an incision during surgery.

It may also prove useful to break down the action of any given movement into separate sequential parts or phases. This is often possible even when these separate phases appear to flow seamlessly one into the other or if the actions of the various constituent parts of a movement, such as the action of different parts of a human body, occur simultaneously. Naturally, if the individual movements overlap or are completely separated by time and occur sequentially, the analysis of the overall action might be much easier. We can conduct the analysis of a walk by looking at the different parts of the body in turn and separately before considering how they work together to form a coherent whole.

The phases of an action may vary somewhat within that action, depending on the inherent nature of the movement or as a result of a particular approach to the action. Some phases may be fast, others slow, some smooth and constant, others more sporadic. These phases can also form part of repeated actions with intermissions between them. They may also be completely cyclical, in which case it could be difficult to ascertain a distinct starting or finishing point; or they may be discrete, unrepeated phases with a very definite beginning and end.

The classification of motor skills as I set here, albeit in a rather incomplete manner, should enable the reader to differentiate between the types of movement of the human figure. In this way we may gain a deeper appreciation of the complexities of the dynamics involved in human action.

There are two distinct areas in which we can begin to look at the way these actions apply to the human figure: movements given to one's own body and movements given to external objects.

Movement Given to One's Own Body

A number of different modes of movement fall into this category, each of which may be separated into subcategories. Naturally, the number of examples of different movements that fall into each of these subcategories is almost limitless; there is not a single way of swimming, for example.

Supported by the ground or other surface:

- Locomotion on foot
- Locomotion on wheels, blades, skis, and other such items
- Rotary locomotion

Supported by water:

- Floating
- Swimming

Suspended and free from support:

- Swinging
- Jumping, flipping, falling

Receiving an impact:

- From one's own body (landing after a jump or fall)
- From an external force (catching, being struck, intercepting an object or figure)

Movement Given to External Objects

- Pushing and pulling
- Twisting and turning
- Lifting and carrying
- Punching
- Striking
- Stroking and rubbing
- Throwing
- Kicking

Some actions involve types of movement that appear in more than one of these categories; by their very nature they are collaborative actions. We will be looking a little more closely at examples from some of these categories later in the text.

As part of the analysis of action, we may also find it useful to identify the primary, secondary, and tertiary elements of the action, which will provide a greater understanding of the nature of the action.

To recap, *primary actions* are actions that are essential to the execution of a movement (such as moving the legs in a walking action) and without which the action would not be possible. *Secondary actions* are actions that are undertaken to assist in an action (such as swinging the arms during a walking action) but are not essential to the action. *Tertiary actions* are those that occur in the overall movement as a *result* of either primary or secondary actions.

You may find it beneficial to link the primary action within the movement you are analyzing to one of these categories. Let's consider a baseball player striking a ball with the bat. This is clearly classified as giving motion to an external object through a striking action, the primary action being the movement of the arms that swing the bat. We could consider the secondary action, the movement of the feet to place the body in the appropriate place in relation to the location of the ball at the time of the strike and to maintain balance in the figure throughout the action. The tertiary actions are normally considered the action of objects external to the figure, such as garments; in this case the term could be applied to the movement of the batter's back foot as it slides across the ground while the figure moves forward through the batting action.

Actions may also be broken further into the different sequential phases of the movement that, when seen together and in order, describe the overall dynamic:

- *Preparatory phase*. During this phase a figure will adopt a posture or stance prior to and in readiness for the action.
- *Execution phase*. During this part of the action the figure applies force to either the figure itself or to an external subject in order for the action to take place.
- *Resulting phase*. The figure enters this phase of the sequence as a result of the release of power or the exertion of force and the desired action having been undertaken.
- *Recovery phase*. Once the action is completed, the figure will return to a rest position, which may either be the original position at the start of the action or a new position arrived at as a result of this action.

To fully appreciate the way in which human movement is achieved, we must not only consider the issues of physiognomy but also take into account a wide range of related issues. Psychological issues, gender and age issues, cultural issues, environmental issues, seasonal issues, economic, and even political issues will often inform the way a figure moves as an individual or as a member of a group; they may even be the determining factor in the movement.

Movement under Loads

The movement of a figure under a load may have a huge effect on that figure's action and greatly determine the nature of its gait. Alternatively, the load may have little effect on the figure and the impact on the action may hardly be noticed at all. Much is determined by the nature of the load, its size, its weight, and the material of which it is made. The action will also vary greatly depending on the structure and size of the figure carrying the load.

It would be expected in ordinary circumstances that there would be a more noticeable effect on the movement of a figure carrying a heavy object than one carrying a light one. The physical implications of carrying a heavy weight may be evidenced in a change to the figure's gait; the length of the stride during walking may shorten and the muscles of the arms may be seen to bulge under the additional tension. Tendons in the neck may tense, and there may even be signs of stress and tension within the facial muscles. The speed of locomotion may slow with the increase in weight, and the striding action during locomotion may become jerky.

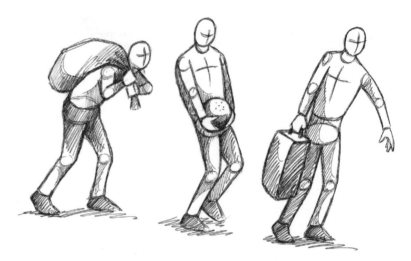

FIG 5.23 Figures carrying heavy loads.

It is not only when a body is under additional stress due to heavy weights that a gait will be altered. Carrying a light load may also result in a figure adapting an unusual gait to effectively undertake the action. Rather than the additional weight, this change may be a matter of balance in an effort to maintain stability.

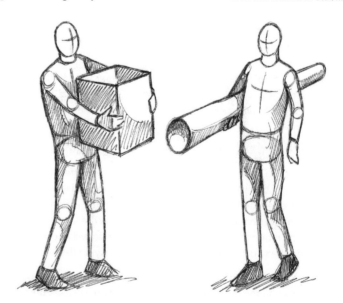

FIG 5.24 Figures carrying light loads.

The nature of the object, its stability, or how delicate it is may be the determining factor in the figure's movement. A lightweight though large and unstable object may require a great deal of effort in maintaining balance. Likewise, a very delicate object such as an unstable explosive device, although not heavy, may also change the nature of the gait, slow the action, and smooth out any movements.

Pushing or pulling a heavy load involves the use of body strength and may also involve the use of body weight as a counterweight to the object being moved. The effectiveness of the effort in achieving the object's movement may not be simply due to the strength and weight of the figure alone; the object's resistance to the forces being applied may vary with the nature of the object, its location, and the surfaces it sits on. A spherical object such as a soccer ball sitting on a flat surface will have a much smaller surface area in contact with the surface than that of a cube of similar size. The potential friction between the two flat surfaces is far greater than that of the spherical surface sitting on a similar surface. Pulling or pushing the cube will result in two surfaces sliding against one another, maximizing the friction between the two, whereas a ball will simply roll with the minimum of friction. Having overcome inertia, the spherical object will gain momentum, which will be more easily maintained by continued force. The friction between the flat surfaces of the cube and ground will not only make the inertia more difficult to overcome, but any momentum will be far more difficult to maintain, requiring far greater and more consistent force. The friction between the ball and the ground will eventually bring it to a halt, but the friction between the cube and the ground will bring the object to a halt far more quickly.

FIG 5.25 Figures pushing and pulling heavy objects with and without the assistance of the use of wheels.

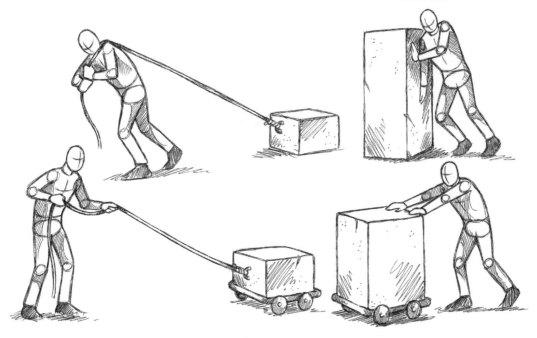

The use of wheels to assist in either pushing or pulling movements as in the use of a wheelbarrow avoids such high levels of friction and greatly assists pushing and pulling actions.

Some of these actions as well as specific examples are covered in much more detail later in the chapter.

Figurative Interaction

Once figures begin to work in tandem with others and interact either directly or indirectly with individuals or groups, the nature of the action alters. The manner of these changes is determined by the nature of the interaction either being spontaneous and unstructured or more planned and structured and involving teamwork. The action is also determined by the shared task and energy costs to the individual. Not all interactions are collaborative or shared actions involving direct physical engagement. Collaborations may also be at distance, as in sports activities, dance, or other choreographed teamwork actions.

To better understand the nature of such interactions, consider their categorizations:

- Momentary interactions: touching, shaking hands, mimicking
- Sustained interactions: shared labor, dance
- Sympathetic actions: musical performances
- Collaborative actions: rowing, sailing, lifting
- Opposing actions: martial arts, hitting and defensive action
- Team actions: team sports

This categorization of actions does not provide a definitive list. It will be evident to you that many of the actions you will study will fall under two or more of these headings.

When movement is a shared task, whether as choreographed movement, spontaneous actions, or simply a momentary collaboration, the action does not necessarily mean that it is neutral in terms of energy costs. There may clearly be a saving in energy in lifting an object as part of a team. However, the nature of the interaction itself may have additional energy costs, as evidenced in opposing actions that form an important part in sports.

Momentary interactions may be of an extremely dynamic nature, as in an exchange of blows between two prizefighters or a very passive action such as stroking a cat. As with other interactions, they will invariably affect both parties, but it is likely that the action does not affect both parties equally. Hitting will have a very different effect on an individual than being hit.

The act of sharing the load does not necessarily mean that the workload is shared equally between the participants. The proportion of load each takes will vary depending on the individuals involved and the nature of the object being carried. Such a collaborative action is likely to be a dynamic activity; it

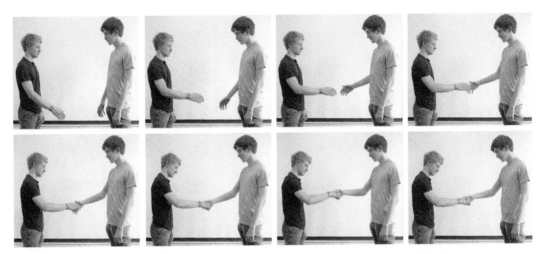

FIG 5.26 Figurative momentary interaction. A handshake sequence.

may be observed that the workload shifts between the participants during the task. We make a more detailed analysis of lifting weights later in the text.

Interaction between figures does not necessarily entail a shared workload or even a physical link between the participants. Dance mostly entails a kind of sympathetic interaction between individuals, with the separate actions of the dancers determined or shaped by the actions of others. Seen in isolation, an individual dancer's movements may not have context; it is only in considering the behavior of the various partners that the dance becomes complete and true interaction takes place.

FIG 5.27 Dance sequences.

(a)

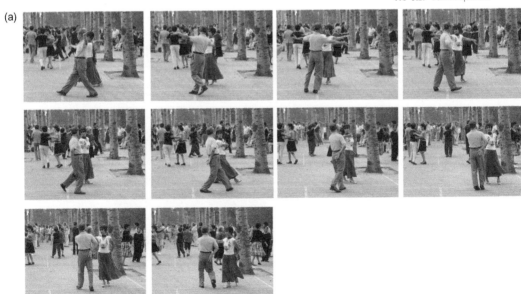

FIG 5.27 Continued

(b)

(c)

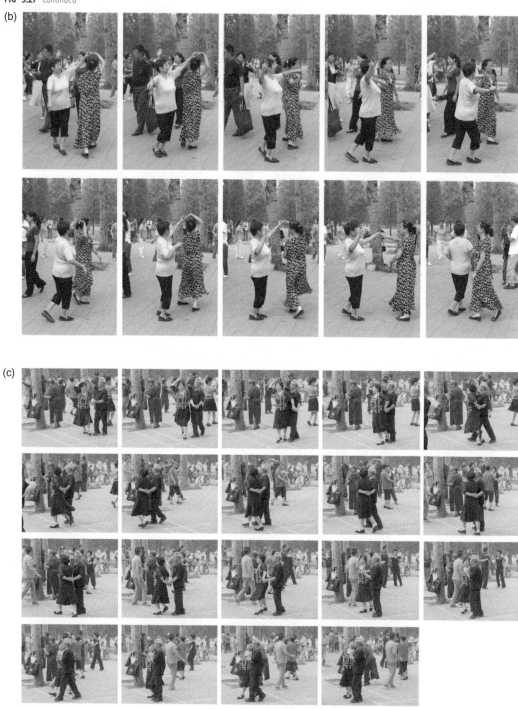

FIG **5.27** Continued

(d)

(e)

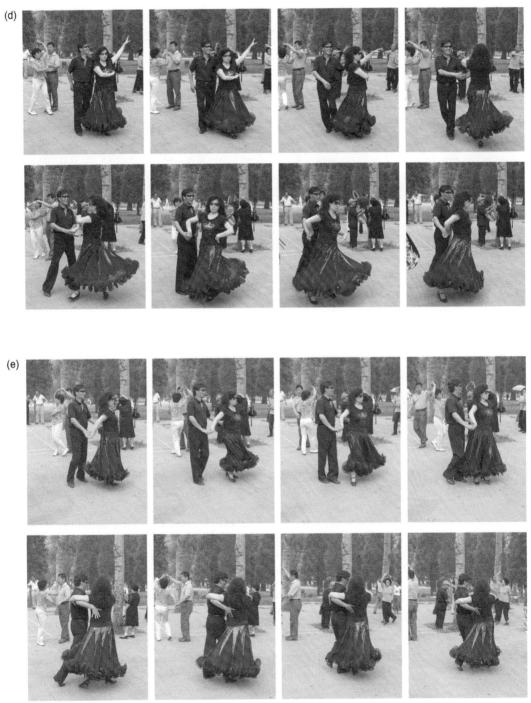

(f)

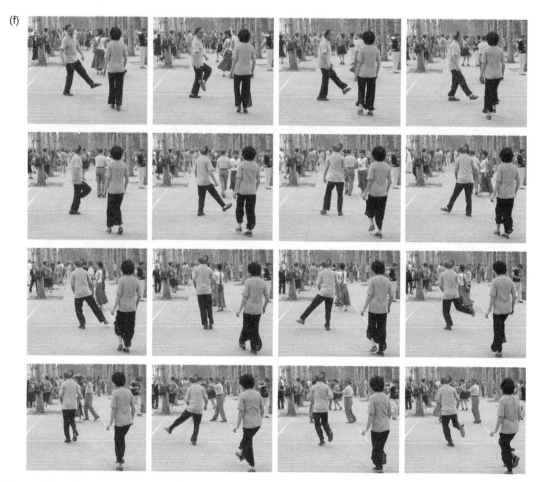

FIG 5.27 Continued

Collaborative interaction may bear a resemblance to dance inasmuch as individuals' actions rely on the other members of the collaboration for the collaboration to work. Such shared tasks depend on the close cooperation of the various participants. In our example we have a figure throwing an object while the second person is assigned the task of catching it. The action of the first (throwing) must be moderated in such a way as to allow the second action (catching) to be possible.

Opposing actions are unlike collaborative actions. In this type of dynamic, the separate actions of the individuals involved exist in response to one another. Although they may share some of the same qualities as dance or collaborative interactions, opposing actions are not intended to work toward achieving a common goal or sharing a workload. Fencers move and respond to the thrust and parry of their opponents and may have the appearance of choreography; however, unlike choreography, here the actions are spontaneous—an individual action is a reaction to either the opponent's movement or lack of movement.

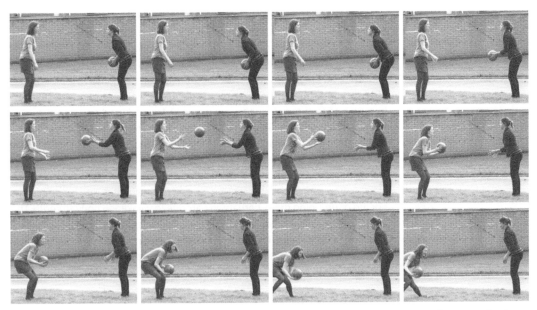

FIG 5.28 Young women throwing and catching a heavy ball.

Children in Motion

Unlike many other animals, human children remain very dependent on their parents for an extended period. They learn to get around independently after only about a year following their birth. To master other tasks may take them many more years. As a result, children's movements often appear awkward and rather clumsy. Inexperience, relatively weaker body strength than the adolescent, and diminutive size all contribute to this impression. Balance in walking and carrying objects takes a while to master, and at age 2 they often still tip drinks from a cup or drop items from plates that they carry.

A 2-year-old child may be able to walk and run freely, but she still has some difficulty climbing stairs and does this by placing both feet on each step, ascending one step at a time. Children generally master climbing stairs with one foot per stair before they manage descending in the same way, and they are around 4 years old before they can master going up and down stairs using only a single foot on each step.

It would seem that balance and coordination skills take a considerable time for humans to master. Initially they may have little coordination or the skills to manipulate objects or undertake delicate or intricate actions. This often leads to frustration, which results in increased clumsiness or mishandling, and as a result they often undertake actions with undue haste.

Movement in the Elderly

As we grow older we continue to undergo physical changes that impact our movement. We gradually become more prone to sickness and ill health, and our body's ability to regenerate or heal is impaired. Movement in the elderly becomes slower; their reaction times become slower as well. As a body ages, a range of health issues may cause changes in gait and the manner in which the person undertakes certain actions. Some actions become increasingly difficult or no longer possible at all. For these reasons, actions of the elderly often resemble those of very young children. For example, as climbing stairs becomes difficult, the elderly person may take to walking up one step at a time, placing both feet on a single step. There will often be a preference for a particular foot to move upward first so that this leg takes the heaviest workload of the climb. Balance often becomes an issue, too, and it is common for the elderly to use walking aids such as sticks or walkers. As with young children, the elderly often find difficulty in carrying certain objects, which may result in them tipping or dropping them, perhaps in part due to weakened body strength. The onset of frailty may increase a person's sense of insecurity and create a lack of confidence, which often results in a shortened walking stride length. This may in turn result in a shuffling gait. The hands are often placed on objects such as rails or furniture or against a wall in an attempt to maintain stability.

Movement and the Environment

It is not only the figure itself or the loads under which it moves that determine the nature of the action. The very environment in which that figure moves will also, to varying degrees, have a discernible impact.

Perhaps the greatest of these environmental issues is the nature of the surface on which a figure moves. Slippery, smooth, uneven or unstable, viscous, dry, or wet surfaces can each result in a different type of action. The surface's quality is most likely to have a noticeable effect on the action. If the surface is firm and stable, a figure will be able to move in an optimum manner. Moving through a field of waist-high grass is very different from strolling along a flat and closely cropped lawn.

Weather conditions and ambient temperature may also affect the nature of an action. Extreme cold or heat may cause a figure to move more slowly in an attempt to either conserve energy and warmth or, in hotter climates, to maintain a cooler body temperature and sustain a physical action that may be more difficult to maintain in high temperatures.

As we have already seen, figures moving at very high altitudes find the physical effort additionally arduous due to thin air and lack of oxygen. This has the effect of slowing actions and increasing fatigue. Some mountain climbers may suffer the effects of altitude sickness when they climb at extreme altitudes. Symptoms of such sickness vary, and not everyone is susceptible to altitude sickness to the same degree or succumbs to the sickness at the same altitude. In extreme cases climbers may be in real physical danger from altitude sickness, and the effects are potentially fatal.

Weather conditions may also result in a change in gait, as in a figure hunching over with head down in a strong wind, heavy rain, or snow.

Walking

The way we move, what we choose to do, and how we choose to do it are largely determined by how we are feeling physically, our moods, and our temperament. Even in the most everyday and prosaic of activities—walking—our moods and temperament will most likely be reflected. An individual who has just received some very good news may walk with a more invigorated stride than normal; conversely, the person who has just received some very sad news may walk more slowly and may hold his body in a more slouched posture. But to start with, let's consider for a moment some of the issues other than physiological ones that can influence a simple and straightforward action such as walking.

A walking man either may choose to or through necessity alter his natural gait at the beginning or at any point during the walk, depending on the environment he finds himself walking in or the ground he is walking on.

Walking on a slippery surface or walking through sticky mud several inches deep will demand a very different approach than strolling along on a firm, flat surface. The length of the stride often shortens when we walk on an icy surface, with the foot being placed flat to the ground along its length, unlike the action in a normal walk, where the heel makes contact with the ground first before the foot is then flattened.

If we're walking through deep mud or snow, the height the foot is lifted from the ground may be higher than normal so that we can extract the foot vertically from the mud or snow. This lifting action is more effective and efficient than attempting to slide the foot forward at the same time as raising it, as in a normal walk. Indeed, the viscous nature of the mud or the depth of the snow may prevent the foot moving forward at all, and the only way to make a stride would be to extract the foot vertically.

Seasonal effects can result in different walks; high temperatures may slow down a walker and make for a rather lethargic gait, whereas walking in heavy rain may create a hunched appearance, with the arms tucked into the body, and a more hurried stride.

Walking on a sloped surface, either upward or downward, will affect a walker's gait, and the nature of the walk will vary depending on the slope's steepness and the nature of the slope's surface.

We may also notice differences in walks as a result of gender. Of course, it's rather dangerous to generalize, but on occasion we can observe very noticeable differences in the walks of men and women. Some men tend to walk in a noticeably heavy manner, with their feet positioned wide apart, whereas some women walk with a stride that places the feet closer together, one in front of the other.

Some heavily pregnant women carry so much weight that they are forced to adjust their posture and walking gait to compensate for the additional load.

This often results in a lateral waddling-type action with a backward tilt of the torso and a noticeable curve in the spine.

The choice of footwear may also make a difference to a walk and can noticeably affect a figure's posture throughout the walking action. This naturally applies equally to men and women. Walking in high-heel shoes, sandals, diving flippers, or steel-toe-capped boots will result in very different types of walks. The actual fit of the shoes may also create different walking actions. If the shoe is too tight, it can restrict the feet and cause discomfort or pain, which in turn can result in a shortening of the stride and a more uncertain and lighter step. When the footwear is too large, as in instances when children wear their parents' shoes, the result is often a shuffling and sliding action of the feet, necessary to keep the shoes in place.

The manner of a walking action may be the result of external factors: environment, shoe type and fit, the weather, and internal factors such as mood and temperament. Some walking actions are a result of the walker's conscious decisions. Some individuals may *choose* to walk in a certain manner for a range of reasons. There are undeniably cultural reasons why some people choose to walk in a particular manner, one that identifies the individual as belonging to a particular group and purposely flagging this fact to others both inside and outside that group. A particular manner of walking may also be used to demonstrate status to other members of the group.

All these examples demonstrate the many variations on an action that to all intents and purposes is the same: using the same form of locomotion (walking) to get from points A to B. If such variations can be found in one action, it follows that similar variations can be found in all actions, though what instigates these actions and creates the variations will no doubt differ.

If we now look in more detail at the process of walking and the basic elements of a walk, we may find ourselves in a better position to understand these kinds of variations.

The average normal human adult walk takes place at speeds of below 2.7 meters per second, with the walk's speed determined by both the stride length and the rate at which each of the steps is taken. Increases in walk speeds may be determined by an increase in either the stride length or the regularity with which the strides are taken. Athletes in walking races are able to increase this average rate to almost double the speed, at around 4.2 meters a second. To achieve these much higher speeds, the walker needs to modify the action beyond simply increasing the stride length and frequency of stride. This is achievable by a modified action of the hips and exaggerated movement of the upper body and arms resulting in the very distinctive waddling type gait we associate with high-speed walking.

Regardless of the reasons for the walking action, as a simple mode of locomotion or as a sporting activity, the action is fundamentally the same, with the figure's balance being altered and adjusted throughout the action. The body shifts from one stable state to another, less stable one and then back to stability, with the body at times appearing to be completely off balance. However unstable the figure is at any given moment in the walk, however, the net result of a walking action is one of stability. Instability is a necessary part of locomotion—so much so that it could be said that a walking gait is little more than controlled falling.

By beginning to analyze the very familiar movement of the walk cycle, breaking it down to its basic components, we reveal the full complexities of the action. We can start to make sense of the different actions within a walk cycle, first by dividing it into two distinct parts; the stride and the passing position. In a full walk cycle, a figure undertakes these two separate parts of the action twice, each corresponding to both the right and left sides of the body. The illustration aims to explain this idea more clearly.

The Stride

The stride describes the position in the walk cycle when the legs are at their most separated point. One leg is fully extended forward, the foot having just made contact with the ground; the other leg is fully extended behind the figure, with the foot maintaining contact with the ground but preparing to lift. At this point the heel of the foot may be raised slightly from the ground. During the stride phase of the walk cycle, the figure is supported by both legs. The length of the stride varies greatly in a walk; the shorter the stride, the more likely it is that the heel of foot in the backward position will be held flat on the ground. We will see how these different component actions vary within the various walks illustrated.

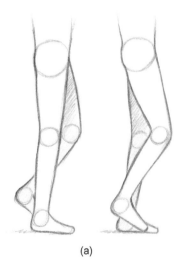

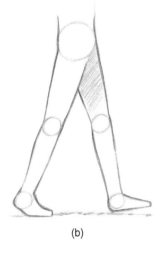

(a)

(b)

FIG 5.29 Walk cycle main key positions. a: The passing position. b: The stride.

219

The Passing Position

The passing position describes the moment in the walk cycle when the body is supported by only one of the legs, which is held in a vertical position with little or no bend at the knee. At this point the leg is positioned directly below and in line with the torso. The other, nonsupporting leg is positioned alongside the weight-bearing leg and swings forward past the supporting leg—hence the term *passing position*. The knee of this leg is bent at this stage to allow the foot to be raised to clear the ground. During the passing position the kinetic energy of the figure's forward movement is converted into gravitational potential energy as the figure rises slightly. This energy is then released as the leg swings forward and the body drops and completes the stride.

If we now take a look at the two passing positions and both the strides as a sequence of keyframes, we can see how the entire cycle works and can analyze it in its simplest form.

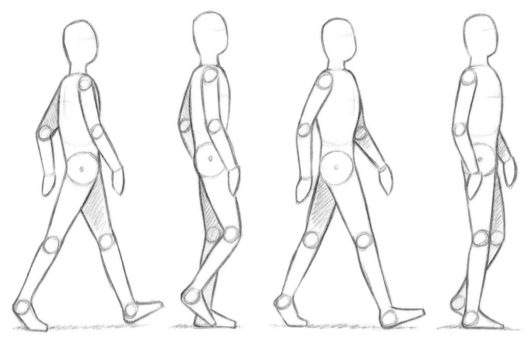

FIG 5.30 The walk cycle keys. From left to right: stride, passing position, stride, passing position.

The leg movement is clearly the primary action of a walk cycle, but the walk action is not limited to the movement of the legs alone. In the following phases of the walk, we can see how all parts of the body work together to produce a complete sequence. The phase order in this instance is an artificial one and quite arbitrary, since there is no distinct beginning or end to this cyclical movement. However, the sequence holds as a general guide, though variations will occur in different walks.

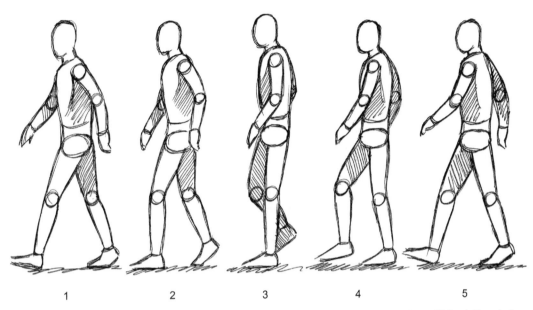

| 1 | 2 | 3 | 4 | 5 |

FIG 5.31 Walk cycle; Phases 1–5.

Phase One: The Stride

- The left leg is thrown forward, the knee is straight, and the foot has just made contact with the ground.
- The right leg extends backward behind the body, the knee is straightened, and there is a bend in the foot as it remains in contact with the ground.
- The right arm is in a forward position, with a slight bend in the elbow and the forearm held in front of the body. The right shoulder is rotated forward.
- The left arm is extended in a backward position prior to its movement forward. There is a slight bend at the elbow and at the wrist. The left shoulder is rotated to a backward position.
- The body is at the lowest point in the cycle. The angle between the legs is at its widest, which places the hips at their closest position to the ground.

Phase Two: Squash

- The left leg moves into a more upright position and begins to take the weight of the body, the foot is flat on the ground, and there is a slight bend at the knee.
- The right leg is now lifted from the ground. There is a slight bend at the knee that ensures the foot clears the ground as the leg begins to swing forward.
- The right arm begins to move backward as the right shoulder rotates backward. The arm is held in front of the body and has a bend at the elbow.

221

- The left arm begins to move forward as the shoulder rotates. The bend at the elbow and wrist remain. There is slight drag on the hand.
- The body remains upright.

Phase Three: The Passing Position

- The left leg now takes the entire weight of the body. It is straightened at the knee and held in a completely upright position directly below the torso.
- The right leg has swung forward to its position alongside the supporting left leg. The knee bends increasingly to ensure that the foot clears the ground.
- The right arm continues to swing backward; the elbow remains slightly bent, with the forearm extending in front of the upper arm.
- The left arm moves forward and is now positioned alongside the body. The elbow remains bent and the hand is located directly below the shoulder.
- The body, head, and hips have risen to their highest positions in the walk cycle. The supporting leg and the torso are vertically aligned.

Phase Four: Stretch

- The left leg now begins to extend backward and is positioned slightly behind the body; the knee remains straightened.
- The right leg swings forward. A bend in the knee means that the lower leg moves ahead of the upper leg in anticipation of the foot contacting the ground.
- The right arm moves backward, with the elbow and forearm extending behind the body. The right shoulder rotates backward.
- The left arm continues to swing forward ahead of the shoulder, which also rotates to a forward position. The bend in the elbow increases slightly.
- The body begins to fall forward from its highest position in the cycle.

Phase Five: The Stride

- The right leg is thrown completely forward; the foot has just made contact with the ground and the knee has straightened.
- The left leg is extended backward behind the body and there is a bend in the foot as it prepares to be lifted from the ground. The knee is straightened.
- The left arm is now in a forward position, with the forearm held in front of the body, a slight bend in the elbow, and the left shoulder rotated forward.
- The right arm is extended backward prior to it moving forward. There is a slight bend at the elbow and wrist. The right shoulder is rotated backward.
- The body once again reaches the lowest point in the cycle, with the angle between the legs placing the hips closer to the ground.

It is important to realize that the sequence described here makes up only half of a complete walk cycle. The second half simply reflects the first, with the opposite limbs undertaking the same actions with the same timings.

If we now consider the timing of the walk, we can see how acceleration and deceleration during certain phases work together to create the whole dynamic. The speeds of the two strides, both left and right, are the same in a normal walk. The timing of the right and left actions may vary and become uneven when a figure walks with a limp or when one side of the figure is constricted in some way or is carrying a heavy load on one side.

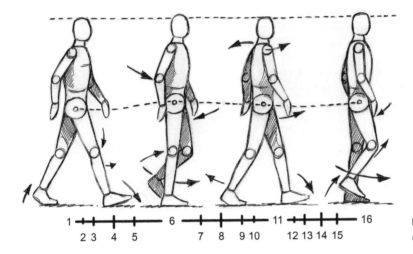

1 2 3 4 5 6 7 8 9 10 11 12 13 14 15 16

FIG 5.32 Basic timing of a walk cycle. 1, 6, 11, and 16 represent keys.

I have lost count of the times young undergraduate animation students have asked me how many frames there are in a walk cycle. This usually happens when they first attempt to animate a human walking. I can understand why they would ask this question as they search for an easy answer to what appears to be a straightforward problem. Unfortunately, there are a number of other texts that state quite clearly a prescribed number of frames for the action. This does little except make for preconceptions and muddy the waters. The truth is that the problem is far from straightforward and the timing of a walk cycle will vary greatly depending on a number of circumstances, many of which we have touched on. The walker's physicality, age, and health; the surface on which she is walking; even the shoes she is wearing may have an effect on the timing of the action as well as the nature of the gait.

It bears repeating that it is both the length of the stride and the frequency with which the steps are taken that determines the speed of a walk.

As the figure goes through the walk cycle, the body rises and falls throughout the action. When the figure reaches the passing position, notice that the head is at its highest point in the cycle. As with the speed of the walk, the degree to which the figure rises and falls is determined by the stride length, but the degree to which the legs are bent at the knees also determines the dip in action. The greater the bend, the bigger the dip is. There are very few examples when a walking figure presents a much flatter action.

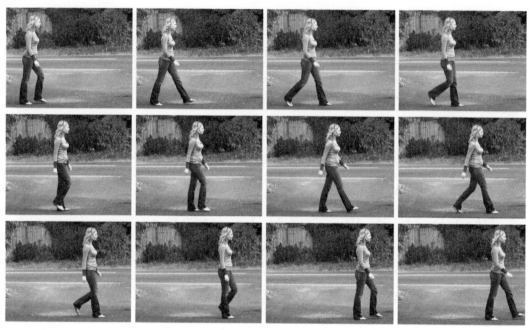

FIG 5.33 Young woman walk sequence on a flat surface.

FIG 5.34 Young man walking up a slope.

The energy cost to a body is less when it's walking downhill than when it's walking on a level surface. As you would expect, the energy cost becomes even greater when we walk up a slope or up steps than when we walk on a flat surface. The gait of a moving figure changes with the angle of the surface the figure walks on. While we're walking up a slope, our stride length may shorten slightly but remain quite wide, though this width shortens as the slope becomes steeper. The body is thrown forward slightly, and once again the inclined angle of the body increases as the angle of the slope increases.

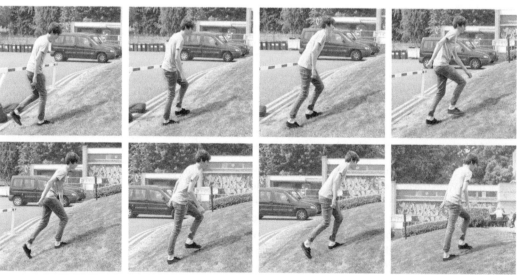

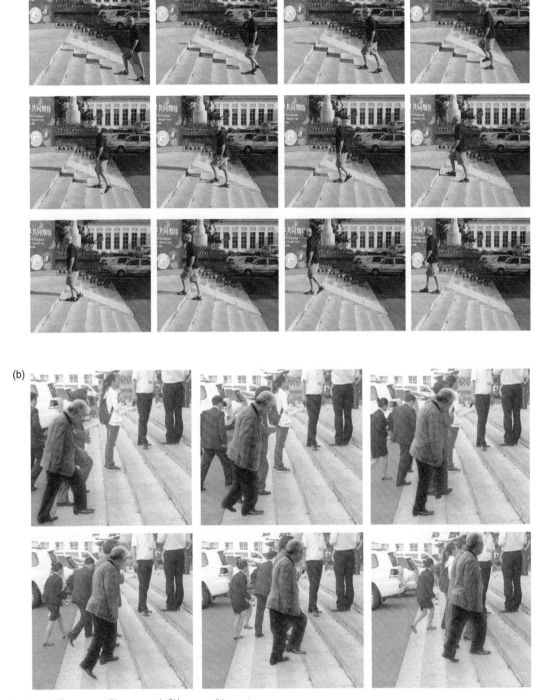

FIG 5.35 a: Young man walking up steps. b: Older man walking up steps.

When the angle of the slope becomes very steep, the walking gait is replaced by a scrambling gait. At this point the hands may be extended forward to be placed on the ground and so provide a little support and assist in achieving stability and balance. Naturally, as the angle of the slope increases, the effort needed to climb the slope also increases.

When a person is walking down a slope or down steps, the body remains in a more upright position and the stride length reduces considerably from that

FIG 5.36 Young man walking down a slope.

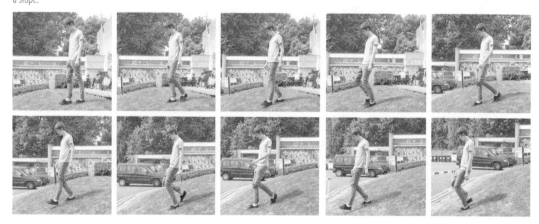

FIG 5.37 Young man walking down steps.

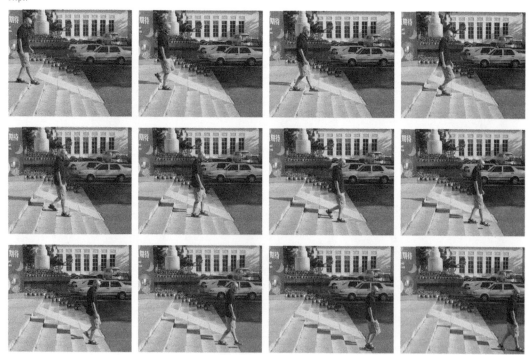

of walking on a flat surface. The figure may then change the angle of descent, scrambling downward with a sideways action and no longer placing the feet down in a forward position but placing them on the ground at an angle to the slope, to gain more purchase. Alternatively, the figure may extend the hands backward, placing the hands on the surface of the slope for support while bending the knees and perhaps even placing the rear end on the slope in a semi-sitting posture. Of course, once the slope becomes so steep that even this action becomes difficult, the figure will turn to face the slope and begin to climb downward. This progression provides us with a very good example of how the nature of a gait can change throughout an action to achieve a more effective and energy-efficient motion.

Walking might not simply be a matter of a person or animal traveling from point A to point B in the most efficient manner possible, but for the most part that's exactly what it is. Given that the action—the moving of legs backward and forward—is the same, it may be a surprise to see that the variations in that action can be huge. A person with very short legs will have a very different walk than someone with very long, thin legs. A person's height and weight will also determine the nature of the walk.

Walking while carrying a load will also affect the nature of a walk, depending on the size, weight, and shape of the load. A heavy load carried on a figure's back may throw the body forward; a heavy load carried in the arms and positioned at the front of the body may result in the body tilting backward. A figure carrying a heavy load on one shoulder will result in a lateral realignment of the body along the coronal plane to ensure that balance is maintained.

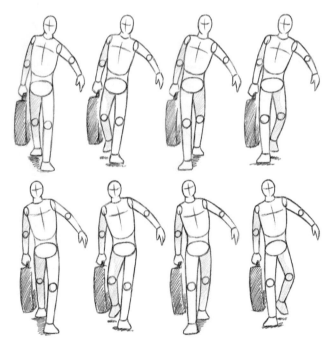

FIG 5.38 Walking carrying a load.

What is very evident here is that although arms may provide additional secondary action that assists a regular walk, walking is not dependent on the action of a person's arms. This is clearly shown in our example.

A Child Walk

The development of a child's walking skills covers an extended period beginning around 6 months, when a baby is able to roll over onto its belly and sit up unaided. Around 9 months the baby is able to crawl. Between 9 months and 1 year she is able to stand unsupported and may be taking a few tentative steps before falling down, usually with a bit of a bump on the behind. By 18 months children have begun to walk around, though at this stage they hold their feet wide apart to achieve a rather uncertain balance, giving the legs a bowed appearance. As the child gains more confidence and begins to master balance, this gap between the feet gradually diminishes with time until the feet move closer together and the legs are straightened. The manner of a young child's walk changes through these early years and remains rather distinct from that of an adult. Generally, it appears to be very much more awkward than an adult walk. Initially a child might hold out his hands sideways, away from his body, along the coronal or lateral plane as an aid to balance.

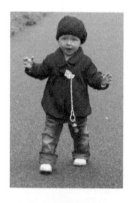 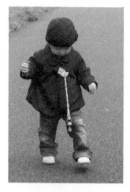 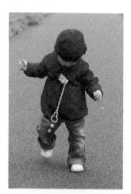

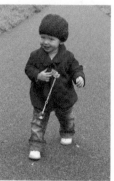 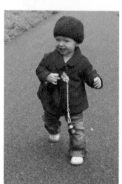 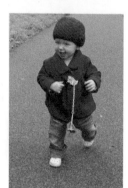

FIG 5.39 A child's walk action.

An Elderly Walk

The elderly often have issues with walking that are very similar to the issues young children face. They may experience difficulty with balance and often lack confidence. Frailty and ill health may affect an individual's strength, resulting in a much slower walk with a much shorter stride length and slower frequency of stride. The surface on which an elderly person walks becomes a far more important factor affecting the gait; any uneven or slippery surface can result in additional anxiety and therefore add to the cautious nature of the action. This uncertainty changes the gait, slows the walk, and further shortens the stride. The knees are often slightly bent, and the figure may increasingly be held in a hunched posture. The hands are often placed on any available firm surfaces to provide additional support and aid balance. The stride is

FIG 5.40 Elderly figures walking on flat, even ground.

(a)

(b)

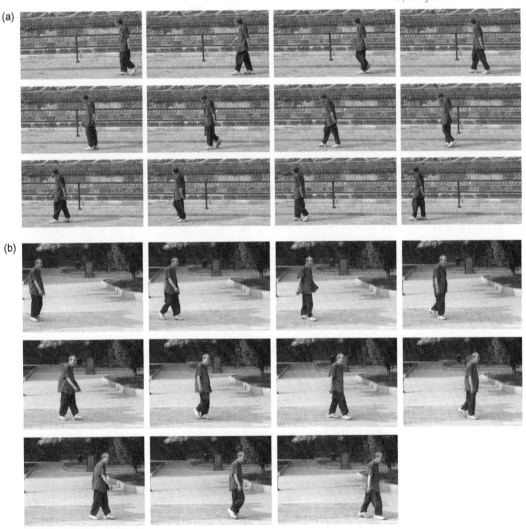

(c)

(d)

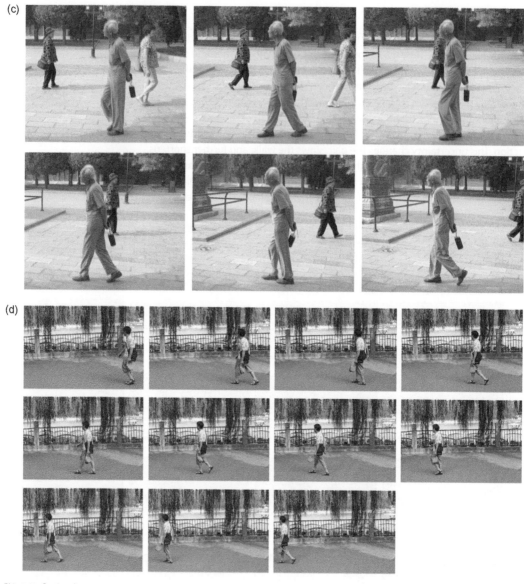

FIG 5.40 Continued

very short, and the steps may be slightly quicker than in younger adults, shortening the periods during which the body is supported by a single leg. Key to this action is the need to remain in a balanced state for longer periods throughout the sequence. In the very frail the feet are often barely lifted from the ground, resulting in a shuffling action.

Many old people gain benefit from the use of a walking stick or other aid to assist with balance and help with support when weaknesses in the legs make walking difficult.

230

A Heavy Walk

This example refers to individuals who are themselves heavier than average, not to individuals carrying additional weight in the form of objects. Naturally some of the effects may be similar in both cases.

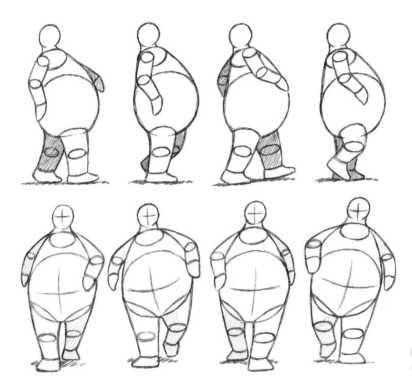

FIG 5.41 Side and front views of the walk cycle of a heavy figure.

As a result of excessive weight, an individual may begin to experience difficulties in mobility, which may increase with the increase in weight. The increase in body mass may also mean an increase in inertia, resulting in slower acceleration rates and lower top speeds during locomotion. Energy expenditure will also be greater.

As a result of the increase in body size, the position of the arms may be forced slightly away from the vertical and away from the body.

If the additional weight is located at the front of the figure, around the waist area, there may be a slight shift in the center of gravity, resulting in the individual beginning to lean slightly backward in an effort to counter the weight and maintain balance. Such a figure standing and walking may then be seen to have a backward lean, which, over time, may develop a slight curve in the spine. Such a posture is clearly evident in women during pregnancy, particularly during the later stages, when considerable additional weight is located at the front of the body.

Although the backward tilt is symptomatic of posture in heavier people, perhaps the most prominent aspect of a heavy walk is the increased sideways movement. This movement is generated at the hips, but it is at its most notable at the shoulders as the figure shifts its weight along the lateral or coronal plane to position itself over the center of gravity. The degree of shift is linked to the size of the figure. This lateral movement may be quite subtle or, in extreme cases—in bodies that are very heavy—it may be quite considerable.

Walking with a Limp

The walks we have considered so far are all fairly standard ones: an adult walk, a child's walk, the walks of the elderly and the overweight. They all have one thing in common: All are symmetrical actions. By contrast, a figure walking with a limp creates a distinctive gait and an asymmetrical walk cycle. However, the gait may vary a great deal, depending on the nature of the limp and the factors that determine the limp. A limp that is a result of a pain in one of the legs or the foot may vary in degree depending on the level of discomfort or

FIG 5.42 Limp: Walking with one leg impeded, side view.

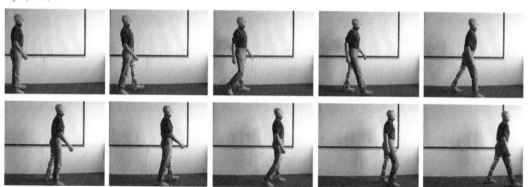

FIG 5.43 Limp: Walking with one leg impeded, side view.

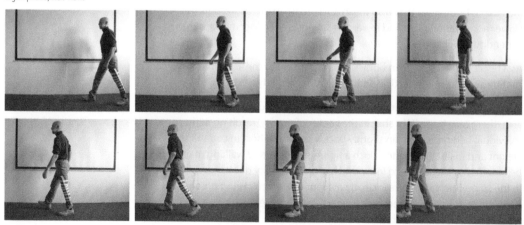

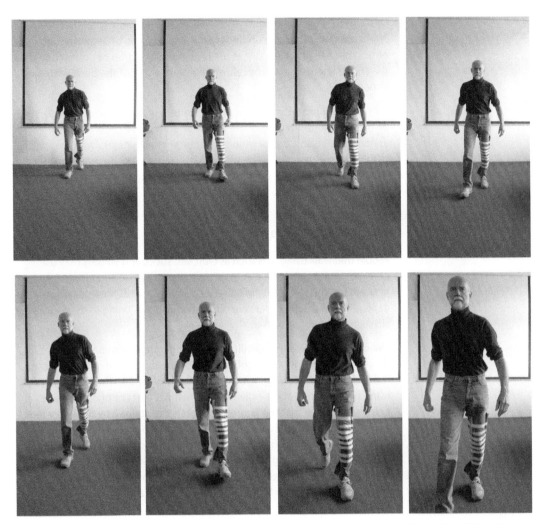

FIG 5.44 Limp: Walking with one leg impeded, front view.

pain experienced. The same or similar effect may be noticed if someone has a stone in her shoe or damage to one of the shoes results in an uneven gait.

If for example the movement of one of the legs is restricted or constrained in some way that prevents the leg from bending at the knee—say, due to a splint or plaster cast—the figure needs to find a way of moving the constricted leg past the supporting leg during the passing-position phase. This is normally achieved by the nonsupporting leg bending at the knee and swinging forward past the supporting leg, with both legs in close proximity to each other. To achieve the necessary action of the constrained leg moving from the backward to the forward position, it may become necessary to swing the leg sideways, away from the body, to ensure that the foot clears the ground. Alternatively, the heel of the supporting foot may be raised off the ground slightly so that the figure

233

can gain a little more height, which will allow the rigidly straightened leg to pass the other one unhindered. There may also be slight though noticeable lateral movement at the hips in the direction opposite to that of the constrained leg, thereby raising slightly the side of the body with the impeded leg.

In an unrestricted and regular walk, the pattern of spacing may be seen to be the same for both sides of the body throughout the cycle. During an asymmetrical gait, a distinct anomaly occurs in the dynamic, with the spacing of the figure varying from one side from the other. If both legs were restricted in a similar manner, a symmetrical albeit rather awkward action would once again be evident and no anomaly would appear.

Walking with an Aid

People that walk using aids such as crutches, sticks, and walkers may use other parts of their bodies to support or at least to aid in support during locomotion. This may result in either a symmetrical or asymmetrical action, depending on whether there are one or two crutches being used or a walking aid such as a geriatric walker.

The use of a single crutch results in an exaggerated asymmetrical movement with a good deal of lateral movement; the use of two crutches results in a forward swinging action of the entire figure. The walking action using two crutches may be divided into distinct parts or phases. In one phase we can see that the figure's support is maintained by the leg or legs while the crutches are swung to the forward position. During the following phase the figure's weight is transferred to the arms via the crutches before the legs are then swung together as a pair, meeting the ground at a position just forward of the crutches. Once the feet are firmly on the ground, the crutches are once more lifted and moved forward as part of the following phase.

FIG 5.45 Young man walking on crutches.

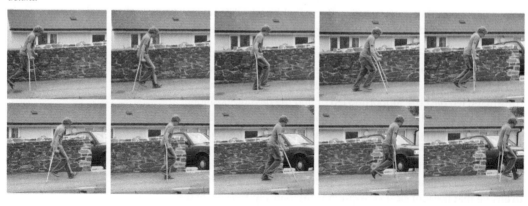

Walking with a walker is similar to the use of crutches in that it results in a noncontinuous action and, like the use of crutches, is executed in two separate and distinctive parts. Initially the walker is lifted or pushed to a forward position. At this point some of the figure's weight is taken by the upper body and arms, but more important, the frame affords the figure a more stable platform and offers increased balance, which enables the figure to walk to the forward position. The walk is then interrupted as the walker device is once again lifted or pushed to the forward position.

Discussing motions that are determined by factors other than an individual's physical aspects or tangible external elements that have an impact on movement leads us to the emotional and psychological factors that instigate and drive our actions. This takes us into a realm of study of the human condition, culture, society, and civilization. These are deep waters. Motivating factors underpin the fourth and highest aspect of the Four A's of Animation: acting. It is performance-based animation that makes up a major part of animation production today in commercials, TV series, shorts, and features. The study and analysis of action to create animated movements that may be considered performance-based animation are the work of a lifetime. This is a topic that deserves more in-depth study, but we can at least begin to take a look at how these emotional factors may influence some of our rather pedestrian and everyday actions.

A Happy Walk

It is evident that the way a figure walks will be determined by mood and emotion. It should not really be necessary to state, though I will, that obviously these states of being vary from individual to individual. Some people keep their emotions hidden and their effect may be difficult to detect; with other people it is only too apparent how they are feeling. How many times have you been able to assess the mood of a friend or a family member by their body language alone?

Let's consider for a moment the nature of a walk cycle that is influenced by happiness. Receiving good news or, for that matter, anything else that puts a person in a good mood and makes them happy may result in that individual walking in a way slightly different from their normal manner. They might move with more of a spring in their step; they might hold their body in a more upright position; the stride may be slightly wider and the walk may be a little quicker. There may be less evidence of a bend in the knee of the supporting leg during the passing position. There may even be evidence in the angle of head to the body; the chin may be held at a more upward angle and stick out a little more. These signs may be very slight and could vary only marginally from a standard walk, but they could be enough to identify the walk as a "happy" one.

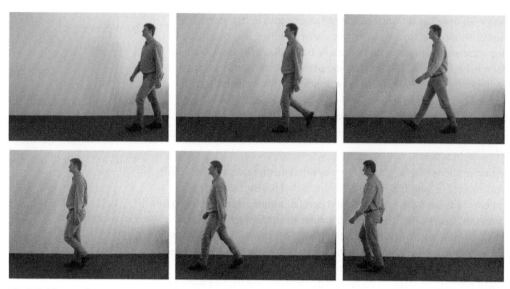

FIG **5.46** A happy walk.

A Sad Walk

The flip side of the coin may be seen in a walk as a result of unhappiness or sadness. The same holds true for this walk in the way emotions are expressed, which may be more or less evident depending on the individual.

FIG **5.47** Sad walks.

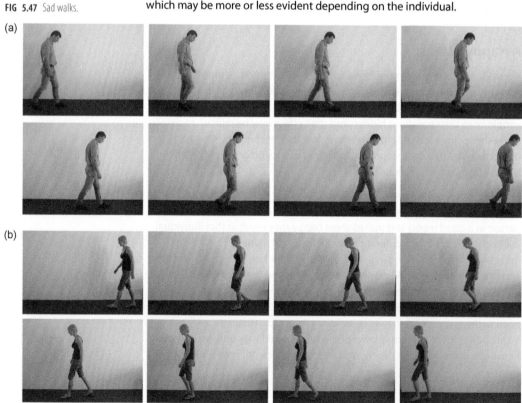

(a)

(b)

A walk that is instigated by sadness may be slightly slower than a standard walk. The stride may shorten, in some instances a great deal. The speed at which the steps are taken will be reduced and there may be a degree more bend at the knees. The figure may be held in a less upright position, with a slight slouching posture, and the head may be held slightly downward. The arms may also demonstrate far less of a swinging action, and there may even be a tendency to walk with hands in pockets. In some extreme cases this type of "sad" walk may result in a shuffling type of gait.

Running

Running is a gait that is undertaken once walking is no longer an effective or efficient mode of locomotion and can no longer provide the required speed of motion. A running gait has similarities with the walk cycle, sharing some of the distinctive phases and, in the same manner as a walk cycle, a running action can be broken into separate phases for ease of analysis.

Although the run cycle includes the passing position, the stride is replaced by a phase that distinguishes the running gait from a walk cycle. This is the *suspended phase*. This phase is the point in the run cycle at which the figure has both feet off the ground and is no longer supported by either foot making contact with the ground. The walk cycle is classified as having at any given point within the action at least one of the feet making contact with the ground. Once both feet are no longer in contact with the ground and the figure is in a state of suspension, the gait is classified as a run.

In addition to the passing position and the suspension phases, I include four other phases in the run cycle, breaking down the action into six distinctive parts in total. These are:

- The push
- The suspended phase
- First contact
- Squash
- The passing position
- The extending phase

The role the arms play in the run remains a secondary action to what they do in a walking gait, though the contribution they make to locomotion is perhaps considerably greater in a running action. This is most evident in sprinters, particularly during that period when they first leave the starting blocks. Movement in the arms is far less extreme during a prolonged running action or a jogging action. The arm action makes a contribution to the overall action, but it is perfectly possible to run while keeping the arms at one's side, though it is rather unnatural. The use of the arms in a run may vary throughout the action and, as already been mentioned, sprinters that accelerate quickly at the beginning of a run demonstrate a greater degree of motion in the arms than they do once they are into their stride.

The rising and falling of a figure during a running action is much more pronounced than in a walk cycle. The rise during the suspension phase is higher, and the squash results in more compression of the leg due to a bend at the knee, locating the figure slightly lower than in a walk.

As with the walk cycle, the nature of the run determines the speed at which the figure is moving. Furthermore, as with the walk cycle, the speed of the run will change with the varying length and frequency of the strides.

To aid our analysis of a running action, I have broken the movement into the key points in the cycle. For our purposes I have limited the keyframes in the illustration to four, though in the phased sequence that follows, where I provide a detailed written description of the actions at the various points of the cycle, I have included two additional phases.

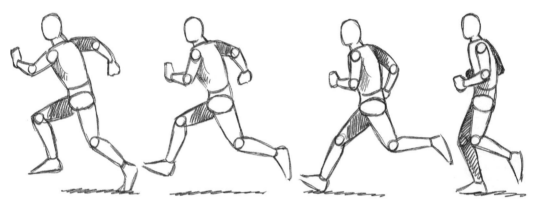

FIG 5.48 Four key positions of a run cycle.

As with the walk cycle, the phase order I present here has no distinct beginning or end. I have started the sequence in the most obvious place (at least it is the most obvious to me): at the moment just before the figure strides forward and both feet leave the ground.

This sequence provides a general guide for a run cycle, but it is clear that many variations will occur in different instances and for different types of figures.

Phase One: The Push
- The left leg is extended fully backward, the knee straightened and the toes pushing against the ground, providing maximum thrust.
- The right leg has swung forward and is bent, allowing the foot to clear the ground. The knee extends forward of the rest of the leg.

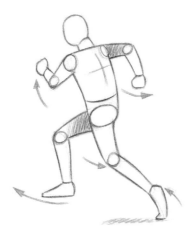

FIG 5.49 The Run Cycle: Phase one, the push.

- The left arm is thrust forward and bent at the elbow. The forearm is held in front of the body around the horizontal.
- The right arm is extended backward and heavily flexed. The upper arm is at the horizontal, with the lower arm being held vertical and at a right angle.
- The body is bent slightly forward of the upright. A rotation in the torso allows for the left shoulder and the right hip to be placed in a forward position.

Phase Two: The Suspension Phase

- The left leg remains extended backward; a bend in the knee occurs at this point because the foot has left the ground.
- The right leg is extended fully forward and begins to straighten for maximum reach in anticipation of the right foot making contact with the ground.
- The left arm remains held in front of the body; rotation in the shoulder begins to move the upper arm backward to a vertical position.
- The right arm begins to swing forward due to a rotation at the shoulder. The angle between forearm and upper arm remains the same.

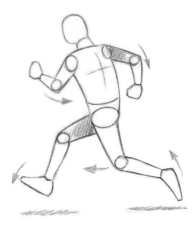

FIG 5.50 The Run Cycle: Phase two, the suspension phase.

239

- The body is unsupported by the ground at this stage of the cycle and has risen to the highest point within the sequence.

Phase Three: First Contact
- The left leg swings forward more quickly; the lower leg increases the flexion action while the knee moves forward to a point just behind the body.
- The right leg is angled less acutely away from the body. The knee is more or less straightened and the left foot makes contact with the ground.
- The left arm continues to moves backward, with the elbow and forearm swinging away from the body to allow it to pass the torso.
- The right arm has been rotated at the shoulder, so the hand is alongside the body, though the angle between upper arm and lower arm remains the same.
- The body has fallen from its high point and is once again supported by the single leg. Counterrotation of both the hips and the shoulders now occurs.

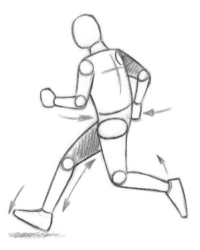

FIG 5.51 The Run Cycle: Phase three, first contact.

Phase Four: Squash
- The left leg has swung to a position whereby the knee is located directly below the body. The lower leg is flexed to the maximum at this point.
- The right leg absorbs the force of the impact with the ground by flexing at the knee. The foot is flat on the ground and directly below the body.
- The left arm is held next to the body. There is an increase in flexion between the upper and lower arms, with the elbow appearing just behind the body.
- The right arm continues to swing to a forward position. The hand is located alongside the hip.
- The body is now supported by a foot directly below the torso. It has reached its lowest point in the cycle as the impact of the contact is absorbed.

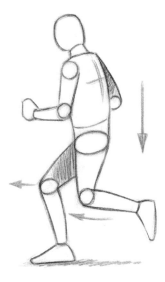

FIG 5.52 The Run Cycle: Phase four, squash.

Phase Five: The Passing Position

- The left leg continues to swing forward, with the knee being located slightly ahead of the body. The knee remains bent and the foot clears the ground.
- The right leg begins to straighten and thrust backward, providing kinetic power for the run. The foot remains flat on the ground.
- The left arm now begins to extend backward, with the elbow clearing the line of the body. The upper and lower arms straighten slightly.
- The right arm begins to swing around the body, with the hand held in front of the torso.
- The body now begins to move upward from the lowest point in the cycle. The hips and shoulders continue to rotate.

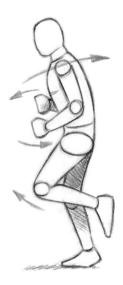

FIG 5.53 The Run Cycle: Phase five, the passing position.

Phase Six: The Extending Phase

- The left leg swings forward, the knee rises, and the lower leg moves to a more vertical position, with the foot clearing the ground.
- The right leg continues to move backward, providing thrust as the foot flexes, with the heel rising and the ball of the foot remaining on the ground.
- The left arm swings backward, the upper arm moving toward the horizontal and the forearm moving toward a more vertical position.
- The right forearm continues to flex while the hand moves a little higher and across the front of the body.
- The body continues to rise. The hips and shoulders rotate, with the left shoulder and right hip facing backward, the right shoulder and hip facing forward.

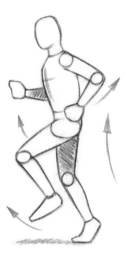

FIG 5.54 The Run Cycle: Phase six, the extending phase.

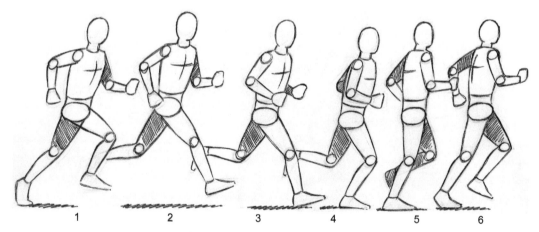

1   2   3   4   5   6

FIG 5.55 The Run Cycle: The Push, the suspended phase, first contact, squash, passing position, and the extending phase; sagittal plane (side view).

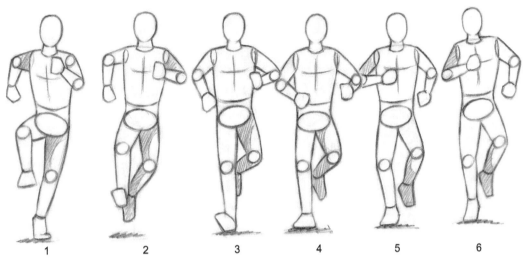

1   2   3   4   5   6

FIG 5.56 The Run Cycle: The push, the suspension phase, first contact, squash, the passing position, and the extending phase; coronal plane (front view).

Timing a Run

Animators timing a run cycle face the same difficulties as with the walk cycle: There is no quick fix and no formula that can be readily applied. However, there are a few principles that may be useful and could help the animator achieve the desired results. Leaving aside such issues as the differences between naturalistic motion and believability and other more abstract and cartoon-based action, we find many cases in a number of texts that provide examples of the cartoon run. I have concentrated here on action analysis and limited my examples to more naturalistic actions.

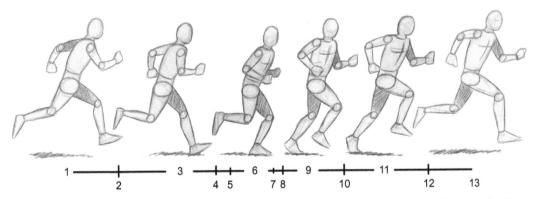

1 ———┼——— 3 —┼—┼— 6 —┼┼— 9 ———┼——— 11 ———┼———
        2   4   5   7 8   10   12   13

FIG 5.57 Human run cycle with an indication of the timing from one suspended phase to the opposite one.

There are almost as many types of run cycles as there are figures that run. The examples here represent only a very limited sample and are simply intended to cover the basic principles. The same issues around age, size, and environment that apply to the walk cycle also apply in this case.

Sprinting

Athletes running a race do not run in the same fashion as a middle-aged man running to catch a bus or a child running with a kite. There are even variations in the ways in which athletes run, and a sprinter has a very different gait from that of someone running a marathon.

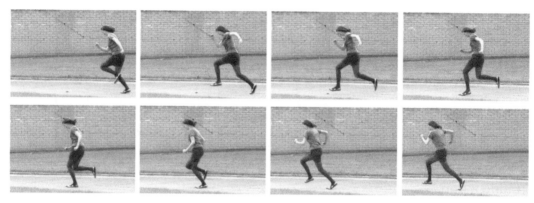

FIG 5.58 Young woman sprinting.

FIG 5.59 Sprint sequence from start position through to steady running position.

In our sprinting example we can see how the runner's action changes from leaving the starting blocks to getting into his regular running stride. You will notice how the angle of the body moves from around 45 degrees to an upright position. The forward tilt of the body during the initial thrust allows more power to be transmitted through the legs to the starting blocks.

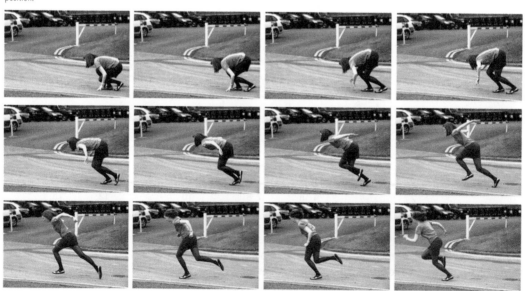

Steady Runs

An adult who is not running as part of some sporting or athletic activity may do so in a very different manner from what we see while watching athletes work out on the track. For most of the adult population, running at speed is something that we do only very occasionally. Therefore the run that is determined by lower stamina and poor technique will probably result in shorter run durations with top speeds much reduced. When athletes run they often make contact with the ground using the ball of the foot, whereas most ordinary people, when running, make contact with the ground using the heel of the foot first before the foot flattens.

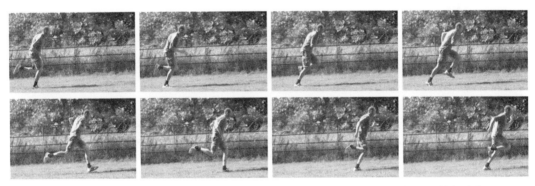

FIG 5.60 Adult male fast run sequence.

An adult running at a much steadier speed may be capable of running for longer durations. The stride length will be noticeably shorter and the frequency of stride slower.

Jogging

The dynamics of a jogging action share many similarities with a regular running action. As you may expect, the overall principles are the same for both. The jog has a suspension phase like the one in a running dynamic. As we have already discussed, it is the inclusion of a suspension phase that differentiates both the run and the jog from a walking action.

There are differences between a run and a jog, though these may be rather subtle and one of degree rather than a clearly defined differentiation, as between a walk and a run. Likewise, the transition between a jogging action and a running action may not be as clear-cut as the transition between a walk and a run or a walk and a jogging action.

In very general terms, the jog action is a much slower action than the run. As we have already seen, the arm action in these forms of locomotion may be considered a secondary action. That is, the arms contribute to the action

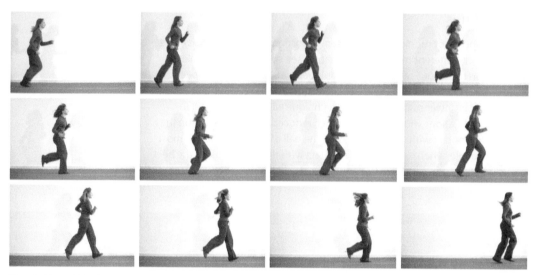

FIG 5.61 Young girl jogging sequence.

and make for more efficient motion, but they do not directly *enable* the action. In a running action the backward and forward swinging action of the arms, synchronized with the movement of the legs, makes a considerable contribution to the effectiveness of the action that is particularly noticeable at very high speeds. There is clear evidence of the contrary action of arms and legs in all running actions, regardless of speed; when the right leg is in the forward position, the right arm is in the backward position; likewise, when the left leg is in the forward position, the left arm is in the backward position. These arm movements become less extreme and not such a great contributing factor at lower speeds, as evidenced by the different actions of a sprinter and a marathon runner.

The movement of the arms during a jogging action is often even more subdued than the action in a sustained run at moderate speeds, such as that of a long distance runner. During a jogging action, arms are generally held quite rigidly, bent at the elbow with the forearms held at the horizontal. The swinging action of the arms tends to rise far less, the forearms being brought across and in front of the torso and the hand seldom rising to a much higher level than halfway up the chest. By comparison, with the action of a sprinter off the blocks, the arms are often raised so high that the hand is brought up to the level of the head.

The stride in a jogging action is often much shorter than in a running action. The legs are lifted a good deal less during the passing position than within the run. There is a much shorter frequency of stride length in a jog than in a run. This, coupled with the far smaller difference in height achieved during the suspended phase, gives the waveform created by a jogging dynamic a much spikier appearance than a regular run. When athletes are running at high speeds, their feet tend to make contact with the ground on the ball of the foot. At lower speeds, such as during jogging, the foot's contact with the ground often seems to be much flatter, with the heel more normally making first contact before the foot flattens onto the floor.

Child Running

When looking and analyzing any figure undertaking any action, we are presented with many difficulties, since by necessity these actions are the result of huge variations in physiognomies and other additional factors. As such we are forced to deal in generalities. The actions of children present us with similar problems; in addition, these actions may vary widely during their developmental stages.

The run action largely depends on the child's age. The running action of a very young child around 2 years old will be very different from a child just a few years older, which will be different again from a child in her teens.

FIG 5.62 Young boy fast run sequence.

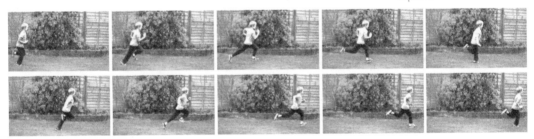

Very young children naturally display rather more uncertain and somewhat awkward gaits. This is largely due to their inexperience, a lack of coordination, and a lack of confidence brought about by uncertain balance. The run itself often has rather shorter strides than a more adult action, with the increase in speed from a walk to a run achieved by the frequency rather than the length of the stride. There is still a suspension phase, though it is very short. The compression action as a result of the bending of the knee once the leading foot makes contact with the ground is far less noticeable in young children. The result is a far more bouncy and rather jerky action than can be found in older children and adults. At this stage the arms will not provide a systematic secondary action that contributes toward the workload of locomotion. Instead they are likely to be held sideways out from the body to provide additional balance. Remaining upright is as much an effort as is actual forward motion; to this end the body is often held in a rigidly upright position with the arms occasionally held in a slightly forward position and the hands held wide open, as if in anticipation of a tumble.

As the child becomes more confident, he uses his arms less and less to maintain balance. The action of the arms begins to synchronize with the action of the legs similarly to what occurs in an adult action.

Lifting

Lifting actions vary a great deal, depending on the object being lifted and the individual or groups involved in the lifting. The required effort and the techniques used for lifting are so varied that it would be difficult to cover all the possible permutations. Even with very similar actions the variations are likely to be considerable. Lifting a cup of coffee for an able-bodied adult is a very different prospect from that of a small child lifting a cup of milk. In very general terms, lifting heavy weights may demand rather more effort than lifting light weights. However, the nature of the object may also have a major impact on the nature of the lift. Very large though rather light objects may require a very distinctive action. Fragile or very delicate objects may also require a different technique. To lift certain objects, it may be necessary for the action to be undertaken by two or more people. In such cases the effort is shared and the actions of the individuals synchronized to affect a lift.

These lifting actions may vary, but they can share distinct phases in the overall dynamic which, if studied, may prove useful for analysis. These phases are more distinct in the lifting actions that entail heavy or awkward weights that require a shifting dynamic throughout the action. The difference in the phases during the lifting of smaller and lighter objects may be far less distinct and give the appearance of a single-phase action.

Lifting a Heavy Weight

FIG 5.63 Sequence of lifting a heavy weight from the ground.

In this example we can see the actions of individuals lifting a heavy weight from the ground. The actions are so extreme that it is easy to identify the separate phases within the actions.

(a)

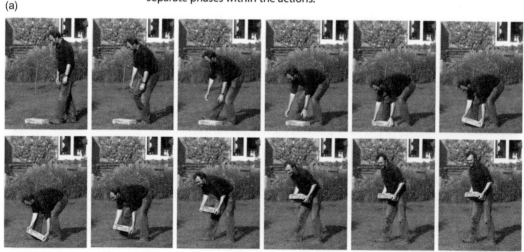

(b)

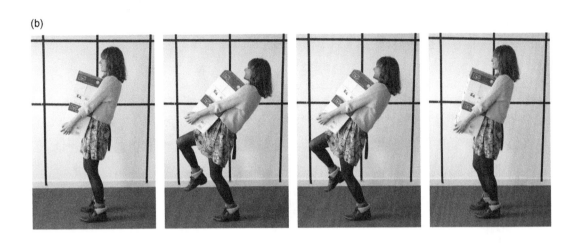

(c)

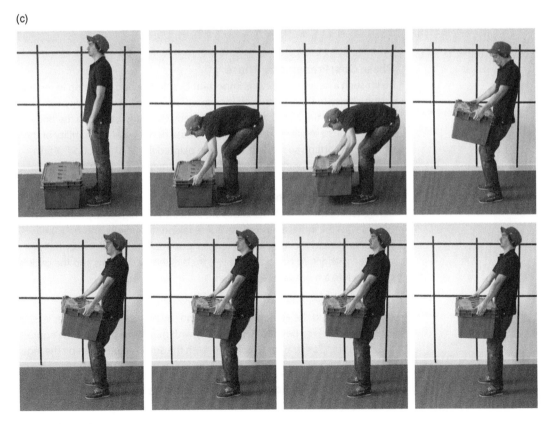

FIG 5.63 Continued

(d)

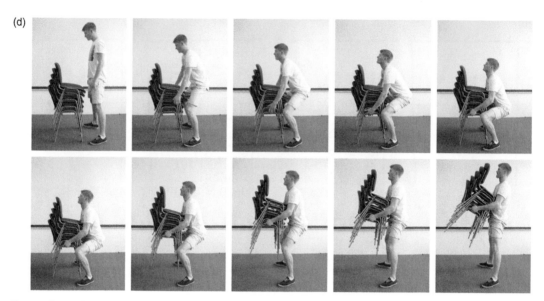

FIG 5.63 Continued

Phase One: Preparatory Phase

To lift such a heavy weight, it is important to shift the body position in relation to the object. In this example, that means placing the body directly over the weight to minimize the angle and thereby cause less stress on the body. Notice how the legs are spread apart to create better balance. Stability of the figure is important, so the feet should be planted flat on the ground. A firm grip is undertaken, with the arms being held straight.

Phase Two: Execution Phase

Before taking the weight, the knees are bent and the hips dropped. The lift begins with the initial action of the figure taking the weight. This may be a small backward movement of the torso, positioning the weight centrally between the feet. At this point the weight is taken by the arms and the back is oriented into a more vertical position.

The lift is then undertaken by the extension of the legs. The knees are straightened and the angle of the femur and the pelvic girdle becomes less acute. If the lift is to be executed properly with minimum strain on the figure, the back is held as straight as possible, with the strain being taken by the legs.

As the figure rises into a near vertical position, the arms may then come into play, lifting the weight to a higher position over the top of the pelvic girdle. This will place the object in a more central position, making balance more easily achievable.

Phase Three: Resulting Phase

As the figure rises into the upright position on completion of the lift, it moves into a position that achieves and maintains maximum balance and stability.

This may require a short step to widen the stance. Once the figure has lifted the weight, it can be seen that the figure is shifted in such a manner that it achieves greater stability around a center of gravity that takes into account both the figure and the object.

Lifting a Light Weight

When a figure undertakes the lifting of a light object, there is often less need to use the entire body as a counterweight and the action may be achieved with the use of arms alone. Because there may be less strain placed on the lower back, the angle of the torso can be held in a less upright position.

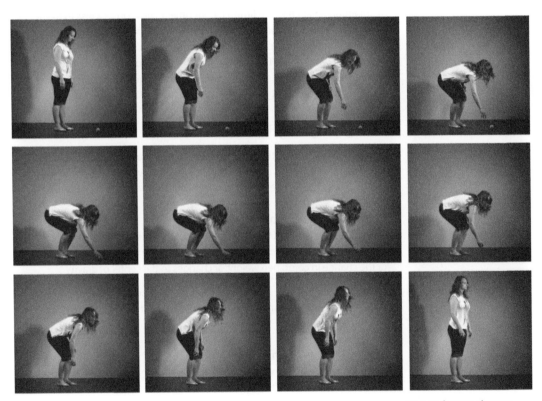

FIG 5.64 Sequence of a young woman lifting a light object from the ground.

Phase One: Preparatory Phase
Any shifting of the body's position in relation to the object may be undertaken not in preparation for taking on the additional weight or to avoid creating additional strain on the body during the lift but rather to simply gain a better hold on the object. Naturally this depends on the shape and size of the object. Moving in preparation just to take hold of an object is very different from a movement that is undertaken to take on large additional weights.

Phase Two: Execution Phase

Taking the weight off a light object may require no adjustment of the position of the figure or result in such a minor movement that any adjustment of the figure is barely perceptible. Picking up a large, light object that entails more movement of the arms may need less adjustment to the balance of the entire figure, since any slight shift of the center of gravity will probably remain within the figure itself. The act of lifting a light object is more likely to be executed with the use of the arms alone, which results in a bend at the elbow and wrist.

Phase Three: Resulting Phase

The attainment and maintenance of stability in a moving figure are common to all actions, though any movement required in achieving stability and maintaining balance when lifting a light object will require a less extreme adjustment of the posture. Any additional weight to be offset by such adjustment around the center of gravity will be less, and therefore the adjustment will be less. The resulting stage, so obvious in lifting a heavy object from the ground, which entails a separate and distinct action, may only be extended to a part of the figure such as the position of the arms and hands.

Lifting a Light Weight with One Hand

Lifting objects simply with the use of the hand, such as the action of lifting a cup, is naturally a far less dynamic action than one involving the use of the entire body. The separate phases of the action may not appear as distinct movements.

Phase One: Preparatory Phase

The preparation required for a less extreme lifting action does not usually entail the shifting of the figure or the alignment of the body to the object in preparation for the change in combined weight or changes to the center of gravity.

Using the hand alone to lift an object may simply require the alignment of the hand to the object and the opening of the hand to expose the palm and extend the fingers.

Phase Two: Execution Phase

The transition into the execution phase, gripping and holding the object and executing the lift, will often follow faster because less time will be needed to prepare for the action. The action of the lift may commence at a slower rate not due to the weight of the object but perhaps as a result of the need to maintain a balance of the object—in the case of lifting a cup of coffee, to avoid spilling a hot liquid. Adjusting the balance of the object throughout the lift may require a fine adjustment of the angle of the hand at the wrist to maintain stability and orientation of the object.

Phase Three: Resulting Phase

On completion of the action, there will be the same requirement to achieve stability, though it may not require a separate and distinct movement to maintain balance within the figure. Depending on the object being lifted, it may be necessary to adjust the orientation of the hand, wrist, and arm to maintain the equilibrium of the object itself.

Cooperation in Lifting Weight

When two or more people work together to lift a weight, the actions of the individuals conducting the lifting must be coordinated to achieve an effective and successful action. The timing of the separate phases of movement may be critical. Communication between the individuals may be an additional aspect that may result in slight pauses between each of the phases. This is perhaps most apparent between the preparatory and execution stages.

FIG 5.65 Cooperation in lifting a weight.

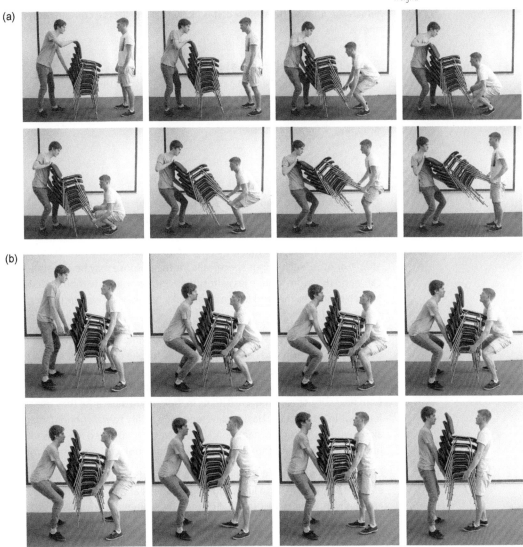

(a)

(b)

Phase One: Preparatory Phase

Shifting the body in part or in its entirety into a position relative to the object and taking hold of the object takes into account the position and grip of each member of the team.

Phase Two: Execution Phase

Taking the weight and adjusting the balance takes into account the position of the team and the support each member offers. The entire group must be seen as a whole at this stage when we're considering the center of gravity and the load supports. The lift itself may be synchronized or executed in a sequential manner, depending on the nature of the object, the need for equilibrium during the lift, or the ease with which the lift may be achieved. It is likely that the lift is a combination of these.

Phase Three: Resulting Phase

The load may be taken across a wide area, with each of the lifting team providing only one of the support points. The position and balance of each of the individual team members is reflected by the center of gravity of the entire grouping of figures and objects.

Carrying

The cost of carrying loads varies depending on the individual and the variables of the object. Once again, the nature of the object, its shape, its weight, its material, and its construction will determine the nature of the carrying action. Objects that are designed to be carried and have handles, straps, or other such things specifically for the purpose may be easier to carry and therefore require less effort than lighter objects without handles. In such examples the workload may actually be less than carrying lighter objects.

Carrying objects in the arms may be the most obvious way of moving an object, and our arms and hands have evolved to take on such tasks. Squirrels may use their front legs rather like arms to reach items such as fruit, nuts, and birds' eggs and use their hands and handle the objects, but they then resort, from necessity, to carrying small items in their mouths because they use all four legs in locomotion. Having developed the ability to walk upright, man, along with some of his distant primate relatives, has liberated the arms to undertake other tasks, carrying and manipulating objects being one of them.

Carrying objects either at the side or at the front of the body is often the most efficient way of carrying a load. Carrying an object at the front of the body enables both arms to be used to distribute the weight more evenly.

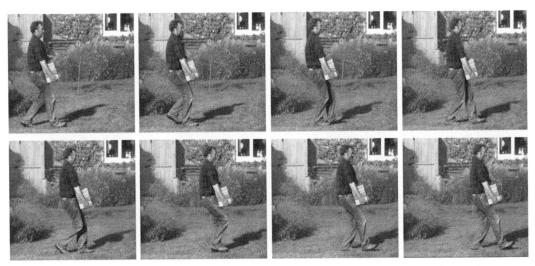

FIG 5.66 Sequence of a man carrying a heavy object.

Carrying loads on the back may enable greater loads to be carried, but in order to maintain stability during locomotion under such a load the figure is thrown forward slightly to place the weight into a more central position.

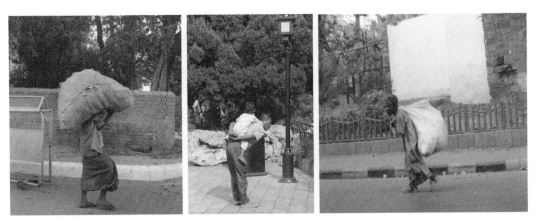

FIG 5.67 Figures carrying burdens on the back and head.

Asymmetrical loading on one side of the body may result in a compensatory shift in the body to maintain balance, which also creates a more efficient and less strenuous way of carrying the load. This may include carrying heavy weights on one shoulder or carrying a weight with one arm.

255

(a)

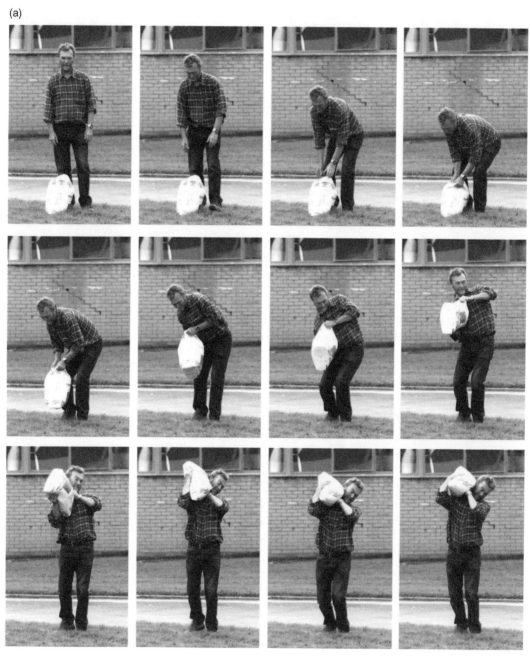

FIG 5.68 a and b: Lifting a weight onto the shoulder. c and d: Carrying a heavy load on the shoulder.

(b)

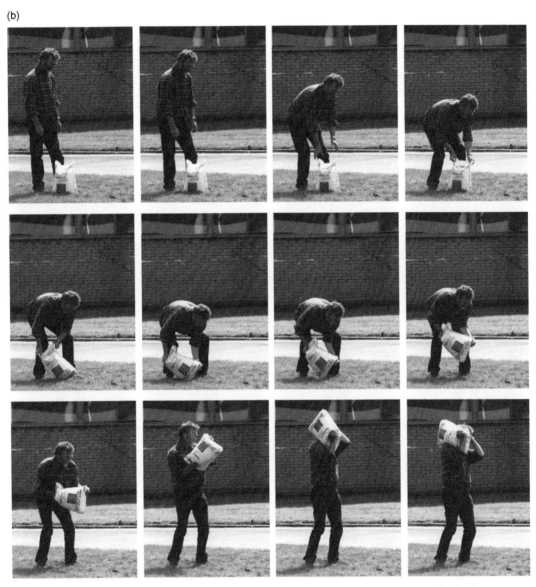

FIG 5.68 Continued

(c)

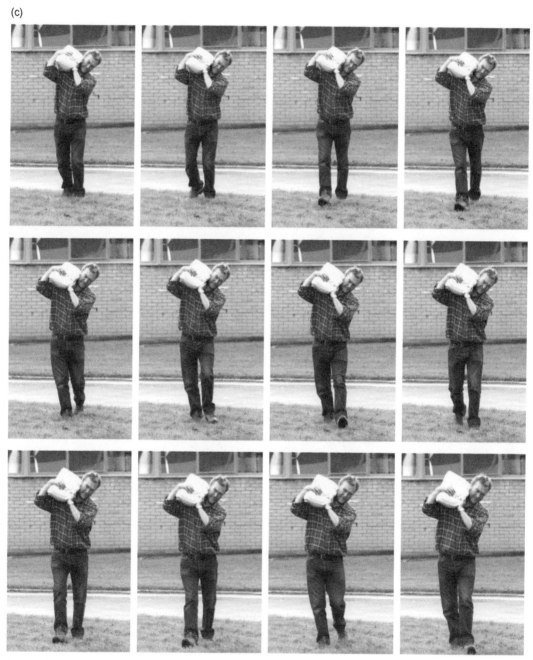

FIG 5.68 Continued

(d)

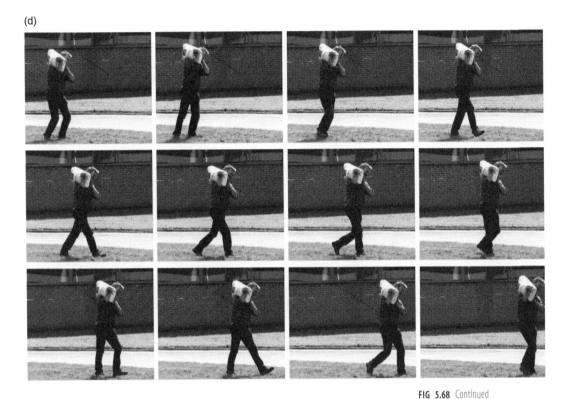

FIG 5.68 Continued

Carrying a heavier object using a single arm may allow the use of the shoulder muscles to take the stain. Carrying a weight using one arm only may also result in a lateral shift of the body in an effort to position the additional weight more centrally over the center of gravity. The arm that is not carrying the burden will often be held away from the body laterally to create a more even balance.

FIG 5.69 Carrying a heavy load with one arm.

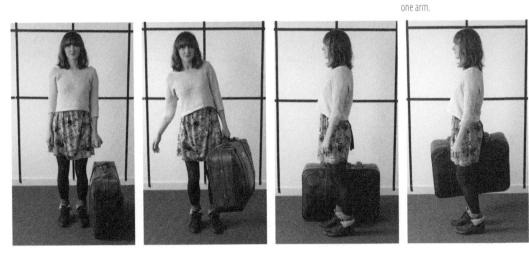

Pushing

As with many actions, the level of force required to complete an action, such as moving an object, determines the nature of the action. Generally speaking, the most efficient method using the minimum of effort applies for all actions.

Pushing a button may require only a very small movement that extends no further than the fingertip. A stronger push may involve the movement of the entire arm, incorporating movement at the wrist, elbow, and shoulder. Pushing an object that offers greater resistance may require the use of the entire body in a way that employs the weight of the body to apply additional force beyond that applied by the effort of the muscles. During this type of push the angle of the body may be positioned not directly above the feet, as in a normal standing or walking gait, but extended beyond the position of the feet in the direction of the object. In this fashion the weight of the body is used to provide the additional force.

Pushing a static object requires a degree of force to overcome the inertia made up of a combination of the object's mass and any friction between the object and the points of contact with any surface on which it sits or

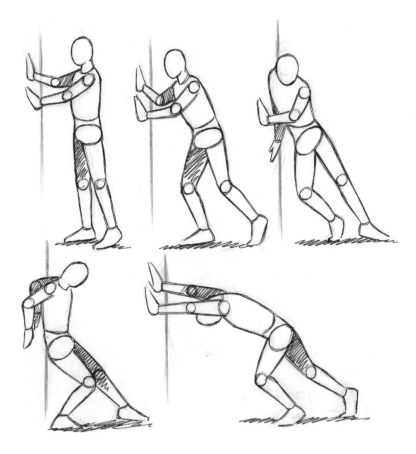

FIG 5.70 Various poses of a figure pushing a static object.

has contact. The more resistance there is at this point, the greater the force required to move the object. There will be a greater level of potential friction between an object sitting on a heavily textured or soft surface than one sitting on a hard, flat, and slippery surface such as ice. Attempting to push an object with a flat bottom may require more effort than pushing a heavier object that either has less friction or is designed to aid smoother movement, such as objects that possess runners, blades, or wheels.

Pushing a wheeled object such as a wheelbarrow requires far less force to overcome inertia and enables far greater loads to be shifted for the same degree of force. The wheel provides a lower level of friction between the

FIG 5.71 a: Man pushing a load on a hand trolley. b: Woman pushing wheelchair on flat even ground. c: Man walking backwards while steadying a wheelchair as it moves down a slope.

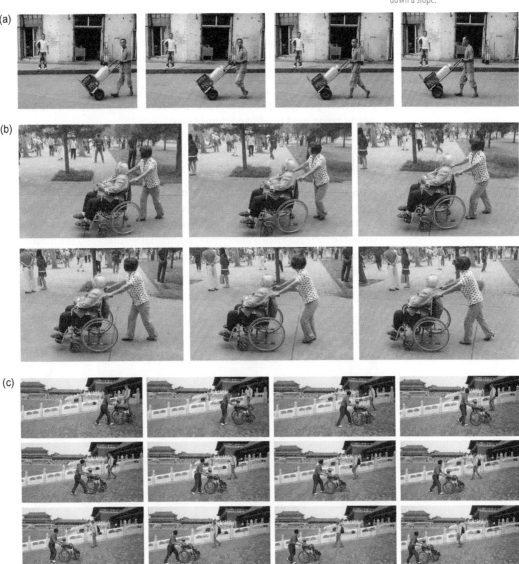

(a)

(b)

(c)

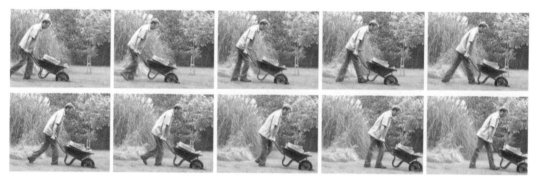

FIG 5.72 Sequence of a man pushing a wheelbarrow with heavy load.

object and the surface through the rolling action as opposed to a sliding action of two flat surfaces. Once inertia has been overcome, forward movement may be maintained by the steady application of force, created as continuous pressure is applied—in this instance, as the figure walks forward. If the weight is very heavy, the pushing figure will tilt forward from the upright position to gain greater purchase with the feet on the ground and the body weight being used to add additional force.

Pulling

Many of the same issues that are evident in a pushing action may also be seen in a pulling action: the need to overcome the inertia of an object and the amount of friction between the object and surfaces and the use of body weight to increase force. Pulling may be undertaken simply by the movement of the fingers. Greater forces may be exerted simply using the hand with a movement at the wrist. Pulling an object by the use of rope, if not too heavy,

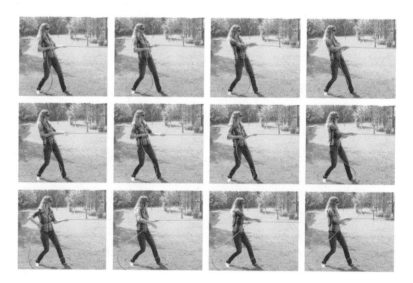

FIG 5.73 Pulling on a rope hand over hand.

may be undertaken by a hand-over-hand action that can only entail the use of the arms. This action entails each arm working in turn to pull on the rope toward the body, one arm pulling on the rope while at the same time the second arm extends forward to gain a grip on the rope in preparation for a subsequent pulling action.

Heavy objects may be moved through a pulling action using the body weight as part of the pull. This can be achieved by the figure facing the object while holding the rope and extending the body away from the object, thereby applying a force using the weight of the body.

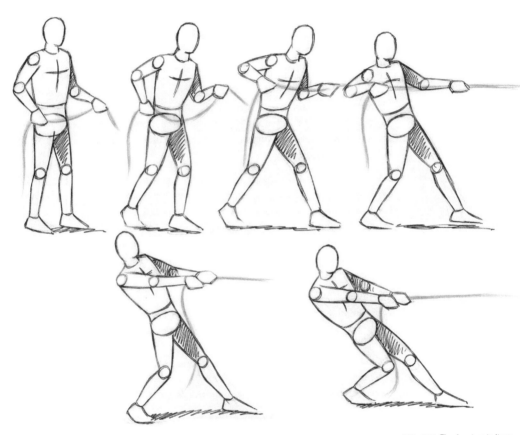

FIG 5.74 The drawings indicate how the weight of the figure is extended beyond the center of gravity using the weight being pulled as a counterbalance.

Alternatively, the body may be turned away from the object with the rope placed over the shoulder and the hands gripping the rope firmly placed close to the body before the figure commences to walk forward. This may entail the body being angled in a position forward of the feet. In this way greater purchase may be gained by the feet on the floor, thereby exerting greater force.

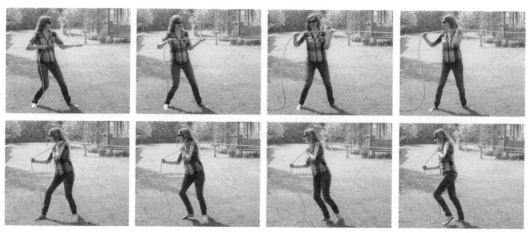

FIG 5.75 Pulling on a rope over the shoulder.

Throwing and Catching

Throwing an object over a distance with any degree of accuracy involves a combination of coordination, synchronized action, control to achieve accuracy, and power to successfully throw the object so that it reaches or penetrates a chosen target.

Using the classification of the objectives of motion, we will find that throwing an object uses balance, projection, a degree of manipulation, and a varying level of effort, depending on the distance required, the weight of the object, and the speed required. At its most basic level, a throwing action can be undertaken by most people, including very young children. However, it may also be a highly skilled activity involving accuracy, speed, and a very precise angle of trajectory.

Techniques for throwing depend largely on the object being thrown. A baseball is a very different object from a soccer ball, both of which are very different from a Frisbee or a javelin. Throwing overarm is a different action from throwing underarm or throwing with a flatter, more horizontal action. Even when the thrown objects are very similar, different throwing actions may be required. Throwing a javelin or a spear, ostensibly the same kind of object, will vary depending on the reason for the throw.

An Olympic athlete attempting to gain the greatest possible distance with a throw will use the entire body and include a run-up in the throw. Distance and not accuracy is the most important objective for such a throw. By comparison, a fisherman using a spear to catch fish will keep his body relatively static in space, with the power of the throw coming from the arms, shoulders, and rotation of the torso. In such a case, gaining maximum distance may not be a requirement, but accuracy to hit the target and power to penetrate the prey are. A dart player attempting to hit a very small and specific area of the dartboard requires far less force because the distance between the thrower and the board is a fixed one

(a)

(b)

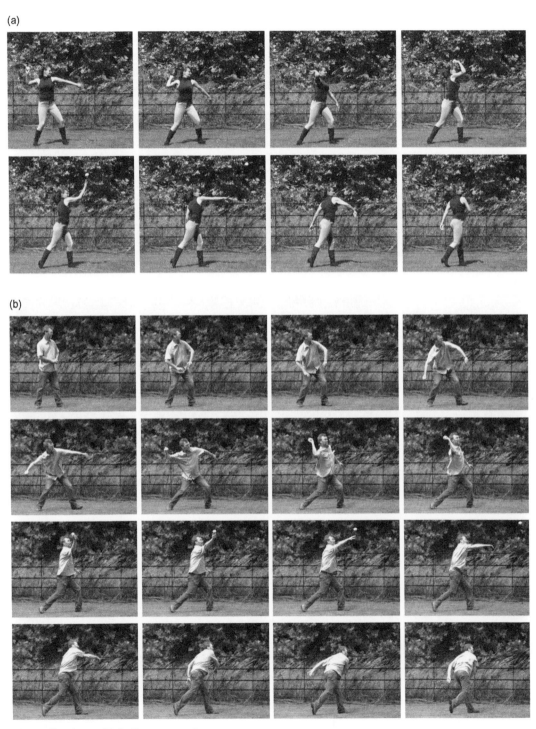

FIG 5.76 Throwing a small ball with an over arm action.

(a)

(b)

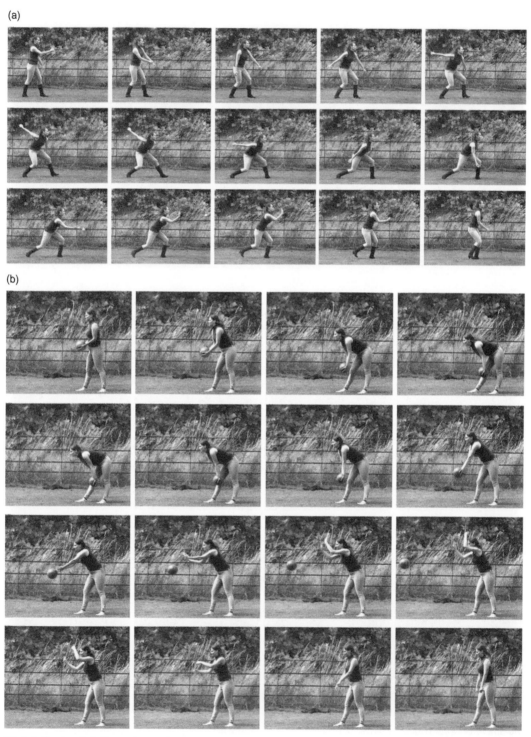

FIG 5.77 Throwing a ball with an underarm action.

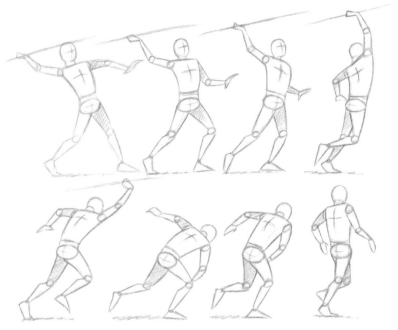

FIG 5.78 Sequence of throwing a javelin from a standing position.

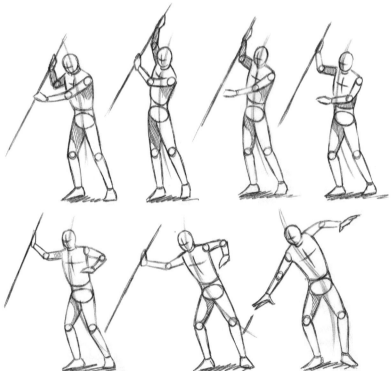

FIG 5.79 Figure throwing a spear with a downwards action.

and easily achievable. The force applied to the dart, though still a critical aspect of the throw, is not so great as to hit and penetrate a moving live prey. However, in this instance extreme accuracy is vitally important; the difference between success and failure is a matter of millimeters. It would seem to follow that, in throwing actions, power and speed are achieved at the expense of accuracy.

The separate phases of a throwing action are easily identified, as shown in the following example of an overarm throwing action.

Phase One: Preparatory Phase
- The figure begins with both legs side by side, holding a ball in one hand and facing in the direction in which the throw will be made.
- A step is taken backward into the anticipation position. This is achieved by the leg on the same side of the body as the arm that will throw the ball moving into a position backward of the body. The legs are now held apart, one in front of the other, with the body no longer facing squarely in the direction of the throw but angled slightly. The body is completely balanced at this point.
- The head continues to face in the direction of the throw, with eye contact being maintained on the target.
- The throwing arm is extended backward, with the ball held up around shoulder level. The nonthrowing arm may be held slightly away from the body and in the direction in which the throw will be made.

Phase Two: Execution Phase
- The second phase of the action generally begins with a movement at the ankles. At this point the entire figure begins to pivot forward.
- This is followed quickly by a forward movement of the legs. This action continues quickly with a dynamic action moving through the body upward to the hips, a rotation in the torso that generates momentum in the upper body. The throwing arm is still held in a backward position at this point.
- This action continues with the rotation of the shoulders that now coincides with the forward motion of the upper arm.
- The nonthrowing arm is held out from the body and rotates backward as a result of the twist at the shoulders.
- The whole of the upper body rotates and moves forward, with the weight of the body almost entirely being shifted onto the front foot while the nonthrowing arm, still held away from the body, swings backward.
- The throwing arm now quickly moves forward, with the forearm extending forward of the body.

Phase Three: Resulting Phase
- The throwing arm has now become fully extended, with the result that the ball is propelled forward from the hand at speed. Additional thrust is added by a rapid forward movement at the wrist while the fingers extend, resulting in the hand being held in an open position.

- Having released the ball, the throwing arm swings forward, downward, and across the body. The nonthrowing arm, held away from the body, swings to a backward position.
- The body continues to move forward, with the weight of the figure now being taken by the leading leg and the trailing leg lifted from the ground and swinging forward into a passing position.
- The upper torso is angled sharply downward, having completed a rapid forward movement that provided additional force to the throw via the shoulders.

Phase Four: Recovery Phase
- The figure continues to move forward and completes the striding action.
- The body straightens up and returns to an upright position. The throwing arm once again is moved across the body and returns to the side of the body.
- Both arms are held at the side and closer to the body.
- The figure regains a stable balanced state.

Catching an object may require a high degree of coordinated action. It certainly entails the catcher keeping his eyes firmly fixed on the object. This requires the head to face toward the object so that both eyes are able to fix on it. It is through our eyes' binocular vision that we are better able to assess spatial depth. To successfully intercept a moving object, hand/eye coordination is vital. To catch an object such as a ball on the move, the

FIG 5.80 Young woman catching a ball with a high trajectory.

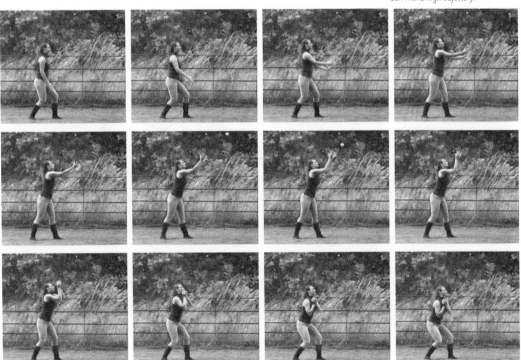

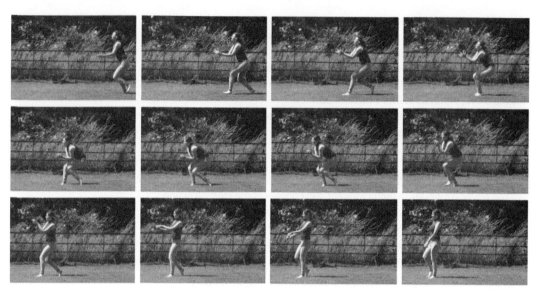

FIG 5.81 Young woman moving forward to catch a ball with a low trajectory.

FIG 5.82 Figure diving to make a catch.

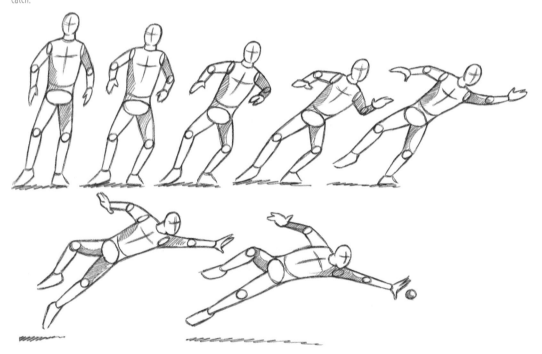

alignment of the body and the hands to the object is critical. In many sports it is often necessary to move to position the body, in some instances over great distances, to take the catch. It then becomes necessary to gauge the trajectory and speed of the ball to move into a convergent catching position. The actual catching of the object may be undertaken with either a single hand or both hands, depending on the nature of the object or the security required of the catch. Cricketers may often choose to take a two-handed catch even though a cricket ball will sit comfortably within one hand.

Maintaining balance throughout the catching action may be important for stability, though to achieve certain catches it is necessary to dive toward the ball, in which case the entire figure may be in motion and, at the moment of completing the catch, not at all in a balanced state.

Kicking

Kicking is a striking action that is undertaken with a foot. Although other examples of striking are covered a little in the text, it might be worth covering this specific action in a little more detail. Kicking, as with so many other actions, is determined by the nature and intention of the strike. Kicking an object such as a ball with the foot as part of a field sport such as football may involve a very different set of issues and require a different approach than, say, a kick intended to inflict a blow to an opponent as part of a martial arts activity.

FIG 5.83 Man kicking a ball.

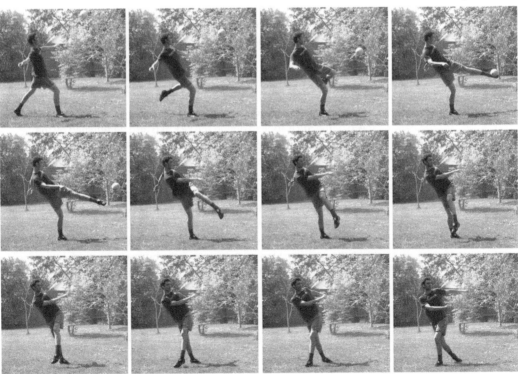

Kicking a ball to move it in a certain direction at a given speed and with the intention of the ball landing on a chosen target requires a high degree of control and accuracy. In addition, it may require speed and power if a great distance is to be covered. However, as we have seen previously in our discussions of throwing actions, the need for power may come at the expense of accuracy. Kicking an opponent as part of an attack is generally intended to cause pain and damage, with power and speed the most important factors and far less emphasis placed on precision and finesse. For either of these actions to be successful, precise timing of the action may be required.

As with a catching action, kicking requires spatial awareness and a high degree of eye/body coordination. Naturally enough, maintaining balance of the entire figure throughout the action is an important aspect of a kicking action because it requires a major shift of balance as at least one leg changes task, from supporting the body to striking. A kicking action that is little more than a slight flexing of the leg at the knee and hip will require only a very slight shift in the figure. A more vigorous kick, such as an overhead kick, may actually *require* movement of the entire body. In such a case the figure may be in a very unstable state as the action unfolds, with stability returning only on completion of the action during the recovery phase.

Kicking a ball, as opposed to throwing a ball, is differentiated by *momentary* contact with the ball, as opposed to the extended contact that occurs during a throwing action. The movement imparted to the ball is a result of the striking action that may be achieved with the use of different parts of the foot. Using the toe may generate a good deal of power, but it may also result in a lack of control over direction the object takes. Using the instep may provide a good deal of power and better control, resulting in greater accuracy; striking a ball using the outside of the foot may increase spin.

The movement of a struck ball is determined not only by the amount and speed of the force applied during the kick. It is also determined by the direction from which the force is applied. The greater the force applied, the further the ball will travel, and a ball struck squarely will tend to travel in a straight line. Variations on this linear movement of a ball can be imparted through differences in the striking or throwing actions. Cricketers expend a great deal of effort in bowling (a particular kind of throwing action) a cricket ball to create spin and movement of the ball as it travels through the air. The variation of air pressure created by the spinning action creates the in-swinger (the ball moving toward the batsman) or the out-swinger (the ball moving away from the batsman). Soccer players may create similar swerving actions on the ball by striking it obliquely. Striking the ball to one side or another will impart spin, and as we have already seen, this spin will affect the nature of the ball's flight through the air. Tennis players achieve the same results by striking the ball with a racket, creating topspin, backspin, and curving actions. This rather goes back to our discussions on dynamics and the laws of motion.

Jumping

The aim of a jump is generally to cover a distance or height that cannot be achieved by other modes of locomotion or movement, such as an ordinary or extended stride as part of walking. Jumping to achieve maximum height requires a very different action for jumping to achieve maximum horizontal distance. Athletes engaged in the long jump, triple jump, and high jump require very different techniques from one another, as does jumping straight into the air from a standing start position.

FIG 5.84 Youth jumping forwards from a run.

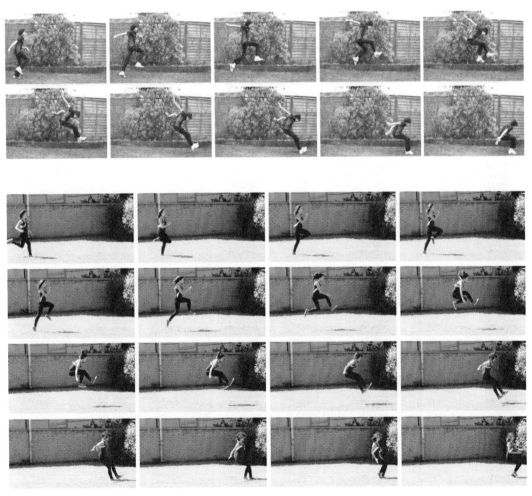

FIG 5.85 Young woman leaping forward from a standing position.

The anticipatory actions for each of the jumps are generally very distinct and quite extreme; actions as part of the preparatory phase of the jump may be considered as separate actions in their own right.

273

An athlete engaged in the high jump takes a run-up along a curving path to approach the bar at an oblique angle. The body is held at an angle to the ground before straightening up while simultaneously turning away from the obstacle just before launching from the ground in order for the spine to face the bar as the figure rolls over the obstacle.

A long jumper demonstrates a very different technique with a much longer and faster run-up and a flailing action in the legs during the phase when the jumper is off the ground.

A triple jumper also takes a long run-up at great speed but is required to include a separate and distinctive striding action as part of the jump and prior to the main launching into the air.

Jumping straight up into the air from a standing position requires a different technique again. In this instance all the height is gained through vertical movement with no run-up. To gain maximum height, the jumper squats low to the ground to gain more thrust on the upward action by fully flexing and extending the legs.

FIG 5.86 Young man jumping upwards from a standing position.

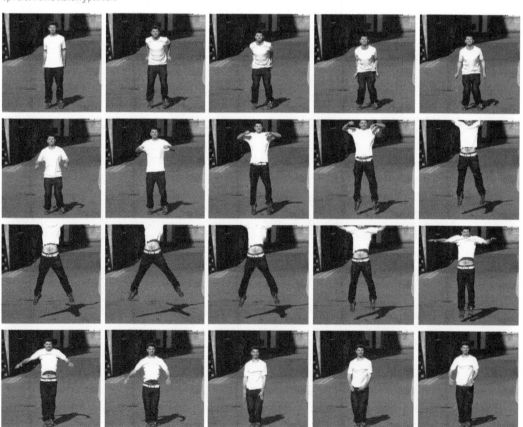

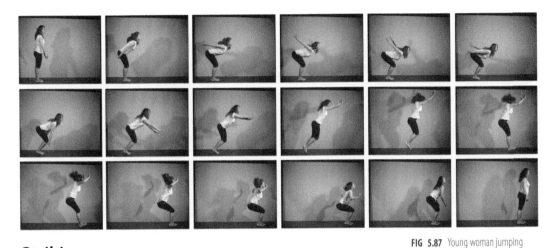

FIG 5.87 Young woman jumping forward from a standing start.

Striking

Striking actions may involve an impact with a part of the body such as the hand, fist, foot, elbow, knee, or head, in which case the power of the blow is delivered through that part of the body. A striking action may also involve the use of an object such as a bat, racket, stick, sword, or club, in which case the point of contact is located outside and beyond the body. Depending on the nature of the object used, it may be possible to exert a great deal more force to the blow.

When we strike a ball using a tennis racket, the point of contact is beyond the reach of the arm; as such the swing carries greater force at the point of contact. Likewise, it is the length of the golf club and the arc described by the head of the club as it swings around toward the ball that enables a great deal of force to be imparted to the ball on contact.

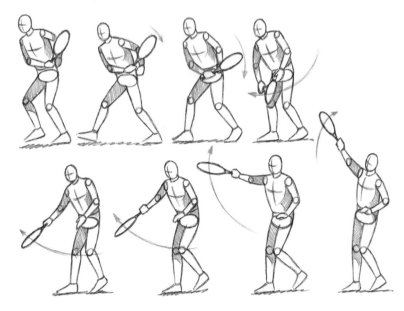

FIG 5.88 Striking sequence. Backhand action.

275

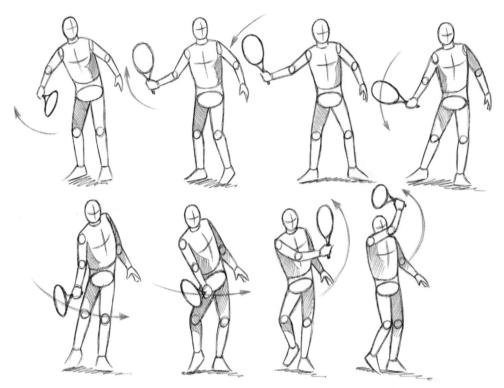

FIG 5.89 Striking Sequence. Forehand.

(a)

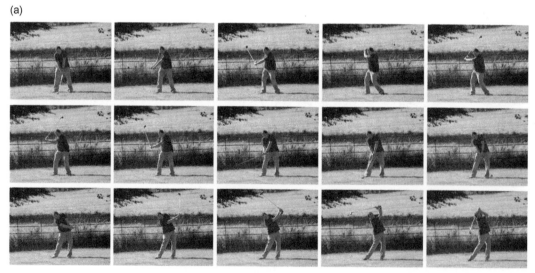

FIG 5.90 a: Golf drive, front view. b: Golf drive, side view. c: Golf chip, side view.

(b)

(c)

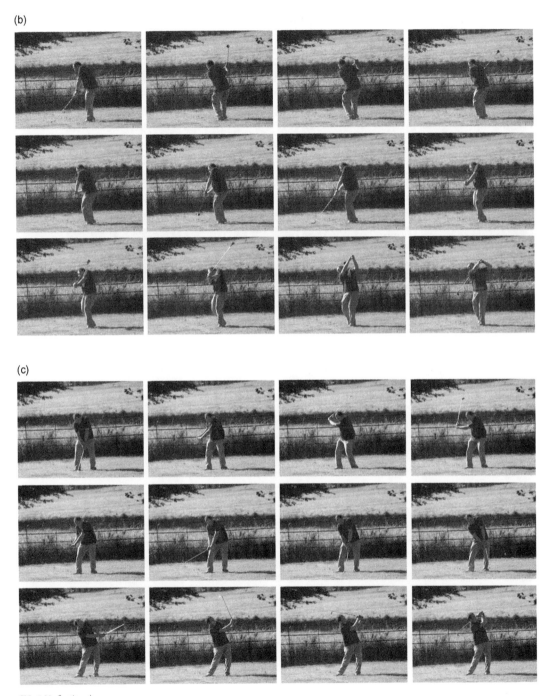

FIG 5.90 Continued

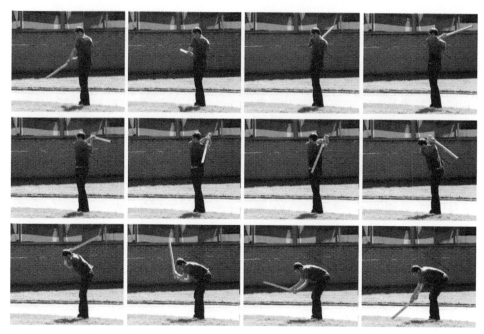

FIG 5.91 Downward strike with a stick.

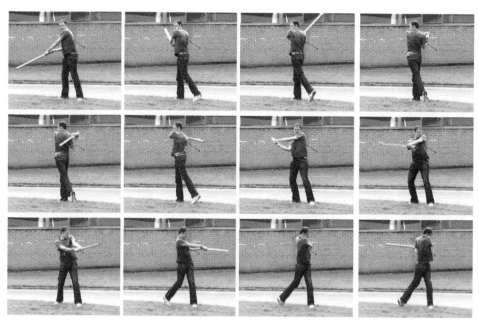

FIG 5.92 Sideways strike with a stick.

The types of striking actions are very different depending on the nature of the activity or sport. A golf swing demands a combination of power, control, and timing. Once again, there may a loss of control in exchange for increased force, as discussed in the section on kicking.

Using Hands and Articulation

The use of tools distinguishes mankind from other animals. We are the technological animal. Early humans fashioned tools from bone and stone; then later, after they had mastered the use of fire, they discovered the secrets of bronze and iron. From there humans' tools became ever more elaborate. We are now so technically advanced that we are able, with the assistance of precision engineering, to make tools and machines so advanced that we can reach out to the stars.

Our own basic tools, our hands, have not developed for hundreds of thousands of years. The articulation of the hands provides the necessary dexterity that allows the most subtle and delicate of actions of the artist, the musician, and the surgeon. Hands also provide power and strength and the

(a)

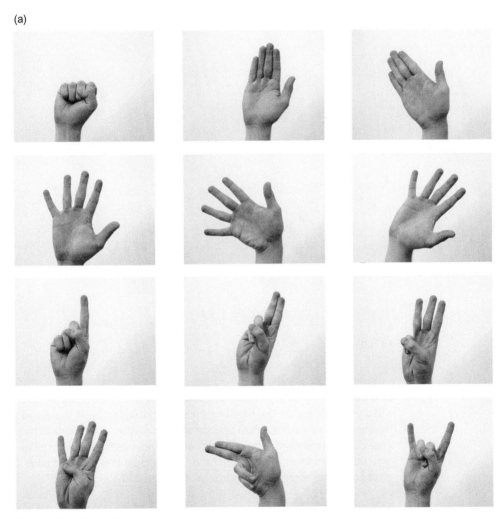

FIG 5.93 Articulation of hands.

(b)

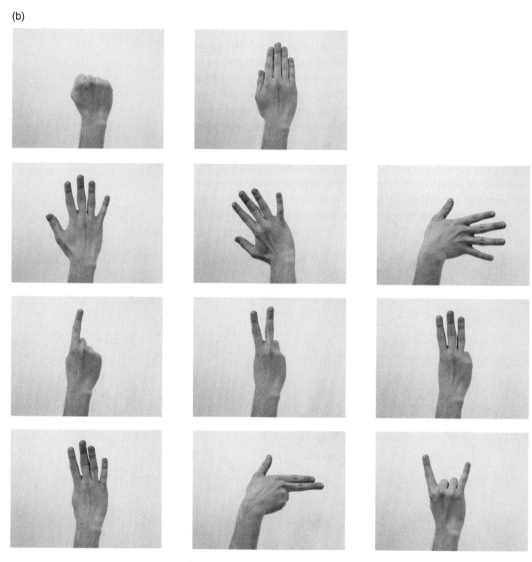

FIG 5.93 Continued

ability to absorb great pressure, stresses, and impacts required by the athlete and the manual worker. Our hands enable us to chop wood, break stone, and hammer nails, to make the most delicate of incisions with a blade, create the most beautiful mark with a brush or pen, and manipulate fine thread to tie the most intricate of knots. Through our hands we are capable of demonstrating great power and aggression as well as gentleness and love.

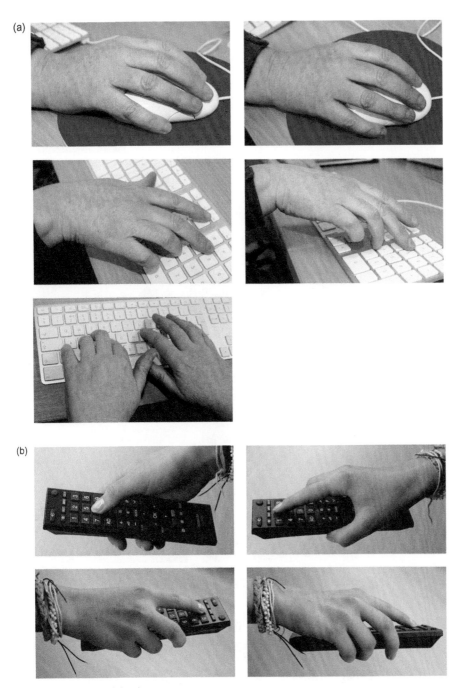

FIG 5.94 Hands: Using tools (a – e).

(c)

(d)

(e)

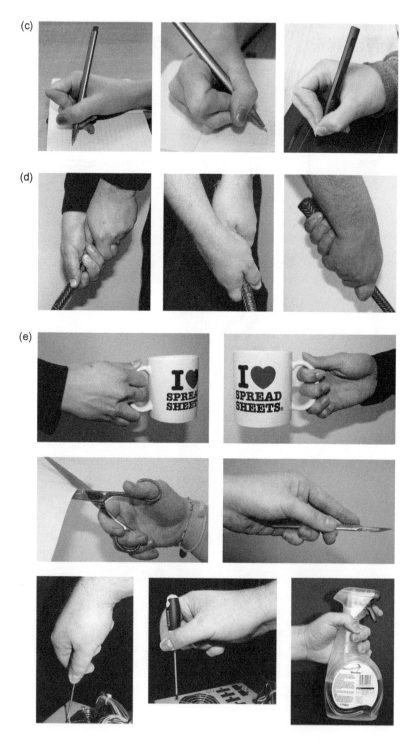

FIG 5.94 Continued

Other than the human face, the hands are the most expressive part of the human body. For an animator creating performance-based animation, the study of the hands may also provide an insight into the character, personality, and temperament of a character.

Facial Movement

The range of facial movements that humans are capable of making allows for an intricate pattern of visual communication in addition to the vocalization skills we possess. Many of these signifiers transcend linguistic or cultural differences. We are able perhaps to express our emotional state more than any other animal, though this ability to communicate through facial expressions is something we share with our primate cousins. This has been covered at some length in the chapter on action in performance and acting. We will therefore limit the text at this point to cover the range of facial motion and the muscles of the face.

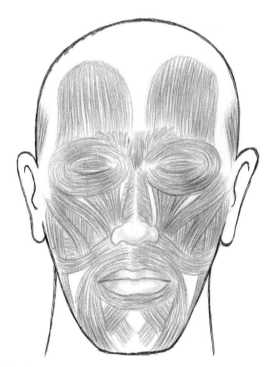

FIG 5.95 Facial muscles.

(a)

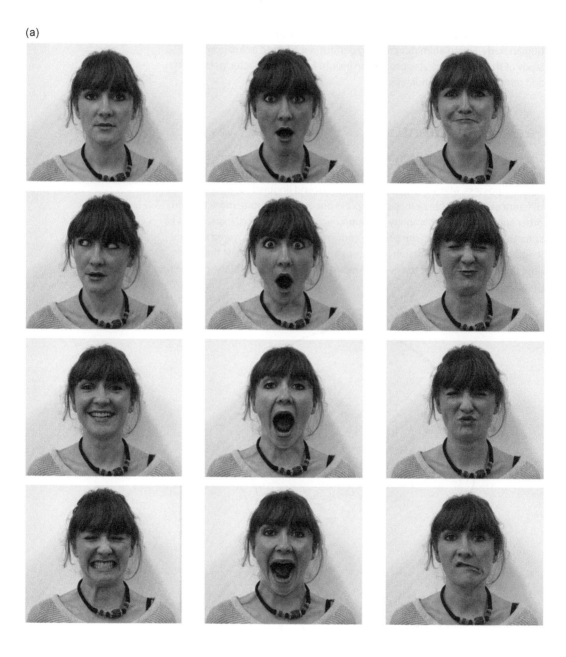

(b)

(c)

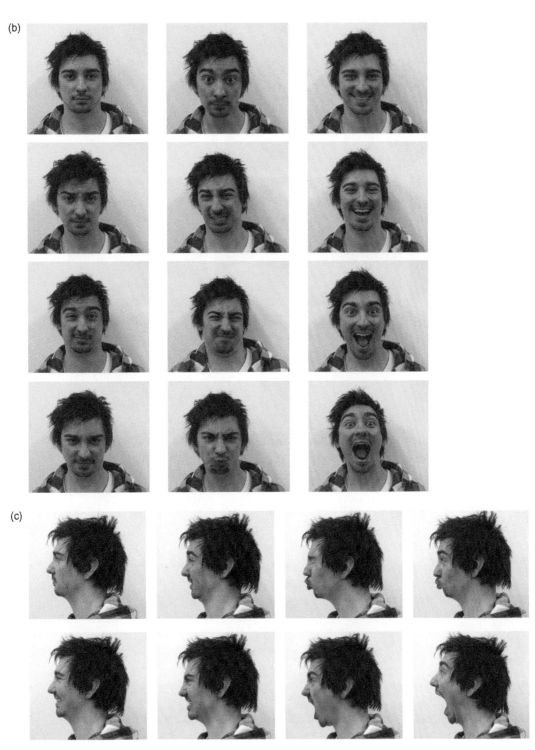

FIG 5.96 Facial movements.

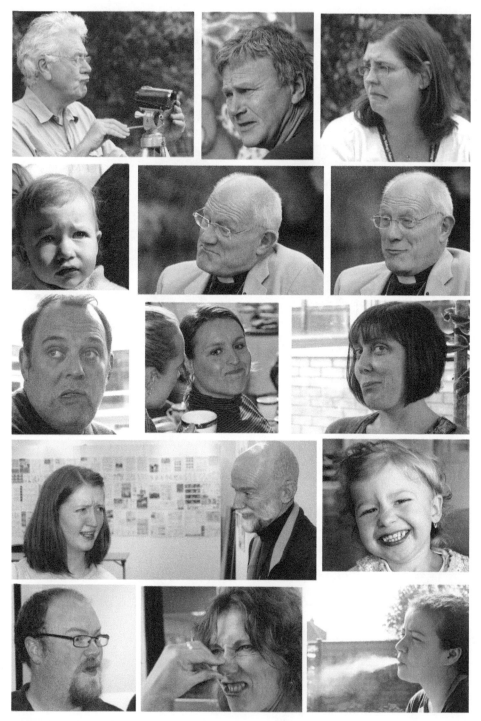

FIG 5.97 Facial expressions demonstrate mood, emotions, concentration, and form a major part of our communication.

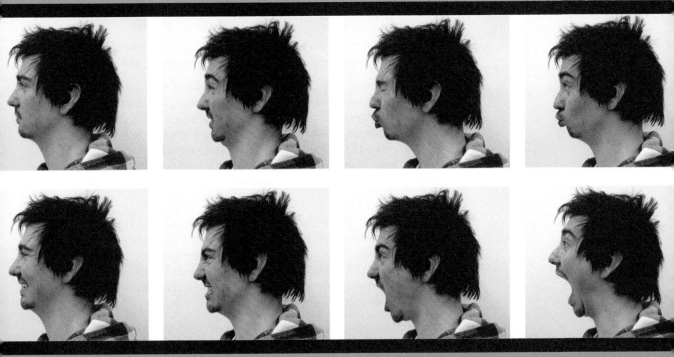

CHAPTER 6

Action in Performance and Acting

A great deal of the animation that is made using all kinds of techniques and intended for distribution through different formats concentrates on performance-based animation. Not all of it involves performance, of course, but such a large proportion of animation does involve acting and performance, whether for the obvious formats such as feature films and TV or the less obvious ones such as commercials, corporate video, and interactive work, that it becomes essential for all animators who want to work commercially to give this serious consideration. Acting and performance constitute such a big topic that to cover it extensively and comprehensively would be a work of considerable magnitude dedicated to this subject alone. This chapter does little more than touch on the subject and point out how animators may begin to use observation and analysis to deconstruct performance, to look at the structures that make up a performance and that will ideally lead to a more in-depth study and *practice* of acting. I encourage animators to look beyond animation for guidance here. Few texts are dedicated to the topic of performance and acting specifically for animation, but many more cover the subject in a live-action context, whether for screen or stage. As I have stated elsewhere, we should be looking beyond animation for our sources of inspiration and guidance; nowhere is this more evident than in acting.

From the earliest examples of animated film created by Emile Cohl, J. S. Blackton, and Winsor McCay, animation meant one thing, and that was entertainment. Entertainment meant the telling of stories. McCay's work clearly attempted to instill personality into his characters, but the even earlier examples created by Cohl and Blackton were a little light on sophisticated narrative, being little more than figures moving around in a fairly simplistic manner and undertaking very obvious actions—and *action* is very different from *acting*.

Action does play a vital role in all animated performances and is a fundamental part of acting, but that's not to say that all animated performances depend on movement and action in the same way. If our animation is not to be reduced to simply moving objects around on the screen, we need an understanding of how dynamics and animation timing create a performance and underpin acting.

The reason that millions of people go to the movies to watch animated feature films is not because of the quality of the animation or the particular technology being used; it's because of the story and the performance. Without a doubt there are occasions when technology has created an added attraction, as with the advent—or more correctly the reemergence—of stereoscopic 3D films such as James Cameron's *Avatar* (2009). It is quite interesting to consider how the novelty factor has played an important part in the development of film. From the outset audiences were drawn to the very novelty of the art form. They were amazed at the Lumière Brothers' *Baby's Breakfast* and were happy to pay simply to see the movement on screen. Later audiences were amazed at being able to hear *The Jazz Singer*. With the advent of color and every technical refinement that followed, including 3D film, audiences continued to come in droves. Regardless of the advances in technology and production processes and despite the modes of distribution, audiences continue to be drawn to film for the same reason they have always been drawn to it: stories—interesting stories full of interesting people doing interesting things. Underpinning all of this was the script.

I have written this before and elsewhere but it holds true for the purpose of this text and illustrates how storytelling underpins all successful animated films:

> *Good Idea + Poor Animation = Good Film*

> *Poor Idea + Good Animation = Poor Film*

> *Poor Idea + Poor Animation = Stinker*

> *Good Idea + Good Animation = Award Winner*

There is yet another issue that goes some considerable way to ensuring a film's success, and that is performance. Even with a good script and good animation—that is, the demonstration of good craft skills in animation and animation timing—it is still necessary that the animation be delivered through a good performance. What creates a good performance is open to interpretation, however. Rather than try to categorize performance in a way that formulaically lays down those traits that make a good performance, it would be better to look at appropriate performances. Drama is not the same as comedy, though comedy may be dramatic and drama often has comedic elements. For that matter, not all dramas or comedies are alike, so to consider only one type of performance as suitable for *any* genre would be a big mistake. Let's take, for example, the animation performances that are used in the TV show *South Park* and the film *The Incredibles*. It would be foolish to judge one against the other in terms of good or bad animation timing, just as it would be to make such a judgment on the performances. It is far better for us to consider both the animation and the performances as being *appropriate* to each of the works. The complexity of performance in *The Incredibles* would be totally out of place on *South Park*, and vice versa.

Whichever way one undertakes to make a performance, it is clearly yet another skill that the animator needs to acquire. Other than mastering animation timing, performance is perhaps *the* key skill for animators who create character-based animation.

I firmly believe that the basic skills in animation can be learned in a relatively short time, at least to the point where animators are capable of producing very competent and believable animation. The numbers of undergraduate students we have seen through our doors and the level of animation they manage to achieve seem to be testament to that belief. However, conquering the art of acting and performance may take a little longer. Indeed, I think it is this aspect of animation that takes a lifetime. It is not that relatively inexperienced animators are incapable of producing good performances. On the contrary, some animators are naturally gifted actors and find it relatively easy to turn animation into a performance. My point here is that good animators just get better and better with time, practice, and experience as they develop and hone their craft skills, in exactly the same way that all actors have the capacity to improve their craft. Along with this experience and mastery of animation timing comes an ability to create ever more subtle and crisp performances. Performance makes a script come to life, and good acting sits at the very heart of all performances.

Acting is undoubtedly a major part of a performance, but it is not the only part. Creating a good performance also depends on the standard of the directing, enhanced by design, sound design, music, staging, and the overall production values.

We have looked at the necessity for animators to study and analyze action and motion to gain a deeper understanding of timing and dynamics. In the same way, I believe it is very useful for animators to undertake the analysis of acting and performance so that they can create their own performances. However, before we look at how we go about doing that, we should take a little step backward and examine once again, albeit briefly, the subject of timing.

Timing Gives Meaning to Motion

As stated previously, animation timing is at the heart of *all* animation. You will find it difficult to create any kind of believable performance if the meaning is missing from the motion. Without a deep understanding and appreciation of animation timing, it is impossible to create believable motion, let alone the degree of acting that underpins performance, which in turn delivers an engaging and interesting narrative. Without the sophisticated use of animation timing, we are left with simple movement that has little to do with believable animation. It is through understanding and applying animation timing that we are able to give believability to an action. Although timing forms the basis for all performance-based animation, it does not *provide* that performance; it simply provides the believable movement that underpins acting. Timing gives meaning to motion, and without this meaning we are left with simple activity.

Body Language

Let's briefly extend the topic of body language to look beyond the gait and movement of individual subjects and begin to look at how this topic links with performance.

We have seen how an analysis of physiognomy can give insight into movement and how a range of movements is, to a large extent, dependent on and limited by physiognomy. We should now take a look at how other aspects of an individual can be ascertained from his posture and the manner in which his body is held when both motionless and moving.

Body language can be an indication of an individual's condition well beyond the physicality of the subject. In its simplest form, it can describe the age and health of an individual, but body language can also indicate other personal aspects such as emotion and mood. It may also be a good indicator of certain cultural traits, traditions, choices, and origins. As animators, the observation of body language may provide us with a wealth of information about our subject and assist us not only in the creation of a believable performance but also in the creation of believable characters with distinct and recognizable personalities.

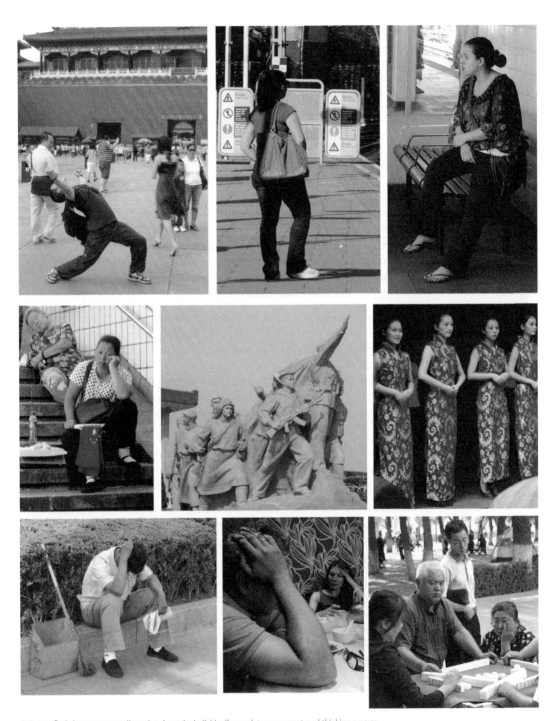

FIG 6.1 Body language can tell us a lot about the individual's mood, temperament, and thinking process.

A number of aspects related to an individual's body language may be indicative of a wide range of external influencing factors. These may become evident in varying degrees through the very particular types of body language that are expressed—a very useful starting point to animators and designers when considering the development of personality for a character.

Some examples of body language and posture can be identified as typical to particular groups, cultures, genders, ages, health, physiognomy, moods, temperaments, personalities. The way an individual moves may also go some way to identifying that individual as belonging to a particular group, whether social, sexual, cultural, and so on. We are on difficult ground here in which it would be easy to stereotype; without wishing to generalize to the point of causing offense, I believe it is very apparent that certain individuals move in certain ways because of their background, traditions, and gender. I would suggest that these movements are to a large degree inherited, whereas other forms of movement and posture may be a matter of choice. Some individuals make a conscious *choice* to move in a specific manner that indicates belonging to a particular social group.

Men and women often (but not always) demonstrate very different body language; they may walk, sit, and stand in slightly or very different ways. There is a certain form of masculine movement that typifies a male walk, which may be exaggerated by men who want to assert their masculinity—often depicted in animation as walking with their chests puffed out and exaggerated swinging of rather stiffly held arms. In some circles this takes the form of a swagger that would seem to typify the movement of male gang members.

Female models have a rather distinctive walk that does not typify a generalized female walk pattern but is reserved for the catwalk. It may be stereotypical, but some male gays have been depicted as having very distinctive mannerisms, including a distinctive walk.

That's all very simplistic, I know, and there are many exceptions to these generalizations, but to deny that in some instances such differences in body language and movement exist in an effort to conform to some form of political correctness would, I believe, be foolish.

It is very important to acknowledge that the recognition of body language associated with any particular group can only ever provide a starting point for our study and understanding of body language. This approach to studying body language may indicate a characteristic or personality *type,* but it will *not* necessarily provide an indication of body language for an individual. If we rely too much on this rather broad interpretation of body language, we will simply create stereotypes and reinforce a stereotypical viewpoint of collective groupings of various kinds. But even this stereotypical approach may have its uses. Such a generalist approach may prove all that is required to deal with a subject we need not explore fully; a man running down a street may look very different from a woman running down a street, and this may be the only differentiation we need.

The debate over whether we are hardwired to behave in given ways is clearly still ongoing, and I am in no position to state a case one way or the other. Clearly, research makes its way into the world through scientific papers and then into the wider world and becomes "fact." This may be quite dangerous if these research findings and conclusions are then set in stone. It would seem that the manner in which we behave is due to both nature *and* nurture. It is a complicated mix in which there are evidently some inborn gender influences. It would be wise to recognize this, though equally we should do well to avoid readily depending on explaining individuals' behavior as being determined by genes or hormones. We must also be aware that we are not brought up in a gender-neutral environment. This will almost inevitably result in the shaping of our behavior and the perpetuating of social norms.

To illustrate, a group of characters you're animating may require very little difference among the group members, such as a group of soldiers undertaking a rigid group activity such as marching. This homogenous approach to movement will soon break down if the animator then needs to explore the *individual* personality of one of the group, such as an individual soldier undertaking action other than a group activity. The soldier's body language may well indicate a level of fitness and training shared by all his colleagues, but there may well be personal traits that set him apart from other individuals. Clearly, the exploration of this individuality becomes really necessary only if you need to showcase this individual.

The observation of body language can provide a basis on which to build a performance; the use of body language alone may be enough to provide the animator with a basis for building a performance. There are clearly performances that depend on little other than body language—purely physical performances. Before the use of sound in cinema, actors had to depend heavily on the physicality of their performances. Harold Lloyd, Charlie Chaplin, and Buster Keaton depended almost entirely on the use of body language; yet this seems to have provided very little restriction to their art and craft, since these three performers managed to develop very distinctive personalities. The inference here is that it is the body language that provides an illustration of personality.

With the advent of sound in cinema, the craft of acting obviously changed considerably. It could be argued that this change allowed for far more subtlety in performances.

Mood and Psychology

An individual's physicality is clearly very important in setting out to create a performance, because the body will either allow or restrict a certain range of movements. Just as important, or maybe even more so, is the psychological makeup of a character. In creating a performance, animators' work becomes more complex, considering the mood and temperament the individual character is required to display throughout the performance.

It is as well to state the obvious here: that all the actions, emotions, and displays of mood and temperament that make up a performance come from the animator and the skills he or she possesses as an animator and as an *actor*. Animators are not just technicians, artists, and filmmakers; above all else they are actors. They simply send their drawings or models onto the screen instead of treading the boards themselves. The animated characters do not possess this skill themselves; they are just puppets, drawings, or pixels, and without the animator's highly developed acting skills they will be little more than the walking dead.

Looking at great animated performances we can see that the great animators' acting abilities easily equal the very best stage or screen actors, unlike some live action actors who become renowned for one particular type of performance or, worse, become typecast. Most animators specializing in performance-based animation need to be far more versatile. Not only do animators need to be able to portray a broad range of human subjects (male and female), animals, and inanimate objects, they need to portray animals and inanimate objects with *personality*.

Characters with distinct personalities, along with their mood and temperament, are generated in a script, but it is in the animation that they become central to the animated performance. The problem animators face is the replication of those issues that appear in the script, and it is the animation of the character that brings these to the forefront.

Let's start by considering an everyday action such as walking. The principle of a walk for all individuals remains the same, involving the stride and the passing position, the swinging arms, the rise and fall of the figure, and the shifting balance throughout. There will naturally be variations that are a result of both internal and external physical elements. However, other variations will be a result of the personality, mood, or temperament displayed by that individual.

A happy walk, a sad walk, an angry walk, a frightened walk, a joyful walk—all conform to the principle we've set out, and any variations are not due to the individual's physiognomy but because of the character's emotion, mood, and psychological state. This concept is covered in more detail in the chapter on figures in motion.

These variations, which are a result of psychological conditions, may be extended to all manner of actions. Take, for example, the manner in which an individual eats a plate of food. This might not only depend on the character; it might also depend on the type of food that person is eating and the circumstances in which it is being eaten. We would expect that there would be a very different approach to eating an ice cream cone on a beach during a sunny day in summer than eating a plate of unappetizing prison food in a communal and perhaps even dangerous environment. If we take these two very extreme examples, we can establish that the manner in which they are animated will vary from individual to individual. The animation will be driven largely by the character's personality. An individual who has perhaps become used to life in prison and the prison regime and who is no longer fazed by the experience will behave in a very different manner from someone who finds himself in an unfamiliar and rather scary environment. Similarly, eating ice cream on a beach will, for some, be the most natural, comfortable, and relaxing thing in the world; for others, even this seemingly innocuous event could prove stressful and a completely uncomfortable thing to do.

Any action has the potential to create tension between normal patterns of behavior or has the potential to cross accepted behavior lines associated with a group to which an individual belongs. The "normal" behavior may reflect the stereotypical behavior patterns that an individual has willingly embraced or has learned as part of a cultural heritage.

In thinking about the behavior of a character, it is as well to consider those external incidents and situations that act as drivers for a performance and that underpin intentional and unintentional movement (*reflex responses*). The mix of reflexive and thoughtful responses to external drivers (things that happen to a character) and internal drivers (the character's emotional response to those things) creates a very elaborate set of issues. The way individuals respond to any given situation will vary greatly; what seems of little significance to one individual may prove of immense importance to a second individual. A situation that creates blind panic in one character may well result in another individual becoming stronger and acting in a calm and altogether more steadfast manner. You can see from this that there is no formulaic approach an animator can rely on to create a performance. Each one is unique. However, there are tools an animator can use to gain a better understanding of behavior in order to build these performances.

One of the most obvious tools is learning to read facial expressions. This is something that we do from birth. We are probably hardwired genetically, at least to some degree, to make and read certain expressions as part of our communication.

Facial Motion and Expression

The most expressive part of the human figure and the one we use most to communicate with, other than the voice, is the face. This is something that we have in common with many animals, particularly the primates. Naturally, the importance of the face in communication varies from species to species. Some animals are almost incapable of any expression at all. The physicality of human and primate faces allows for a very high level of expression. Other species such as reptiles have a much more limited range of facial expressions. It might be easy to recognize when a human child is happy simply by looking at the smile on her face; however, the inscrutable grin of a crocodile is not much of an indicator of its emotional state. Obviously, such a face remains totally expressionless, and the grin we perceive is only our anthropomorphic interpretation. We attribute an emotion where none exists by misreading the animal's "grin" or "smile."

The showing of emotion through facial expressions is not limited to humans. A number of animals do indeed use the face to express emotion. The most obvious expression is the baring of teeth as a warning sign and a sign of aggression. Some apes have a complex system of signs that use the color around the face, which seems to emphasize the message.

There has been considerable debate regarding the way facial expressions may be interpreted and the emotions that certain facial expressions denote and the possible cultural variants across races. However, it would seem that at least some of these expressions are common throughout all peoples and that we are hardwired to express and read certain emotions in a specific way.

The face's flexibility allows for a wide range of movement, and not simply to eat food. Facial expressions such as the smile may be indicative of a certain type of emotion or mood (pleasure or enjoyment), but it does not necessarily follow that all subjects will smile in the same way or for the same reasons. It may be reasonably safe to say that a smiling face denotes good humor, but it would be completely wrong to suggest that this is the only way pleasure and enjoyment will be expressed or that smiling does not indicate other emotions, such as vindictiveness or hatred. This is determined by the individual, the context, the circumstances, and above all, the individual's personality.

The expression of mood, anger, love, and tenderness may be determined through facial expression and body language, and though these are not an exact science, they do give us some useful pointers toward reading one another and, for us as animators, in creating performance. Our moods are not always easily read on our faces; hiding our emotions may be a part of a survival strategy. It might not always be to our advantage to show outwardly what we are experiencing inwardly. Poker players take great care not to give away any signs that may possibly indicate the hand of cards they hold. They purposefully intend for their expression to be misread, but the misreading of expression can also be quite unintentional. Some individuals may have faces that tend toward the less expressive, retaining a more neutral expression; others express their inner feelings more clearly.

Much can be learned from a curl of the lips, the furrowing of a brow, the angle of eyebrows, and narrowing of the eyes—even coloration on the cheeks; blushing red or becoming pale and drained of color. All these are indicators of some internal emotional state.

The range of emotions or mental states is extensive and complex, so differentiating all of them may be near impossible. A number of universally recognized emotional states can be expressed through facial expressions and are understood regardless of cultural traditions; happiness, sadness, anger, fear, surprise, disgust, and contempt. Other expressions can be easily read by a wide range of people, but it is argued that these are more subject to interpretation and may be subject to cultural variations, a matter of nurture rather than nature: excitement, concentration, confusion, frustration, and desire.

This very simplistic diagram is intended to demonstrate how such expressions can be read. Simply by altering one or two of the very simplistic elements that make up the face, different emotional states can be achieved. Given the bare minimum of information in the diagram, it is evident that, if we look at the complexity of the human face by comparison, we can easily see how we become capable of a very broad range of expressions and emotions. Some of the signals that we send out to each other may be universal and have evolved to be easily read by others in a group. Some of these signals may be easily read by strangers, but the level of understanding of very subtle signs increases with familiarity of the subject. Small telltale signs that could go unnoticed by a stranger may be picked up very clearly by someone who is familiar with a person. Strangers, acquaintances, friends, and family will all pick up on signals of varying subtlety.

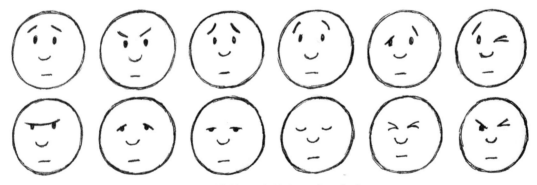

FIG 6.2 Visual communication is possible even in very simplified faces and with the use of just a few lines.

We may all be well aware of this in our day-to-day life as animators, but it is part of our job to ensure that our audience reads these messages loud and clear. At the most subtle level we may even need to identify the signaling that takes the form of personal traits identified with a given character.

When we communicate with each other, we tend to look in each other's eyes, or not, largely as a result of a combination of our particular personalities as well as cultural traditions and accepted modes of behavior.

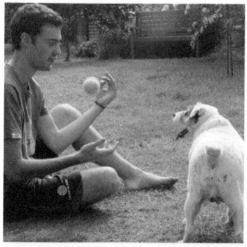
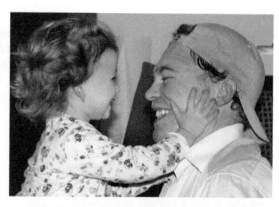
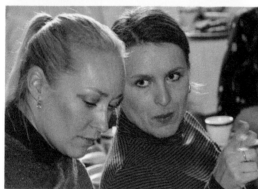
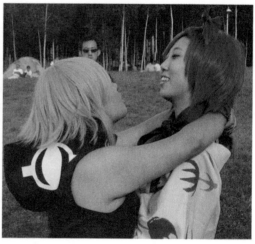

FIG 6.3 Eye contact between individuals may convey a great deal of information. For animators this is an important part of creating a performance.

The scope for the expression of human emotion not only lies in an individual's physical appearance but is also determined by that person's personality and nature. We are all aware that some people are quicker to smile and laugh than others, but it does not necessarily follow that they have a more friendly disposition. However, we can often detect the insincere smile. It is easier to smile by simply using facial muscles to stretch the lips into a grin, revealing the teeth, but a true smile can be seen in the eyes.

In certain cultures it is a matter of respect to avert the gaze and to avoid looking directly into an individual's eyes. However, in other cultures this avoidance may be read as guardedness, and as a result the observer may be critical of people who won't meet their gaze and engage in direct eye contact. This behavior could be a sign, wrongly read, of distrust and suspicion. On the other hand, individuals who stare into the face of another with unbroken eye contact during communication may be seen to be intense, overbearing, and strange, even by people from a culture where making eye contact is the accepted norm.

Our use of our eyes is a major part of performance; eye contact can be very revealing. The way couples in love gaze into each other's eyes is very different from the look of a mother to her child, though both examples have their roots in love.

Public speakers often strive to gain eye contact with many members of an audience to convey a message directly to them or create the illusion of personal communication. This kind of direct eye contact is intended to command attention; it may have the added effect of giving the impression of confidence where none actually exists, of sincerity where there is none, and of engaging on a personal level where doing so might be impossible. However, as we have already seen, direct eye contact may also be perceived as threatening. Politicians beware.

The study of expression and emotion has been undertaken by a number of specialists, perhaps none more eminent than the psychologist Paul Ekman, who developed a system of analyzing human emotions through facial expressions. His research resulted in the creation of the Facial Action Coding System (FACS), in which he managed to cover a vast range of facial expressions using thousands of case studies. Ekman's research extended into nonverbalized behavior that also included body language as applied to the analysis of lies and lying. Animators will find his work and the FACS system to be a very useful and powerful tool in helping them fully appreciate the flexibility and potential for expressing emotion through behavior.

On a very practical level, animators working with characters will find it very important to ensure that eye contact is maintained between those characters that you want to interact. Obviously, the exact nature of the interaction and level of eye contact depends on the context. The result of characters that do *not* maintain eye contact is an exchange lacking in believability, a disconnected performance that has little to do with real engagement. In such a situation it is difficult to create a connection between the individuals, let alone warmth of feeling between them.

But it is perhaps through the eyes that we are best able to gain insight into what an individual is thinking. A person might be saying one thing but thinking something quite different. As animators, we are best able to create a performance by tapping into characters' thought processes and the visualization of those thoughts.

The Thinking Process

It has been claimed that all acting has its roots in and is initiated by the thought process. As a result of the thinking process, such motivated movement occurs and transcends reflexive movement. I have written elsewhere that timing gives meaning to motion. We could expand on this idea a little and suggest that emotion gives meaning to movement. Such movements have a motive, they are undertaken for a purpose, and it is this purpose that creates the meaning. No performance is built simply on the movement of actors from point A to point B.

The unspoken words and the thinking process are internal processes that not only drive action; they may be made visible through facial and body movement, pose, gait, and timing. This is true even with the simplest of actions. Walking or running may simply be a way of getting from A to B at different speeds, but it may also be possible to ascertain the emotional state of a character through the choice of movement; then the run or walk becomes a physical manifestation of mood. An angry or agitated person may express his state of mind through very different kinds of movement. Because we may have no other way of conveying characters' emotions except through the physicality of movement, the animator needs to create the *illusion* of thought, which is central to good acting and performance. Performances are based and built on the thinking processes, and characters' changing moods and emotional states and their interactions are a result of these thought processes.

In developing your acting skills as an animator, it is important not to simply look toward other animation as a reference point. Looking toward other performers and actors in film, on television, and in theater will enable you to gain an understanding of how these actors develop their craft. This will be of real benefit to your craft, but perhaps the best source of inspiration for performance is not to refer to other actors or animators but go directly to the source: real people leading real lives. Learning to read body language and facial expressions will give you insight into human behavior, and it is that after all that we want to bring to the screen in the animated characters we create.

I do not wish to give the impression here that all emotion and performances depend on a character's movement and expression. A good deal of thought and much of what constitutes a performance can be illustrated through silences and stillness. Consider for a moment the point in the film *The Incredibles* when Mrs. Incredible discovers a long blond hair on her husband's clothing. Her reaction, so natural and so believable, comes from an understanding of the human condition. We can see all those thoughts rushing through her mind; she loves her husband but there are doubts, and we can see them reflected in her facial expressions. Who does this hair belong to? Has he been having an affair? What has he been up to on these business trips? The audience can read all these thoughts in a glance, in the silence of the moment. Stillness and silence often allow the action that sits at either side of the stillness time to breathe. The stillness often contextualizes the action by giving meaning to the dynamic; it punctuates dynamic action with motivating thought.

Many young animators make the simple mistake of overanimating their characters. I have found this particularly true of stopframe animators, though no doubt other animators working with other techniques are equally guilty; they simply don't seem comfortable leaving their model or puppet alone for more than a few frames. The result is that the model is forever on the move. This might be perfectly acceptable for scenes that are action packed, but it is a far less satisfactory approach to acting. As we have seen elsewhere in this text, most actions can be broken down into phases, which can move from one into the other in an almost seamless manner, but they are *distinctive* phases.

The illustration of the thought process in acting demands an even more subtle approach to animation timing. Because it is thinking that instigates *most* movement and action, the ability to demonstrate this thinking is a valuable tool for the animator. If your audience is to understand the reason for the movement, they must understand or at least be aware of the thinking behind the action. It is far too simplistic to consider the thinking process as a separate and distinct action. Animating the thought process in this simplistic action-thinking-action way will only lead to very strange and rather unconvincing acting. Depending on the context, the thinking process may be something as subtle as a narrowing of the eyes or a slight pause in movement. Consider the moment in *Bambi* when the young deer meets the prince of the forest for the first time and hears the dreadful news: "Your mother can't be with you anymore, Bambi." The expression on Bambi's face, the very slow drooping of his ears followed by the downward movement of his head and the very slight narrowing of his eyes, clearly shows the audience that the magnitude of the news has hit home and Bambi realizes that he now faces life alone.

On the other hand, the thinking process may be a more protracted event, resulting in a series of actions: opening a bottle and pouring a drink, standing up and walking across a room, or a sequence where the character uses a prop. As with most good acting, there is no formula for animating this thought process; you will find your own way of dealing with it. Largely it will be down to the characters you are working with, the context they appear in, their individual personalities, their intentions, and their motives. Noticing how people's behavior and their use of everyday objects display their emotional state will prove a very useful exercise for the animator.

Lip Sync

Perhaps the most familiar form of action analysis for animators is the use of lip sync guides. These have been around for a very long time but were missing from the very first text on making animation, *Animated Cartoons; How They Are Made, Their Origins and Development,* by E. G. Lutz, published in 1920, when movies were still silent. It does contain a series of drawings that illustrate a method of animating a baby crying, complete with a text substitute for the actual sound. Interestingly, the illustrated guides for creating walk cycles in the same text are as valid now as they were then, clearly demonstrating that there is no sell-by date on the principles of animation and action analysis.

The nature and the design of a character's face will determine the type of lip sync that an animator will find possible. However, the principles that underpin the lip sync remain the same for all examples.

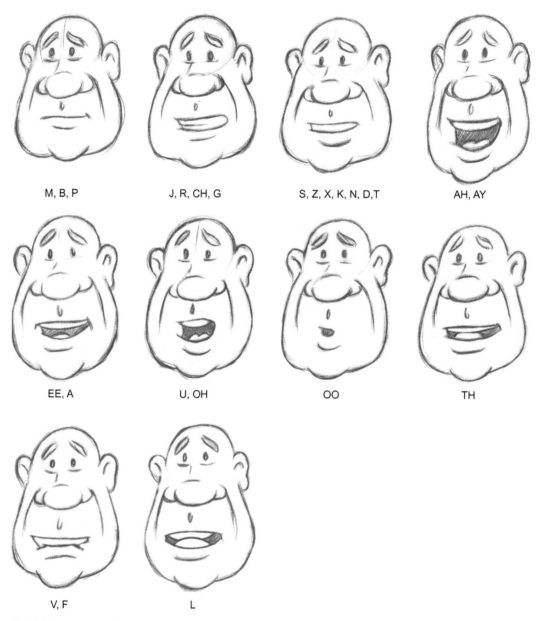

M, B, P   J, R, CH, G   S, Z, X, K, N, D,T   AH, AY

EE, A   U, OH   OO   TH

V, F   L

FIG 6.4 Lip sync guides may be useful to the animator but they do not provide the full range movements possible.

Lip sync guides appear in many texts on animation production and are readily available to animators, and it is true that they can prove very useful in creating believable lip sync. However, I believe they should be used only as a guide; they cannot provide a foolproof solution to lip sync problems. Indeed, I am very suspicious of any kind of guide that claims to offer a one-size-fits-all solution to any animation or design problem.

The range of mouth movements made to articulate a given word or phrase will vary a great deal and depend not only on the character's physiognomy but also on the context of what is being said. There are thousands of ways one can say the same words, each way of which will create various facial movements. There are few generalizations, but it may be true to say that the louder one speaks or shouts, the greater the facial movement. This is where many of the lip sync guides prove inadequate as a template. The illustrations are generally far too extreme in the mouth shapes and a more subtle version is often called for, particularly in more naturalistic animation.

The illustration included here demonstrates the differences between a guide and the actual thing.

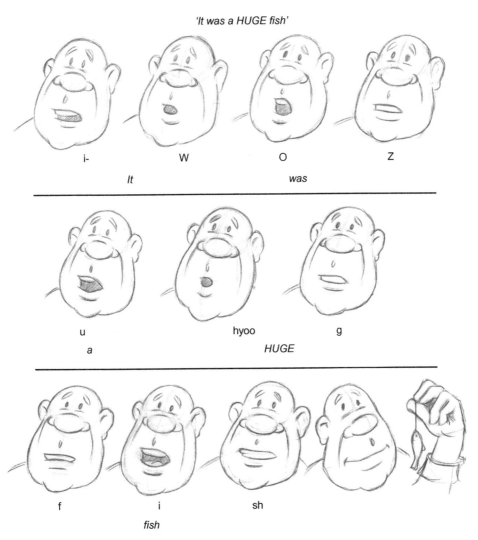

FIG 6.5 Example of lip sync being used to illustrate dialogue.

Motivated Movements

The motivation for an individual character's actions largely depends on the character's nature and personality coupled with the motivating factor. This combination may result in a series of actions or patterns of behavior specific to that individual character. What constitutes a motivating factor and instigates a particular action for one person clearly does not necessarily motivate other individuals.

These motivating factors can be made apparent in a performance; indeed, they can form the basis for analysis. This is where people watching can be of real value. Watching how individuals react differently in similar situations can be very revealing. The way people behave when they are stuck in a traffic jam, queuing for service at the post office, or waiting in line for a taxi clearly demonstrates these personal traits. Observing these behaviors reveals how different people deal with and react to particular situations—which become bored, which become impatient, and which behave in a more stoic and calm manner. It interesting to witness what this rather prosaic situation motivates them to do as a result.

The things that motivate one person into action, and in some instances rather extreme forms of action, may have little if any effect on another person. What upsets one character will not have the same effect on others. Indeed, it could result in an altogether different action. You can probably see how important it is for the animator to begin to gain a reasonable if not in-depth understanding of the human condition. After all, it is the human condition on which much of your work will be based.

Characterization

Animators' ability to attribute personality and psychological traits to characters is one of the fundamental skills for working with character-based animation. It follows, then, that the study of character will prove useful. For the purpose of this text, I differentiate between the terms *character* and *personality,* but clearly they are interrelated though not necessarily the same.

It might be possible to categorize character types (in a very incomplete and simplistic way) by taking into account external factors, such as where they live, their jobs, or their hobbies. Personalities, on the other hand, might be seen as more individualistic and related to the nature of that individual: morose, happy-go-lucky, serious, daydreamer, panicky, steadfast, and so on.

Character Types

You must consider the individual characters in your animation. The interaction between individuals is what makes a performance interesting; let's face it, that's what makes *life* interesting. There could be some truth to the old saying, "Birds of a feather flock together." Initially we might be attracted to like-minded, people but interesting interaction comes from the juxtaposition of *different* types of people. Interesting narratives are generally centered on and around the interaction of different character types. If all your characters were the same, your story would be bland and uninteresting; if everyone in the world were the same, that would be less vibrant too.

Simplistic and rather formulaic narratives depend heavily on the villain and the hero, stereotyped characters that are often depicted in an oversimplified manner. Cowboys in black hats = baddies, cowboys in white hats = goodies. Superman is perhaps the epitome of a stereotyped hero; clean shaven, clean living, healthy, moral, kind, and honest with a good physique, nice haircut … and he's young.

Character types extend to cover the kind of professions they undertake, either by choice or by tradition. For individuals that have the freedom to choose a profession, it might be worth considering whether they are drawn to a particular way of earning a living or a lifestyle because of their personalities. Is there something there you can identify that links them to one particular thing or another? The demands of some occupations seem to suggest that some individuals are more suited to that occupation than others. Working as a lumberjack obviously requires a certain physicality to be able to do the job and, if not an affinity with the great outdoors, at least the capacity to tolerate it. A lab scientist, on the other hand, would seem to suggest a need for a higher-than-average level of intelligence and perhaps a lesser dependence on physical strength. People that are drawn to the caring professions probably possess an enhanced degree of people skills and a level of compassion that enables them to be successful at what they do.

Perhaps I should refrain from suggesting what character types are best suited to life as politicians—or animators for that matter.

Personality

It has been said that we are all prisoners of our own personalities. I find it difficult to attest to that, but it would seem that our personalities are what determines, at least to some degree, the way we deal with life, our circumstances, and the manner in which we interact with the people we meet.

The range of personalities is almost without limit, so any classification is really rather unsatisfactory and of limited use. I am sure that most of us know or have met individuals at some point in our lives who have personalities we are able to describe in fairly simplistic ways. This may be as simple as a tendency to demonstrate a positive or pessimistic outlook on life; they may see their glass as being either half full or half empty. Others may be described as generous, kind, loving, or thoughtful. We may even know people who possess a short temper or a tendency to demonstrate violence. These labels clearly don't provide a full profile of a person, but they do provide a kind of useful shorthand for describing them.

There has been a considerable amount of research and debate around the shaping of an individual's personality and attempts to establish whether personality is determined by either nature or nurture: inherited genetic traits (nature) or an individual's upbringing and experiences (nurture).

The personalities of the characters we animate need to shine through in any of the performances we create. Naturally, this is only essential if a degree of acting is called for. We can't expect our audience to engage, sympathize, or empathize with characters that lack personalities; they become nothing more than manikins moving from A to B and undertaking action without any apparent emotional engagement.

Performance Dynamics

There are many separate aspects of animation production, each requiring not only very specialist knowledge in the particular area but also an understanding of how the areas relate to each other. In addition, an understanding, or at least an overview, of the entire process is invaluable. An audience going to a cinema to watch a feature film is naturally drawn to the narrative and content of the film and not the processes required to get it on screen. John Lasseter has famously said that the three most important aspects of any film are the script, the script, and the script. However, to bring the script to life, the performance becomes all-important. The overall performance is usually made up of a number of separate periods (either shots or scenes) that each has its own pace. When these shots or scenes are placed alongside one another, a performance dynamic is created, generally considered the film's *pacing*.

If we look at the dynamics of a performance in much the same way as we have animation timing, we will be able to see how a performance can be analyzed in terms of a dynamic flow. To this end it might be useful to revisit those classifications of animation timing: timing, phrasing, and pacing.

- *Timing.* The term *animation timing* simply describes the speed at which an object or a figure moves. Timing is the building block of animation, so without a good understanding of timing it is difficult to create good performance.
- *Phrasing.* This term describes the relationship of separate actions of varying lengths that make up a sequence. The contrasting speed between the actions and the changes of speed within the action create a dynamic arc in a way that's very similar to choreographed dance. The phrasing of action creates temperament and mood and a reaction to changing circumstances in short a performance.
- *Pacing.* This term describes the dynamic of an extended narrative, the story in its entirety. Pacing shapes the film and determines how the story develops over an extended period. Pacing is illustrated by the manner in which separate shots and scenes of different duration and varied dynamics and phrasing come together to form a coherent entity.

The pacing of a film is based on the script, but it is ultimately determined by the director and his or her individual approach to storytelling. Naturally this varies from film to film and from director to director. However, it is ultimately the animator who creates the performance in animation, rather like the actor who creates the performance in front of the camera. There is only so much a director can do; ultimately creating a performance is down to the animator's acting and performance skills.

Action Analysis and Acting

We have covered many of the issues related to analyzing action elsewhere in this text; now let's give some consideration to the analysis of acting and the physicality of performance. Action analysis, as we have considered it so far, has been limited to a figure's dynamics that have largely been based around the physicality of the subject and the actions that are undertaken simply for locomotion or those other task-based actions that have little to do with performance. This study has been relatively straightforward; our attention has been placed on the action alone and far less on the motivation behind that action. The difficulty we face in analyzing action in acting and performance is the contextualization of that action. The important aspect of the analysis of action in acting is emotional engagement and the personality of the protagonists associated with the action.

In analyzing acting, the reasons behind an action, the motivating factors, and the way actions are determined by relationships, the interactivity between individuals and the response to changing emotional states of the protagonists are more important than the actions themselves. Studying and understanding the reasons behind the action will enhance your own acting and performance skills. A simple action such as placing a cup on a table, when seen as an animated action, focuses on issues such as weight, timing, overlapping action, drag, squash and stretch, and so on. However, even such an innocuous action as putting a cup down can be laden with meaning. It may be done gently, with love, or in anger or fear, or any one of a hundred other emotional states. But the general action remains the same: the cup is placed on a table, but the small telltale signs—hesitation, speed, tension in the grip of the hand on the handle—all make visible those otherwise invisible emotional states.

To analyze acting and performance, we need to consider the story or the reasons behind the movements. Tapping into the reasons and motivation behind movements creates acting. Insight into the motivation of the action of a given shot is not necessarily evident from the shot itself; we gain a benefit from viewing the shot within the broader context of the scene or the extended sequence. Seen in isolation, actions rarely reveal the true context.

Film can provide a great source of inspiration for the aspiring animator, but you must look beyond the timing and dynamic. In learning your craft as an animator—and I strongly suspect the same can be said of any creative practitioner—it becomes difficult to experience the results of that creativity simply as a consumer. Part of your experience will almost invariably involve, at least to some degree, an analysis of the work being experienced. In becoming a practitioner involved in the making of creative work, it is difficult to leave behind a level of critical analysis. That I fear is part and parcel of being a creative practitioner: You must know the tricks of your trade. Similarly, with acting there are techniques and methods that are perhaps appreciated by other performers that the ordinary consumer is blissfully unaware of. Whether this insider knowledge makes for a richer experience is open to debate.

One way you could begin to analyze performance is to initially watch a film in its entirety and try to enjoy the experience as it was intended—as an entertainment. Do not start to pull the film apart at this stage; just watch. Having experienced the entire thing, you can then make a start in analyzing it by giving some very general thought to the relationships depicted in the film and the emotional dynamics between the actors. Try to identify the particular emotional traits and personalities of the characters. Begin to ask questions about the main characters. Why did they behave in such a manner to a given situation? How did the interaction between the individual personalities contribute to the behavior? How did the behavior of each character shift throughout the narrative?

Choose a sequence from the film, preferably one with a dynamic arc that demonstrates a change of behavior or thinking in more than one character. For this purpose I often recommend the sequence in *Toy Story* in which Buzz Lightyear and Woody first meet on Andy's bed.

The sequence starts with Buzz investigating a strange and alien environment. His inquisitiveness turns initially to alarm when Woody surprises him by popping up out of nowhere. This action results in extreme caution as Buzz strikes a defensive mode, aiming a laser weapon at Woody's head—no doubt a result of his thorough training as a space ranger. Woody, on the other hand, is relatively relaxed though rather anxious about the possibility of being replaced in Andy's affections by a new toy. On catching sight of the sheriff's badge on Woody's vest, Buzz immediately relaxes; he now sees not a threat but a fellow law enforcement enforcer. Unfortunately Woody's anxiety is a little less easily dispelled. When the other toys join the pair on the bed, Buzz takes it into his own hands to protect Woody from this newly perceived threat by throwing him to the ground and protecting him with his own body.

You may find it a useful exercise to ask yourself some questions about this sequence:

- What is the emotional state of each character as he begins the sequence, and how are these states made evident through the characters' actions, expressions, and dialogue?
- How does the emotional dynamic between the characters shift during the sequence?

- How are the changes in emotions displayed in action, speech, and facial expression?
- How do the characters respond to one another, and how does their behavior alter as a result of the presence of other characters?
- How does the sequence conclude? How have the characters changed as a result of the encounter?

This exercise will provide you with a starting point for the analysis of acting. Through such systematic study, you will continue to learn more about your craft.

Now consider another short example of how emotional states can be manifest in very different ways, depending on the nature of the character involved. Two very well-known and beloved characters, Bugs Bunny and Daffy Duck, would respond in very different ways to the same event; even if they were both driven to high levels of annoyance, they would demonstrate it in very different ways. If pushed to the extreme limits of his tolerance, Bugs would announce to his antagonist in the calmest but tensest of voices, "You realize, of course, that this means war." Daffy, on the other hand, would behave entirely differently—far from being calm cool and collected, his reaction would be more extreme, more physical, and probably a lot louder. A slight closing of the eyes and a smile playing around the lips would suffice for Bugs; nothing but a raging tantrum would be sufficient for Daffy to express his displeasure.

Group Actions and Dynamics

At the root of any great performance is an understanding of movement, but for animators working with performance-based animation—through the movement of objects, animals, or more complex personalities—interactivity is key. Performances are seldom a solitary activity; though there are some very obvious and excellent examples of this, more often than not a performance is an interactive event between two or more characters.

An individual's behavior may change a good deal once that character is in the company of others. An individual's behavior may be reinforced by the presence of others; the result may be to encourage a certain type of behavior, or it may repress it. The company of strangers could have a liberating effect on an individual who may feel somehow restricted in the presence of people that know him or, conversely, the confidence that family or peer groups bring may evaporate. A degree of competitiveness within the group may emerge. We can often see this in the behavior of children that become more excitable in the presence of other children.

Once individuals come together, they begin to interact in various ways. Groups may decide to collaborate and begin to work in teams, or they may interact in other ways—perhaps in partnership or as antagonists—and the composition of the group may determine the action of the group and the individuals in it. Groups may either suppress or amplify given modes of behavior. Groups of strangers may suppress individual behavior, resulting in conforming to what passes as a given norm. Groups of like-minded individuals, particularly those that know one another, may result in those norms being accepted by a wider society and breaking down, to be replaced by behavior that would be considered a norm by and for that group.

Action within a group often displays a dynamic that has fluidity as certain activities move throughout the group and are shared among group members. However, this is not true of all actions or all groups. Not all members of a group necessarily take part in actions either together or to the same degree or even at all; there is often a clearly discernible pecking order. This is as true for some groups of people as it is for some groups of animals.

It is interesting to observe the way that actions flow throughout a group, instigated by an individual and with others in the group subsequently responding. Such actions may pass from one group member to another in turn or then result in group collaborative action. The exact nature of the action will obviously vary a great deal, but the action does flow throughout the group.

Collaborative effort presents an opportunity for another area of study. Working as a team may involve people with the same physical attributes and skills or may involve individuals with different skills who are working toward a common goal. Consider team games with players taking different team roles, each of them making a specific and often unique contribution to the group.

Dance and Choreography

Dance is a rather distinctive form of performance that clearly entails a degree of acting on the part of the dancers. During a dance, individuals take on the role of dancer, which is outside of everyday activity, though the act of dancing may relate very closely to everyday activities. The reasons behind dancing are almost as varied as the number of dance styles; it may be ceremonial or linked to cultural, religious, or social traditions. Dance, along with music, may be seen as an art form through which cultural identity is expressed. There can't be a single society on the planet that does not have both dance and music as a central part of its cultural heritage. As a nonverbal form of communication, dance may be used to tell stories, to demonstrate feelings toward one another, or to reinforce social structures or groupings. Dance may involve large groups of people or it may be a solo event undertaken by one individual. In this instance it may be a way of establishing that the individual concerned belongs to a specific group or used as a way of identifying an allegiance with a group. For some communities, the dance of an individual or group takes on a ritualistic nature and provides a way of connecting with the spiritual aspects of the wider society, serving a very real and important role for the entire community. Early rock paintings discovered in India depict dancing figures that date back 9,000 years. The study of dance and dance theory is a broad subject and may also be linked directly to many other fields of study, including anthropology, culture, gender, and ethnography.

The study and analysis of movement, choreography, and the language of dance constitute an art in itself and is covered extensively and systematically by Rudolf Laban. Born in Hungary in 1879, Laban became interested in human movement in relation to space during his studies as an architect. He established a systematic way of notating dance movement based around four main categories: body, effort, shape, and space. Laban's system, first published in 1928, later became known as Labanotation and remains in use as a form of dance notation. His system not only found application for dance and choreographed movement but also in industrial time-and-motion studies in an effort to reduce wasted time, effort, and energy.

It is important that we see the kind of systematic approaches to the analysis of movement as created by the likes of Laban and Ekman as tools for the analysis and understanding of that movement and, in the case of Ekman, the associated emotions to movement. These approaches *cannot* be seen to be formulaic processes whereby performance through movement, as covered within each of the systems, can be made. They are akin to musical notation systems. Music notation provides a way of recording the *underpinning idea* of the music, but it neither records the actual music nor provides a way to create a Mozart.

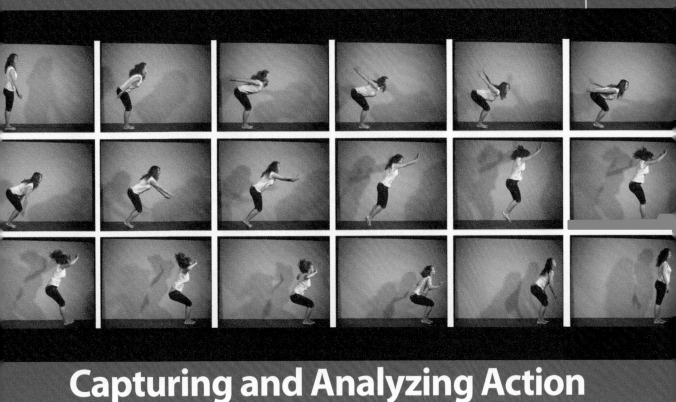

CHAPTER 7

Capturing and Analyzing Action

To undertake any serious study we must consider the importance of research and the issue of identifying and gaining access to the relevant source material that will underpin this research. Using reference material from a range of sources can be of great benefit to artists and designers of all kinds. Animators who want to analyze action can gain a great deal from such material. Unlike animation's pioneers, who had little access to the kind of research material that makes action analysis possible, we are in the very fortunate position of having a wealth of material on which to draw.

Despite the fact that animation as an art form is still very much in its infancy at only around a hundred years old, there are plenty of books, videos, and online examples that provide a huge and very valuable reference library. However, this wealth of readily available material often falls short of the exact requirements. The material may not fit the bill exactly or not come close enough to provide a useful substitute for first-hand research, in which case it may be preferable for animators to undertake their own research and create material *exactly* suited to the task at hand. Clearly, some animators never bother much with action analysis let alone gathering or creating their own reference material for the study of motion and dynamics. Perhaps they don't see the value in studying animation in such an analytical manner.

Obviously, the need for such an analytical approach to dynamics is largely dependent on the work being undertaken. It is difficult to see how the detailed study of rabbits or ducks would have helped the likes of Chuck Jones or Tex Avery in creating their particular brands of cartoon-based animation for Bugs Bunny or Daffy Duck. So, for some animators such in-depth study might not be relevant, but for others, particularly those working with figurative performance-based subjects, such study is vital and the rewards of those efforts will be very great. However, even for cartoonists such as Avery and Jones or animators making completely abstract animation that, at least on the face of it, requires less in-depth study of particular subjects, the study of motion and dynamics will still repay the effort. If you choose to undertake a serious analysis of action, I can almost guarantee that you will be a better animator as a result.

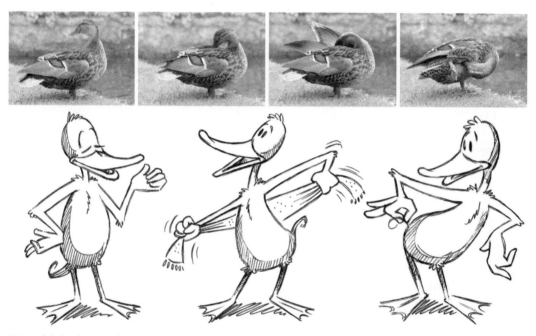

FIG 7.1 A duck and a cartoon duck clean and preen in very different ways.

Capturing Action

A range of methods and techniques is available to animators who want to capture and record action for analysis that will suit the needs and fall within the scope of the individual animator or studio, regardless of size. Some of these methods are very specialized and require very specialized equipment that is often rather expensive. However, options are available even to the animation student who has somewhat limited resources. Here we consider some cheaper options as well as the more elaborate and costly ones and see how they can be applied to the study of dynamics. However, capturing and analyzing action does not have to depend on technology at all; after all, for centuries artists depended on little other than their own first-hand observations, and this lack of technology didn't seem a serious hindrance for them.

First-Hand Observation

Perhaps the most obvious analysis technique and one that is often overlooked for a variety of reasons (not least of which is the modern tendency to depend on technology and gadgets for everything) is first-hand observation on the part of the artist. Observation and the skill of "seeing" served many of the greatest artists that ever lived, and the earliest pioneering animators depended on their own observations of action and movement. Try to get into

FIG 7.2 First-hand observation, just looking, will result in a greater understanding and appreciation of movement.

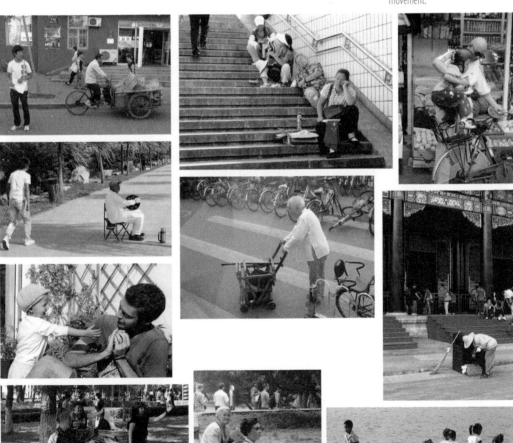

the habit of observing all types of action, not just the very dynamic ones such as dance or the ones you see at sports events. Everyday mundane actions are worthy of analysis and will probably be of more direct benefit to you than very unusual, if highly energetic, actions on the sports field. As an animator, it is critical that you develop an eye for the way things move and behave in regard to everything from how people walk, the action of wind on water, and the flight of birds to running horses. To get started in this level of research, you don't need any special equipment, you don't need to go anywhere special, you don't even need to *do* anything very special: just stop looking and begin to *see*.

Start to observe the way people move around and interact. See how body language reflects the mood of a person and observe how different people move in different situations. See how young children and old people walk and compare the two. Notice how they pick up things with confidence or uncertainty. See how people use simple tools such as pens or keys. Analyze how different people open doors or run for a bus or lift a cup of tea to their mouths to take a drink. Begin to see the differences of people making a simple action like taking a drink, depending on who is drinking, what they are drinking, and where and in what company they are doing the drinking. Start to notice how fast things and people move. Even a simple activity such as taking the dog for a walk can provide a lesson in dynamics.

Once you have started this level of first-hand observation you will soon find it becomes second nature and you'll be surprised how much you start to notice the things that once went unnoticed and how much you begin understand about movement. This kind of first-hand observational research will provide you with a very useful point on which you can start building throughout your animation career.

Becoming the Reference

The access to and use of really good reference material is important in making believable animation. We have very many sources to draw on in this effort. One very rich and useful source of information that is readily available to us all but that animators often overlook is their own bodies.

Faced with the problem of animating the performance of a particular figure, you will find that one of the quickest and easiest solutions is to observe a real figure going through the same action that's required for the animation. Having a model on hand to undertake a series of actions that animators might want to study is highly impractical. However, animators might choose to work together, each providing the movements for the other to study. In this way they can direct the figure to undertake the *exact* action they require. Working as partners they can quickly explore alternative actions and make changes to any planned action *before* they begin animation, thereby saving a lot of time and effort.

In addition to such processes or for animators who don't have colleagues or friends to assist with the action, they can go through the required action themselves. There are many additional benefits to this type of personal study of movement. Animators who undertake a particular action will be much better placed to analyze that action; they will gain a deeper appreciation of the dynamics than they can achieve by simply recording an action. By undertaking the action him- or herself, the animator will be able to feel the stresses and tensions in the body and the manner in which these shift as the movement develops and changes. The animator will be able to feel where the figure's weight and balance are throughout the motion. This is something that can only be felt, not seen. Learning how to see through to the underpinning aspects of a subject, rather than just looking at the subject in a superficial way, is not as simple as it sounds and will come only with practice.

If an animator is able to "act out" a particular sequence in the manner of the subject she is animating—that is, not just going through the motions but moving as the subject would move—she is likely to gain an even deeper insight into the performance, not just the movement. There is a big difference between the two; performance may be beyond some animators' abilities, but movement might not be.

It is perfectly possible for animators to become the subject of their own research. They can use and study their own bodies, the kinds of actions they are capable of and the manner in which they move, as a way of understanding movement. Many animators begin a study of a particular movement they are trying to capture by making similar movements of their own to gain an idea of the performance they are searching for. This exercise enables them to see the action, but what's far more useful is that it enables them to *feel* the action at the same time, giving them even more information about movement. Going through an action, you will be able to feel where the weight is, where the tensions are, and how the weight and balance shift as a movement progresses. Mirrors can be very useful tools for animators, allowing them to both see and feel a movement at the same time. A full-length mirror can provide a new perspective on the figure in its entirety. Though using a full-length mirror may be impractical in some situations, even a smaller mirror could help with details such as movement of the head and facial expressions. A smaller mirror positioned on the animator's desk will be of great value to the study of mouth movements during lip sync. One of the biggest problems for inexperienced animators is overanimating the lip sync. We discussed this in some detail in the previous chapter, but it is well worth repeating.

Such a study of movement that involves the animator's own body does not need to be limited to animation of figures that reflect the animator's own physiognomy, age, gender, or even species. I have seen animators use the technique of studying their own actions for a wide range of subjects, including dragging themselves along with the aid of crutches to gain a better

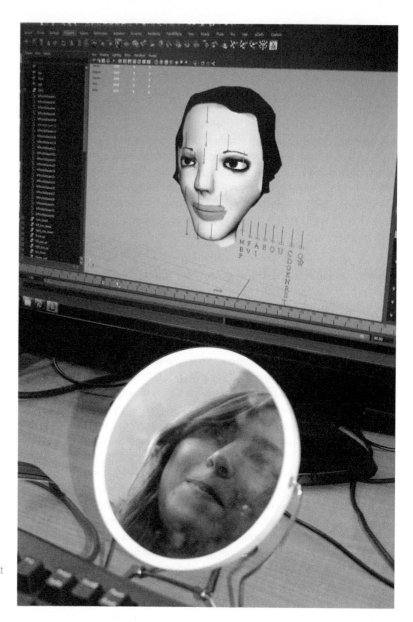

FIG 7.3 The use of mirrors will assist the animator in analyzing action and is particularly useful during lip sync.

understanding of how a mortally wounded pterodactyl might struggle along a beach prior to its final collapse and death.

In the case of performance-based work, animators could find the use of props of immense value. The task of animating a figure picking up a box from the floor would benefit from the use of an actual box. Substituting an animated prop with a physical object of a similar size and weight will also help the animator gain a deeper insight into the potential for movement. Using a short

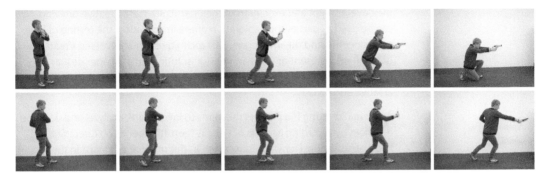

FIG 7.4 Acting out a sequence, particularly with the use of props, will allow the animator to gain a much clearer idea about the nature of the movement.

stick as an ersatz sword will give the animator and would-be swordsman a good indication of swordplay, and on top of that it will probably be a lot safer than using the real thing.

This approach to acting out an action can be very useful, providing very good reference material, but it might not suit everyone. Some people won't feel comfortable acting out what may seem to be rather ridiculous and foolish actions, particularly in a studio environment, or even in private for that matter. For those individuals there are still plenty of alternatives. One of the best of these is life drawing.

Drawing from Life

Drawing underpins many of the graphic visual arts and a broad range of art and design disciplines. First let's establish how drawing can be used as a discipline in its own right—a platform for individual creative expression. In addition, it is a vehicle for research, the exploration of subjects, and the development of a deeper understanding of subject matter. There is overlap between the two approaches, but it might be useful to differentiate between the two. The former, drawing as a creative endeavor in its own right, has its roots in the imagination and is an interpretive and responsive activity. It is an approach that may be highly subjective; in addition to being a creative process in its own right, it may play a vital role in the creative processes in other art and design practices. Academic drawing, on the other hand, presents a more objective approach to a subject, one in which drawing is underpinned by direct observation, experience, and analysis rather than imagination. This approach serves an entirely different function, the value of which is to explore a subject in an objective manner, to evidence what *is* rather than what *thought* to be as an emotional response to the subject, and with little regard to how the artist feels about the subject.

This distinction between the two approaches is not an argument for one form of drawing over the other; rather, it is the recognition that both approaches may serve the artist, designer, and animator in different ways in the development and execution of their particular craft. Creative drawing can be used as part of the exploration of the imagination, the testing of ideas and concepts, and the investigation of techniques and processes. Creative drawing may present options and design solutions in a broader design context or be an end in itself, with the drawing becoming the artifact of the creative endeavor.

Academic drawing is a process that aims to investigate, analyze, and describe a subject by recording aspects of what is seen. It depends on direct first-hand observation. Drawing undertaken in this manner will assist in the development of skills, both practical and observational, that may then be used to underpin other creative efforts while extending the animator's knowledge and understanding of the subject matter.

It would be a big mistake to consider life drawing as simply being useful to artists who use drawing as part of their practice. I have seen many young students and aspiring computer animators make this mistake and neglect drawing as a way of developing observational and action analysis skills, only to regret it later. Life drawing, or should I say drawing from life, provides all practitioners with the opportunity to observe the way things are, not simply the way things are imagined to be, and to develop a keen ability for observation that will then aid visualization.

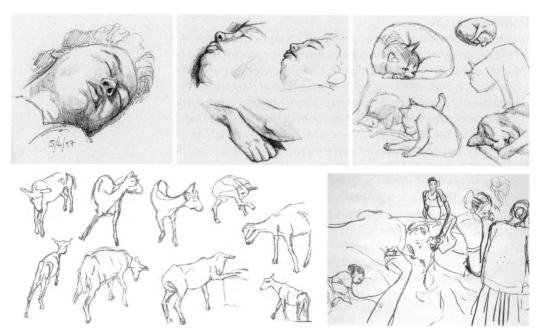

FIG 7.5 Drawing is not necessarily about making beautiful drawings, it allows one to observe more closely a subject and to see things otherwise missed.

Drawing from life is not so much about making marks than it is about observation and seeing; *not* just looking is the most important aspect of life drawing. This skill takes time and practice to develop.

The great cartoon animator Chuck Jones, in his book *Chuck Amuck*, spoke about his life drawing teacher, who is reputed to have said that each artist had 100,000 bad drawings in them and the sooner they worked through those to reach the better ones underneath, the better. I couldn't agree more. Life drawing, according to Richard Williams, is the antidote to those artists and designers that have found a formula to drawing solutions, formulas that rely on the tricks they have learned, the shortcuts and simplistic visual symbols that present a substitute for the real thing. Academic drawing provides an understanding of form, line, and volume and enables the artist to look with a keener and more critical eye.

Before you even start to make a drawing, you need to give some consideration to what it is you want the drawing to achieve. Establish the reason you are making the drawing and what your drawing is about. This might sound obvious, but unless you have established these goals at the outset, you will have no way to measure whether the drawing is a successful one or not. If you have no clear aims for your drawings, they are more likely to become unfocused, failing to provide you with any really useful information or extend your knowledge of a subject. Without a clear aim for your drawings, they cannot help solve any of the problems you intended the drawing process to address in the first place.

By limiting the scope of your drawing, the more likely your drawing is to surrender the results you are looking for. You should aim for a drawing to address only a single topic at a time, or at least a very limited range of topics. Issues such as volume or weight, line, light, space, or any one of a hundred other different topics are more likely to be fully explored and therefore likely

FIG 7.6 Line work.

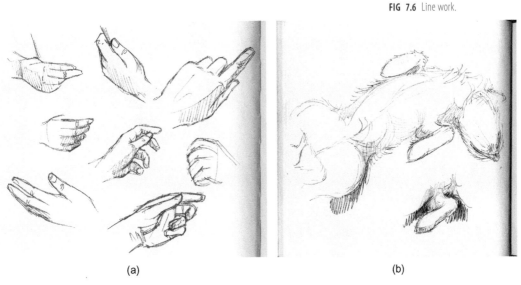

(a)   (b)

to be more successful if you make the drawing with a single clear aim in mind. It is far better and you will learn much more by making a number of different drawings that explore the same topic using different techniques for different reasons. As a subject for analytical study, it is important not to overburden your drawing by making it deal with too many issues.

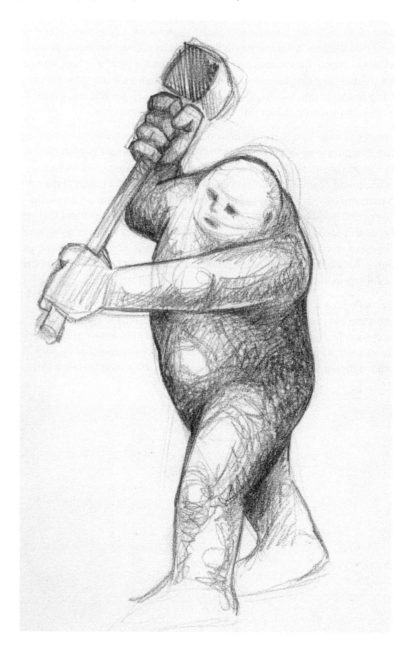

FIG 7.7 Volume and weight being illustrated through the use of tone.

By setting such constraints at the outset, you are then free to give consideration to particular aspects of the subject and omit information that is either unnecessary or at least of lesser importance to the immediate needs of the research. You can see that there will almost certainly be a need to create many such drawings, each of which deals with a different aspect of a subject.

Anatomy

The study of basic human anatomy can be a very useful undertaking for artists, designers, and animators. However, it might not be necessary for them to have a particularly in-depth knowledge of the workings of the human body in order for their particular practice to gain a great deal from such study. Much of animation deals with the human figure, even though a lot of the animation may be abstracted to some degree and in extreme cases the anatomy and movement of human characters may barely resemble the human form at all. Nonetheless, an understanding of the human form, the way it works and the range of movements it is capable of making will inform the animator's work. In a similar way, understanding the basic anatomy of quadrupeds will also prove of some use. To help with this idea, there are some first-rate texts on human and animal anatomy specifically aimed at the artist. In addition to the chapters in this book, I have listed a few texts in the bibliography that you may find of some use for further study.

Construction

Drawing the human figure can be a rather daunting undertaking. To make things a little clearer, particularly when you're drawing a figure for animation purposes, it might be useful to try to see past all the surface detail to its underpinning structure. If we can begin to understand how a figure is structured, we will be better placed to draw and animate it. The aim is to simplify a complex structure to a level whereby the action and dynamics can be more clearly captured, reproduced, and understood. Animators in the Disney studio did much to promote this way of animating using a simplified structure that was designed specifically to disregard all the unnecessary detail that wasn't immediately relevant to the action, movement, and performance of the piece. In this way the most complex structures are reduced to a series of spheres, cubes, cones, and cylinders. If we understand the construction of figures in these simple terms, it becomes easier to interpret rather complex structures in terms of movement, stripped away of unnecessary detail and information that can only confuse the issue. Of course, once the movement is captured to the animator's liking, it is then possible to add the necessary detail. In this way the process of animation can be differentiated from that of drawing. This concept is particularly important for animators specializing in 2D classical animation.

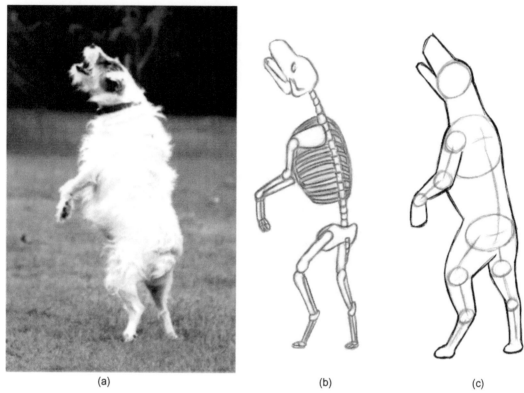

(a)　　　　　　　　　　(b)　　　　　　　　　　(c)

FIG 7.8 Construction of a figure may make the animation of complex figures far easier. a: Photo of dog leaping for a treat. b: Skeletal drawing of the same action. c: The simplified drawing of the dog leaping, identifying the joints, connecting long bones, and the bulk of the body.

This approach to using construction to simplify a figure applies not only to animation; it may be a very useful technique for making sketches of figures when speed is important and you want to capture only posture, body language, or animation.

Materials and Mark Making

The choice of suitable materials for life drawing is really important in getting the results you require. Furthermore, to achieve a range of types of drawing, it is necessary to use a range of materials. Some of these materials will be suited to a particular approach to drawing or to a particular type of image making. The scale and size of the drawing may be determined in part by the materials you use. Fine-line pens, dip pens, and pencils are all suited to making small to medium-sized drawings. Drawings of this kind might be preferable when you're working in public places or in small sketchbooks.

Large drawings may be suited to exploring particular aspects of a subject that are difficult to deal with using drawing materials that create finer marks.

(a)

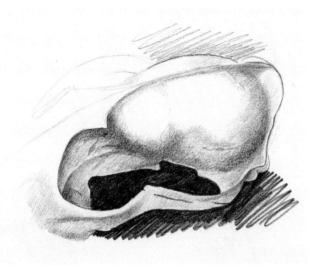

(b)

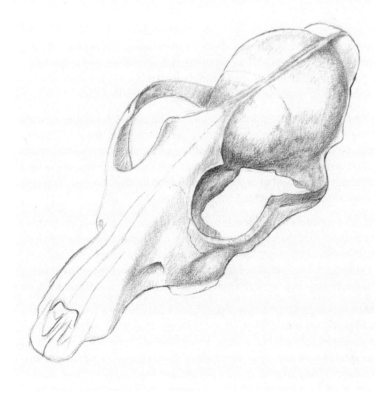

(c)

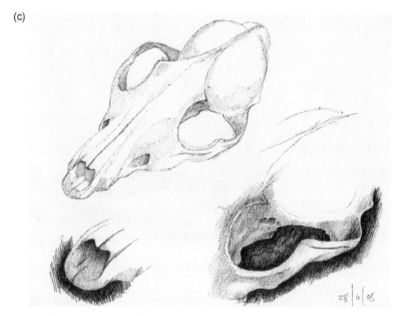

FIG 7.9 a: Tone work used to depict form and texture. b: Tone is used to describe the volume of this fox skull; pencil. c: Tone work used to describe form and negative space; pen and ink.

Although large drawings can clearly be made using a wide range of materials, some materials, such as charcoal and pastel, are more suited to the task. Charcoal and pastel may also be more suited to drawings that deal with tone, whereas other materials are perhaps more suited to line work.

Drawing with a brush using either paint or ink can result in large or small drawings. It might be more difficult to use this medium in a public place, but the nature of the drawing and what paint and ink have to offer make the effort well worthwhile. The flowing lines that brushwork can achieve lend themselves very well to capturing movement; the use of a wash to create shade is suited to describing volume and weight.

Whichever medium you decide to use—paint, pens and ink, pencil, charcoal, or pastels—the choice of drawing surface is an equally important aspect of drawing. Lightweight, heavyweight, smooth, and rough surfaces will surrender different results. Sketchbooks are available with different weights of paper; heavier paper may be more suited to watercolor and drawing with ink.

Mark making and the scope of possibilities afforded by a broad range of tools and processes enable the artist and animator to explore various aspects of movement. Soft graphite pencils provide line and tone; harder pencils may be used to generate crisp lines; the traditional dip pen and ink demand a certainty of approach since they are perhaps less forgiving. These, along with markers and pens, allow for immediacy. Pens of various types give

(a)

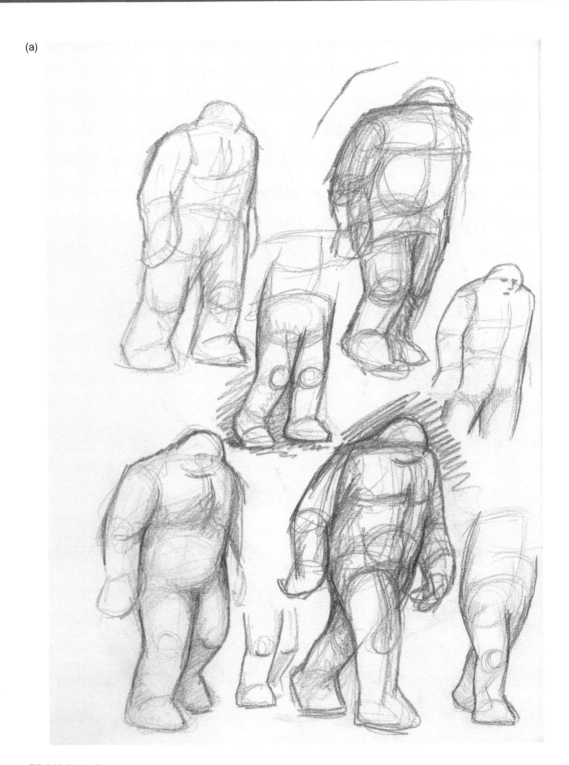

FIG 7.10 Continued

(b)

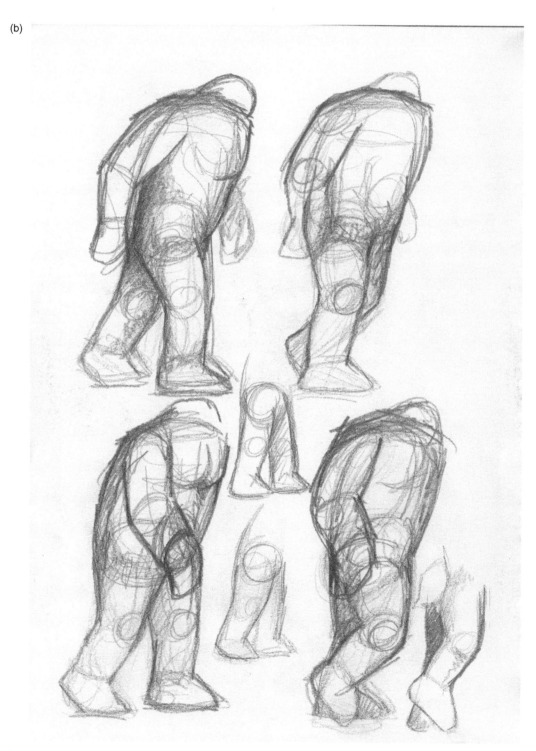

FIG 7.10 Continued

(c)

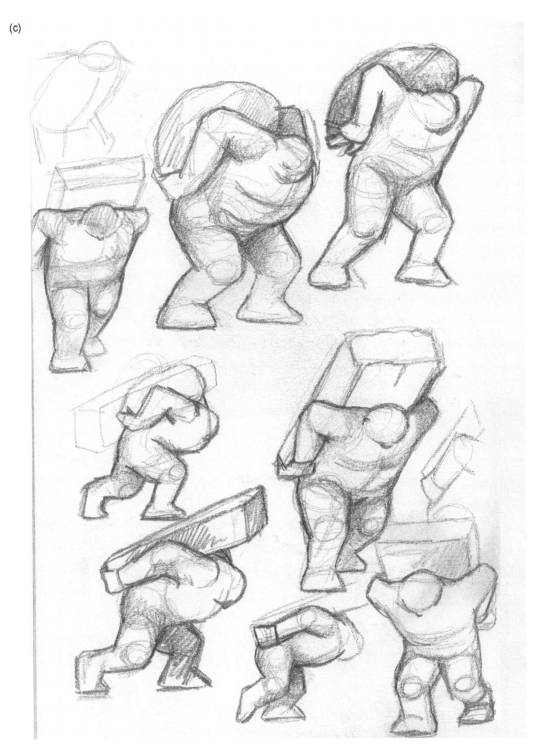

FIG 7.10 Continued

329

(d)

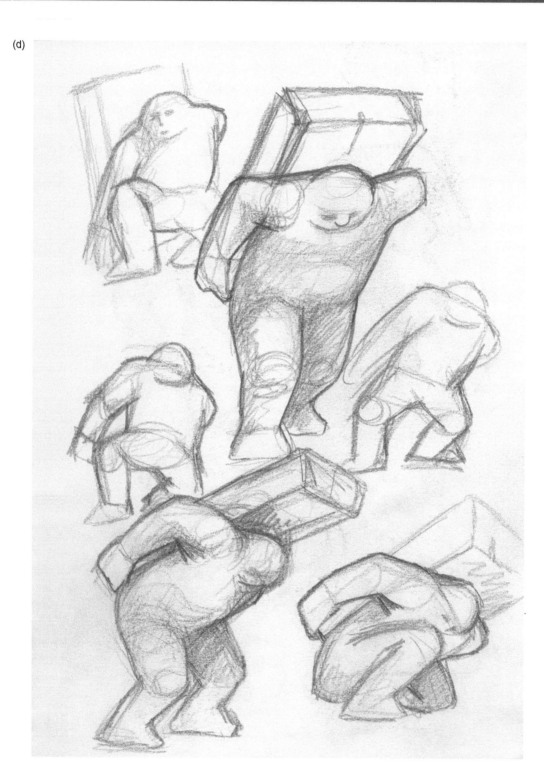

FIG 7.10 Continued

(e)

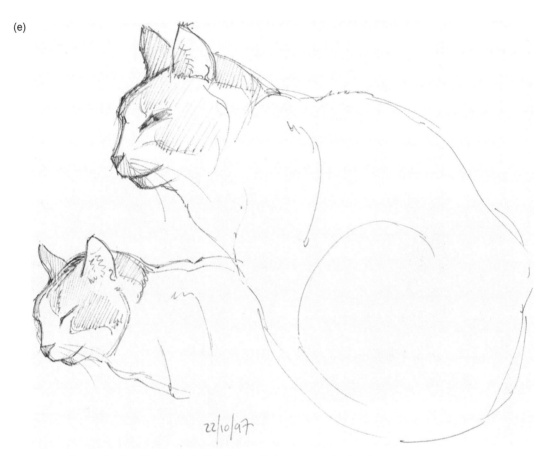

22/10/97

FIG 7.10 a–d: The use of a soft pencil helps when dealing with tone and volume and makes for strong forms. e: Fine pens are useful for line work and allow the artist to pick out the necessary detail.

different results, though they are all rather unforgiving in that once a mark has been committed to the page, it is there to stay. The use of pencils almost encourages you to erase a mark, avoiding commitment to the image. Pens encourage a certain level of involvement with the process, but it could be argued that they also require a higher level of observation before a mark is made. It may also be worthwhile to experiment by drawing with an eraser, making an image by taking away rather than adding to the drawing. Drawings using tone, texture, color, and line all have their place in exploring the various aspects of a subject.

Sketchbooks
There is a long tradition of artists and designers keeping sketchbooks, notebooks, and journals in which they develop their work. These books serve to test ideas, explore possibilities, experiment with techniques, and explore different processes. Sketchbooks provide a private place for a kind of exploration, investigation, experimentation, and study that is not part

of a broader, more public aspect of practice. The benefits of the private nature of sketchbooks and journals are that the results are kept hidden from prying eyes, which can only encourage a level of risk taking in drawing. It is important not to get too precious about the use of sketchbooks, though; the purpose of sketchbook work is to provide a support for practice and a way of helping practice to develop. They are seldom used as part of the practice itself.

FIG 7.11 Choose the right size of sketchbook for the subject and location.

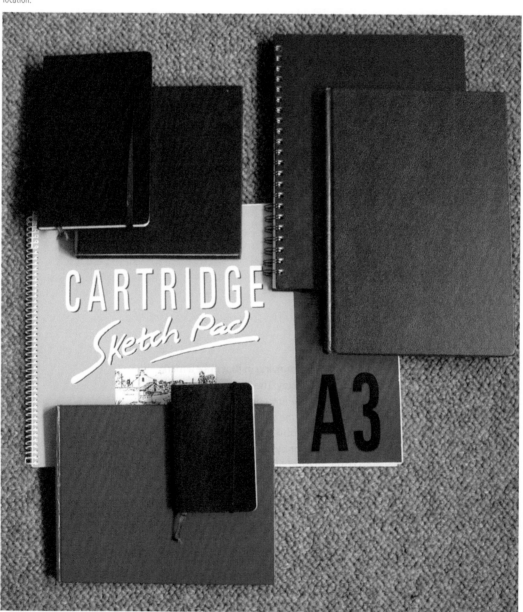

You may find it useful to own a number of sketchbooks of various sizes, each of which can be useful in various situations and environments. Larger-format sketchbooks are perhaps more suited to a studio environment, or at least somewhere the artist has a little more room that will allow work on a larger scale. Making larger drawings enables the use of more materials such as charcoal and pastel, which often need a certain scale to exploit their finer qualities. Large sketchbooks also allow for a broader type of drawing. Drawing at a larger scale often requires a drawing action that is generated from movement at the elbow and even the shoulder for even broader actions. Drawing on a smaller scale generally requires much finer movements that are generated at the wrist or even the fingertips, with the elbow and the shoulder remaining locked. Working at larger scales also allows the animator to make a series of drawings on the same page, creating a sequence of images, one flowing into the other, or making alternative drawings of the same subject.

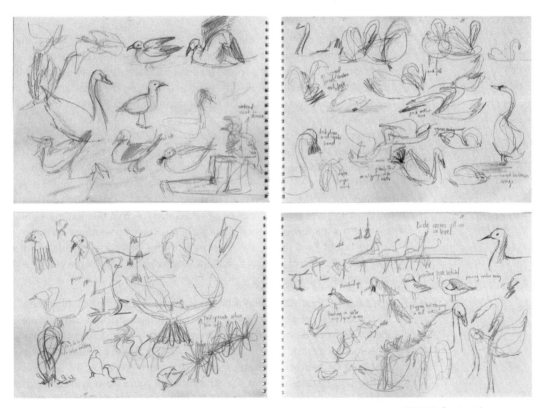

FIG 7.12 Drawing in large sketchbooks allows for larger mark making and bolder drawings.

Small sketchbooks can be very useful if you want to make drawings on location in a particular environment. If you expect to go out and about drawing in public, you may feel the need to be more surreptitious in your approach. Studying the movement of people in public spaces requires a

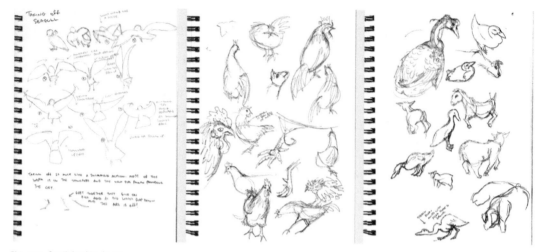

FIG 7.13 Small sketchbooks may allow for a more discrete approach to drawing. They fit easily into a pocket or bag and you can take them almost anywhere.

degree of discretion, particularly in situations such as coffee shops and the markets or on the bus or train, where you will be relatively conspicuous and close to your subject. It would be unfair to make people feel awkward if they knew you were closely observing and drawing them, so take a degree of care to avoid that. Using a small, discrete sketchbook will help. Sketching people going about their daily business at the market, in parks, and at sports events is not easily done with large, cumbersome sketchbooks and a bag full of art materials. This is where the small sketchbook and fine-line pens really come into their own. Working in this way requires speed; you will not have the luxury of spending minutes over rendering a particular aspect of a life model. The subjects will be constantly on the move and the nature of pen and ink dictates that the first mark you make is the mark you are then stuck with. Yes, you can overdraw on the image, but you will not be able to erase with the same ease as you can with a pencil. This type of observational drawing helps you develop a very keen observational eye.

The different kinds of sketchbook bindings also have a bearing on which ones you choose for a particular purpose. I find that small hardback sketchbooks are ideal for working on location because they are small enough to be stuffed into bags and pockets and the hardback offers the protection to the individual pages that I look for. Sketchbooks with a spiral binding allow you to fold the book back on itself, again something that is very handy when you're drawing in confined spaces. I find stitched bindings much better than glued bindings because they seem to be able to take more punishment. I particularly like larger sketchbooks with soft covers to be spiralbound along the top edge. Again, this allows me to fold back the pad on itself and keep the binding well out of the way of my hand as I draw. These are my personal choices; you will no doubt discover your own preferences through experience. There are plenty of options out there.

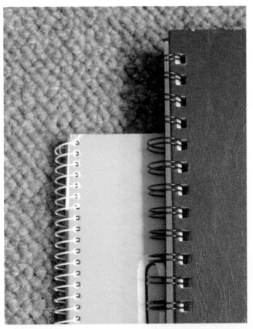
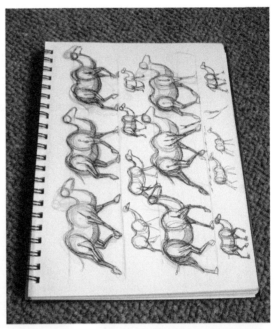
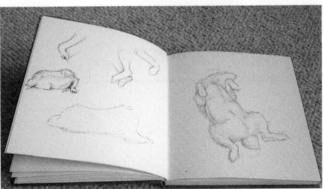
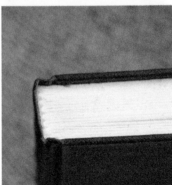

FIG 7.14 Sketchbooks come in a variety of different bindings, those that open flat may be better for use on location, particularly if the size of the sketchbook proves to be a problem. Don't choose sketchbooks with poor bindings as these will almost invariably fall apart.

There are many very good texts available at reasonable prices to help you get started with life drawing or more general drawing from life, some of which are specifically aimed at animators. I have listed a few in the reference section to help you make your choice. As good as these books are, there is little substitute for attending life drawing classes under the guidance of an experienced drawing teacher. You should be able to find life drawing classes in most towns. Failing that, you should use these texts as a guide then use your friends, family, and pets as subject matter.

Finally, a word of caution about the value of the drawings you make for the purpose of analysis. Be very careful not to become too precious about the drawings themselves. No doubt some of the drawings you make will be first rate, but the likelihood is that many of them will have flaws, be incomplete, and disappoint in one way or another. This is not a bad thing; it's normal. Remember, such drawings are made as part of a critical analysis of a subject; they are simply a by-product of that investigation. Their main

(a)

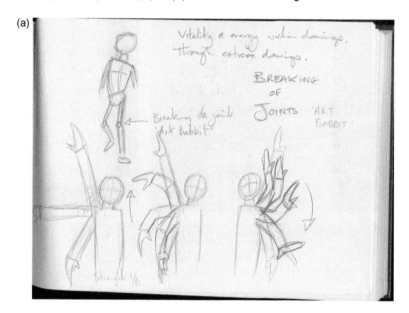

(b)

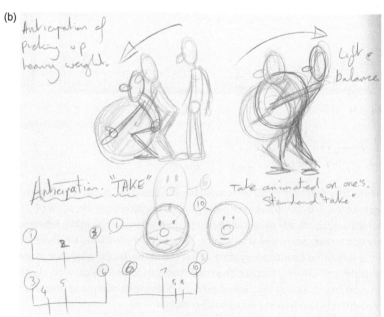

FIG 7.15 Notes and drawings made during an animation lecture.

function is not as an art object in their own right, to be hung on the wall of a gallery, but to help you get through to a deeper understanding of the subject. The real value of such drawings lies in the level of understanding they have helped you gain and the role they have played in developing your ability to more clearly observe, record, and analyze. The drawings themselves may have little value as art objects, and though they might not be the most beautiful things in the world, the learning they will facilitate is beyond price.

It is one thing to say that drawing should make a major contribution to the development of a visual arts craft; it is quite another thing to implement this contribution. For some, the very process of drawing is rather intimidating. For animators who simply find drawing too much of a chore, photography offers a different kind of vehicle for action analysis.

Photographing Action

For many animators who want to analyze action, photography offers one of the easiest and quickest ways to capture and record movement. Photography could be a particularly useful technique for animators who feel less confident with other methods, such as drawing. Photography can also be good news for people who are less comfortable with technology, because it doesn't have to entail highly complicated equipment (though it can) or be prohibitively expensive (ditto). Equipment can be simple, quick, and easy to use. I am not trying to present photography as a better alternative to drawing; it is simply a *different* alternative to drawing. Where possible I would advocate the use of both drawing and photography. Photography offers a contrast to drawing and provides a different perspective on a subject's movement. It offers an opportunity for a different kind of investigation of a subject and provides the animator with different but complementary information. Unless one takes a purely creative approach to photographing, in which the aesthetic nature of the image itself is important and represents an *interpretation* or *representation* of the subject, I would argue that creating a photographic image is rather less subjective than drawing. A photographer may choose to make a selection of a particular part or aspect of a subject, but the focus of attention in a photograph is rather less selective than in a drawing. It takes in the entire field of vision and, in rather general terms, treats each part of the frame with equanimity. The recording of an image in this way is less subjective, and outside certain parameters, such as focus, depth of field, and exposure, it has the potential to provide a more objective approach to capturing an image or sequence. I would not go so far as to say it offers a more truthful representation of a subject, though. If it offers any truth at all it must be considered as one particular truth, a different truth to that provided by drawing.

The sequential photographic work of Eadweard Muybridge was groundbreaking in its day, providing information about movement that was hitherto unknown. To this day his photographs still provide us with an invaluable resource and remain perhaps the most famous examples of this objective approach to capturing movement and analyzing dynamics.

Drawing is clearly a very useful approach to observation and action analysis, but photography is far more suited to recording a specific range of subjects. In doing so it provides reference material that is objective. With the use of very high shutter speeds, cameras are able to freeze a single moment in a very rapid action that even the keenest eye could otherwise miss.

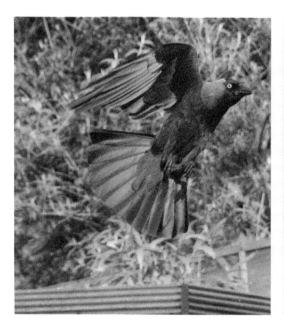 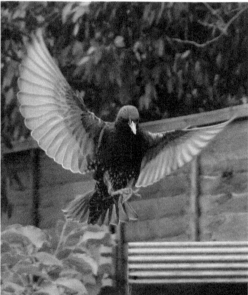

FIG 7.16 Recording fast action will provide details that the human eye may miss.

Single images may be useful for gaining information on the details of a figure in motion, though on their own, without subsequent related images, they may prove of rather limited value. A single frozen moment from within a movement can provide an indication of an action such as balance, positioning of the limbs, rotation of the torso, or angle of the head, but on its own the single image might not be enough to gauge the dynamic nature of the entire movement.

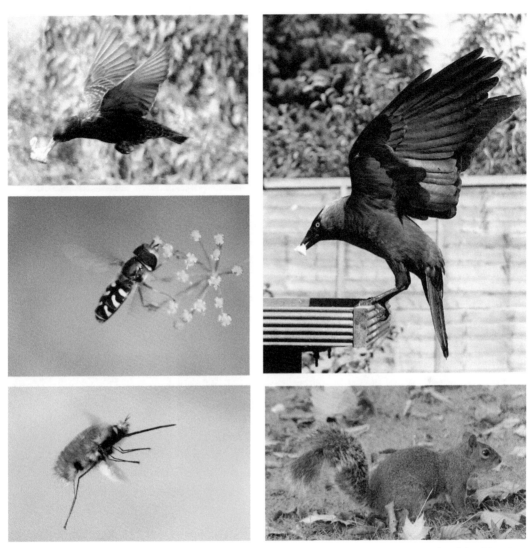

FIG 7.17 A good idea of the action of a figure in motion can still be gained from a single still image that illustrates balance, gait, and posture.

Sequential images are much more likely to provide relevant information on the development and progression of an action over time and demonstrate how the combined dynamics of separate parts of a figure work together to create the entire action. Sequences of still images may provide useful information on the overall dynamics, whereas the individual frames from within the sequence may provide specific information on key moments within the action. These individual images could prove very useful as a guide for creating keyframes for an animated sequence. Rather than using the entire sequence of images, as in rotoscoping, the use of individual images as *guides*

339

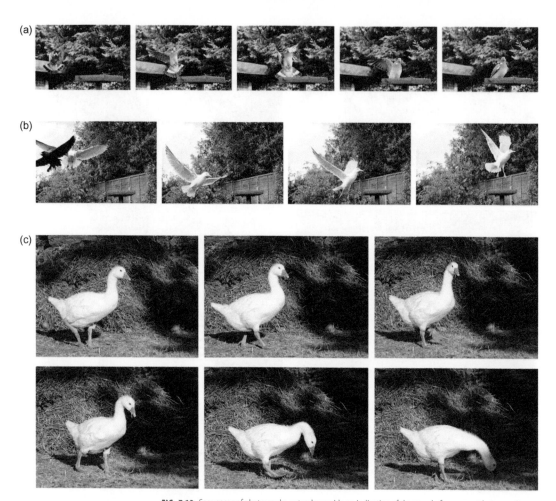

FIG 7.18 Sequences of photographs not only provide an indication of the speed of movement but may give additional information on the action of a figure, its balance, and its dynamic.

for keyframes will allow the animator to make the required adjustments to timing, slowing the movement down or speeding it up. In this way sequential images of a chosen subject may be useful in creating animation of a subject that might be different from the one in the reference material, substituting one figure for another. A running male figure could provide key information for a running woman, for example. Obviously there are limits to the ways in which reference materials can be of use to the animator, though I have seen students successfully using footage of themselves as reference for the animation of a dog—and it worked!

The rate at which technology advances makes discussion of the relative merits and qualities of individual pieces of photographic equipment somewhat irrelevant in this text. So here we deal only with the principles of capturing and recording action for action analysis. For readers who require more in-depth information on technology issues, many very good books and periodicals offer up-to-date information on photography and photographic equipment. I have listed a few in the section on research, though these lists are by no means exhaustive.

Whatever camera you choose to use, it is very worthwhile for you take time to become familiar with your equipment and what it is capable of producing. That way you are sure to make the best use of your time when you're filming your chosen subject. When you're doing research, you need to concentrate your efforts on the nature of the movement, not on solving problems with handling the equipment. Poor results can lead only to frustration and reluctance to engage any further.

Film Cameras

Although film cameras can provide extremely high-resolution images, this form of photography can be very expensive and rather time consuming. The cost of film stock and the processing and printing processes really make this an expensive alternative. As an art form, film photography provides remarkable results; however, for a way of simply recording images to analyze movement, film becomes a somewhat less viable method, particularly measured against a digital alternative. For the nonprofessional or occasional photographer, the advent of digital photography has made creating detailed reference material far easier. Digital technology has made this form of research and action analysis not only much more achievable but far more cost effective.

Compact Digital Cameras

Today you can choose from among a wide range of compact digital cameras that provide first-rate images of high resolution. Just as important, these cameras are relatively inexpensive, very easy to use, and very convenient and are easily carried in a pocket or a bag. These smaller compact digital cameras might not offer the same range of features as a digital single-lens reflex (SLR) camera, but the options that are available enable macro photography, nighttime photography, landscapes, and portraits. They have a built-in flash unit, a timer that allows for delayed exposures (particularly useful for self-portraits), and a facility that allows for zoom and digital zoom. This last feature is very useful for extreme closeup work, particularly if the quality of the final image is not critical, since images made using digital zoom usually result in more "noise," or graininess, on the image. These cameras generally don't have a multiple-exposure option, so sequencing of rapid action is a little more difficult. Compact digital cameras are usually semiautomatic and do not have manual override, which means they do not give you the option to select shutter speed. Although they have zoom facilities, they do not have interchangeable lenses. So, there are clearly are some limitations to this type of camera, but they are more than capable of giving some excellent results and remain a very valuable tool for action analysis.

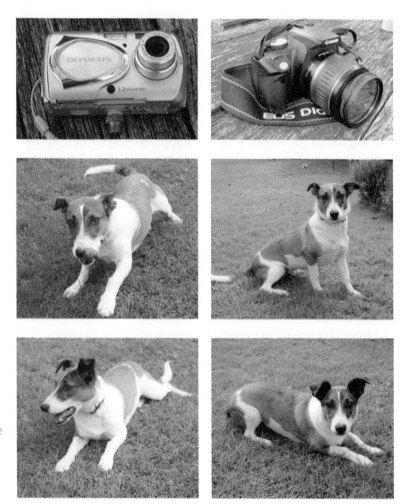

FIG 7.19 You do not need expensive camera equipment to achieve good results. Most inexpensive compact digital cameras may suffice for most of your research.

Digital SLR Cameras

Digital SLRs (DSLRs) offer more control and have more features than compact digital cameras. The most noted of these features is the fact that they offer the opportunity to change lenses. Other than that, the DSLR offers a range of modes in which to operate. In manual mode, the DSLR allows a highly flexible range of functions that include focusing and selecting shutter speeds, ISO ratings, white balance, and sequencing. Very long exposures are possible with DSLRs, as are very fast shutter speeds that allow you to capture very fast actions.

Unlike traditional film cameras where the subject's latent image is captured on the surface of a plastic film coated with light-sensitive material to be processed and then transferred to a second piece of light-sensitive material, in digital cameras the image is first captured on a sensor, a charge-coupled device (CCD), that offers varying degrees of resolution measured in megapixels. This device responds to light falling onto it in a similar manner to film. After the device captures the image at the moment the shutter is opened, a second stage occurs during which the image is downloaded to a memory card inside the camera, where the image is then stored. Unlike film, the CCD does not retain the image forever but is cleared and is then ready to capture the next image.

Film Speeds

Traditional photographic film still meets the needs of a certain part of the market, though digital photography has largely taken over in the enthusiast and hobbyist market. However, film speeds are not simply of interest to those working with more traditional technologies. Film speeds differentiate between the light-sensitive qualities of different types of film stock; these qualities are available to the photographer using digital technology.

The rate at which photographic film material reacts to light is known as the film's *speed*. The faster the film reacts to light, the higher the speed rating of the film. Digital cameras do not use film stock, but the sensors of digital cameras react to light in the same way film does. Unlike film stock, which has a predetermined sensitivity, the sensitivity of the CCD sensor can be

FIG 7.20 Images created using different ISO setting allow for the capture of action in different situations. a: Slow action allows for greater detail to be captured. b: A high ISO setting allows for much higher camera speeds, though this results in image "noise." c: Low light conditions calls for higher ISO settings that allow you to use the shutter speeds required to capture the action, even if it is a slow action. d: This low ISO setting allowed for capture of detail even with a shallow depth of field.

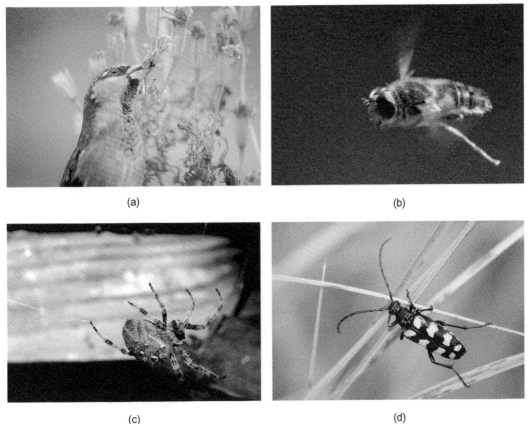

(a)

(b)

(c)

(d)

adjusted. This is done through setting the sensitivity rating known as the International Standards Organization (ISO) number, and in this way it reflects the capabilities of a range of different film stocks.

The range of settings is commonly between 200 and 800 ISO, with the higher numbers representing the greater sensitivity and faster film speed. The lower numbers represent less sensitivity and slower film speeds. There are advantages and disadvantages to both fast and slow film speeds as well as high and low ISO ratings.

Fast film, because it reacts more quickly to light, allows for very high shutter speeds, which make it rather more suited to capturing fast action such as sports events or animals in motion. In this way you can ensure that the moving image is recorded sharply in focus. The other advantage of high-speed film or high ISO numbers is that they are suited for low-light conditions, enabling shutter speeds fast enough to capture action where lower film speeds would require such slow shutter speeds that image sharpness would be more difficult to achieve. However, there are downsides to high film speeds and high ISO ratings. The higher sensitivity of photographic film is due to the coarseness of the grains in the film emulsion. This then results in grainier images. Likewise, digital images taken with a high ISO setting have a higher level of digital "noise," which looks rather like the grain in film stock. The lower the ISO number and the slower the film speed, the finer the detail of the final image.

Lower ISO settings may result in much finer detail in the resulting image, but the cost of achieving this higher detail is a less sensitive CCD that then requires slower shutter speeds to achieve correct exposures. This makes it rather more difficult to capture fast action and at very slow shutter speeds makes the whole process more vulnerable to camera shake.

Lower ISO numbers around 200 result in crisper images; higher ISO ratings, up to 800 or more, generate higher levels of digital noise, making them grainy and less clear. This choice is the kind of compromise that you need to assess in each situation.

You will probably find that the quality of the image needed for action analysis can be kept to a reasonably low level. As long as the images are clear enough for your research purposes, there should be no need to take the level of care generally desired for high-quality prints.

Technical Issues

You need to take into account a number of technical considerations when you choose photography as a medium for capturing action. However, these considerations don't need to be restrictive or become an overriding issue. Your images don't need to be works of art for them to make analysis worthwhile. You just need to ensure that the photographs are at least reasonably well framed, sharp, and correctly exposed.

Exposure

Achieving a correctly exposed image involves a combination of separate elements that require different settings on the camera. *Exposure* refers to the amount of light falling onto a light-sensitive material or surface. Exposure is determined by the shutter speed and the aperture setting. The correct exposure of any given subject will vary under different light conditions and is controlled by the photographer, who determines exactly how much light should fall on the light-sensitive material, either film or the CCD in a digital camera. Too much light and the image will be overexposed and too light; too little light and the image will be underexposed and too dark. This is not necessarily determined by either dark or bright conditions; the exposure can be adjusted to account for that. The exposure is controlled by the amount and duration of light falling onto the sensor and may be varied by changing the shutter speed (the duration of light) or the aperture (the intensity of light). It is often difficult to achieve a correct exposure for all elements in an image, so some aspects may be under- or overexposed while the main element of the photograph is correctly exposed.

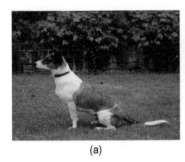 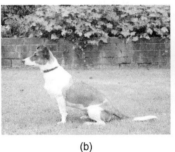 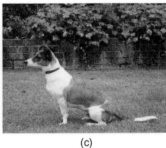

(a)   (b)   (c)

FIG 7.21 a: Underexposed. b: Overexposed. c: Correct exposure.

Lens Aperture

We have seen how the intensity of light is one element that determines the exposure of an image. This intensity is controlled by the size of the aperture that allows light to fall on the sensor. Rather like the eye's iris, the mechanism in the camera, also called the *iris*, may be adjusted to allow more or less light onto the sensor. The aperture may be opened or closed through a series of settings across a range of diameters. These diameters are measured in units known as f-stops. The lowest f-stop numbers denote the widest aperture settings. The widest aperture setting, allowing the most light in, is f2.8; the smallest aperture setting, allowing the least light in, is f22. A range of f-stops is available between these two extreme settings, and cameras vary in how these are adjusted. Some allow for third- or half-stop increments. In this way very fine adjustments can be made.

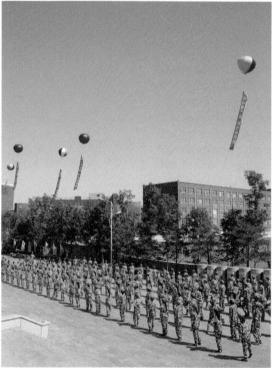

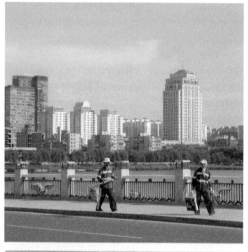

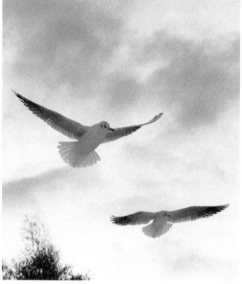

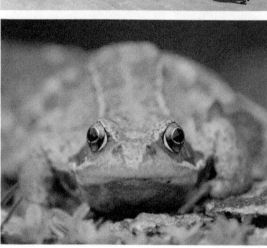

FIG 7.22 Different f-stops combined with different shutter speeds will allow you to achieve different results: deep or shallow depths of field, high or low shutter speeds to capture action, and of course recording the subject in different light conditions.

Shutter Speeds

The shutter speed determines how long the shutter remains open, thereby varying the amount of light it allows in. Digital compact cameras are fully automated and do not have the facility to change the length of exposures. In Digital SLRs, when in manual or certain semiautomatic modes, the shutter speed can be adjusted. Long exposures are achieved by very slow shutter

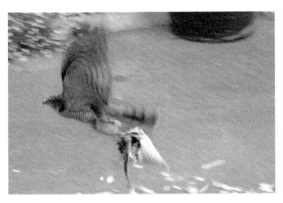

(a)

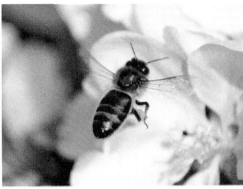

(b)

speeds that can be of an almost indefinite length; this may be very useful for photographing subjects in very low light conditions, but such long exposure times may not be of particular use when you're trying to capture action. Short exposures are achieved by fast shutter speeds up to 1/2000th of a second. Such high shutter speeds are critical for capturing actions. The faster the action, the faster the shutter speeds you'll need.

In addition to the duration and intensity of light, we have already seen how the sensitivity of the film or the digital sensor also plays its part in determining the amount of light required to achieve a correctly exposed image.

FIG 7.23 Choosing the right shutter speed is important. a: A relatively slow shutter speed has resulted in motion blur. b: A faster shutter speed has allowed the detail of the wing to be captured.

Depth of Field

Depth of field refers to the distance that extends in front of and behind a chosen subject, which remains sharp and in focus. A really deep depth of field may extend a great distance, from a few meters away from the camera all the way to the horizon. A very shallow depth of field may extend over only a few millimeters. A shallow depth of field can be used in a very creative manner for the purposes of capturing images as part of your research into action analysis, but a greater depth of field can provide images of a subject that is in focus in its entirety. Fully sharp images from front to back should at least allow for a more thorough analysis of your subject.

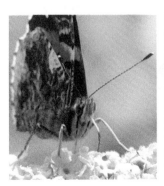

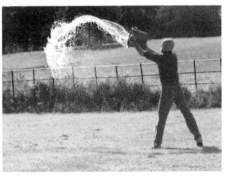

FIG 7.24 The appropriate depth of field (sometimes shallow, sometimes deep) may make the analysis of action easier.

347

The depth of field may be determined by a number of factors, such as the lens aperture, the distance of the subject from the camera, and the focal length of the lens being used. The depth of field may be adjusted using a combination of these controls to create the desired effect:

- *Lens aperture.* The wider the aperture the iris is set at, the shallower the depth of field becomes; the narrower the aperture, the greater the depth of field. When you're adjusting the lens aperture, you can ensure the correct exposure if you compensate for the light levels by the duration of the exposure. Increasing the lens aperture will not only let more light fall onto the sensor, it will shorten the depth of field. As a result of the increase in light, a faster shutter speed will be required to maintain the required exposure. Conversely, by decreasing the aperture, less light will fall on the sensor; therefore slower shutter speeds are required to achieve a correct exposure. As a result of this narrower aperture, the depth of field will be lengthened.
- *Focal length of the lens.* The focal lengths of different lenses will result in varying depths of field in specific series of shots. With the figure at a given distance from the camera, the depth of field is increased as the focal length of the lens is decreased. In this instance a wide-angle lens with a shorter focal length, such as a 28mm lens, has a greater depth than a standard 50mm lens, which will in turn have a greater depth of field than a telephoto lens with a focal length of 300mm.
- *Distance of subject from camera.* The depth of field will also change in relation to the distance the subject is to the camera. Using the same lens of the same focal length with the same aperture setting, the depth of field will increase the further the subject is from the camera. This principle applies to lenses of all focal lengths.

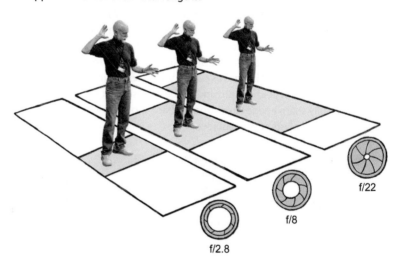

FIG 7.25 A wider aperture (low f-stop value) results in a shallower depth of field.

Lighting and the use of flash photography enable another approach to action analysis, though one that needs a higher level of control and thereby has built-in limitations. *Chronophotography* is the recording of several images onto a single frame. These photographs are achievable by the use of strobe lighting in a studio environment, though similar results may be achieved by the layering of images using Photoshop.

Using a DSLR, the photographer has the option of a fully manual mode, semiautomatic modes, or fully automatic modes. They all have their advantages. If you choose a fully automatic mode, the camera selects the appropriate combination of shutter speed and aperture to ensure a correctly exposed image and focuses on the subject. Other semiautomatic settings allow you to prioritize either the shutter speed or the aperture setting. If you select the shutter speed as priority, the camera selects the aperture setting required to create a correctly exposed image. If the aperture is set as a priority, the camera will select the appropriate shutter speed to achieve a correct exposure. It is also possible to allow the camera to automatically focus on the subject, though this could result in the camera focusing on the wrong element in the frame. In the fully manual mode, the photographer determines all settings as well as focus. This approach does offer maximum control, but it also requires more effort. In very pressured situations, when the photographer needs to act quickly, it might not be the best option. Each situation requires its own approach.

You need to give some consideration to the desired resolution of your images and the format in which you want to use them. If you intend to print your images, you will need to increase the resolution, though the file size will increase along with it. The higher the resolution, the better the quality of the image. Unless you are preparing work that is intended for commercial print purposes, images that range between 150dpi to 300dpi should be high enough for most personal uses. The resolution is one of the determining factors in the file size. The other is the area size of your image. If you intend to use the images only as screen-based resources, 72dpi should be adequate. It will certainly make for much smaller file sizes while maintaining decent quality.

Photoshop is a very powerful tool with very many features and uses. Unfortunately, there is simply no room here to do anything other than discuss this tool in the simplest of terms. You'll find some first-rate texts out there that deal with Photoshop and photography. Once again, in the resources section I list a few that I have found very useful.

Photoshop can be used for a wide range of purposes though I have restricted the discussion here to the way I use it for processing images for the purpose of action analysis. I also use it extensively for my other photographic work and my animation but in very different ways. For action analysis I simply use it to process my digital images for printing or for screen-based reference. I never go beyond making the images as clear as possible, and to that end I rarely give the making of these images any purely aesthetic considerations. For the most part, when I use Photoshop to process images for action analysis, I crop the image to the frame format I require and change the contrast, image, and resolution. The batch processing of multiple images using the actions facility in Photoshop is very useful and saves me a lot of time. I then save the files as JPEGs for ease of use. I am sure that you will find your own way of processing your images.

Lenses

Using different lenses present the photographer with many more options for capturing action. Compact digital cameras offer a zoom facility that allows for a range of shots using telephoto and wide angle options as well as a digital zoom, which enables extreme closeups, though with a loss of some quality by way of noise; however, the DSLR enables the use of interchangeable lenses. The digital zoom mode on compact digital cameras can prove pretty useful for achieving closeup shots of wildlife and the like.

DSLRs offer more flexibility through the use of different interchangeable lenses, of which there is a very wide choice on offer. Lenses fall into two general categories: prime lenses with a fixed focal length and zoom lenses.

Wide-angle lenses range from the ultra-wide-angle lens of around 14mm to those with a focal length of around 28mm. These are very useful for landscapes, interiors, and portraiture.

Standard lenses have a focal length around 50mm and are useful for a range of subjects, from landscapes to portraiture.

Telephoto lenses range in focal length from around 75mm to 500mm and are used to photograph subjects at a distance. Telephoto lenses are ideal for sports and wildlife photography.

Zoom lenses offer variable ranges of focal length in a single lens. These focal lengths generally fall within a particular range, though there are lenses that offer a much wider focal range. Zoom lenses of the type in which the focal length and field of view can be adjusted without the need to refocus are standard in digital compact cameras. Lenses range from ultra-wide-angle ones to large telephoto lenses. Each lens has its particular qualities and uses and is suited to different situations. For this reason, photographers often own a range of lenses to cover the demands of different subjects. Possessing a number of lenses with different focal lengths can be very expensive; you can achieve a lot with a single lens with a modest range of focal lengths. You should be aware that lenses with a very wide range of focal lengths, from the wide angle to extreme telephoto, are likely to produce images of lower quality. As with so many other matters, the choice of lenses appears to be a matter of compromise and personal needs.

A number of specialist lenses are available that come in different forms and are intended for a relatively narrow range of uses. Macro lenses permit very close focus, allowing the study of very small subjects or extreme closeups of a subject. Super-telephoto lenses allow for photographing subjects at extreme distances; fisheye lenses achieve the unusual effect of creating an extremely curved image; tilt-shift lenses allow for the manipulation of perspective by adjusting horizontal and vertical planes. Most of these lenses are not used in general photography and may be of limited use in capturing action for analysis.

A tripod provides additional stability for your camera and helps reduce camera shake, allowing for slower shutter speeds, which may prove useful for recording slower actions. Recording fast action requires a much faster shutter speed that might not require the use of a tripod. However, the stability of a tripod enables a consistent framing of the background to be achieved over a number of frames as the subject travels through a series of shots.

FIG 7.26 Sequence of a subject moving through a shot.

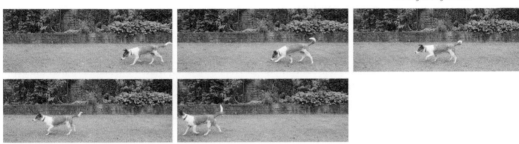

A good, robust tripod with a smooth action will not only provide a stable platform for the camera, it will allow for a constant panning shot to follow the subject as it moves through the environment. This action may be a little awkward if you have to pan the camera and press the shutter release set on multiple shots at the same time; it is more useful for video.

FIG 7.27 Following the subject with the camera keeps the subject in the center of the frame.

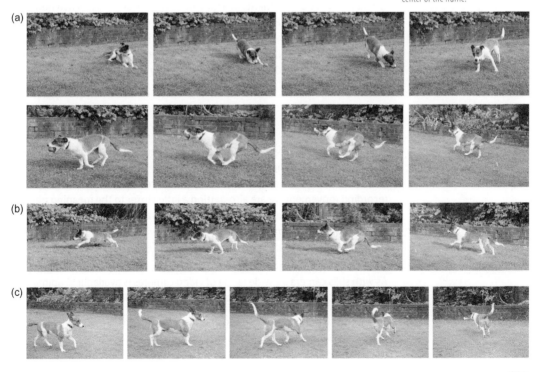

Studio-based photography could be an option for you. If so, strobe images provide a series of images on a single frame, which can give you additional information about a figure in motion, such as the distance between particular points on a figure: elbows, knees, and shoulders. Compositing a number of separate images onto a single frame using Photoshop provides another way of achieving the same result.

Mobile Phones

Over recent years the inclusion of cameras in mobile phones has become the norm. Use of these cameras has grown increasingly popular as the quality of lenses and the images mobile phones can produce have also improved. The resolution these cameras provide might not match the standard that the SLR or even a compact digital camera can achieve, but many are capable of giving more than acceptable results. They have fewer features, but their ease of use and the fact that they are so very convenient make them very useful tools in capturing, recording, and studying action. Most mobile phones also have the capacity to record video, though the screen might not be large. As a result some of the detail may be difficult to fully analyze, but they are still a powerful tool for the animator.

As with any other camera, it is important to hold the mobile phone steady while either taking photographs or recording video footage. Try to follow the action by moving with a steady motion while keeping the image well in the frame. Try not to be tempted to keep moving the camera in a random fashion to focus on different elements of a moving subject; don't try to film a number of different aspects of a moving subject in one go. This approach will just create a sequence with very distracting camera movements and make analysis very difficult at best, impossible at worst. The more camera movement within a sequence, the more difficult it will be to get any useful information from the resulting images.

Filming Action

Video footage of a moving subject obviously offers the animator an additional element that photography, drawing, or even first-hand experience can provide. As I have said elsewhere, *timing gives meaning to motion* and by recording movement we are also getting a little closer to the meaning of the motion. It is the inclusion of a timeline that gives an indication not only of what happened but *when* these things happen within the course of an action.

Video Cameras

As with stills cameras, a wide range of video cameras is available to animators, and not all of these cameras are prohibitively expensive.

The normal filming rate, recording and playback, for video is 25 frames per second for PAL and 30 frames per second for NTSC. However, it is possible to film footage at a higher film rate that when played back at normal speeds creates a slowed-down action. The high-speed camera I have used in creating some of the sequences in this text is capable of taking up to 1100 frames per second. Considering that a standard filming rate is 25 frames a second, you can see that this enabled a thorough analysis of high-speed action by slowing it down a great deal. Choosing the appropriate record speed was an important part of this filming. If I filmed the subject with too slow a record rate, the full detail of the motion would not be captured; too fast a record speed and the action is slowed down so much that a clear analysis becomes more difficult. I found that ordinary actions such as walking or running filmed at 250 frames a second offered the detail I was looking for while maintaining a sense of the dynamic. For actions such as splashing water, breaking glass, galloping horses, flying birds, or fast-action sports, speeds of 1000 frames a second captured all aspects of very fast motion.

FIG 7.28 This is the hide I use to record birds in my garden. a: Exterior. b: Interior. c and d: The camera being used in the studio.

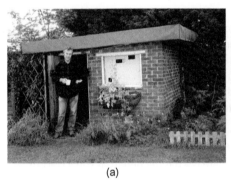

(a)

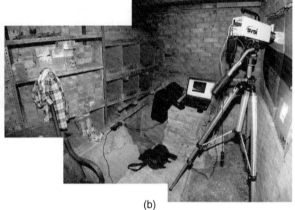

(b)

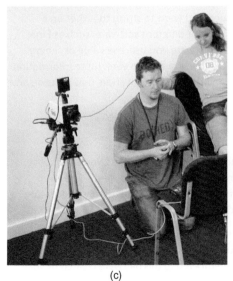

(c)

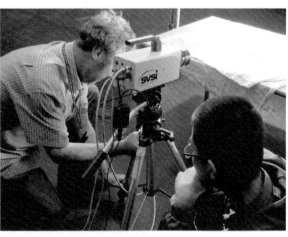

(d)

Of course, recording and playing back in real time are options that present the most accurate timing and reflect exactly the movement of the action. However, footage viewed in real time may be less good at showing the full details of an action and may in some regard limit the analysis of a particular aspect of a movement or make the analysis that much more difficult, particularly with very fast actions.

As with still photography, it is important to ensure that video footage is sharp and correctly exposed if you are to be able to analyze the action fully. Footage taken using a handheld camera is obviously more subject to camera shake than that captured using a tripod, so wherever possible use a sturdy tripod when you're filming subjects for action analysis. Since the primary reason for recording the moving image is for the study of motion and not the creative or aesthetic use of the footage, it seems sensible to aim for the most stable form of capturing the moving image.

Creating Movies

Having filmed the work, it would be useful to have it in a form that can be easily stored and retrieved. Saving the footage as QuickTime movies and storing them on an external hard drive will provide an original source of reference. Unless, of course, you intend to create an archive of different actions, you will probably find that you will need to store only a relatively small amount of work for a limited time.

You may also find it useful to edit the research footage of different actions to create a sequence of different shots. This would certainly help in building performances, but there is a danger here that you'll start to take away from the creative performance-based aspect of animation. I would recommend that such sequences form the basis of study rather than straight imitation. For editing sequences together, I tend to use Adobe Premiere to edit any sequences I want to string together on a timeline, but others will no doubt favor different software, such as Final Cut Pro. Regardless of the editing software you use, the value of seeing different shots in a sequence will allow you to gain even more information about an action and how it fits in with the action of shots that precede and follow it.

Motion Capture

For completely accurate capturing and analysis of actions, you can choose from among a number of automated motion capture systems. These are becoming more prevalent, particularly in the computer games and feature film sectors of the animation industry.

The first automated systems for the capturing of information based on kinetic movement and the analysis of such movements were mechanical. The best of these and the ones that are remembered to this day were created by Jules

Marey. You'll find more about these in the chapter on the study of motion.
The origins of digital motion capture began with the scientific use of motion-
tracking technology, developed in the 1970s and 1980s. This was undertaken
as part of research into biomechanics, for much the same purposes as Marey's
early devices. Since the first development of digital motion capture there
have been many applications of this technology, including military, scientific,
medical, sports, and other uses, to gain accurate information and create equally
accurate simulations. Motion capture allows us to analyze the movement of
humans and animals, which is very useful in assessing the performance of
athletes and analyzing the gaits of animals. Given the cost of thoroughbred
horses, capturing and analyzing their actions and thus assessing their potential
could make a great deal of difference to their value as breeding stock.

(a)

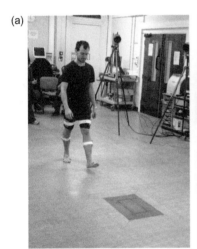
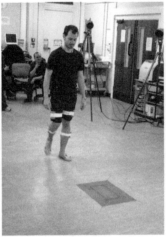
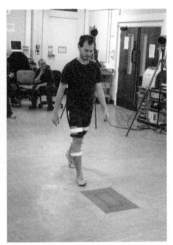
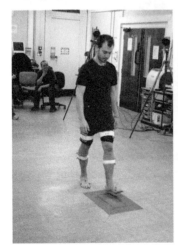
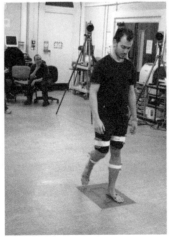
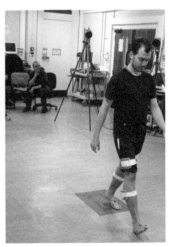

FIG 7.29 Continued

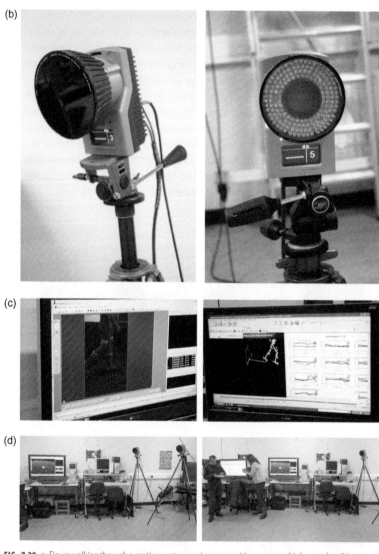

FIG 7.29 a: Figure walking through a motion capture environment with sensors on his legs and walking over a pressure pad set in the floor. b: Motion capture cameras. c: Motion capture results displayed on the computer. d: Motion capture studio.

In filmmaking, motion capture is more often used for more creative, interpretational, and entertainment purposes, to create animation for digital characters.

Automated Systems
Motion capture is a process that captures and records detailed information usually of the movement of humans and animals in digital form which is then translated onto a digital model of varying types.

The use of motion capture extends beyond capturing and recording figurative movement: it also incorporates the capture of facial expressions. Motion-capture techniques and processes used in conjunction with an actor as a subject have created some remarkable performances. They played a major role in creating the performance of Gollum in the *Lord of the Rings* films. This was achieved by a mixture of the movements of performer Andy Serkis, who gave life to Gollum, and the CG animators, who used more traditional keyframing techniques. The movements are captured as data, and while they are conformed around the general physiognomy of the performer or subject, they do not include all the performer's physical details. Therefore the movements of one subject may be easily mapped onto a character of different design. The technique allows for a speedy and relatively inexpensive way of creating naturalistic action on which the animators can then build. This efficiency has been a boon to the features and games industry, which uses these systems to great effect.

Camera moves may also be recorded using these techniques so that the performance, captured digitally, can be mapped onto previously recorded live-action camera moves. Match moving allows for camera tracking of digital camera moves and the live-action moves and for accurate compositing of the different elements to integrate them seamlessly into the same scene. Camera tracking and match-moving techniques are not only responsible for some of the more spectacular shots in feature films; they are also starting to appear regularly in other forms of filmmaking, including wildlife documentaries.

There are a number of systems available for motion capture. They fall into two distinct areas: optical and nonoptical systems.

Optical systems operate by tracking markers placed on the subject that are detected by an array of electromagnetic sensors positioned in such a way as to create a performance area. Within this area the movement is triangulated by a given number of sensors. This number may vary; the greater is the number of sensors, the more detail that can be gathered on the subject. This raw data then needs to undergo a level of processing before it is applied to a computer model. Animators may then work with this automated movement to refine or add additional movements.

Nonoptical systems fall into several categories. Some systems use a series of gyroscopes to make the necessary measurements of movement, but these inertial systems currently lack the accuracy of other systems. However, they are much cheaper systems than optical systems.

The mechanical motion system gathers motion data directly from sensors placed at specific points on a data-capture suit. This works rather like an exoskeleton because the sensors form a rigid structure comprising a number of linked, jointed rods that correspond to the subject's physiognomy. Sensors placed at the joints then detect the relative movement of the performer's arms, legs, and so on. The nonoptical mechanical systems clearly have their applications, but they are capable of achieving more limited data-capture volumes than the electromagnetic optical systems.

Rotoscoping

Rotoscoping is a process of copying a subject's actions, *not* directly recording them. One of the earliest rotoscoping systems was developed in New York in 1917 by the Fleischer brothers. The first experiments were undertaken in an effort to make the level of fluid animation achieved by Winsor McCay, though with more efficiency and requiring less skill. McCay was, after all, a superlative draftsman and a remarkable animator with a highly developed sense of timing, and there was certainly a shortage of those at the beginning of the 20th century. Max Fleischer devised a process in which a subject's movements were initially filmed in live action and then the individual frames were traced, providing slight exaggerations to the action to fit in with the cartoonal images they required. Along with his brother Joe, Max built a system that was later to help provide much of the animation for one of their most famous and enduring creations, Koko the Clown, in the *Out of the Inkwell* series of films. Max's other brother Dave proved to be an excellent subject for these first experiments, which were quickly used for animation production.

Analyzing Action

Once an action or a sequence has been recorded or captured as a series of drawings, photographs, or moving images, the next stage is to systematically analyze the action. There certainly are processes that will assist in this analysis. The aim of this exercise is to observe things as they actually are and not as we suppose or expect them to be. This takes a little time to learn since we seem to be preconditioned to see things in a certain manner. This truism has been evident in the number of occasions I have seen student animations in which they get the sequence of arm and leg movements in a human walk cycle wrong and are unable to see for themselves the errors they have made. I have seen this time after time; some of these young animators remain oblivious to their mistakes until it is pointed out to them, at which point they are amazed that they made such fundamental errors.

Regardless of the depth of action analysis or the reason for undertaking it, the analysis benefits from a systematic approach. This approach can include observational analysis and the categorization of actions, deconstruction of actions, a mechanical analysis through the measurement of forces, movement, and the gathering of the data related to the action. Much of this type of analysis may be of interest only to scientists who require very specific and highly accurate information for very specific reasons. The consumption of energy may surrender information on the efficiency of muscles under certain conditions; the detailed analysis of a horse in motion may provide valuable information on injuries or the potential for performance. The projection of performance under any given situation may have very important implications. The manner in which certain materials perform and the effect of external forces on them could result in bridges staying upright, nuclear power resources remaining within safe operational limits, and other things that we all have a vested interest in. Clearly, for animators' purposes, the analysis of action need not to be this detailed; the outcomes of our analysis might not have such far-reaching or critical implications.

Of course, the analysis of action varies depending on the medium involved. Viewing live footage depends on the use of a timeline, which might or might not include a time code. Analysis of the moving image can be undertaken as a continuous sequence or frame by frame; each has its benefits. Analysis of the moving image can also provide individual images taken from video footage to identify possible key poses. Some aspects of analysis are common to the moving recorded image, first-hand observation, or the still image, one of which is the deconstruction of movement in an attempt to better understand the movements. This should lead you to the identification of primary action: the source of the action, secondary action, and tertiary actions found in both still and moving reference material.

You can deconstruct action for analysis in a number of ways. Here we concentrate on three of them, each of which will yield a different understanding of movement: the Four A's of Animation, the hierarchy of action, and phases of action. Let's start with my own breakdown and classification of animated movement, the Four A's of Animation.

Four A's of Animation

I have divided animated action into four individual elements, each of which represents a different level of movement. If you can identify the movement you are studying as within one or more of these categories or possessing aspects of these elements, you are in a better position to more clearly analyze the movement. As a result you may be in a better position to replicate this movement in your animation. The Four A's are:

- Acting
- Animation
- Action
- Activity

These categories are arranged in a hierarchical manner, activity the lowest and acting the highest. I believe that an appreciation of these categories will make an invaluable contribution to your understanding of action and help you develop your practice to the highest level.

Activity

Activities are the most basic forms of movements that are not associated with any kind of recognizable action. The term simply denotes movement of an object across time and space. The movement may display variable dynamics, but it does not describe any recognizable action. This type of action can be illustrated by such subjects as animated titles (text rolling across the screen); it is animated action but it does not relate to anything seen in nature or that is character driven.

Action

Action refers to a type of animated movement that we can associate directly with a particular object or thing. In this type of movement we can see the way things behave when affected by external forces. We can see the action of waves on water, leaves on the trees being blown by the breeze, or the way objects fall. Consider the behavior of balls made from different kinds of material as they roll along a surface. Each one would a demonstrate different action, depending on a range of circumstances: its size, mass, shape, the material it's made of, flexibility, and so on.

Animation

Animation is a type of movement that is instigated from within a particular animal. This type of movement carries some degree of intention; an animal considers moving and then undertakes that movement because of the original intention and *not* simply as a result of external forces. The nature of the movement will be determined by the motivating factor. The complexity and variety of such animated movements are enormous. The big difference between animation and action is that animation is an *intentional* motion, whereas action is a *consequential* motion.

Acting

The highest category of animated action is acting. Acting movements are determined by the subject's psychological conditions. Not only are such movements also subject to the laws of nature, as with actions; they are intentionally undertaken (as in animation) but they are also motivated by thinking and the emotional condition of the subject. This is the foundation of performance and acting.

We already covered some of this concept in the chapter on the principles of animation, but I think it is worth repeating here.

Analyzing the Moving Image

The best way to study motion is to look at motion, but unless this is done through keen observation and an understanding of what we are looking at, we are likely to remain passive viewers, *not* observers. There is a big difference between the two. There are two separate ways of analyzing the moving image: one, through first-hand observation, being there as the movement happens, and the other, the analysis of a recorded action. Both methods have advantages, and if possible both should be undertaken.

It could be argued that first-hand observation allows for a fuller appreciation of the overall three-dimensional actions of a subject as it moves through space, without any of the depth of image compromised, as happens when the action is captured on film or video, essentially two-dimensional formats. However, first-hand observation demands a great deal of concentration, and if a given action is not repeated, much of the important detail of an action may be overlooked, particularly if the action is a fast one. For example, a running figure repeats the action over and again, thereby allowing the study of the separate elements that make up the action, whereas a jumping figure may be an unrepeated action, one that cannot be fully grasped in all its complexities if seen only once. It could also be argued that a greater sense of the actual timing of an action is gleaned from observing the movement first hand, the action being experienced as it happens, in the same timeframe.

The recorded image has the advantage that the recording can be manipulated in a number of ways to assist the analysis of action. The footage may be stopped, rewound, slowed down, and sped up. It can also be viewed again and again at the animator's leisure. The recorded image does flatten the space, but this does not often present a difficulty, though the quality of the filming and resulting footage obviously has an impact on the analysis. Slowing images down does not necessarily provide a clearer and therefore better understanding of the action since a soft-focused subject and motion blur may obscure the details. Some of Muybridge's original photographs suffer this way, particularly those depicting the fast action of birds in flight, where a combination of the subject's speed and the occasionally rather ambiguous outline of the birds' wings serve to obscure the nature of the action. Though these images managed to capture general motion of a figure, they failed to capture the necessary detail.

Let's look at how we can begin to analyze the recorded moving image. You might want to take notes on key moments within the sequence using the time code as a reference, though you might not need this level of accuracy.

1. Begin by establishing which part of the action you want to analyze. It might not be the entire sequence, or it might be just a single part of the moving figure.
2. Start by viewing the action in its entirety, trying to get a feel for the overall speed and dynamic of the movement.
3. Run the sequence through a few times, but at this stage try not to focus on any one aspect of the figure. Your aim should be to gain an overall impression of the subject's movement as it travels through space.
4. Note where the action begins to speed up or slow down or whether the figure moves at a constant rate throughout the action. Get a feel for the variations in timing.
5. Once you have done this and are satisfied that you have a feel for the overall timing, start to look for the source of the action. This is the primary action. View the sequence a few more times.
6. Now scroll through the action at a slower rate still, concentrating on the principle source of action, and begin to look for the key moments in the movement. These moments will vary depending on the nature of the action. It could be when a foot makes contact with the ground, when a hand takes hold of an object, or when the subject's torso becomes fully straightened. The variables are almost endless.

7. Try to identify the various phases of the action, such as the preparatory phase, the execution phase, the resulting phase, the recovery phase (see the following for a fuller example). Depending on the nature of the action, not all of these phases may apply.
8. If necessary, start to view the detail of a *specific* action frame by frame, shuttling backward and forward to reveal all the detail.
9. Now begin to compare the different states and positions of the various parts of the figure at a given moment. When one foot makes contact with the ground, for instance, notice what the other feet are doing.
10. Go through these separate stages of analysis for each of the actions: primary, secondary, and tertiary.
11. Finally, view the footage again in real time, this time observing how each of the three categories of action (primary, secondary, and tertiary) work together to create the entire movement.

Analysis of Timing

Timing gives meaning to motion. In animation, timing is everything, and without controlled motion through timing we are left with movement that is little more than simple activity—objects moving through space and time without any indication of purpose. Timing provides the *illusion* of speed, weight, and balance—and ultimately character and personality.

So, how do we go about making an analysis of motion? To start with, we need to understand the importance of being able to discern the subtle differences in timing. This is fundamental to the development of animation skills. As animators we need to develop a highly evolved appreciation of timing, rather like a photographer has a highly developed appreciation of light. Animators use timing as a raw material the way painters use paint or masons use stone and fashion designers use fabrics. Time is the raw material for animation, and the basic unit of time is the *frame*. The great animator Norman McLaren knew full well the importance of the frame. He said:

> Animation is not the art of drawings that move but the art of movements that are drawn; what happens between each frame is much more important than what exists on each frame. Animation is therefore the art of manipulating the invisible interstices that lie between the frames.

The analysis of timing takes practice and it takes patience, and it can be learned through a systematic approach. When students first begin to study animation, they tend to make things move in a rather crude manner, and they find it very difficult to analyze the action they have created. Many of them find it very difficult to discern between footage that they themselves have shot on one, two, or three frames and are generally amazed when these variations are pointed out to them. Within a matter of two or three weeks of practicing animation—and more important, analyzing their animation—they too are capable of undertaking subtle analysis of timing and recognizing errors of a single frame in a sequence.

In addition to this appreciation of timing, animators need the ability to analyze action by breaking it down into constituent parts, to identify the subtleties of dynamics, recognize the complexities of acceleration and deceleration, and appreciate the details of an object moving through space.

When you're starting to analyze an action, however simple, or a group of actions, don't try to take in all the separate aspects of the action(s) all at once. Instead, take a systematic approach to the analysis. It is likely that on first viewing the action you will not be aware of all its complexities; these will become apparent only once you begin to deconstruct the action. Instead you should concentrate on one aspect of the movement at a time. If necessary, take notes in a notebook; if you're looking at live action, identify the point on the time code where a particular action occurs.

- It might sound obvious, but you should start by establishing exactly what it is that you need to analyze in the action; it might not be the action in its entirety.
- Go on to identify the start and end of the action you want to analyze. This might not be the start and end of the footage; it might occur at some point in the sequence.
- Then try to get a sense of the overall speed of the subject and its movement through space.
- Take a note of the phrasing of the action, identifying when the movement speeds up and when it slows down.

Only after you have gained a feel for the overall action should you go on to the next stage of analysis, in which you should look for and identify the three categories of the hierarchy of action:

- Primary action
- Secondary action
- Tertiary action

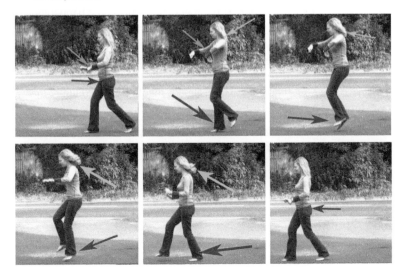

FIG 7.30 In this example primary action is indicated by the red arrows. Secondary action is indicated by the blue ones, and tertiary action is identified by the green arrows.

Do this in a systematic manner, and don't be tempted to skip from one to the other. We covered these classifications earlier in the text, but it is timely to discuss them here as well. The following list of the four stages of analysis is not exhaustive, though it does provide a good working framework for your analysis:

1. Start by identifying the primary sources of the animation; these are the parts of the figure that are the driving force behind the motion. Depending on what the action is, it might be provided by the legs, the arms, the torso, the head, or a combination of these. Identify whether the source of primary action shifts throughout an action—for instance, in rising from a chair, a figure might start with the primary action in the torso, then shift to include the arms, and then shift again to the legs.

2. Once you have taken note of the primary source of animation, look to those other movements that assist the action and make the action easier or more efficient but that are not the driving force behind the movement. An example is the swinging arms during a walk cycle. They assist with the movement but are not essential to it.

3. Once you are happy with noting the secondary actions, go on to identify tertiary actions—the actions that happen simply as a result of the primary and secondary actions and that play no part in motivating or causing the overall movement. An example might be the movement of a horse's tail as it walks. The tail's action is a result of the walking and does not contribute to the walk.

4. Finally, you should go back to looking at the action overall, trying to assess how all these different elements fit and work together to create a cohesive whole.

It is important to understand that all actions do not fall neatly into simple classifications, nor do they necessarily occur one after another. Actions can occur as simultaneous actions (a number of different actions occurring at the same time), combination actions (a number of different actions happening at the same time to create a single dynamic), or sequential actions (one discrete action following on from a previous action). However, most movements, even a very short sequence of movements, involve more than one of these different classifications of action throughout. The trick to getting a full idea of the dynamic is close observation. As I have already mentioned many times, this takes time and it takes practice.

In addition to the other classifications of movement, an action may be deconstructed and broken down into different phases:

*   Preparatory phase
*   Execution phase
*   Resulting phase
*   Recovery phase

Not all actions demonstrate each of these phases. Furthermore, there is an additional phase—the return phase—that can occur when a figure moves back into its initial state before the preparatory phase. This is common among cyclic actions such as a repeated hammering action.

To fully understand a particular movement, we might find it useful to look at the action and its various phases rather than try to analyze the overall movement. There might simply be too much detail to take in all at once. As we have already seen, there is some value in initially looking at the overall action to get a feel for what is happening. It will then become useful to break down the action into a series of separate parts or phases. This exercise will be beneficial even if these separate parts or phases appear to flow smoothly from one to the other or if the actions of different elements of a subject happen at the same time, are staggered, or have different and variable timings. Indeed, only by splitting up an action in this way will you be able to fully appreciate all its detail and complexity. As part of this process, identifying the start and end points of an action is vital.

Preparatory Phase
You may find that the preparatory phase of an action is commonly referred to in many animation textbooks and by most animators as *anticipation*. In limited animation or actions using very broad cartoonal animation conventions, anticipation becomes an important part of reading a sequence. During this phase the subject generally adopts a posture or position in preparation for the subsequent action. For a figure to leap, for example, it might be necessary to bend the knees; to throw a punch, it is necessary to draw the arm backwards in preparation for the next phase.

Execution Phase
During the execution phase, the subject expends the force so that the action can take place. The nature of this phase may be fast, extremely powerful, and dynamic, as in a hammer being brought down onto a nail, or it may be a small, subtle, and gentle action, as in a surgeon's knife cutting into a patient.

Resulting Phase
The resulting phase may be an extended phase or a rather short phase, depending on the nature of the action. The extension of the arm at the extremity of a throw may be momentary before the figure begins to recover from the action or the throw. In jumping, the resulting phase would be part of the action during which the figure lands, the feet make contact with the ground, and the knees are compressed.

Recovery Phase
During the recovery phase the figure, having completed the main part of the action through preparation, execution, and resulting phases, moves into a more stable and balanced posture.

Let's take a look at these different phases and how they apply to a specific action. In this case we will look at a figure jumping from a standing-at-rest position. We may consider the action here in two distinct parts: taking off and landing.

Taking Off
Preparatory Phase
The figure begins the preparatory phase by standing completely relaxed in an upright position. The figure then bends at the knees with the torso tilting forward to around 45 degrees. At the same time, the arms move backward, rotating at the shoulder; the head pivots at the neck to maintain a horizontal and forward-looking gaze. The three distinct actions—the bend in the knees, the movement of the arms, and the tilt of the torso—occur simultaneously, though only the bend in the knees is a primary action; the others are secondary.

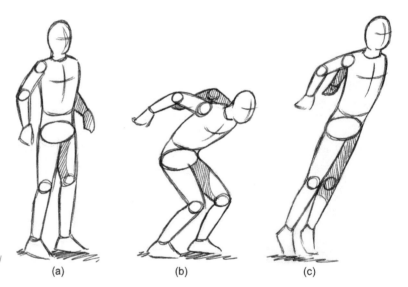

FIG 7.31 The phased sequence of a jump. a: Starting position. b: Preparatory phase. c: Execution phase.

(a)　　　(b)　　　(c)

Execution Phase
The knees are flexed rapidly, providing the thrust for the jump the arms swing quickly forward and the torso straightens. The head pivots to maintain a horizontal alignment of the eyes. These actions are combination actions because they work together to create the single action, though they are slightly staggered. The legs and the flexing of the torso are primary actions; the movement of the arms is a strong secondary action. The movement of the hair is a tertiary action and happens only as a result of the other movements.

Resulting Phase
The figure is propelled through the air as a result of the previous actions. The period during which the figure is moving through the air is as a direct result of the preparatory and execution phases.

Landing
Preparatory Phase
The resulting phase of the takeoff is quickly followed by another action that may be considered a second preparatory phase as the figure swings the legs forward in anticipation of landing. The torso straightens and the head rotates to maintain its horizontal orientation.

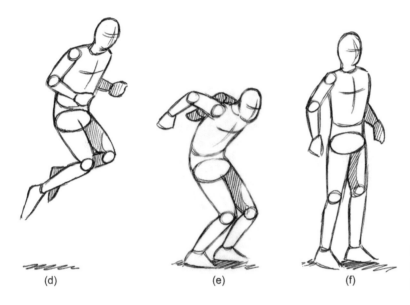

(d)   (e)   (f)

FIG 7.32 The phased sequence of a jump. d: Resulting phase. e and f: Recovery phase.

Execution Phase
The legs are extended ahead of the torso, and as the feet make contact with the ground they quickly flatten from their initial contact point on the heels. The knees then begin to bend, acting as shock absorbers.

Recovery Phase
During this part of the action the figure returns to its original standing position and once again is at rest.

Cyclical actions may have another distinctive phase—the return phase—as the figure moves back each time to a position that preceded the preparatory phase. Actions that have a clear beginning and end, such as a chopping action, clearly demonstrate this phase. However, in some cyclical actions that are more or less continuous, such as a walk cycle, a return phase is not evident because there is no distinctive start position.

As we have discussed elsewhere in this text, identifying the primary, secondary, and tertiary elements of an action, along with the separate phases, will go a long way toward providing us with a thorough and proper analysis of an action.

Reading a Sequence

The way we look at individual actions and the manner in which they can be deconstructed leads us to the analysis of a sequence of movements. *Reading* such a sequence of movements adds yet another level of complexity to the process of action analysis, but once again, if undertaken systematically, it need not present too difficult a problem.

Here we attempt to establish the timing of animation in a sequence. Unlike the timing of an individual action, simply called *animation timing*, the timing of a sequence of actions is known as *phrasing*. This term describes the way that separate movements work together sequentially to create an extended movement that in some instances could be described as a dynamic narrative. The separate actions that form the sequence often have their own distinct dynamics and timing that, seen together as a sequence, form a series of variable timings, rather like a dance with fast, slow, and intermediate phases. These sequences are sometimes linked through sudden transitions from one state to another; at other times there may be a slower and more steady transition from one phase to another. Let's consider for a moment an athlete undertaking a triple long jump. This will involve a number of separate and

FIG 7.33 Jumping action illustrating all phases and how the figure moves from one to the other.

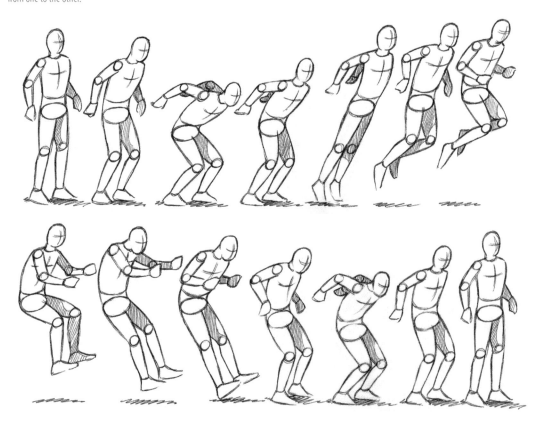

distinct actions that each can be broken into the separate phases described earlier, but they may also be analyzed as a sequence of actions that create the whole.

- The preparation for the jump may be a rather slow one, with the athlete rocking backward and forward, shifting his weight from one foot to the other, with slight adjustments to the arms to maintain balance as he psyches himself up for the jump.
- There will be a transition phase from this state into the full run down the track.
- The run itself will increase steadily in speed as the athlete prepares for the jump itself.
- The sequence then moves into a phase where the athlete takes an initial short jump from one foot, landing on the other foot.
- The next movement is the second and larger jump, during which the athlete undertakes a series of movements using the arms and legs to help propel him through the air.
- At the end of this action the figure lands in the sand pit with his feet extended fully forward.
- The final action is where the figure recovers from the landing and stands up.

Breaking down this sequence in this way, we can see how it is constructed from a series of complex actions, each of which has its own timings. To read a sequence and analyze the various actions, we need to approach it in a logical manner.

It is important in analyzing a sequence, as it is with the analysis of a single action, to start by gaining an overall impression of the sequence. Begin by identifying the aspects of the sequence you are interested in analyzing. It may be the entire sequence or just part of it. Start by viewing the sequence as a whole a few times and in doing so aim to get a sense of the dynamic shifts: when does it move quickly and when more slowly? The next step is to identify the various actions that make up the sequence. Try to notice how these actions link with one another. Are there smooth transitions from one action into another? Do they suddenly change from one action to another? Is there a discrete linking action that sits between two or more fundamental actions? It is perfectly possible for each of these transformations to occur in a single sequence.

Once you have got a feel for the individual actions, start to look at the pauses or spaces between the separate actions. These are just as important as the actions themselves. Rarely are the periods between the actions completely without a motion of their own. Although they might not be as dynamic as the main actions, they do need to be identified and understood as actions in their own right. Look for any shifts in emphasis in actions throughout the sequence. It is these shifts that give a sequence a choreographed feeling.

Staging Actions and Choreography

Many of the simplest of the actions we undertake are often planned before they happen and staged in such a way as to achieve a very specific goal. These staged actions are not necessary as part of a performance but are done to produce a very particular result or a more efficient manner of locomotion. Driving a car involves a series of synchronized actions that by necessity are planned to a high degree. If they weren't staged in a particular way, the very act of driving would be impossible. The example we saw of the athlete undertaking a long jump can be seen as a series of staged actions. Each of the actions was predetermined and planned, with the body undergoing actions in a particular order, at a given speed, with various parts of the body behaving in a very specific manner, bearing just the right amount of load or providing the right amount of force.

These actions, although staged and choreographed, might not be conscious decisions on the part of the figure—just a natural process, either learned or developed instinctively or both.

The choreography of action does not apply to dance actions alone but can include regular and repeated events in an overall movement. These may well conform to a distinct rhythm, the kind that you might find in dance movements. Even the hammering of nails into wood demonstrates a rhythm, and the example we have already used, that of driving a car, is a form of choreography.

Choreographed action is also demonstrated during the interaction of individuals engaged in collaborative actions. These can be either physically integrated actions that demand the efforts of a number of individuals to achieve a single physical task or a choreographed action, or one that does not involve a common workload but still involves teamwork. An integrated action may be one in which two or more individuals act in unison to achieve a particular task and contribute to a unified single action, such as two figures engaged in lifting a single object. The choreography of the individuals' action is fundamental to achieving the goal. Choreographed action may involve actions that aren't integrated but still involve work from individuals acting as a team. Through necessity and structured behavior their actions allow them to achieve a common goal. All team sports such as baseball, football, and rugby conform to this form of choreographed action. The different team members undertake separate and distinct actions and may have very different workloads, but each action is synchronized and choreographed in such a way as to achieve a single performance and objective.

While we're analyzing this kind of character interaction, group actions, and choreography in the same way and following exactly the same processes as the analysis of a single action, there are additional elements to look out for:

- Look for any hierarchy within the action and whether a particular individual within the group instigates the action.

- See if you can determine a reason for this instigation. Is there one individual stronger than the others, or is it a leader within a group? Animals working in groups often display strong hierarchical pecking orders.
- See if the dynamic shifts throughout the action. Do members of the group take the leadership role in turns? If so, can you determine any pattern to this?
- Establish the level of synchronization within the group. This will vary from example to example. A skein of geese in migratory flight will synchronize their wing beats to the lead bird in order to cut down on drag and gain greater energy efficiency, but there will be a slight delay in their individual actions as the birds move from one type of action (powered flight) to another (gliding) and back again. Some groups, such as synchronized swimmers, require some of the actions of the entire group to happen exactly at the same time.
- Look for the distribution of labor in a group and identify whether there are individuals taking on the majority of the work and the reasons for this.
- Look for specialist activities within the group. Some groups may display none at all, such as a group of hunting wolves, or there may be a great deal of specialist activity within the group, as in football teams.

Analysis of Performance

During the analysis of action, we have mostly been concerned with looking at identifying the nature of the action, categorizing actions, ways to recognize differences in timing, identifying key moments in an action and in a sequence of actions. We've looked at changes of pace and direction, and we've looked at effort. We've considered individuals and groups and intention and goals as instigating factors in creating action. All this has been focused on the physical. In the analysis of performance, we need to take this much further than looking at the physical aspects of an action; we need to look beyond the actions themselves to the causes of the actions.

It is useful to be able to recognize the instigating factors for actions and how physical actions come about and change as a result of emotional shifts. We need to identify how physical actions are driven by psychological states, feelings, moods, and temperament. A character's action is not simply a result of his physiognomy but also of his personality. This type of performance-based movement is at the heart of much of what we do as animators, and if we are to fully develop these skills we should have an appreciation of these motivating factors. Performance is not simply the movement through time and space of a figure or the actions necessary to complete a task; it is based on the rationale for the movement and points to a wider contextualization and underpinning narrative. Understanding this and mastering the art of creating such movement is the highest of my Four A's of Animation. It is called *acting*.

However, not all performances should be classified as acting. Each of us chooses to behave in a given way that will shift and change depending on our situation and circumstances at the time. People reinvent themselves all the time and modify their behavior accordingly. Our "performance" when we are with our friends will be very different from our performance when we are with our work colleagues or with strangers or in a strange town or country. Even when with different members of our own families, we are likely to modify our behavior and "perform" in different ways. We reinvent ourselves constantly, and to appreciate these changes the student of action analysis needs to become more than an observer of the physical—she or he needs to become one that attempts to understand and appreciate the human condition.

The actions of people we observe who are motivated by psychological rather than simply physical issues are complex. It is practically impossible to claim with absolute certainty how and why a figure chooses to move in any given manner, because the factors governing those actions are so complex. External factors are not specific to the individual but could affect that person's behavior. Cultural issues may influence a person's actions; what is deemed to be acceptable and perfectly normal in one society may be frowned on in another. Sociopolitical aspects will in some instances impact behavior, as may the class or status of an individual in a society. Gender, upbringing, education, and employment will all determine, to a greater or lesser extent, the nature of actions and performances.

The nature of the performance is also determined by the personal as well as the social and is subject to nature as well as nurture. Mood, temperament, and personality can be shaped by external factors and are, it could be argued, to some degree attributable to social groupings, but they are in general considered solely the nature of the individual.

We can undertake the analysis of performance in several ways, each of which will provide us with different results. From the outset I would urge animators *not* to immediately turn to animation for the study of performance. I am not suggesting for one minute that the study of animation for animators is not a worthwhile activity and that you will not benefit from such study; far from it. However, I am claiming that animators who turn *only* to animation for their study of performance are severely restricting the development of their understanding of performance and in doing so limiting their own creative potential.

First-hand observation remains one of the best ways to gain an understanding of the ways people behave. This is the raw material of performance, the stuff of which performances are built. To gain first-hand experience of how "performances" are put together and structured, you could do a lot worse than use the theater as a school for the study of human behavior within a narrative.

Those who can't or choose not to go to the theater can access another first-rate resource of performances. Use a range of film and television performances, either in the form of animation or live action. If you are to get the best out of this kind of reference material, you need to shift from being an ordinary member of the viewing public to become an analyst of the action.

Animation provides invaluable insight into how other animators undertake an interpretation of a performance; live action offers a record of how people move within their environments and respond to each other. Live-action performances, though not necessarily ordinary and in some cases rather artificial and extreme, are not mediated by a separate artificial process through drawing or modeling.

Look initially at the nature of the performance. Is it a drama, is it a documentary, is it poetic, is it naturalistic, is it humorous? To properly analyze a performance we must first be aware of what we are watching. This is relevant if you are to understand the nature of the dynamics and timing that *may* be associated with different types of performance. Comedy, for instance, is largely determined by timing, which is critical if it is to be successful and funny. Any comedian or comedic actor will tell you that timing in comedy is everything.

- Look for the dynamic in the narrative, how the shifts in the story are reflected in the changes in the action.
- Look at each character separately and in turn, then begin to analyze the role each character takes in the sequence. Is this individual driving the narrative, responding to others, or remaining passive?
- Begin to analyze the way the characters interact. Look for links and tensions between the different performers, and look for the way the characters influence one another and the situation.
- Make a note of the delivery of dialogue, the tone in which it is delivered, the volume, the intonation. Don't just listen to the words being spoken; listen to what is being said. The two are not always the same.
- Take note of how a character responds to dialogue, the emotional change that comes about as a result of the words and the physical action that comes about as a result of the thinking about what is being said.
- Take note of the eye contact between characters. A lot can be understood about the relationship between individuals from a simple exchange of glances.

This topic is covered in more detail in the chapter on action in performance and acting.

Analyzing Still Images

Still images have a more limited use for the analysis of action because they contain less information than a sequence of images that track the direction over a series of images or the moving image that depicts speed and events over time. However, a single image does have value. A single image may be difficult to gain much information from with regard to the speed of the subject, but it may still provide an indication of the balance of the figure, the direction of movement, and some inference can be gained about the period before the image was taken, and even a suggestion of the movement that may follow the second that is captured within the still. Of course, there can be little certainty regarding the speed of the action, but even a still image will give *some* indication of speed.

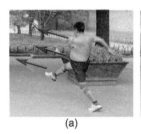 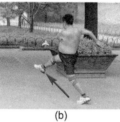 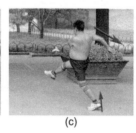 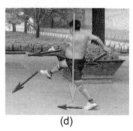

(a)   (b)   (c)   (d)

FIG 7.34 It is possible to make an analysis of motion even within the single image. a: Gives an indication of the general direction of the motion. b: Illustrates the start and end position of the foot and the direction of action. c: Indicates the upward action of the supporting foot during the kick, the rotation of the upper body and the backward motion of the arm. d: Indicates the center of gravity and the potential position of different parts of the figure as the movement progresses.

Clearly, a sequence of images will reveal more information than a single image. Viewing several stills together will clearly show the shift of balance and the sequence of movement of the individual elements of a figure. For many years animators have used the still images produced by Eadweard Muybridge to good effect.

Analyzing Animation

So far we have looked at the analysis of action as video, still photographs, sequences of images, or first-hand observation of movement. Now let's turn our attention to analyzing animation that we have created.

Learning to animate involves far more than sitting in front of a computer or at a lightbox creating images or manipulating puppets. Developing your craft skills in animation takes the form of experiential learning. We learn by doing. Rather like learning to ride a bicycle, animation cannot be done simply by reading books, watching films, or attending lectures, although all of these help. Animation is learned by animating. However, unlike riding a bicycle, animation is also learned through analyzing and by reflecting on completed work, making an evaluation of that work before going on to make more work. I suggest that the evaluative process is more important to learning how to animate than simply animating. This is why the ability to analyze your work clearly and honestly is vital.

Walt Disney understood the value of analyzing animation and the importance of this analysis in creating believable acting and performances that were at the heart of the films he made. He would gather together with his animators to view the results of their efforts in what became known as *sweatbox sessions,* to make observations and comments and call for amendments and changes.

Practice is essential if you are to make the required improvements to your work, so making animation on a regular basis will allow you to progress, develop your skills, and gain an understanding of your craft. However, I would argue that the real learning process takes place *after* the animation has been completed. Through analyzing your work and reflecting on your efforts, applying methodical objectivity, a deeper understanding can be gained. Undertaking such analysis of your own work on your own will yield results, but better yet is to review and analyze work in a group situation.

It becomes difficult at times to recognize the quality in the animation we ourselves have made. Often it's easier for others to recognize these qualities, both good and bad, in the animation we produce. People who have had no involvement in making the work won't be as close to the animation and can often see through some of the baggage that you inevitably develop during the act of making the work. You might find it difficult to see past issues you encountered while making the sequence and your value judgments that have evolved as you made the work. It is easy to be dismissive of our own efforts. It is also easy to fool ourselves into thinking that our aims have been achieved with a particular piece of animation. It might be that the thing you are trying to achieve with your animation is very evident to you, but it might not be so apparent to others, particularly those who get to see the work only once. Never forget: It is for people who get to see the results of your efforts only *once* that we make our work in the first place.

Analyzing work in groups will provide a deeper insight into the true nature of the completed work. For this you will need mutual support. That does not mean that it should become a cozy, mutually backslapping group. Supporting others means telling them exactly how you see it. You need to have confidence in each other and be able to rely on each other's judgment. Criticism should be qualified with full commentary and feedback. Simply stating that something is "cool" or, on the other hand, "rubbish" is less than helpful. It is important to state *why* something is good and *why* something is poor. This should be followed by suggestions for improvements. Of course, these comments can be made only if those analyzing the work fully understand the animator's aims and what the animator is trying to achieve. By fully articulating your thoughts on the detail of the animation, the individual or group not only helps the animator make an assessment of his work, but those making the comments are also developing their own powers of observation and analysis. This is what is called a win/win situation. In fully analyzing your work, you will be in a better position to reflect on the results and make the necessary amendments and improvements. Remember, it is easier to identify the aspects of the animation that are poor and that can be improved by amendments; it is far less easy to identify those good qualities. We are far more apt to accept that something is successful and then quickly move on to the next task at hand. This is a serious mistake. If we are unable to identify and state *why* a piece of animation is successful, we are far less likely to be able to replicate our successes. We will simply be depending on chance. This is not good enough. It is therefore necessary to assert the *reasons* that the animation either works or doesn't work.

The analysis and reflective process is a cyclical one:

1. Establish the aims.
2. Gain a general impression of the work.
3. Undertake more detailed analysis of the work.
4. Reflect on the findings.
5. Identify problems.
6. Establish solutions to the problems.
7. Implement the changes.
8. Begin the analytical process again.

A systematic approach should be taken to the analysis of your work and undertaken in several separate stages:

1. You will need to establish exactly what you are trying to achieve with any given piece of animation. This goal can be identified in a storyboard or an animatic, and you may have clear instructions from the director. If you are unclear as to your aims or what you are trying achieve before you commence the animation, how will it be possible for you make an assessment of the success (or otherwise) of your work once you have completed it?
2. Don't be in too much of a rush to make a judgment about your work. It is natural that you will make an assessment of the work *as you make it,* but you should avoid making a decision regarding the animation's success until you have fully analyzed the shot. You should wait until you have completed a shot or sequence before you even attempt to make a thorough assessment of the work.
3. You will find that using a notebook to identify the good and bad points of the work will help you in your objective analysis. *Do not* try to remember the good or bad aspects of your work; write them down, making a note of when they occur within the sequence. At this stage do not be in a hurry to write down the solutions to the problems; simply identify the problems. You need to give yourself time for reflection before you attempt to create solutions to problems.
4. If you date the comments on the work you are analyzing in your notebook, you may find it useful to look back on and identify the progress, or otherwise, you have made over an extended period.

5. Start the analysis by viewing the work all the way through a number of times in real time to gain a general impression of the timing and the phrasing. This will allow you to gain an overview of the work.

6. Once this is done, begin to note specifics about the animation, such as character interaction, weight and balance, follow-through, squash and stretch, and so on. Begin by identifying the primary animation, moving onto secondary then tertiary dynamics.

7. To analyze the separate elements fully, you will probably benefit from viewing the work a number of times by scrolling through the sequence frame by frame and, if necessary, scrolling backward and forward over just a few frames.

8. Through this more detailed analysis you should simply identify the good points in the work and list them. Go on to identify the problems separately, making a list of them also. Make a note of time codes, frame numbers, or drawing numbers. This will help you identify exactly where the problems are. It helps if you are making rough line tests that the drawing numbers are clearly visible on the pencil tests.

9. You should remember to view the work in the context in which the audience will experience it. Looking at lip sync without sound is completely useless. Likewise, viewing a shot in isolation may well provide you with detailed information about that shot, but it will do little to identify any problems with continuity in a longer sequence. Wherever possible, take a look at the shot you are working on alongside the shots that precede and follow that one. You are then able to ensure that there are no continuity problems and that the animation is in keeping with the rest of the work. By cutting the animation into the appropriate point in the animatic, you will be able to check for errors or problems as the production progresses and make any ongoing alterations before the final edit. It is essential to check the quality of the animation as it is being made, particularly if more than one animator is creating it. The end result should look like the entire animation was created by a single hand.

10. Give yourself space between making the work and assessing the work. First impressions are important, but they can also be deceptive. Good points can be easily overlooked in the heat of a moment. Only after a reflective period should you establish what changes are required.

Making a systematic analysis of your work in this manner will yield results quite quickly. I think you will be surprised at the progress you make through such analysis. At first you might find it difficult to identify problems with your work. Remember you are learning to see, not simply to look.

Of course, it is possible to test animation at various stages as it is being made and before the animation is complete. Those of you familiar with traditional drawn techniques using paper on a lightbox will no doubt be familiar with flipping and rolling techniques, which enable the animator to check a number of drawings against one another.

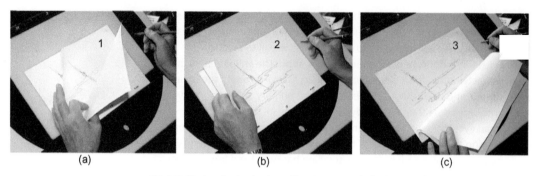

FIG 7.35 Flipping animation drawings. a: The animator views the first drawing in the sequence. b: The wrist is quickly rotated forward and the fingers closed to reveal the second drawing in the sequence. c: The hand is then moved backward to reveal the third and final image within the sequence.

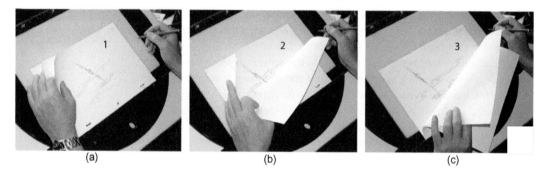

FIG 7.36 Rolling animation drawings is more straightforward, revealing the drawings in sequence. a: Drawing 1. b: Drawing 2. c: Drawing 3.

You can also test the rough drawn animation without making the finished drawings. Making final animation drawings may be very time consuming because they are often full of design detail that could have little to do with the actual action. It is therefore often very useful, particularly for the inexperienced animator, to check the timings before committing to final drawings. It might be useful at this point to make a distinction between the separate processes of animation and drawing. When making drawn animation, it is useful to work with a very rough version of the drawing, omitting as much detail as possible while keeping the structure. By keeping the drawings simple you can get results very quickly, finalize the animation, and then go on to make the final animation drawings, including all the design detail.

It is possible to test your 2D animation even before the in-betweens have been made. Known as a *key pose test,* this allows an animator to gain an impression of the general timing of an action before committing to making the in-betweens. Once again, this step can be useful and save rather a lot of time, particularly if the sequence is a long and complex one. On completing the keyframes and the animation timing breakdowns for the in-betweens, but *not* the in-betweens, the animator may test the keys by shooting the drawings in the same way as normal but assigning the number of frames to each of the key drawings based on the number of planned in-betweens. These timings are likely to differ between keys, some demanding more in-betweens than others. If followed closely, an accurate impression of the animation timing can be assessed—that is, certain key positions will occur at a very specific moment in the action, but the movement will remain very simplistic and jerky. It is possible to gain an impression of the overall movement and assess whether the number of required in-betweens is accurate.

It is only when all the drawings are tested that a *full* analysis of the movement can be made. To better analyze the dynamics of a movement in a line test, you may find it necessary to shoot the work in such a way as to make the action clear. At this stage it is important to remember that you are trying to analyze the action, not shoot final finished footage. The way the animation is shot at this stage should not necessarily conform to the way the shot will appear in its final form in the context of a film sequence. Individual shots are often cut on the action to enable a more fluid and dynamic sequence. This often entails very rapid action from the very first frame until the last, with movement throughout the shot. This is particularly common in high-action sequences. If you choose to shoot a line test that conforms to the nature of the final shot, it might not allow you to undertake a full and thorough analysis of the action. The action will be so quick that you could miss some detail that is important. It might be preferable to shoot the first image in the sequence over a longer time than it will appear for in the finished shot. Shooting it this way allows the brain enough time to register the image before the action begins. I often get my students to shoot the first image for 25 frames (1 second) before the movement proper begins. Obviously, when this shot is placed in context, it is edited without these extra frames in accordance with the animatic. Similarly, it might be beneficial to frame a line test differently from the way it will appear in the final shot. Shooting a closeup of the movement at this line-test stage might enable a more thorough analysis of the action as it will appear larger on screen. It may also be useful for animators to test the different aspects of action within a given shot separately, particularly if there are multiple characters on screen at any one time. This will make the individual animation elements easier to analyze without any unnecessary distractions from other movement. Obviously this cannot be done if any element of character interaction is evident in the shot. Such choreographed movement involving multiple elements interacting is always best viewed as multiple elements. Only then can a true assessment of the interaction be made.

With experience an animator could feel that some of the action is so simplistic that making a line test is unnecessary. This will obviously vary depending on the animation's complexity and the animator's level of experience. With practice it is possible to take a look at a number of animation drawings and the timing breakdowns on the keys and gain a fairly good idea of the dynamics, though this can only ever give an indication of the timing. As I say, this skill comes with practice.

Similar tests can be made when you're working with other animation techniques and processes. Making computer animation with complex geometric models can be undertaken in a similar manner that provides the same benefits of saving time and effort. Using simplistic versions of the model to block out the animation before commencing the final animation with all the necessary detail will provide the same level of information about the phrasing of a sequence and even give an indication as to the animation timing. Placing the models at a particular point within the screen space and at a particular point on the timeline will provide you with the keyframes that can then be further developed and worked on by adding additional detail to the action. The position on the screen and along the timeline will provide you with variable speeds of actions throughout the shot.

The way digital animation is made offers the animator the opportunity to make amendments to the work on the fly, incorporating changes as the work is actually being made. Shifting the keyframes along the timeline, moving the model either in its totality or in its separate elements, adding or removing holds—all are easy to achieve and appear to give the animator an easier time of things. However, these alterations are so quick and easy to make that doing so could lead to a tendency to analyze each small section of the action without seeing the entire shot in its full context. Try not to be tempted to make too many final decisions regarding the success of your animation before you have seen it as a whole. Working in this way may also make it that much more difficult to put a little space between you and your animation before arriving at a conclusion about the action.

You might find it helpful to consider making animation as similar to adding different and additional levels of complexity, one on top of the other, until you have your final results. Rather like building a house, you start with the foundation, lay your first course of breeze blocks, then go on to add the bricks. A rough render is added to the inside; later this is plastered over before the whole thing is finally decorated. You build layer upon layer until finally you have a very complex and highly finished result.

This layering of the animation can take the form of keyframes or block animation followed by the in-betweens or tween frames. This can then be added to with secondary actions and finally the tertiary movements. In this way the animator can concentrate her efforts on individual elements and aspects of a movement, at each stage adding more and more refinements until the shot is completed in all its glory.

Unfortunately, people making animation with stopframe techniques using models or puppets will find it a good deal more difficult to make animation tests that can then form part of the finished work. This is due to the nature of production. Each frame of stopframe animation is a unique record of a unique event, and once the model is moved to a new position, it is difficult to exactly replicate that previous position. Unlike CG animation or tradition 2D animation, with stopframe there is no lingering artifact—a drawing or separate data file among which it is easy to insert additional drawings or files. Once stopframe animation is done, it's done. Any errors and you are probably going to have to reshoot the entire thing.

Of course, it is perfectly possible for the animator to practice the shot or elements of the shot before undertaking the animation proper. I am sure that such practice efforts will be repaid in the form of better-quality animation, but this process will be much more time consuming because it will probably be impossible for the test animation to be incorporated into the final sequence. I suppose that one additional benefit of making test animation with a puppet is to test the capabilities of the model itself, identifying the movement it will allow and how far the animator can manipulate it without it either breaking or looking implausible.

Whatever form your animation practice takes, from the simplest low-tech forms to the most advanced and complex processes, the analysis of action will help you improve your skills. The ability to analyze action does not depend on technology or process. Undertaking thorough action analysis will provide you with a good understanding of timing and dynamics, transferable skills that will last a lifetime and on which you can build for a lifetime in animation.

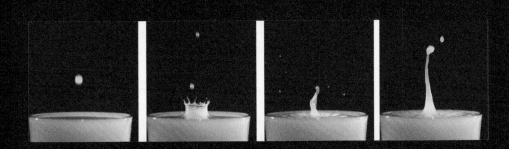

CHAPTER 8

Research

Information is not Knowledge
Knowledge is not Truth
Truth is not Wisdom
Wisdom is not Beauty.

Reference and Research

If students of animation are to make the most of their studies to progress their practice, it is important to develop a healthy relationship between research and practice. As you might expect, any research that is linked to theoretical study alone and completely divorced from practice will not allow for the application of any knowledge gained through that research in the progression of the necessary practical skills in animation. This could make for a rather dry and incomplete form of study. On the other hand, practice undertaken without any underpinning or complementary theoretical study supported by relevant and thorough research is in danger of becoming a form of craft that relies on supposition and preconceived notions. It could result in a form of simplistic mimicry of what has gone before and what others have already produced, without any kind of appreciation or true understanding of the underlying principles. Once again, I am reminded of that great quote from Walt Disney:

In order to achieve the fantastic we must first know the real.

It is through research and methodical study that we begin to know the real. Through our practice, we are able to take this knowledge and apply it to make the fantastic.

Unfortunately, we still get some students who make the big mistake of concentrating entirely on the "making" process without giving due consideration to either the underpinning principles of their chosen disciple or the wider theoretical aspects of their practice. Their practice is left impoverished as a result, and they rarely manage to fulfill their true creative potential.

Far too often student animators seem to see research as scary, the prerogative of "academics" or other "clever people," undertaken solely for academic purposes. This is absolute nonsense. Unfortunately, some of these preconceptions about research have been perpetuated by the academic community itself. I realize that this is a rather contentious statement that will ruffle a few feathers. No doubt some of my colleagues will completely refute it. It remains a fact, however, that some students consider research at best irrelevant, a rather unnecessary part of their studies and surplus to requirements. Some even find the thought of research rather threatening and beyond them. This is, of course, far from reality. The truth is, those engaged in a creative practice such as animation will invariably already be engaged in research of some sort or another. However, whether they recognize that what they do as research is another thing entirely. It is even more doubtful that they would claim to be undertaking research; nonetheless, the activity that they *are* engaged in may indeed include research. For students of animation it might be worthwhile to consider what activities you already undertake as part of your practice and then make an assessment if this does actually include research. You might be surprised. I am sure that if you see it in these simple terms, you will find the whole thing a lot less intimidating and even of great value.

It is difficult to overstate the importance of research and its contribution to a creative arts practice. Without the appropriate level of research, your depth of knowledge and understanding will be substantially less and you will not achieve the full potential for your ongoing creative development.

There is not one single way of doing research. You can choose from among various methods, but naturally enough, some methods are more appropriate to particular areas of study, and you might find that you are more suited to one kind of research method than another. Here we take a look at a few of these methods and hopefully along the way simplify them and dispel some of the misconceptions about research.

For the student of animation, research and practice should be seen not as two distinct activities that sit apart from one another but rather as integrated parts of a single endeavor. They should work together to improve and develop your animation practice. The practical and creative aspects of production should help steer research and provide you with the research questions, and the research findings and knowledge gained should inform and broaden your animation practice, which then in turn will generate additional research questions. As you can see, this has the potential to be an ongoing and beneficial process, one that is mutually dependent on both research and practice.

It would be a big mistake to think that conducting research into action analysis for animation simply entails watching animation or looking at the work of animators or filmmakers who have inspired you. Of course, there is nothing wrong with any of that; we all gain inspiration from other practitioners of our craft. But there is a big difference between being a fan of animation and being a creative practitioner of animation. Far too often this approach simply leads to a concentration on what is current, popular, or just downright fashionable. The net result of this kind of "research" is a second-rate regurgitation of what already exists that in no way enhances your knowledge or understanding as an animator. At worst it turns animation into a simple trick that can be learned without underpinning knowledge. This applies not only to the practical issues of animation timing; it also extends to other creative aspects of animation. I have lost count of how many portfolios I have seen from young, aspiring animators that are full of third-rate Tim Burton look-alike work.

We can see some evidence of this lack of research in the work of many of the early animation pioneers. These animators at the beginning of the 20th century were breaking new ground and had few texts to guide them, let alone examples of movement in the form of film or even a tradition in the animation art form. This, coupled with the pressures of demand for product, resulted in much of the produced work being rather simplistic and formulaic in terms of animation timing or dynamics. It was very inventive, and the audiences were clearly intrigued by these drawings that moved, but at that point it was not possible to draw on the underpinning principles that we rely on these days, nor did those animators tap into sound research in dynamics. For the most part research did not exist in a form easily accessible to animators. In most studios there was very little in the way of action analysis. There were some major exceptions, however; the likes of Grim Natwick, Otto Messmer, and Winsor McCay left an indelible mark on the development of the art form. Although there were a few individuals who undertook serious research into action analysis, it was the Disney studios that really took this effort to a new level and emphasized the importance of this kind of research.

If you have any doubt about the relevance of research to your own work, you should be aware that not only can it save you a lot of time, effort, and money; it will also almost invariably improve the standard of the work you produce.

On occasion I have heard students of animation say that using research material in the form of reference material is in some way "cheating." This thinking is very wrong headed; for the life of me I fail to see how this can be a reasonable assessment of the benefit of research or the proper use of reference material. How else are we to gain knowledge about the real unless we study the real? Once we have acquired such knowledge, are we not then allowed to use and apply it?

In the most simple terms, research may be described as a search for knowledge through a number of systematic processes and techniques. Through research, we are able to formulate new ideas; through these new ideas we are then able to develop new theories, and through these new theories we are able to find solutions to the problems we face.

We may be able to separate research into two distinct areas. Though neither one is better than the other, both may prove to have their benefits for our work:

- Scientific research
- Artistic research

The scientific method of research is intended to provide the researcher with scientific information that goes some way toward explaining aspects of nature and the various properties nature displays, information that gives a rationale for the phenomena we witness or experience. Knowledge and information gathered through the scientific methods of research often form the basis for the further development of existing theories or the creation of new ones.

The artistic research methods offer an alternative to methods that are of a purely scientific nature. Such research may be considered practice-based research, the subject of the research and the practice itself being one and the same. Using this research method we can consider that undertaking the work itself is a form of research through which we can gain a deeper understanding of the practice, techniques, and methodologies.

Let's also look at two other distinctions in types of research: primary research and secondary research.

Primary Research

Primary research is a term that describes gaining information that does not exist elsewhere. Primary research might involve direct action and observation on the researcher's part, perhaps based on information and knowledge already acquired. In this instance the research may be targeted at very specific areas of interest based on that information. The exact manner in which the information or material is collected is determined by the researcher and will vary depending on the area of enquiry. This may require fieldwork, research on location, or research under a very particular set of circumstances. Primary research offers an opportunity to gather information in the most appropriate manner, which, for action analysis, could include filming, photography, drawing, or simply observing and note taking, or a combination of any of these. It can also include the researcher undertaking the actions himself.

Two major advantages of this kind of primary research is that any material gathered or generated is very specific to the researcher's questions and needs, and it is entirely owned by the researcher, who is then free to do with this material as she will.

However, primary research can be rather time consuming and, depending on the subject, could prove rather difficult to undertake. Primary research into fish behavior, for example, may entail actually getting into the water. Primary research into shark-feeding behavior may also present the researcher with some interesting demands. Obviously, this kind of research is not always practical nor indeed the most effective or efficient method of research.

Secondary Research

Secondary research is a term used for acquiring information that already exists and is available to the researcher. This may entail collecting data from a number of sources and, having gathered it, making a further study of it in such a manner that results cast new light on the subject. The researcher may make a review of the findings of other research or information and, as part of the secondary research, undertake the synthesis of this information and publish it in a new form.

Unlike primary research, which may involve fieldwork, much of this secondary research may be undertaken from within a studio or office environment.

In recent years the greatest source of material for secondary research has been the Internet. This is a very rich seam of material, but the researcher does face certain difficulties in this type of approach. For a start, the sheer volume of material available on the Internet demands a degree of editing and collating, sifting the relevant from the irrelevant. Establishing the veracity of the information you find may also be problematic. Just because the material is widely available does not mean it's accurate. The quality of the available information is highly variable and the sources might not always be reliable.

In addition, the information acquired during secondary research may originally have been generated for very different purposes from our own needs, which means that it might not be entirely suited or appropriate to our immediate research investigations. It is likely that this secondary research will not be as well controlled or as well targeted as primary research. Still, this may be the only practical manner of getting the necessary material. But swimming with hungry sharks to study feeding behavior might not be everyone's cup of tea.

By comparison to those pioneers of animation, we are in a very privileged position to be able to access such a vast wealth of material, so we should make the most of it.

There are two other classifications of research that you might find useful to understand: quantitative research and qualitative research.

In the simplest terms, *quantitative research* deals with numbers, measurements, and statistics (quantities); *qualitative research* deals with more intangible matter, the nature of behavior, feelings, and perceptions (qualities). Both research types have their benefits, though one or the other might be best suited to studying certain subjects. These methods often require different techniques, and they may provide very different kinds of results that present the researcher with different kinds of information and data.

You might find that your own research will demand one or the other approach, but you may also find that your work will benefit from a combination of both types of research. It is important to appreciate that these approaches to research are not mutually exclusive. The researcher may apply both approaches as appropriate.

Quantitative Research

Quantitative research deals with subjects and phenomena that can be measured using instrumentation or techniques that give results expressed in the form of figures. Once gathered, these figures may be presented as hard data that in turn may then be analyzed and turned into useful information. This kind of data may then form the basis for predictive modeling, providing possible outcomes to future events. In this way quantitative research may involve experimentation and the control of variables. The observed results of such models may then take a form that provides the basis for further investigation, study, and additional experimentation.

This form of research is usually undertaken as part of the scientific research method. The use of statistics naturally depends on accurate figures being provided by quantitative research.

Researchers engaged in action analysis may use this kind of approach and the resulting data to examine the efficiency of movement under certain conditions, such as the measurement of the energy requirements for locomotion, athletes' performance under given conditions, and the effectiveness of sports equipment in enhancing performance.

Qualitative Research

Qualitative research is often undertaken to explore human and animal behavior and to investigate the reasons behind those behaviors. It may be used to look for patterns in behavior and to identify possible causes in any changes in behavior. It may be used to look at decision making, cultural differences, practices and traditions, and belief systems. It may be used to conduct research into how people feel and how they then behave as a result of those feelings. Quantitative research may also be used to provide statistical data on such behavior.

This qualitative research approach can be used to investigate the nature of movement in animals and may provide useful information through the comparative analysis of types of movements achieved by animals of similar species. This could include research into the variable nature of flight in birds as a result of the physiological differences between them determined by the size, shape, and aspect ratio of wings or the manner in which feeding behavior differs between bird species and is determined by such things as the availability and the nature of the food source and the shape and size of beaks.

Information gathered using qualitative research may provide the researcher with a set of impressions of the subject. These impressions can then form the basis for further analysis, which could in turn then require further work using quantitative research methods to gain numerical data. As we can see, research is not a one-size-fits-all process.

Research Methods

The purpose of research is to discover new knowledge and provide a solid underpinning of the work of any given practitioner. Given that, it would seem to follow that a number of options are open to you, including your choice of research methods that you can employ in your studies in a particular discipline or of a given subject.

The subject of research and the research questions we ask on a subject may determine the nature of the research and the kind of research techniques we adopt. As we have already seen, some approaches and methods may be more appropriate than others, depending on the subject and results we seek. It might be perfectly feasible and appropriate to use more than one method that will provide different kinds of data or information.

Here I categorize a few of the main research methods in an attempt to simplify the terminology that some may find a little confusing. I have attempted to make that language clearer and perhaps a little less off-putting.

This list is not comprehensive, but it does cover some of the research methods you might come across elsewhere.

Heuristic

Heuristic is a term for a kind of research that depends on a researcher's direct experience and relies more on his intuition and application of common sense than would a more scientific approach or the gathering of scientific data. Heuristic research relies on a trial-and-error approach to problem solving, using a rule-of-thumb methodology and taking an educated guess. It relies on the researcher's "gut feeling," and as a result tends to provide information that is in principle accurate though perhaps less reliable in providing completely accurate and detailed data. This approach to research may be perfectly acceptable if the results you are seeking do not need to stand up to scientific rigor or the work you are undertaking is not so dependent on the findings' scientific accuracy. Such results may be well suited to the kind of action analysis that supports the vast majority of animation production. A good rule of thumb we may often rely on is that if the animation *looks* correct, it *is* correct. If you are looking to create a representation of an action, that rule of thumb might be perfectly acceptable. If you are looking to create a *simulation* of an action, it might not be satisfactory.

Direct observation may be a very productive technique for this kind of research.

Phenomenology

The term *phenomenology* refers to the study of any events or occurrences that may be observed and that happen as a result or as a consequence of other conditions. In the simplest of terms, phenomenology is the observation and recording of phenomena. However, it does rely on the empirical evidence of those observations. Phenomenology is a common term used in both scientific methods of research and in philosophy.

One aspect of phenomenology is that it requires the researcher to use techniques that measure those observations in such a way that the results provide data for further analysis. Any research of a subject that provides the *perception* of events or conditions by individuals must, using phenomenology, be gathered in such a manner that these findings can be attributed with a numerical value. Results that are described in mathematical terms may then provide more concrete data, enabling the researcher to undertake further analysis.

It is through empirical evidence that phenomenology sets out to describe events not as they appear to an individual but as they appear to any and all individuals.

Action Research

The term *action research* refers to an approach that is dependant completely on practical activities. Such activities may be rather like performing an experiment: A range of actions may be undertaken to test ideas and acquire information on the action and in doing so provide a deeper knowledge of the nature of the action that may be difficult to gain using other research methods. By the researcher undertaking the actions herself, she may gain a direct experience of the subject of the research as well as an understanding of how such actions *feel*. Simple observation and even scientific measurements may provide accurate data, but they cannot provide the researcher with information gained through action research. If such research is undertaken by the researcher herself, she gains direct experience of how it *feels* to undertake such actions. This kind of direct and personal experience may provide valuable information, but by its very nature it may be limited to the researcher's personal feelings, which are variable and subjective. Such findings may only apply to a very specific subject: researchers themselves.

Watching someone undertake an action such as lifting a heavy object can provide the observer with a good deal of information, but undertaking that action oneself will provide additional information that can *only* be gained through that direct experience. The direct experience of the weight, the feeling of tensions and stresses within the body, and gaining a sense of the center of gravity and the shift in the point of balance throughout the lift can only really be gained by undertaking the action. This approach to research entails direct participation; it is an empirical process that provides direct results.

Employing a range of individuals to undertake given actions may provide researchers with useful results suitable for comparative analysis, which in turn may provide data suitable for further synthesis.

Participant Observer

The aim of *participant observer research* is to become intimately familiar with a group of individuals to gain insight into behavior, practices, and the environment in which such groups operate. This approach is often used in cultural anthropology, in which groups, communities, societies, or religions are either the subject of the research or central to the study. It is used to gain an intimate insight into the behavior, belief systems, and practices of groups or communities and may use a number of different techniques, such as direct observation, interviews, and the direct involvement of the researcher, who may participate in the activities of the study group.

This kind of research involving investigation into group behavior and the like is often conducted over an extended period, since it may take time to gain the trust of the research subjects. In such situations, the closer the researcher becomes involved with the group, the better the information the researcher gathers. It might even be necessary for researchers involved in social anthropology to be involved with a group over many years. Through direct participation in a group it may be possible to discern the difference between what is said or thought to be happening in that group and what actually happens. Familiarity with a group and trust between researcher and subject will enable a more accurate picture to be formed. This takes time.

Ethnographic Research

The term *ethnographic research* refers to the kind of research undertaken into cultures and societies. This could include issues specific to a group, shared with other groups or societies, or focused on the differences among groups, cultures, and societies. This kind of research can involve techniques used in participant observation, though it is not necessarily limited to those techniques. Ethnographic research often involves primary research, but it might also be possible to undertake secondary research by accessing existing material and information. Indeed, research into remote communities and cultures or those that have either changed over time and are no longer represented by the contemporary society or no longer exist may be the only practical approach in which research can be undertaken.

Ethnographic research is a method that may also be used by people interested in history, folklore, cultural studies, and the study of linguistics. It can provide valuable information on the behavior of cultural groups that might be useful to an animator involved in creating performance-based animation. It may also be useful for animators who are developing narratives involving identifiable cultures or groups, particularly if these activities need to be represented accurately.

Sources

In recent years the Internet has become a valuable resource for research, providing a fantastic range of reference material, information, and support for research and study. Web sites of all descriptions provide easy access to text and sound and both the moving and still image. There are hundreds of thousands of blogs of practitioners at all levels that give a very personal take on subjects and insight into the most current processes and methodologies. Though the Internet presents a wealth of material at your fingertips, much of the available material is of a very particular nature and probably created for purposes other than the ones for which you want to use it. Still, you will no doubt find some of it very useful.

I would suggest at this point that you seek out information from a range of sources. Trawling the Internet could return some very useful stuff, but the Internet is not the only source, and I would like to make a plea here for a varied approach to research and varied reference material that includes online references but also includes real-life observation, DVDs, and good old-fashioned books. There is a considerable range of texts that will assist you in your efforts. You will find work of the very highest quality from all manner of experts; this work has undergone some form of editing, verification, and mediation. Unfortunately, that's not always the case with material you find on the Internet.

Creating Your Own Reference Library

This is my call to all serious students of animation to create their own collection of references, their own library of information, research, films, stills, and drawings. The beauty of this kind of collection is that it could contain different types of material in different formats, both digital material and hard copies. Making your own reference resource can be very valuable. It will consist of the very things you are interested in and will be directly related to your very particular and individual practice. In time it will perhaps provide you with a rather unique resource. It is the individual creative voice of an artist, filmmaker, or animator that makes for long-term success. Your research will assist you in developing that voice.

Gathering such a collection can take a long time; my own has taken over 30 years and is still growing. But you should be in no hurry; you will gather your information and material as your practice develops and your experience progresses. Your own notes, production journals, sketchbooks, photographs, and moving images will be of immense value to you and will form a central part of your reference library. A word of caution here: Be careful what you throw away; if you keep it, it could have very real value to you and your practice one day.

Even in this digital age, good old-fashioned books form an important part of my reference material, but I admit that this due in large part to my love of books. However, books can be costly, and the expense of building up such a reference library, particularly if like me you get hooked on books, can be very considerable. Having said that, there is no need to look for rare books or first editions; there are plenty of cheaper alternatives. Good second-hand books are available from a number of web sites and plenty of other online material is available to you for free.

If you are going to be able to use your reference material in a sensible and useful manner, you need to give some thought to storing and organizing it in such a way that you can find, access, and retrieve it with ease. Books and DVDs sit on a shelf, so no problem there, but data and other digital resources that reside on your computer or external hard drives or in your Favorites list on your Web browser might need to be classified in some way. This classification will entail good file management methods and using appropriate naming conventions.

A little time spent organizing your material will save you a lot of time and potentially a lot of money later on.

Further Reading and Viewing

There are a number of books in the bibliography that you may find useful. Here I have specifically recommended a few of those texts. However, it is important to state clearly that these books represent my own very personal choices and are not intended to imply that these are of more value than any others listed in the bibliography or those that I have omitted completely. As I say, this is a personal list and is simply intended to get you started. Do your own research and no doubt you will find plenty of other material that's far more appropriate to your own individual practice.

Action Analysis

Alexander, R. McNeill (2006) *Principles of Animal Locomotion*, Princeton University Press. A very clear text covering a wide range of subjects; easily understood, though the author also provides the mathematical formulas that explain such issues as the energy costs of given actions.

Alexander, D. E. (2002) *Nature's Flyers: Birds, Insects, and the Biomechanics of Flight*, John Hopkins University Press. This is a very thorough text on all manner of flight in nature: insects, birds and bats, even the gliding action of seeds, it's all here. The text is written in such a way that makes technical issues easily accessible, even for the nonspecialist.

Hamilton, N., and Luttgens, K. (2002) *Kinesiology: Scientific Basis of Human Motion*, McGraw-Hill, New York. The average animator might find this a rather technical and dry text, though it does give some very useful and detailed information on the anatomy of human muscular/skeletal structures, which it covers in great detail.

Muybridge, E. (1957) *Animals in Motion*, Dover, New York. After all these years, this book provides a very useful resource for animators. The images are not always of the best quality, but given the time period in which they were created, they provide a fantastic addition to any animator's reference library.

Muybridge, E. (1955) *The Human Figure in Motion*, Dover, New York. As above, but even better.

Practical Guides

Brown, B. (2002) *Cinematography, Theory & Practice,* Focal Press, Oxford. If you are looking for one book that will assist you with the techniques and principles of cinematography, look no further. A very useful book.

Culhane, S. (1988) *From Script to Screen*, Columbus, London. Very lively in content from one of the great classical animators. It seems a little dated in the way it is written, but the principles that are laid out here are timeless.

Eisner, W. (1985) *Comics and Sequential Art*, Poorhouse Press, Florida. A first-rate book for animators who want to develop the craft of storyboarding and sequential imaging.

Halas, J., and Whitaker, H. (1981) *Timing for Animation*, Focal Press, Oxford. *The* must-have book. If there was one book any student animator should own, it's this one. Written in an accessible style, it covers all the principles of animation with easy-to-understand examples and plenty of illustrations. It is a little old-fashioned, perhaps, but it's none the worse for that. Affordable for most students, it is in my opinion *the* animator's bible.

Hooks, E. (2000) *Acting for Animators: A Complete Guide to Performance Animation*, Greenwood Press. There are few books that cover this topic, and no doubt animators will find this one a useful addition to their collections. It is an easily accessible read, though it could have dealt with the topics in more depth. This is a minor criticism; I would recommend that all animators take a look at this volume.

Kuperberg, M. (2002) *A Guide to Computer Animation*, Focal Press, Oxford. An okay introduction, though students will have to dig deeper to find more specifics on software.

Laybourn, K. (1998) *The Animation Book*, Three Rivers Press, NY. A great book. This covers a lot of ground. Still, a little old-fashioned despite some updated information that covers aspects of computer animation. A very good addition to a collection and a real must-have book for teachers of animation and those working in mixed media.

Shaw, S. (2003) *Stop Motion: Craft Skills for Model Animation,* Focal Press, Oxford. An excellent book that covers all the essential basics of modeling and preparing to make 3D stop-motion animation, including materials and armatures. Few if any books deal with this subject in such a clear and concise manner, which makes it a very useful and most welcome guide to this discipline. This is a vital book for the serious stopframe animator.

Thomas, F., and Johnson, O. (1985) *The Illusion of Life*, Hyperion. A brilliant book. Written by two of the masters of animation from the Disney stable. The book is in two distinct parts. The first covers the historic background of the Disney studio and some of its greatest animators. Though this part is interesting and informative, it is of little direct use in developing skills. The second, more practical part of the book is pure gold. This is also a must-have book for the serious animator.

Williams, R. (2001) *The Animator's Survival Kit*, Faber & Faber, New York. Another brilliant book. Written by a master animator and director with years of experience, including *Who Framed Roger Rabbit* and the ill-fated *Cobbler and the Thief*. The book covers, in plenty of detail, all the principles of animation, explained clearly with loads of illustrations. Written in a very open and accessible style, it includes anecdotes from Williams's career that are much more than amusing stories; they are lessons in themselves. Computer animators should not be put off by the emphasis on drawn animation; the principles apply to your work, too. A must-have book for serious animators.

Winder, C., and Dowlata, Z. (2001) *Producing Animation*, Focal Press, Oxford. A first-rate book. A must-have for independent animators and serious animation students alike. If you buy only one book on production and production management, make it this one.

Webster, C (2005) *Animation: The Mechanics of Motion*, Focal Press, Oxford. Difficult to say much because it is my own book. There are some useful things in it, not just for 2D animators, particularly on timing for animation.

Theory

Furnis, M. (1998) *Art in Motion Animation Aesthetics,* John Libbey, Sydney. Another first-rate book that deals with a broad range of issues such as representation, audience, and gender.

Pilling, J., ed. (1997) *A Reader in Animation Studies,* John Libbey, London. Another first-rate book that deals with a broad range of issues such as representation, audience, and gender.

Wells, P. (1998) *Understanding Animation*, Routledge, London. This is a very good text if you want to get to grips with the contextualization of animation in media production. Entertaining and well written, with a light touch (a lamentably rare quality in such books, unfortunately).

Finally, I will once again urge you to look toward material and disciplines other than animation for inspiration. Live action, photography, illustration, graphic design, theater, film, literature, interactive media, painting, and sculpture will all provide you with a rich source of inspiration and knowledge. Your research will form the basis of an invaluable source of information, inspiration, and reference material that will find its way into the remainder of your animation practice.

Index

Page numbers followed by *f* indicates a figure and *t* indicates a table.

Printed and bound by CPI Group (UK) Ltd, Croydon, CR0 4YY

21/10/2024

01777057-0013